INEQUALITY | A New Zealand Crisis

Chapters

Max Rashbrooke
Robert Wade
Ganesh Nana
Jonathan Boston
Karlo Mila
Philippa Howden-Chapman
Sarah Bierre
Chris Cunningham
Kim Workman
Tracey McIntosh
Cathy Wylie
Evan Te Ahu Poata-Smith
Paul Barber
Paul Dalziel
Nigel Haworth
Mike O'Brien
Linda Tuhiwai Smith

Viewpoints

Ian Taylor
Kristine and Craig Absolum
Damian Christie
Pete Bryant
Tamara Baddeley
Chris Harris
Mary Richardson
Stan Coster
Asher Emanuel
Anake Goodall
Kate Frykberg
Kelly Belcher
Susan Guthrie
Gareth Morgan

INEQUALITY
A New Zealand Crisis

Edited by Max Rashbrooke

BRIDGET WILLIAMS BOOKS

First published in 2013 by Bridget Williams Books Limited
P O Box 12 474, Wellington, New Zealand

Book © Max Rashbrooke, 2013
Essays © The Contributors, 2013

This book is copyright. Apart from fair dealing for the purpose of private study, research, criticism or review, permitted under the Copyright Act, no part may be reproduced by any process without the prior permission of the copyright holders and the publisher. Inquiries should be made to Bridget Williams Books.

ISBN: 9781927131510
ISTC: A0220120000222C3

Editorial note: Macrons are used on Māori words and proper names (for example, iwi and hapū), and on names of organisations where the words would have a macron applied in modern usage. They are applied in quotations and book titles only where they were used in the original text. All dollar figures are in 2013 New Zealand dollars unless otherwise stated.

Acknowledgements
The publishers thank the groups who have generously supported the publication of *Inequality: A New Zealand Crisis*: the New Zealand Council of Christian Social Services, the J. R. McKenzie Trust and Paul and Peter Monin. BWB's publishing is supported by the BWB Publishing Trust, and the G & N Trust; this too is gratefully acknowledged. Max Rashbrooke thanks the Bruce Jesson Foundation and the G Trust, for their commitment to his work on the project. The views expressed in this book are not necessarily those of any group providing support for the project.

National Library of New Zealand Cataloguing-in-Publication Data
Inequality (2013)
Inequality : a New Zealand crisis / edited by Max Rashbrooke.
Includes index.
ISBN 978-1-927131-51-0
1. Income distribution—New Zealand. 2. Poverty—New Zealand.
3. Wealth—New Zealand. 4. Equality—New Zealand. I. Rashbrooke, Max. II. Title.
339.20993—dc 23

Cover and internal design by Neil Pardington, Base Two
Edited by Tom Rennie
Production by Philip Rainer, Jo Scully, Megan Simpson
Typeset by Tina Delceg
Printed by Printlink, Wellington

Contents

List of Viewpoints	vi
List of Figures and Tables	vii
List of Contributors	viii
Acknowledgements	x
Preface Jonathan Boston and Max Rashbrooke	xi
PART ONE: INTRODUCTION	**xv**
1 **Why Inequality Matters** Max Rashbrooke	1
2 **Inequality and New Zealand** Max Rashbrooke	20
PART TWO: ISSUES AND DEBATES	**37**
3 **Inequality and the West** Robert Wade	39
4 **The Cost of Inequality** Ganesh Nana	55
5 **What Kind of Equality Matters?** Jonathan Boston	70
PART THREE: CONSEQUENCES	**89**
6 **Only One Deck** Karlo Mila	91
7 **Building Inequality** Philippa Howden-Chapman, Sarah Bierre and Chris Cunningham	105
8 **Crime, Imprisonment and Poverty** Kim Workman and Tracey McIntosh	120
9 **Schools and Inequality** Cathy Wylie	134
10 **Inequality and Māori** Evan Te Ahu Poata-Smith	148
PART FOUR: LOOKING AHEAD	**165**
11 **Reducing Inequality** Paul Barber	167
12 **Education and Skills** Paul Dalziel	184
13 **The Rewards of Work** Nigel Haworth	198
14 **A Better Welfare System** Mike O'Brien	213
15 **The Future is Now** Linda Tuhiwai Smith	228
Glossary	236
Endnotes	243
Index	272

Viewpoints

1	Not in it for the money	Ian Taylor	18
2	In the middle	Kristine and Craig Absolum	35
3	Don't let it get entrenched	Damian Christie	53
4	The value of support	Pete Bryant	68
5	Income, not budgeting, is the issue	Tamara Baddeley	87
6	A divided Auckland?	Chris Harris	102
7	Rebuilding divisions?	Mary Richardson	118
8	The State as parent and warden: Stan's story	Stan Coster	132
9	So, what school did you go to?	Asher Emanuel	145
10	Back to the Māori future?	Anake Goodall	159
11	On generosity and restraint	Kate Frykberg	181
12	Just so many obstacles	Kelly Belcher	195
13	A collaborative approach	DSK Engineering	210
14	Unconditional basic income	Gareth Morgan and Susan Guthrie	225

Figures and Tables

Figure 1.1	Health and social problems index and income inequality	13
Figure 2.1	Step by step: New Zealand's income ladder	21
Table 2.1	Relativity: how your household's disposable income compares to others	22
Figure 2.2	Wealth in New Zealand	23
Figure 2.3	The Gini coefficient in 34 OECD countries, 2010	24
Figure 2.4	The top 1 per cent's share of personal (pre-tax) income in New Zealand, 1921–2009	26
Figure 2.5	The rich and the rest: how the gap widened	28
Figure 3.1	Share of top 1 per cent in US income, 1913–2006	40
Figure 3.2	Share of US income deciles, 1947–2009	42
Table 3.1	Decile shares (per cent) of national income, US and average for 133 countries, 2009	43
Figure 4.1	Relationship between economic analysis and social outcomes	57
Figure 4.2	The inter-relationships of income, wealth and opportunity	59
Figure 6.1	Unemployment rates for Pacific peoples and the total New Zealand population, 1987–2012	97
Figure 7.1	Housing tenure in New Zealand, 1916–2006	111
Table 10.1	Wealth distribution between major ethnic groups	155
Table 12.1	Distribution of total personal incomes of the New Zealand usually resident population aged 35–39 years, by ethnic group, 2006	186
Table 12.2	Top 20 occupations requiring a Level 4 qualification ranked by number of employees, 2006	187
Figure 13.1	Income: how it is shared	199
Figure 14.1	The widening gap: benefits and average wages, 1980–2010	217
Table 14.1	Benefit rates in New Zealand, 2012	219

Contributors

Paul Barber is a policy advisor at the New Zealand Council of Christian Social Services (NZCCSS) and leads the council's flagship programme, *Closer Together Whakatata Mai – reducing inequalities*.

Sarah Bierre is a research fellow in the He Kainga Oranga / Housing and Health Research Programme, at the University of Otago, Wellington.

Jonathan Boston is the Director of the Institute for Governance and Policy Studies in the School of Government at Victoria University of Wellington. The author of numerous books and articles, Professor Boston is a leading contributor to policy debate in New Zealand on a range of issues, and was the co-chair of the Children's Commissioner's Expert Advisory Group on Solutions to Child Poverty in 2012.

Chris Cunningham (Ngāti Toa, Ngāti Raukawa) is the Director of the Research Centre for Māori Health and Development at Massey University, Wellington. He is a co-director of He Kainga Oranga / Housing and Health Research Programme.

Paul Dalziel is Professor of Economics at Lincoln University, and was the leader of one strand of a recent major research project looking at the links between education and employment.

Nigel Haworth is a labour market specialist at the University of Auckland, and a former chair of the Partnership Research Centre and the Centre for Housing Research. He fulfils a number of roles, in and outside the university, including membership of the New Zealand Labour Party's Policy Council and the International Labour Organization's Century Project.

Philippa Howden-Chapman is an expert on health inequalities at the University of Otago, Wellington and the author of research on poor housing and health. Professor Howden-Chapman is director of He Kainga Oranga / Housing and Health Research Programme and the New Zealand Centre for Sustainable Cities. She has received a number of national awards.

Tracey McIntosh (Tūhoe) is a Senior Lecturer at the University of Auckland. She has extensively researched issues around Māori development, imprisonment and marginalisation. A former director of the Centre of Research Excellence Ngā Pae o te Māramatanga, she was also a co-chair of the Children's Commissioner's Expert Advisory Group on Solutions to Child Poverty.

Karlo Mila's work spans the arts, commentary and academia. An award-winning poet of Tongan, Samoan and Palagi descent, she has also worked on Pacific health research, been a columnist for the *Dominion Post*, and recently completed a PhD in sociology on Pacific peoples.

Ganesh Nana is Chief Economist at research and consultancy firm Business and Economic Research Limited (BERL). He has over 30 years' experience in economics, including as a lecturer at Victoria University of Wellington and working overseas. He is a regular commentator on the New Zealand economy for various media.

Mike O'Brien is Associate Professor at the University of Auckland, and the Convenor of the Child Poverty Action Group. A leading figure in welfare debates, he was also the head of the Alternative Welfare Working Group.

Evan Te Ahu Poata-Smith (Te Rarawa, Ngāti Kahu) is head of Indigenous Studies at the University of Wollongong. Prior to this he taught at the Auckland University of Technology and the University of Canterbury. More recently he was a Fulbright Scholar-in-Residence at Northern Arizona University where he taught in the Applied Indigenous Studies and Sociology programmes. His research focuses on Māori political and social change.

Max Rashbrooke has written for national newspapers and magazines in Britain and New Zealand, including the *Guardian*, the *National Business Review* and the *Listener*. He was the recipient of the 2011 Bruce Jesson Senior Journalism Award.

Linda Tuhiwai Smith (Ngāti Awa, Ngāti Porou) is Pro-Vice Chancellor Māori and Dean of Te Pua Wānanga ki te Ao School of Māori and Pacific Development at the University of Waikato. Professor Smith is the author of the influential book *Decolonizing Methodologies: research and indigenous peoples,* first published in 1999.

Robert Wade is Professor of Political Economy at the London School of Economics. A New Zealander, Robert H. Wade is a leading international writer on globalisation, inequality and world financial systems, author of the award-winning book *Governing the Market*, and winner of the Leontief Prize in Economics, 2008.

Kim Workman (Ngāti Kahungunu ki Wairarapa, Rangitāne) is founder and director of Rethinking Crime and Punishment. He was head of the prison service 1989–93, among other public service roles. He received the International Prize for Restorative Justice in 2005, and was awarded a QSO in 2007.

Cathy Wylie is chief researcher at the New Zealand Council for Educational Research. She leads Competent Children, Competent Learners, a longitudinal study of children's development, and has just published *Vital Transitions*, a major book on the school system.

Acknowledgements

This book has drawn on a wide range of expertise and support, as the preface acknowledges. In our warm thanks for advice and commentary, we acknowledge that the responsibility for the text lies finally with the authors.

The advisory group included Jonathan Boston (chair), Paul Callister, Len Cook, Philippa Howden-Chapman, Tracey McIntosh, Bridget Robson, Bob Stephens and Kim Workman. Others who contributed to early discussions include Colin James, Charlotte Macdonald and Tapu Misa. Valuable comments were provided by Carol Archie, Geoff Bertram, Simon Chapple, Joris de Bres, Tim Hazledine, Jim McAloon, John O'Neill, Richard Pamatatau, John Pratt, Keith Rankin, Bill Rosenberg, Susan St John, Māmari Stephens, Geoff Walker and Denis Welch.

Many others have assisted with this project: Tim Davies-Colley, the staff of the Porirua Citizens Advice Bureau, Michele Whiting, Blair Badcock, and the Wesley Community Action team in Waitangirua, especially Lizzie McMillan-Makalio; Lyndy McIntyre; Stephanie McIntyre; Jeff Drane, Graham Howell, Mike Leon, the staff of the Wellington City Mission and the Wellington soup kitchen; Charles Waldegrave; Robert Whitaker and Ben McKeown; Julie Timmins; and Peter Malcolm and others in the Equality Network. Wide-ranging interviews were conducted for the personal viewpoints; some will be published subsequently (including those with Faye Rhodes and her partner Donny, and Puke from the Downtown Community Ministry's consumers group).

Copyright material has been reproduced with the permission of the following individuals and organisations. For Chapter 6, Woodcut Productions, on behalf of Tyree Tautogia, for Smashproof lyrics; Universal Music Publishing, representing Alan Jansson and Pauly Fuemana, for OMC Lyrics; Huia Publishers, for the poem by Karlo Mila. For graphs and tables, as acknowledged on the page: *The Spirit Level*, Penguin Books (London); Bryan Perry, Ministry of Social Development; Oxford University Press and John Wiley & Sons; Te Ara, Ministry for Culture and Heritage; Bill Rosenberg, New Zealand Council of Trade Unions; Statistics New Zealand.

Bridget Williams would like to offer special thanks to those who have provided funding support, as acknowledged in the preface and on the imprint page, for their critical role in making this book a reality.

As the book's originator and editor, Max Rashbrooke has the final word, with thanks to the publishers for a strong commitment to this project, and to his family and friends.

Bridget Williams, Publisher   *Max Rashbrooke, Editor*

the book's advisory group and other specialists who have given generously of their time and knowledge.

Support from a number of funders has been essential to this publication. Max Rashbrooke's work was supported by the Bruce Jesson Senior Journalism Award and by the G Trust. The New Zealand Council of Christian Social Services made an early contribution to ensure that independent research and writing on this critical issue was published. The J.R. McKenzie Trust has also provided invaluable support to enable wider discussion of the issue. Paul and Peter Monin have continued their commitment to the publishing of good books on New Zealand issues. Behind all BWB publishing projects stands the BWB Publishing Trust, with the G&N Trust. Funders have provided support independently of each other and the writing process, and are not necessarily identified with any views expressed in the book. We would like to join the publisher, Bridget Williams Books, in thanking all these groups most warmly.

Jonathan Boston *Max Rashbrooke*
Chair of the Advisory Group *Editor*

Part One
Introduction

Preface

Rising income inequality in many developed nations has been a source of growing international concern. Large income disparities pose serious economic and political risks, undermine social cohesion and raise acute ethical challenges. Highlighting this, the *Global Risks 2013* analysis prepared for the World Economic Forum summit in Davos, Switzerland, identified 'severe income disparity' as the greatest threat facing the world economy; this assessment was based on a survey of over 1,000 experts from industry, government, academia and civil society. Likewise, the Organisation for Economic Co-operation and Development claims that income inequality threatens global economic growth, and that ignoring it is 'not an option'. The World Health Organisation has initiated a major drive to tackle the inequalities linked to adverse effects on public health. A number of major international publications – including Richard Wilkinson and Kate Pickett's *The Spirit Level* and Joseph Stiglitz's *The Price of Inequality* – have been at the centre of this discussion.

This book investigates the nature, causes and consequences of income inequality in New Zealand – a country where the gap between high and low incomes has widened faster in recent decades than in most other developed nations. It locates income inequality as one of the most significant and complex issues confronting New Zealand today, and explores the many contours of the problem, drawing on a wealth of evidence, analysis and perspectives.

The authors of the book's fifteen chapters include academics, researchers and journalists; their contributions cover many, but by no means all, of the facets of New Zealand's rising income inequality. The views they express are of course their own. No attempt has been made to frame the discussion within a single, unified philosophical approach or advocate an agreed set of conclusions. Nevertheless, the contributors share a common concern about the societal risks posed by severe income disparities, and a desire for the issue and policy options to be properly debated.

To complement the chapters, the book contains a series of shorter, more personal viewpoints; these too are independently written, not linked to any one chapter or endorsing particular perspectives expressed elsewhere in the book.

We would like to thank all the contributors for sharing their expertise and their personal stories. We are also most grateful to those who served on

1   Why Inequality Matters

Max Rashbrooke

High on the hills of eastern Porirua, the new Aotea Block stretches out along the ridgelines and gullies. Sections here sell for over $240,000, while house and land together can cost up to $800,000. On the slopes below, row upon row of older, smaller and often dilapidated houses line the streets: this is Cannons Creek, one of the country's most deprived communities. When the Aotea Block was being built, a road linking it to the suburbs below was proposed, but the idea has languished, passed over as too expensive and having 'little strategic value'.[1] Introducing mixed or social housing was also dismissed as 'not a priority', leaving one community at the top of the hills, the other sitting just below, but living worlds apart.[2]

Disconnected worlds like these are growing steadily more evident in twenty-first century New Zealand, as poverty and wealth create ever-starker contrasts between the lives of those who 'have' and those who 'have not'. Since the 1980s, the number of people who are poor in New Zealand has doubled, with many families living in severe hardship.[3] In the words of one researcher, 'Behind the statistics are real people who are to varying degrees experiencing the stressful and demoralising exclusion from ordinary life that financial strictures and moral hardship bring.' Yet at the same time, New Zealand is now a country where, across all adults, the top 1 per cent owns three times as much wealth as the poorest 50 per cent.[4]

The very distance between these worlds – the widening gap between low-, middle- and high-income New Zealanders – nonetheless connects us all. A rush of statistics is telling us how unequal our society has become, and this unfolding script states emphatically that inequality affects all who live here. As Karlo Mila puts it in Chapter 6, there is 'only one deck'. And this is what the numbers show:

- New Zealand now has the widest income gaps since detailed records began in the early 1980s[5]
- From the mid-1980s to the mid-2000s, the gap between the rich and the rest has widened faster in New Zealand than in any other developed country[6]

- The average household in the top 10 per cent of New Zealand has nine times the income of one in the bottom 10 per cent[7]
- The top 1 per cent of adults own 16 per cent of the country's total wealth, while the bottom half put together have just over 5 per cent.[8]

This book aims to present the story behind these statistics. Why New Zealand incomes have diverged so significantly; how income inequality affects people across the country; and what the consequences might be if this divergence persists. Woven into this story are many kinds of inequality: of opportunity, of status, of rights, of participation.[9] But running through it all is inequality of income. Any free society will always have some differences, but New Zealand's income gaps have now widened to such an extent that they have created something of a crisis: not in the sense of a natural disaster that strikes in an instant, but a gradual shift that builds until it reaches a tipping point. That time is now.

'In addressing inequality in New Zealand,' as Linda Tuhiwai Smith notes in Chapter 15, 'we have to raise poverty, to understand that poverty has direct impacts on society, not simply because we pay for it but because we will keep paying for it over time. Deep poverty is not a temporary event.' This deep poverty has long been a crisis for New Zealand, one confronted by many committed researchers, campaigners and organisations. Most recently, activists and official taskforces have focused on child poverty.[10] New Zealand has between 170,000 and 270,000 children living in poverty (depending on the measure used),[11] and one of the world's worst records of child health and well-being, with alarming rates of preventable diseases amongst children.[12] Children in New Zealand are more likely to be poor, and less likely to feel safe and well, than children in most other developed countries.[13] One major report on children's welfare ranked New Zealand twenty-eighth out of thirty developed countries, better only than Mexico and Turkey.[14] In particular, our rates of preventable diseases, especially among children and the elderly, have been described as a 'national embarrassment'.[15]

By tracing incomes from these deeply deprived communities through to the most affluent – arcing from Cannons Creek to the Aotea Block and far beyond – this book aims to show how, just as concentrated wealth can affect everyone, concentrations of hardship and suffering make us all worse off. The impact of rising income inequality crosses boundaries: for United States President Barack Obama it is 'the defining issue of our time'; for International Monetary Fund (IMF) chief Christine Lagarde it 'is a growing concern for policymakers around the world'; The *Economist* considers it one of our 'biggest social, economic and political challenges.'[16] In this book, New Zealand commentators outline some of these challenges, and identify the urgent need to confront them in this country.

Defining inequality

So what does the phrase 'income inequality' actually mean? In this book the 'income' part generally refers to households' *disposable* income: the amount households have to spend after taxes have been paid and any benefits and tax credits added. To compare like with like, this amount is then adjusted for household size.[17] Two people might both be earning $60,000, but if one was an adult raising two children, they would have a very different standard of living from one who had no children and lived with a partner who earned a further $150,000.[18] 'Income inequality' then looks at the way incomes are distributed unequally across the various participants in an economy. In general, this refers to differences between households, but occasionally it is used to describe differences in individuals' incomes, where that is more relevant.

This book focuses on income inequality because, to put it simply, money matters. It may not be the only thing that makes for a good life,[19] but it is vital. Income is a powerful influence on one's well-being and standard of living. In the words of the New Economics Foundation, a British think-tank, 'How much you earn can determine your lifestyle, where you can afford to live, and your aspirations and status.'[20] Closer to home, the Ministry of Social Development argues that people's living standards are determined by many things other than just their current income – but most of those other things, such as assets, gifts, expected future income and so on, have some kind of monetary basis: 'In this wider sense, it is almost all about income.'[21] Not only does income determine people's ability to afford the basics of life, its absence also limits their access to opportunities, experiences, security and participation in society.

Unequal impacts

A shocking statistic for New Zealand is the disproportionate number of Māori and Pacific people living below the poverty line. Though Pākehā make up the majority (just) of those in poverty, only one in ten Pākehā households is in poverty.[22] In contrast, one in five Māori and Pacific households live in poverty.

This disparity for Māori is traced throughout the book, notably in contributions from Evan Te Ahu Poata-Smith (Chapter 10), Anake

Goodall (Viewpoint 10), and Linda Tuhiwai Smith (Chapter 15). These contributions outline a story in which, as Goodall puts it, the meeting of Māori and Pākehā cultures has been 'a largely one-sided affair'.

Central to this story is the appropriation and alienation of almost 95 per cent of Māori land from the nineteenth century well into the twentieth century.[23] The Treaty settlements process has provided an important form of redress, acknowledging that the Crown's acquisition of land was often flawed 'to a greater or lesser degree', and that 'excessive land loss had a harmful effect on Māori social and economic development in general'.[24] Settlements to date have produced compensation of about $1.48 billion – an amount that has to be considered against the impact of the almost total loss of an economic base over more than a century.[25]

There is growing wealth in Māori society as well as deepening poverty, but the broad picture is one in which Māori are disproportionately represented amongst the poorer part of New Zealand's population. In the early twenty-first century this translates into a heightened risk of poor health, worse school results and reduced opportunities. Continuing structural discrimination in public services means Māori are less likely to be treated for similar health conditions even when they have the same need as Pākehā.[26] The criminal justice system has a disproportionate effect on Māori families (see Chapter 8), while school curriculums are not sufficiently responsive to Māori students' needs (see Chapter 12). Initiatives such as Whānau Ora (which takes a whānau-centred approach) may make a difference. But a wider response is needed if these impacts of income inequality for Māori are to be reduced (see Chapter 15).

Income inequality is also apparent when comparing the incomes of women and men in New Zealand. Over the second half of the twentieth century, the average income for all women (including those not in paid work) as a percentage of men's increased from around 20 per cent in 1951 to around 60 per cent in 1991 – but has stalled at that level ever since.[27]

There are complex reasons for this disparity. While the number of women in paid work has increased, the care of children and other family responsibilities take women (more often than men) out of the paid workforce for long periods. This affects women's incomes in a number of ways over time. Women also do significantly larger amounts of unpaid domestic work than men, as Marilyn Waring set out so plainly in *Counting for Nothing*.[28]

In addition, the welfare system has not always accommodated the position of many women. It is overly reliant on paid work – historically, male wage earners' work – to ensure an adequate income.[29] Many recent initiatives, such as the subsidies for KiwiSaver contributions and some Working for Families tax credits, are available only to those in paid work or, sometimes, in full-time paid work. Since a lower proportion of women are in full-time paid work, they are more likely to be excluded from these initiatives, and more reliant on inadequate state benefits.

In the workplace, the gap between women's and men's earnings has narrowed since the 1972 Equal Pay Act was passed, but progress has slowed in recent years. The gap in average hourly earnings is now about 13 per cent, and is much wider for weekly or annual earnings. Women are over-represented in part-time work and do less overtime.[30]

Another factor in the pay gap is the lower proportion of women promoted to senior positions within almost every occupation, including Parliament and company boards.[31] Women are also concentrated in particular occupations and sectors, many of them low-paid and, arguably, undervalued.[32] Often the skills needed in these kinds of occupations, such as nursing and childcare, are not given the same weight as 'male-type skills'.[33] New Zealand research also suggests that much of the gender pay gap is shaped by 'discriminatory or gender-biased elements'.[34] Because of the constraints of childcare and interruptions to their career, many women are often forced to accept part time, low-paid or low-status work.[35] Māori, Pacific, and immigrant women are particularly over-represented in such low-paid work.

In Chapter 6, Karlo Mila writes about the expectations of people who have come from the Pacific over the last 60 years, looking for a 'land of plenty'. The reality is that they 'have typically started at the bottom rungs of the income ladder … [and] have frequently been the first to be let go.' They have also been hard hit by the disappearance of traditional manufacturing industries, and, although many have upskilled in recent decades, Pacific workers remain concentrated in low-paying sectors, such as cleaning and aged care. The unemployment rate for Pacific people in the past three years has consistently been two to three times higher than the general population's rate; in the words of a recent Salvation Army report, 'Pacific people appear to have been hit more severely by the effects of [the global financial crisis] than other New Zealanders.'[36] And, like Māori, Pacific peoples experience structural discrimination that exacerbates the problems of living in poverty. These issues – of rights, access to work and discrimination – also affect recent immigrants, who suffer worse health, education and employment outcomes than the average population.[37]

This then is the diverse shape of income inequality in New Zealand, a complex picture in which 'The degrees of disadvantage within ethnic categories – for instance, rural and urban Māori, local and foreign-born Pacific people, or long-settled and newly arrived Asian migrants – can be just as significant as those between them.'[38] Amid this complexity stand real people: around 800,000 New Zealanders below the poverty line, amongst whom more are women than men, and a great many are children.[39] Many elderly people also live close to the poverty line, in addition to those who are below it. And against these figures can be set the 29,000 people who hold 16 per cent of New Zealand's wealth or the 13,000 New Zealanders who have incomes over $250,000.[40] It is what happens for all these people, bound together by their lives in these Pacific islands, that this book is about.

But why do low incomes matter?
It is sometimes suggested that anyone in New Zealand, irrespective of their background, can get by if they just budget better. Yet incomes at the bottom are typically too low for people to afford anything other than a life of bare subsistence – and often not even that.

Take, for instance, a typical two-parent family, with two children, living on one minimum wage income. Using 2012 figures, a full-time minimum wage salary of $540 a week becomes $460 after tax. Working for Families and the accommodation supplement might increase that to $790.[41] An average house in eastern Porirua, one of New Zealand's cheapest suburbs, costs $255 to rent,[42] leaving around $540. Other weekly costs soon eat up the rest. Feeding a two-child family well – by meeting nutritional guidelines in the cheapest way possible – costs about $260, even if families buy raw ingredients (rather than packaged meals), and the cheapest meat, fruit and vegetables.[43] That leaves around $280 per week for everything else. Running a car (a necessity for many people to access work) typically costs $85.[44] Power costs can often be $50. So once bare survival is taken care of, just $145 a week may be left for everything else: $5 a day per person to cover clothing, a phone, replacing or repairing appliances, healthcare costs, and so on. It is simply not enough for the most minimal standard of living.[45]

In a real-life example, a single man on the unemployment benefit is living on just $280 a week,[46] with fixed costs that leave him $50 a week for food, clothing, a phone, transport, entertainment and everything else (see Chapter 14). Again, it isn't enough to live on. Around a fifth of poor households report going without several essential items, such as having a decent pair of shoes, heating all the rooms in their house, or giving birthday presents to their family.⁴⁷ In half of poor households, food runs out because there isn't enough money at the end of the week.⁴⁸ Low-decile schools report many children coming to school without being properly fed, or without adequate clothes – again, because their parents, even when working, don't earn enough to pay for these basic necessities.⁴⁹ As British researchers Mark Tomlinson and Robert Walker have written: 'Basics become luxuries that have to be prioritised and saved for. Solutions to one problem create problems of their own, as when saving on heating exacerbates illness.'⁵⁰

Income, not budgeting, is the main problem. There is little evidence that poor people are on average any worse at budgeting than rich people; they just have less money.⁵¹ (See Viewpoint 5.) Poor families are, for instance, just as likely as anyone else to budget a set amount for food each week, and make a shopping list before going to the supermarket.⁵² Nor do the poor spend all their spare cash on luxuries. Figures from 2010 show that the average beneficiary household spends less than $20 a week on alcohol and cigarettes: about enough for a 12-pack of beer, or 3 pints at a pub.⁵³ International evidence indicates that 'most parents living in poverty are remarkably resilient and possess strong coping skills in the face of the adversity in their lives.'⁵⁴ Nor is it true that they are poor principally because they have too many kids. Although large families are more likely to be poor than others, the majority of families below the poverty line have just one or two children.⁵⁵

Why inequality – why not just poverty?

If incomes do matter, the question remains: why put so much stress on a *relative* issue, the difference in incomes between various groups? Why not focus simply on the fact that some people are too poor to get by, in a basic *material* sense?

The short answer is that poverty is not just a problem for the poor; it concerns and involves everyone, including the very well-off. In these pages, we describe the levels of poverty now found in New Zealand as a crisis for the society as a whole. While few New Zealanders may live in absolute poverty in Third World terms, we do not live in a third-world country. And the material poverty we do have is undeniable, and severe. To put it simply, too many people now live in appalling conditions without the income needed for the essentials of life.

But examining the full arc of income inequality also frames poverty in relative terms. To use the words of British sociologist Ruth Lister, poverty can be described as 'a shameful and corrosive social relation'; in these terms, poverty represents not only material hardship but also a 'lack of voice; disrespect; ... powerlessness; denial of rights and diminished citizenship'.[56] As the political economist Adam Smith put it over 200 years ago, the essentials of life are 'not only the commodities which are indispensably necessary for the support of life, but whatever the custom of the country renders it indecent for creditable people ... to be without.'[57] What is needed, then, is what Linda Tuhiwai Smith describes as a 'whole-of-society' response, a recognition that how income is distributed across society shapes everyone's futures.

The argument for reducing differences (in this case, for reducing income inequality) has strong ethical foundations, grounded in the idea that all human beings 'are equal in some fundamental respect' (see Chapter 5). People's ability 'to participate fully in their society and enjoy a sense of belonging' is especially important. While people have a responsibility to contribute to society, they also have a right to share in the rewards of the society that they have helped create. The roadworker, the receptionist and the rigger all contribute to a functioning economy, just as much as the businessman or the board director.

For this reason, the most relevant poverty measures in New Zealand (and for other developed countries) are relative ones: that is, they measure whether a household has less than a certain percentage of the typical household's disposable income.[58] This book generally uses the figure of 60 per cent of typical household income, because New Zealand families in focus groups have reported that they need an income around that mark to provide an 'adequate household expenditure'.[59] Below this level, households struggle to afford the things – like transport and good housing – that allow them to take advantage of opportunities available. These are the households referred to earlier, the 800,000 New Zealanders living in poverty. These households have to meet all their expenses, including housing costs, on less than the following amounts (which are adjusted to reflect the higher expenses of larger households):

single parent, one child:	$26,780 a year	$515 a week
couple with one child:	$35,620	$685
two parents, two children:	$41,600	$800[60]

What about social mobility?

Even if these relative measures matter, aren't they irrelevant if people can move up and down the income ladder, meaning no-one needs to be poor for long? Instead of focusing on inequality of *income*, why isn't the focus on inequality of *opportunity*?

For a start, many people do not rise up the ladder. New Zealand has limited data on social mobility, but available figures show that 45 per cent of the people living in poverty are still there seven years later.[61] Jaine Ikurere, the 63-year-old woman who cleans the Prime Minister's office, is still on just $14.60 an hour after 19 years cleaning at Parliament.[62] Social mobility does not reduce the numbers of people in poverty if pay rates remain low: as people move 'up the ladder', others will simply take their places in poorly paid jobs. Also, if a job is worth doing – as many low-paid jobs clearly are – then people should be able to do it and enjoy a decent life *without* having to move to another job. As the economic historian R. H. Tawney put it, a good society is not just one in which people can rise, but also one in which 'they should be able to lead a life of dignity, whether they rise or not'.[63]

Focusing only on equality of opportunities also overlooks the fact that we cannot separate opportunity from income. When people have hugely different incomes, they have different opportunities – and these differences can persist through generations. As Chapters 7 and 9 indicate, children from high-income families typically go to better-equipped schools than children from low-income families. Geographic differences can define opportunities, since communities with concentrated disadvantage often lack good healthcare facilities, access to affordable and healthy food, and well-supported schools. Low-income New Zealanders often face, in Karlo Mila's phrase, 'constrained' choices rather than real choices (see Chapter 6).

There is also substantial evidence that in more equal societies, people have a greater chance to advance from low incomes than they do in more unequal societies.[64] The United States, for instance, is supposed to be the land of opportunity, but its levels of social mobility are very low thanks to its large income gaps. A son born to a father in the poorest fifth of the population has only an 8 per cent chance of moving into the richest fifth in adulthood; 42 per cent of sons who are born poor, stay poor.[65] By contrast, in Denmark, only 25 per cent of poor sons remain poor, and many experience significant social mobility across their lifetimes.

Countries with the lowest levels of income inequality offer greater equality of opportunities; typically these are societies that invest more in children's early years, spend more on public services, and use tax and benefits to reduce income inequality.[66] Rather than generating complacency or conformity, this investment appears to act as a safety net that encourages greater self-expression, creativity and innovation.[67]

Rightful reward?

If people's incomes were a fair reflection of their worth (however measured) and the result of decisions they had made, income gaps could be seen as simply right and natural. As the columnist and former MP Deborah Coddington argues, 'It is our intelligence, our skills, our capacity for hard work which enables us to generate a good income.'[68] So is it just the case that some individuals need to work harder and make a bigger contribution?

Individual choices and attributes do matter. As Jonathan Boston observes in Chapter 5, rewarding people for their talent, contribution or effort can be seen as socially just: 'A person who makes a huge effort to achieve some particular task is arguably more deserving than someone of equal natural abilities who decides to make absolutely no effort at all.' Yet allocating reward simply on the basis of talent or effort presents some significant challenges. Are people to be rewarded on the basis of an innate ability? Or because they have worked particularly hard? And what role do circumstances play in achievement or success?

Contribution (to society or the economy) is another possible yardstick for measuring reward. But current systems of pay do not necessarily represent the value of people's contributions. For example, using the concept of a 'social return on investment' (the broader benefits to society created by a particular activity), British researchers have suggested that high-paid investment bankers, by engaging in predatory lending and contributing to financial crises, destroy £7 of wider social, economic and environmental value for every £1 of value they create.[69] In contrast, low-paid childcare centre staff help nurture the workers of the future and generate between £7 and £9.50 in value for each £1 they are paid. More broadly, there is little evidence that very high salaries, especially for chief executives, are linked to performance or contribution (see Viewpoint 1).[70]

While it could be argued that some income gaps are justified on the basis of extra hard work, there is little evidence that people on lower incomes work less hard than those at higher levels. The hours worked by low-income New Zealanders have increased significantly since the 1980s, and the falling benefit numbers when there were more jobs available in the early 2000s are testimony to a strong work ethic.[71] In fact, people's rewards are shaped by a range of factors outside of their control. These include what Boston refers to in Chapter 5 as the 'inequalities in the distribution of natural endowments, such as intellectual abilities and physical skills, or economic resources acquired via inheritance or sheer luck', but also wider social forces. These can include social norms, the informal beliefs that govern society's behaviours. In Japan, for instance, excessively high pay is regarded as unacceptable, and chief executive salaries are constrained to just 16 times the average salary, as opposed to 200 or 300 times (depending on the measure) in the United States.[72] And to take a very different social constraint, much of the work mentioned in this book is undervalued simply because it has traditionally been carried out by women.

Power also frames the allocation of reward. If staff bargain collectively through a union, or some other democratic means (such as a cooperative workplace structure), they can act as what economist J. K. Galbraith referred to as 'a countervailing power' to employers. If employees have to bargain individually, their power can be reduced. In contrast, New Zealand research suggests that increases in chief executive pay are explained in part by CEOs' ability to use relationships with board members.[73] In Chapter 15, Linda Tuhiwai Smith discusses further the role that power relations can play in shaping how income inequality is addressed.

Can't economic growth lift us out of this?

But ultimately isn't just growing the New Zealand economy, not redistributing income, the most effective solution? Surely enlarging the 'pie' of income will improve everyone's economic circumstances?

Economic growth, while important, has not yet proven to be a sufficient answer to the problems presented by dramatically increasing inequality. As the last three decades have shown, there is no guarantee that growth will do anything to help those on the lowest rungs of the ladder. In the lowest 10 per cent of incomes, people are no richer now (once housing costs are taken into account) than they were in 1987 (see Chapter 2). In America, there has been significant economic growth in the last 25 years – yet inflation-adjusted incomes for many have actually fallen.[74]

Moreover, a substantial body of research suggests that high levels of income inequality can stifle economic growth. Recent research from the IMF indicates that inequality limits growth in at least three ways: by denying low-income families the money they need to invest in their children's education (and thus their contribution to the economy in later life); by allowing top income earners to influence politicians to pass laws that favour their interests, not the wider economy's; and by making societies more unstable and less able to respond to sudden shocks (see below for more details).[75] Former IMF chief economist Raghuram Rajan, meanwhile, has argued that inequality was one of the drivers of the global financial crisis.[76]

Why inequality matters
A growing body of evidence demonstrates that unequal societies are less functional, less cohesive and less economically sound than their more equal counterparts – and that these weaknesses are felt widely.

Dysfunction: how do unequal societies fail?
Large-scale income inequality prevents a society from functioning as well as it should. That impact has been influentially captured by two health researchers, professors Richard Wilkinson and Kate Pickett, in *The Spirit Level*, published in 2010.[77] Compiling hundreds of different sets of data, across dozens of countries, they make a compelling case that countries with higher levels of income inequality perform worse than more equal countries on a wide range of social measures, from school performance to average lifespans. This thesis has its critics,[78] but Wilkinson and Pickett have provided good answers to those that offer substantive comment. This debate is covered on their website: www.equalitytrust.org.uk.

Wilkinson and Pickett's findings suggest that one of the key connections between income inequality and societal dysfunction is, quite simply, stress.[79] Prolonged exposure to stress damages hearts and immune systems, and is 'seriously detrimental' to health and longevity. Stress can also impair our ability to perform well at school and participate more widely in society.

The Spirit Level also argues that high levels of income inequality dramatically increase what is known as psychosocial stress: the psychological and physical effects of comparing ourselves to others and feeling inferior. Psychosocial stress is, the authors argue, a powerful and insidious force, worsening problems like mental health and obesity throughout society. When added to the effects of material poverty, psychosocial stress is likely to have greater repercussions for those on low incomes. New Zealand's long-running Dunedin survey, for instance, shows that children from poor families are twice as likely to suffer heart disease as children from wealthy families.[80] In other words, poorer children are damaged by growing up in low socio-economic circumstances in a way that later wealth cannot fully erase.

It was health research that laid the foundations for academics examining the impact of income inequality. In 1978, British health

Figure 1.1 Health and social problems index and income inequality

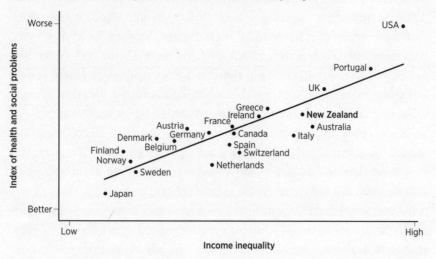

Source: R. Wilkinson & K. Pickett, *The Spirit Level, Why Equality is Better for Everyone*, Penguin, London, 2010, p.20.

researcher Michael Marmot found that heart attacks among UK public sector workers increase significantly *lower* down the income ladder.[81] It is, according to this research, more stressful to be on a low income, probably with less control over one's work or income, than at higher levels, even with the pressures of management and responsibility.

Drawing on Marmot's research and hundreds of other peer-reviewed studies, Wilkinson and Pickett compiled an index of health and social problems (including obesity, life expectancy, imprisonment rates and alcohol abuse) and ranked countries accordingly, as in Figure 1.1.

Countries with lower income gaps, including the Scandinavian countries and the Netherlands, do well, while countries with higher inequality do badly. New Zealand has five times the teenage pregnancy rate of countries such as Sweden and twice as many obese people as countries such as Norway: these are both countries with more equal societies – that is, less income inequality, or smaller gaps between high and low incomes.[82]

One of *The Spirit Level*'s most influential conclusions is that in less equal societies nearly everybody, not just the poor, is adversely affected. For example, Americans die on average 4.5 years earlier than the Japanese, but it is not just low-income Americans dying earlier. Low-income Americans are not sufficiently numerous to be responsible for such a big average gap across hundreds of millions of people in two countries. The gap makes sense only if *most* Americans have reduced life expectancy compared to their Japanese counterparts.[83]

Division: How does inequality break down social cohesion?

Another important conclusion that Wilkinson and Pickett draw from their research is that more equal societies are likely to have more social cohesion – people feel they have more in common with each other, and are more trusting.[84] In contrast, significant income gaps can leave people living very different lives, weakening bonds between different groups, widening divisions and reducing opportunities. They encourage a focus on competition and conspicuous consumption, rather than collaboration. 'Living in unequal ... societies, we use possessions to show ourselves in a good light, to make a positive impression, and to avoid appearing incompetent or inadequate in the eyes of others.'[85]

When people have very different incomes, they also begin to lose their ability to understand and empathise with others. Recent surveys suggest that New Zealanders' trust in others has typically been strong in the past, but is falling sharply.[86] And according to Wilson and Pickett's research,[87] New Zealanders are likely to become less trusting if inequality becomes entrenched.

Current urban planning is likely to exacerbate a decline in social cohesion. A limited supply of homes and rising high incomes put many housing areas out of reach of low-income families. In the absence of state house building programmes or policies to build mixed communities, social isolation and segmentation has increased. As a report by the Auckland Communities Foundation noted, '[Auckland] suburbs are each becoming more homogeneous internally'.[88] The same is true in Porirua, a city that graphically represents what is known as a 'hollowed-out' income distribution pattern. It has about 20,000 people with incomes in the lowest fifth of all New Zealand incomes, many of them in Cannons Creek and Waitangirua; about 15,000 with incomes amongst the highest fifth of all incomes, in Whitby and other suburbs; and a remaining few from middle-income groups scattered through the city.[89] A similar picture can be seen in rural areas: a socio-economic map of Northland, for instance, shows areas of relative affluence right next to concentrations of extreme deprivation.[90]

Inadequate housing policies play a role in this segregation (see Chapter 7), and create huge problems for schools that are dealing with concentrations of disadvantage and struggling learners (see Chapter 9). Children can grow up with limited worldviews: those brought up in well-off households in affluent suburbs 'have virtually no direct experience of material deprivation or hardship'.[91] As Auckland's different groups become less linked with each other, the communities foundation's report found, those who could lend a helping hand seldom take their skills and resources out of their own communities to where they are most needed. This finding matches international research such as Robert Putnam's *Bowling Alone,* which charts how a decline in 'social capital' (people's networks and community bonds) leads to lower participation in joint activities, reciprocity and community-building initiatives.[92]

Low-income communities can be cut off in quite literal ways. They tend to be located at some distance from urban centres and from employment. As Viewpoint 6 notes, some children from low-income suburbs have never been to their nearby city centres. In some New Zealand research, three-quarters of the long-term unemployed found mobility a significant barrier to getting a job.[93] Travel costs can make work barely worth the effort when the jobs available are often temporary shift work or other low-quality employment, which through its shifting, unstable nature can also damage people's health.[94]

The effects of segregation are, in the end, seen most profoundly in the poverty traps common to more deprived areas. Families whose health is already poor because of their housing may find that their low-income suburb lacks shops that stock 'affordable and healthy food'.[95] People who struggle to get credit are preyed upon by finance companies that target low-income areas, offering loans at extortionate rates. Poorer communities, as Chapter 7 points out, often lack adequate GP clinics and other health services.

As the American philosopher Michael Sandel has noted, the segregation of our society ultimately has consequences for democracy, which requires that citizens 'share a common life':

> What matters is that people of different social backgrounds, different walks of life, encounter one another, bump up against one another, in the course of everyday life. Because this is how we come to negotiate and abide our differences, and this is how we come to care for the common good.[96]

Stagnation: how does inequality weaken growth?
A growing body of international research suggests that high levels of income inequality may be harmful for economic growth.[97] One major piece of international research at the IMF, for example, finds that although short-term growth can be generated with either high or low inequality, narrower income gaps are good for *long-term* economic growth. The latter is exactly what New Zealand needs.[98]

Entrenched inequality can weaken the economy by depriving it of the ability of a broad spectrum of the population; a more equal economy draws on the strengths of a wider workforce. Inequality means that fewer talented children from poor families will rise to the positions where they could make the most difference, as Ganesh Nana argues in Chapter 4. In the words of the Organisation for Economic Co-operation and Development (OECD) secretary-general Angel Gurría, 'Greater income inequality stifles upward mobility between generations, making it harder for talented and hard-working people to get the rewards they deserve. Ignoring increasing inequality is not an option.'[99] In contrast, a more equal economy rewards workers more fairly, and research suggests they may in turn work harder and generate more income.[100] Drawing on the ideas and innovation of the whole workforce, not just a select few, can result in higher performing companies and economies.

Secondly, in countries with large concentrations of income, the wealthy can use their power to argue for policies that further their interests rather than those of the economy as a whole. The absence of curbs on big financial companies in the US and UK is just one example of what Robert Wade, in Chapter 3, calls 'state capture' by the 1 per cent. More equal economies, in contrast, are more likely to crack down harder on monopolies and cartels, both of which limit growth by keeping out new entrants and driving up prices.

Thirdly, high income inequality can weaken the economy by depriving people of the spending power needed to buy the goods and services it produces. This weakening takes money away from those at the lowest end, whose income is (of necessity) mostly committed to expenditure and thus stimulates the economy, and transfers it to the wealthy, who typically save 15–25 per cent of their income or spend it overseas. And, as the economist Joseph Stiglitz points out, a lack of money makes it difficult for lower- and middle-income families to invest in their children's education, especially at university or polytechnic, thus lowering the supply of skilled workers.[101]

An unequal economy is also more prone to financial instability. A top-heavy concentration of wealth means surplus cash often gets invested in property and other asset bubbles, or is lent to people trying to supplement very low incomes, who may struggle to repay the loans. Such borrowing was, according to a recent IMF study, a major factor in the global financial crisis.[102] Some economists also claim significant income inequality can lead to socio-political instability, which may frighten investors.[103]

Finally, a more equal economy can be more efficient. Economies run best on trust, limiting the time and money spent on drawing up contracts or monitoring others. In unequal economies, where trust is low and people may behave more self-interestedly, transaction costs can soar and productivity fall.[104] More equal economies can also save large amounts of money by investing upfront in programmes that help people before things go wrong. Money spent on free, universal early childhood education, for example, could save New Zealand anywhere between $3 and $17 for each dollar spent, since well-educated and socialised children are less likely to incur health, crime and other costs as they get older.[105]

Where to from here?

We are all worse off for having wide income gaps in New Zealand. The next chapter sets out how those gaps opened up, and just how wide they really are. These themes are then expanded in Part Two, 'Issues and Debates', which tracks the rapid growth in inequality right across the developed world, and outlines the economic and ethical challenges that this raises. Part Three, 'Consequences', looks in detail at some of the social effects of inequality: the damage it does to our health, education and imprisonment rates, and the way that these effects have been felt in Māori and Pacific communities. Finally, Part Four, 'Looking Ahead', begins the debate about how best to narrow our growing income gaps.

Not in it for the money

Ian Taylor is the chief executive of Animation Research, a leading computer animation company that he founded as a joint venture in 1991. He was named Māori business leader of the year in 2013, and was interviewed for this viewpoint by Max Rashbrooke.

When Ian Taylor saw pay rises for company directors being defended in the *New Zealand Herald* with the line, 'If you pay peanuts, you get monkeys', he responded strongly. In a letter to the newspaper, he wrote: 'If that means I have joined our fellow primates ... then I know who I would rather spend my time with: them and the countless other CEOs and management of small New Zealand companies who still live in the real world.'

Taylor, a former television presenter and *North and South* New Zealander of the year, established Animation Research with four others in 1991. Considered one of the country's top computer animation firms, it employs thirty people doing pioneering work for sports broadcasts, television programmes and advertising. The company's work is used in countries around the world.

Taylor spoke out because he felt uncomfortable with the levels of top salaries. 'When large amounts are being paid to some, and the family down the road is not able to feed their two or three kids ... that inequality just seems wrong, and it doesn't seem to make sense. It's pretty basic.'

Taylor himself is financially 'comfortable', he says. 'You want to be able to retire with savings, you want to know that you can pay your bills ... I'm not saying that people shouldn't be paid well, but they need to be paid well *and* their staff too.' On that basis, he hasn't taken a pay rise in ten years. 'Until everybody here at Animation Research is paid what they are worth, I'm staying where I am.'

High salaries are also unnecessary, Taylor argues, citing the example of TrustPower chief executive Vince Hawkesworth, whose estimated $580,000 salary is a third of those at comparable companies. 'We get these stories that you need to pay $1.5 million. But we need to understand that there are some hugely talented people out there who actually manage to do the same if not a better job for less – and consider themselves to be well rewarded.'

High pay is not even a sensible motivator, Taylor adds. 'If you have got people running companies whose focus is on the size of their pay packet, then I don't think they should be running them.' And while he's not sure that lower CEO pay could be 'mandated', the idea 'needs to be thrown out there and discussed. You need to have the community and the country understand that there are people like Hawkesworth.'

Taylor vehemently rejects claims that high salaries are needed to reward hard work, talent or innovation. 'Most of the people who have been the most innovative … when they started doing it, it wasn't about money. How many of them started in a garage because it was challenging, because it was exciting, because it was fun?' At Animation Research, he says, 'We have never done anything for the money.'

He also rejects the idea that letting the market determine salaries is the best way to allocate resources efficiently. Noting the sudden rises and falls to which the stockmarket is prone, he says: 'That's the market? It's sort of like people rolling dice all over the place. It seems to be as random as just about anything.'

Taylor's concerns go beyond chief executive pay. He worries that very narrow goals – financial bottom lines and shareholder dividends – have taken the place of making sure that the economy generates enough income for everyone. 'Even when we look at government support for companies in New Zealand, there doesn't seem to be any consideration around the jobs that might be created – better salaries, more even salaries; instead, it seems to be about shareholder wealth.'

The alternative is to believe that, as he puts it, 'The country is a better place to live in if everybody can afford to live in it.' For business people, that means focusing on staff. 'For me, the first people on your list of concerns when you get up every morning should be the people who work with you. That's it.' Rather than chief executives being rewarded for cutting staff and thus reducing costs, their pay 'should be measured by how well he or she protects jobs and should bear a direct relationship to how well the employees … are paid'.

To argue that this approach is incompatible with running a successful business is 'ridiculous', says Taylor. If staff are your first priority, 'then profits and finding jobs is the corollary of that'. It is for that reason that he maintains a punishing schedule travelling the world to drum up business: 'Not because I like it, but because I know that's how to find work for the people that are here.'

Within Animation Research itself, there is a culture in which people look out for each other – and are loyal. During a difficult spell a few years ago, when the company was running with just a month's worth of reserves, the staff said, 'OK, let's go month by month.' No one left. The company also runs on a reciprocity-based Māori principle, ako, which means that 'there is no management, there are no workers – we are all management, we are all workers.'

Taylor would ultimately like New Zealanders to rethink their attitudes to wealth and income. People, especially those who are paid well, need to ask themselves: 'Are you happy that there are people out there who are working in old people's homes, people cleaning the Beehive, [who] have to take three jobs in order to feed their kids?' Shareholders, meanwhile, should think of wealth not as higher dividends, but as the chance 'to live in a society that is really harmonious – because nobody wants for anything'. In other words, we need to realise that profits and people are not separate. 'They go hand in hand.'

2 Inequality and New Zealand

Max Rashbrooke

How large is the gap between the rich and the rest in New Zealand? When has this gap changed? And how has this divergence happened? In learning what New Zealanders earn and own, we can start to understand the forces that help shape income inequality.

Who earns what?
How much does an individual have to make in a year to get into the top 10 per cent of income earners in New Zealand – $200,000, $500,000, $1 million? The answer is just $72,000.[1] Anyone earning above that is richer than 90 per cent of the country.

The distribution of incomes across New Zealand is represented in the 'income ladder' opposite. (The incomes referred to here are the pre-tax incomes of individuals.) The bottom half of the ladder – representing half of the total population – earns less than $24,000. Among them are beneficiaries: those on the unemployment benefit receive $11,900 a year before tax, someone on the domestic purposes benefit (DPB) gets $17,300, and pensioners receive $20,800 each.[2]

Moving up the ladder, 70 per cent of New Zealanders earn under $43,000. A full-time minimum-wage salary, for example, equates to $28,600 a year, while a 'living wage' worker gets $38,270 (see Chapter 11). On these lower rungs are cleaners, many of whom earn less than $30,000 a year.[3] Further up, 90 per cent of New Zealanders earn less than $72,000. Senior firefighters earn no more than $57,000 a year,[4] while the basic maximum income for teachers is $73,000.[5]

Up the top of the ladder, the remaining 5 per cent – the highest earning New Zealanders – earn a minimum of $93,000 each.[6] The top 2 per cent earn over $131,000, including MPs, on a minimum of $141,800,[7] as well as chief financial officers[8] and principal accountants.[9] To be in New Zealand's top 1 per cent you would have to earn over $170,000, while the top 0.4 per cent (some 13,000 people) earn over $250,000 each. In this latter group are the most senior managers in government departments and public sector bodies (where more than 250 staff are on over $250,000 each),[10] and the highest-paid staff in large companies, where the average salary for chief executives is $1.5 million.[11]

Figure 2.1 Step by step: New Zealand's income ladder

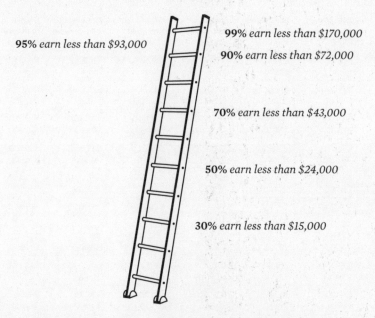

95% earn less than $93,000
99% earn less than $170,000
90% earn less than $72,000
70% earn less than $43,000
50% earn less than $24,000
30% earn less than $15,000

Source: Inland Revenue, Income distribution of individual customers, 2002 to 2011, http://www.ird.govt.nz/aboutir/external-stats/revenue-refunds/inc-dist-of-ind/ (accessed 31 May 2013).

These figures for pre-tax income help give a sense of people's salaries. But to understand actual living standards across New Zealand, some further context is required. As Chapter 1 explained, a household's total income is a more revealing measure than individual income alone. And both the taxes people pay and the Working for Families tax credits they earn make a big difference to their final income. So to understand the spread of living standards and how New Zealand households compare with others of their type, we need to look at the figures for households' after-tax incomes (that is, disposable incomes), as set out in Table 2.1.[12]

The rungs on the ladder in Figure 2.1 correspond to the decile numbers in the table. To work out where a given household sits, just find the column that represents that household's type, before reading down the column to locate its annual after-tax income. For example, a couple with two children on $60,600 after tax would be broadly in the middle of New Zealand's income distribution. With $143,200, they'd be near the top.

Who owns what?

Like annual incomes, net wealth in New Zealand (as measured by how much people own in cash and assets, once money owed is subtracted) is unequally distributed. Together, New Zealand's 2.9 million adults own almost $470 billion. Of that, the top 1 per cent of the adult population

Table 2.1 Relativity: how your household's disposable income compares to others

	One person, no children	Sole parent with one child	Couple or two adults sharing	Couple with one child	Couple with two children	Couple with three children
Decile 10	$66,000 or more	$92,400 or more	$101,600 or more	$122,800 or more	$143,200 or more	$160,400 or more
Decile 9	$51,400–66,000	$72,000–92,400	$79,200–101,600	$95,600–122,800	$111,600–143,200	$124,900–160,400
Decile 8	$43,500–51,400	$60,900–72,000	$67,000–79,200	$81,000–95,600	$94,500–111,600	$105,800–124,900
Decile 7	$36,700–43,500	$51,400–60,900	$56,500–67,000	$68,200–81,000	$79,600–94,500	$89,100–105,800
Decile 6	$31,900–36,700	$44,600–51,400	$49,100–56,500	$59,300–68,200	$69,200–79,600	$77,400–89,100
Decile 5	$27,900–31,900	$39,100–44,600	$43,000–49,100	$51,900–59,300	$60,600–69,200	$67,800–77,400
Decile 4	$23,800–27,900	$33,300–39,100	$36,600–43,000	$44,200–51,900	$51,500–60,600	$57,700–67,800
Decile 3	$19,900–23,800	$27,900–33,300	$30,700–36,600	$37,100–44,200	$43,200–51,500	$48,400–57,700
Decile 2	$16,600–19,900	$23,300–27,900	$25,600–30,700	$31,000–37,100	$36,100–43,200	$40,400–48,400
Decile 1	$16,600 or less	$23,300 or less	$25,600 or less	$31,000 or less	$36,100 or less	$40,400 or less

Note: This table shows some typical household types, and how incomes are spread between them. Each 'decile' represents one-tenth of the population, so decile 1 is the lowest tenth of households, while decile 10 is the top.

Source: Adapted from Bryan Perry, *Household Incomes in New Zealand: Trends in Indicators of Inequality and Hardship 1982 to 2011*, Ministry of Social Development, Wellington, 2012, p.45.

alone own 16 per cent of the total wealth, as set out in Figure 2.2. That's just under $77 billion owned by around 29,000 adults. This group and the rest of New Zealand's wealthiest 10 per cent own over half the country's total wealth.[13]

For many New Zealanders in the lowest 50 per cent, the picture is one not of wealth but of debt: the 200,000 poorest (in wealth terms) *owe* a combined $4.7 billion. No one in the poorest fifth of New Zealand owns more than $6,000 in assets. The typical household has a net worth of just under $70,000.[14] Between them, the entire lower half of the country's adults, some 1.45 million people, own just 5 per cent of all wealth, around $23 billion. In other words, the wealthiest 1 per cent of New Zealanders together own three times as much as is owned collectively by the poorest 50 per cent of the population.

More unequal than most

So how does New Zealand's level of income inequality compare internationally? A common way to determine this is the Gini coefficient, a scale in

Figure 2.2 Wealth in New Zealand

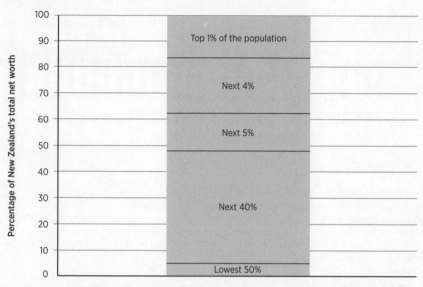

Note: The chart shows how much of New Zealand's $467.67 billion in net wealth is owned by different groups.
Source: Jit Cheung, *Wealth Disparities in New Zealand*, Statistics New Zealand, Wellington, 2007, p.8. Licensed by Statistics NZ for re-use under the Creative Commons Attribution 3.0 New Zealand Licence.

which 100 represents all the income going to one person, and 0 represents income being evenly divided among everyone. The lower the score, the lower the level of income inequality.[15]

New Zealand was historically one of the developed world's more equal societies.[16] But following the unprecedented increase in income inequality between the mid-1980s and mid-1990s, we have fallen in the rankings. Figure 2.3 shows the Gini coefficients in the OECD's thirty-four developed countries in 2010; New Zealand is ranked down at twentieth.[17] And that assessment is arguably flattering, as New Zealand's recorded inequality dipped below-trend in 2010 (to 31.7), only to rise sharply above-trend in 2011 (to around 34). New Zealand's true position is probably around twenty-third, next to Australia.[18]

What we don't measure

It is important to acknowledge that our understanding of income inequality in New Zealand is far from complete (especially compared with the domestic data available in many OECD countries). Despite committed and ongoing research by academics, commentators and various organisations and government departments (notably, the Ministry of Social Development), significant gaps in our knowledge remain.[19]

One gap is the lack of detailed information on the top 10 per cent of incomes (especially the top 1 per cent), including the composition of those

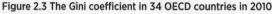

Figure 2.3 The Gini coefficient in 34 OECD countries in 2010

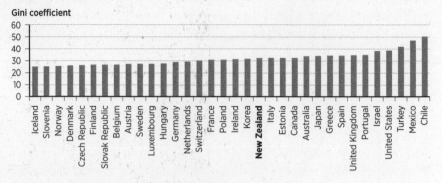

Note: The Gini coefficient measures income inequality. A score of 100 represents all the income going to one person, and 0 represents income being evenly divided among everyone.

Source: Derived from the figures and data in OECD, *Crisis Squeezes Income and Puts Pressure on Inequality and Poverty*, May 2013, Figure 4, 'Gini Coefficient of Household Disposable Income and Gap Between Richest and Poorest 10%, 2010', http://www.oecd.org/els/soc/OECD2013-Inequality-and-Poverty-8p.pdf (accessed 28 May 2013).

incomes and how they have been earned. No country has a complete record of top incomes, which are difficult to sample accurately and can be obscured by tax avoidance. In New Zealand, for example, family trusts are used to avoid an estimated $300 million in tax each year.[20] But New Zealand has less data than many countries, because we do not tax or record capital gains – an issue of policy as well as measurement. New Zealand researchers are also deprived of important income data because this country chooses not to participate in the flagship Luxembourg Income Study.

Only chief executive pay for the period 1997–2002 has been studied in-depth, and New Zealand has relatively little data about how much this pay has increased, what form it takes, and why it has risen.[21] Slightly further down the income ladder, we know even less about pay for senior managers and company directors, and the means by which these salaries are set. The only significant analysis of wealth in New Zealand is based on 2003 data.[22]

We have relatively little information about long-term social mobility, and our research into attitudes towards inequality has been limited. Our reporting of social indicators, many of which are tied to inequality, could be improved. The Ministry of Social Development's *Social Report*, for example, has been reduced in frequency from once a year to once every three years at most. New Zealand has recently been excluded from an international league table of children's health because our data are so poor.[23]

One other, temporary limitation is that the delay of the New Zealand Census until 2013 leaves researchers reliant on data from the 2006 Census.

Equality in New Zealand – truth and myth

Today's extremes of wealth and poverty in New Zealand are striking – especially because, after the Second World War, we were one of the world's more equal societies.[24] Landmark reforms by two governments, the Liberals from 1890 to 1912 and Labour from 1935 to 1949, helped make New Zealand a notably egalitarian country by world standards.

The Liberal Government broke up big estates and distributed land widely, introduced income taxes and the world's first state pension,[25] and passed the Industrial Conciliation and Arbitration Act 1894, which allowed the government to help set minimum pay levels. The First Labour Government introduced the Social Security Act in 1938, explicitly designed to end poverty.[26] It extended old-age pensions to all, created a free healthcare system and introduced a universal family benefit. A 'cradle-to-grave' welfare state and an extensive state-house building programme completed the support package. To fund it, Labour brought in 'hefty' death duties, and raised the top rate of income tax to 77.5 per cent.[27] Thanks to these reforms, and trade union achievements such as the eight-hour working day,[28] New Zealand was said to be leading the world in creating 'a modern, inclusivist liberal democracy'.[29] In the words of the political scientist Leslie Lipson, where America had the Statue of Liberty, New Zealand might have erected a 'Statue of Equality' in Auckland harbour.[30]

But as labour historian Melanie Nolan has observed, New Zealand's history of equality is 'a rich amalgam of truth and myth'.[31] Fused into this history is the disproportionate impact of income inequality, identified in Chapter 1. Māori were systematically excluded by settler governments from many egalitarian measures. The Liberals, for example, while reducing inequality among Pākehā, continued the disenfranchisement of Māori, buying 3.1 million acres of their land, often through punitive or coercive means, in what one historian has called 'a massive land grab'.[32] Much later, when many Māori families migrated to urban areas in the 1950s, they were often forced by poverty and discrimination into poor-quality housing, with knock-on effects for their health and well-being (see Chapters 7 and 10). At the same time, few New Zealand women were able to earn an income of their own: less than 10 per cent of married women were in paid work in the early 1950s, half the level of the US and the UK. And even when in paid work, women were often not considered to have 'dependants', and were therefore paid less.[33]

A snapshot of this varied history is captured in Figure 2.4, which tracks the proportion of income going to New Zealand's top 1 per cent of earners across the twentieth century.[34] It shows how, despite the Liberals' efforts,

Figure 2.4 The top 1 per cent's share of personal (pre-tax) income, 1921–2009

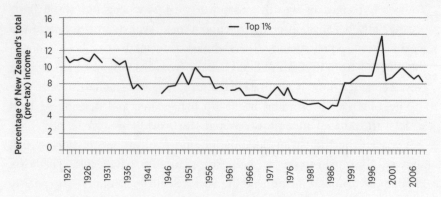

Source: Derived from figures in the World Top Incomes Database, for New Zealand, 1921–2009, http://topincomes.gmond.parisschoolofeconomics.eu (accessed 14 March 2013).

the top 1 per cent still held nearly 12 per cent of all pre-tax income by the 1920s, and maintained that share until roughly the time of Labour's election in 1935. But although this share rose again immediately after the Second World War, it fell steadily from the 1950s to reach an all-time low of around 5 per cent in 1984. This decline was sustained under Labour governments and throughout Keith Holyoake's 1960–1972 National Government. New Zealand's experience was mirrored internationally with income gaps narrowing right across the developed post-war world, in what the economist Paul Krugman has called 'the great convergence'.[35]

A turning tide

During this time of convergence, the international post-war recovery delivered exceptional economic gains: world GDP growth averaged 4.8 per cent between 1950 and 1973, compared to 3.2 per cent in the period 1980–2009.[36] This growth was shared widely, with a large proportion of profits going to wage and salary earners rather than lenders and investors.[37] In New Zealand, women and Māori did not necessarily share in this income distribution. However, the gender gap was reducing, with the average income for all women (including those not in paid work) rising from 20 per cent of men's in 1951 to 54 per cent by 1986. Average Māori incomes rose from 50 per cent of non-Māori income to 62 per cent over the same period.[38]

But by the 1970s this 'great convergence' faced challenges on several fronts. Internationally, the economic shocks and high inflation created by oil shortages in the 1970s put significant pressure on existing economic and political models.[39] New Zealand's economic performance began to lag, and the country slid down the world's economic rankings.[40] High tariffs and extensive controls on importing goods had insulated many New Zealand industries from competition. The economy was over-reliant on meat exports to Britain, and these began to drop off. Revenue fell, and inflation surged, as global oil prices rose sharply. The 'Think Big' public works failed to stimulate the economy.[41] Into the 1980s New Zealand was borrowing well beyond its means: government debt ballooned (it hit 60 per cent of national income in 1984 and 75 per cent by 1987),[42] and, by the 1984 general election, the country had just about exhausted its stocks of foreign currency.[43]

Major structural changes followed as the next two governments, Labour (1984–1990) and National (1990–99), opened up every aspect of the economy to 'radical change'.[44] Over two decades they deregulated markets; removed controls on the flow of finance into New Zealand; reduced tariffs and trade barriers; weakened the bargaining power of unions; reduced taxes and benefits; and privatised or corporatised government activities.[45] It was transformation on a scale not witnessed since the 1930s, profoundly altering not only the economy but also the social fabric.

The great divergence

In the two decades framing these changes, the gap between those at the top and bottom of the income ladder in New Zealand opened up more rapidly than in any other comparable society.[46] These changing fortunes are shown in Figure 2.5, splitting New Zealanders into four groups: those in the lowest 10 per cent of incomes, the middle, the top 10 per cent, and the top 1 per cent.

The figures used in the first three lines (the lowest 10 per cent, middle, and top 10 per cent) are the yearly after-tax (or disposable) income of an average single-person household in that group.[47] The top line represents the annual pre-tax income of the average individual in the top 1 per cent.[48] All the incomes have been adjusted for inflation.

Tracing these four groups across the graph reveals that, while incomes at the top have increased sharply, those in the lower and middle have either stagnated or increased only slightly. Across all four groups, women's incomes have been stuck at 61 per cent of men's since 1991, while Māori incomes have fallen further behind those of Pākehā since the mid-1980s.[49]

The strong correlation between the structural reforms and this 'great divergence' bears careful examination. For some economists there is a 'prima facie' case for connecting the reforms with rising income inequality, while for others the causations are more complex.[50]

Some striking contrasts are revealed by comparing New Zealand's income inequality rates with those of other countries that modernised

Figure 2.5 The rich and the rest: how the gap widened

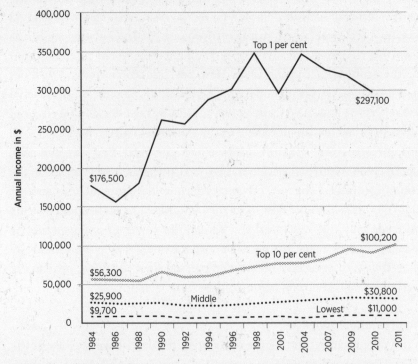

Note: Annual average incomes are in 2010 dollars, and have been adjusted for inflation. The figures for the lowest 10 per cent, middle and top 10 per cent are the yearly disposable income of an average single-person household in that group. The figures for the top 1 per cent are the annual pre-tax income of the average individual in that group.

Source: Adapted from Perry, *Household Incomes in New Zealand*, p.218, and figures in the World Top Incomes Database, for New Zealand, 1921–2009, http://topincomes.gmond.parisschoolofeconomics.eu/ (accessed 14 March 2013).

their economies over the same period. Denmark, for example, developed a fully open, modern economy while *reducing* inequality from the mid-1980s to mid-2000s.[51] Indeed, during the last forty years, the more egalitarian economies of Sweden, Denmark, Norway and the Netherlands have generally grown as fast as or faster than the more unequal economies of the US, Australia, Britain, Canada and New Zealand.[52]

Going nowhere

New Zealand's lowest incomes – shown as the bottom line in Figure 2.5 – had only a minimal increase during the last three decades. A single-person household disposable income in this group of $9,700 a year in 1984 has risen to just $11,000 a year in 2011. And if housing costs are deducted from those figures, these households actually have *less* money to spend than they did in the early 1980s.[53]

This low-income stagnation is due largely to a combination of two factors: a growing number of people on benefits, and sharp cuts in the value of those benefits.[54] The number of people out of work, which had been negligible in the 1960s and 1970s, was still under 4 per cent in the mid-1980s. But by the early 1990s it shot up to 11 per cent, as reforms cut jobs in the public sector and removed the barriers protecting New Zealand companies from overseas competition. Māori and Pacific workers were hit hard: for both groups unemployment was over 15 per cent throughout the period 1989–99, hitting 25 per cent in the early 1990s.[55] Although total unemployment later fell to 3.8 per cent in 2007, full employment was never regained, and by early 2013 over 330,000 people were either jobless or seeking more work.[56]

As unemployment increased during the 1980s and 1990s, the number of people on other benefits (including the invalid's benefit and the DPB) also rose sharply.[57] At the same time, New Zealand began taking an increasingly punitive approach to beneficiaries (see Chapter 14). The 1991 Budget cut the value of the unemployment benefit from $144 to $130 a week, which has not been restored, only adjusted for inflation.[58] The DPB was also cut by around 20 per cent and a number of forms of support have been removed over the last thirty years, including the universal family benefit.

Some changes over the last decade have benefited low-income families, notably a higher minimum wage and Working for Families (a government scheme offering tax credits to families with dependent children). But beneficiary households have gained little from an increased minimum wage, and do not receive some Working for Families tax credits. More broadly, increased housing costs, charges for previously free public services and for tertiary education, and rising power prices will have outweighed many gains for low-income New Zealanders.[59] Low-income families have also been hit hardest by the regressive flat-rate goods and services tax (GST), introduced in the 1980s and recently increased to 15 per cent. This is a tax that falls disproportionately on low-income families, as most of their expenditure is likely to be on items attracting GST (such as food and clothing); for the wealthy, less than half their expenditure is likely to attract GST.[60]

Many on low incomes in New Zealand would be still worse off if they had not been working increasingly long hours since the early 1980s. According to one recent study, the extra hours worked by low-income staff in the 1980s and 1990s were so great their incomes kept pace with those of their higher-paid counterparts, despite their actual hourly wages falling significantly behind.[61]

The struggling middle

While low incomes have remained stagnant, the recent story for New Zealand's middle-income households is not much better. The income of a typical single-person household, in the middle of the income distribution – the second line in Figure 2.5 – has increased by less than 20 per cent since 1984, from $25,900 to just $30,800 in 2011. That income is generated through work (wages and salaries) and through welfare (tax credits and benefits), but, remarkably, the income from work has not increased for these households *at all* since 1987.[62] The only reason these households are doing slightly better than they were thirty years ago is Working for Families tax credits and other government support.

Various factors help explain these relatively poor results for middle-income households. Across the developed world, globalisation has played a role in restricting work incomes for these households. As trade barriers have been removed, unskilled and semi-skilled manufacturing and related jobs (that were traditionally quite well-paid) have typically shifted to developing countries with cheaper labour. The jobs available domestically in their place have often been in the service industries and other low-paid occupations. The resulting 'hollowing out' of the workforce has led to a polarisation between well-educated and well-paid workers at the top, and poorly educated and poorly paid workers in the lower levels.[63]

However, this explanation for middle-income stagnation is not applicable to all developed countries, suggesting that other contributing factors are at work in shaping income inequality. While globalisation has widespread impacts, not all countries have soaring top 1 per cent incomes or spiralling inequality. France and Japan have held their top 1 per cent income shares relatively stable since the 1980s,[64] while Denmark reduced inequality from the mid-1980s to the mid-2000s. The correlation between income and education (or skill) is another factor to take into account. Obviously, levels of education and skill are likely to increase up the income ladder, but the correlation is not exact and there is little to suggest that recent dramatic increases in income inequality reflect equivalent differences in education or skill. For example, very high income earners (the 1 per cent) are not necessarily better educated than, say, others in the top 10 per cent of income earners (in New Zealand, those with incomes over $72,000).[65] And although New Zealand has had the world's largest increase in inequality since the 1980s, this country has a relatively small earnings advantage for those with degrees.[66] Overall, recent international evidence suggests the 'hollowing out' of the workforce has been going on for decades, even during times of narrowing income gaps.[67]

New Zealand's productivity levels over this period offer few clues as to why work incomes for many low- and middle-income households have stalled. According to mainstream economic theory, as people work more efficiently and intelligently, producing more in each hour worked, their hourly wage should increase at the same speed. In 1989, the average hourly wage in New Zealand was $21.49 (in 2011 dollar terms). If salaries had increased in line with national productivity since then, the average hourly wage in 2011 would have been $31.85.[68] But it was only $24.43 – about the same as it was in 1972.[69] That's a difference of more than $7 an hour, or $300 a week, or $15,000 a year. The average employee, who today earns $50,000, should therefore be getting $65,000 a year.

One possible factor, beyond globalisation and productivity, for stalling work incomes is the workforce's declining power.[70] Union membership in New Zealand fell from nearly 70 per cent of all workers in 1980 to just over 20 per cent by 1999.[71] Over the same period, the share of national income going to wage and salary-earners dropped from 60 per cent in the 1980s to a little over 45 per cent by 2002.[72] This is lower than in almost any other developed country.[73] Other factors reducing New Zealand's lower and middle household incomes include changes in household structure, particularly the increased number of sole-parent households, and the growing tendency for people of similar backgrounds and income levels to 'partner up', which can concentrate income higher up the ladder.[74]

Compounding the slow growth in low and middle incomes, the gap between incomes and living costs (especially housing costs) for many New Zealanders has widened significantly in recent decades.[75] In consequence, private borrowing has soared, from around 60 per cent of households' disposable income in 1991 to over 140 per cent now, the bulk of it in mortgages.[76] Since 2009 middle incomes have fallen again[77] and half of New Zealanders are now living from pay cheque to pay cheque.[78]

Up, up and away

The top 10 per cent of New Zealand single-person households – the third line in Figure 2.5 – have seen their incomes increase by nearly 80 per cent between 1984 and 2011. Within this group, pre-tax incomes for the top 1 per cent – the top line – have more than doubled over the same period.

In the mid-1980s, incomes for the top 10 per cent were roughly five to six times those in the bottom 10 per cent. Although incomes for the top 10 per cent did not rise significantly while the economy struggled from 1984 to 1992, they have since risen rapidly to reach an average of over $100,000 by 2011 – more than nine times the income of those at the bottom.

The incomes of the top 1 per cent appear to have become detached from those of the rest of the country: they soared from the mid-1980s until the late 1990s, even as GDP per person fell and the stock market crashed. From an average of $156,000 in 1986, top incomes more than doubled to $348,000 in 2004, before fluctuating sharply in later years. Some commentators have seen this increase as an unleashing of previously shackled ability, the fruit of 'opportunity, challenge, and the fierce heat of competition.'[79] Others believe it was more the result of the growth of the 'finance, speculative and property sector'.[80] Whatever the cause, the share of national income for New Zealand's top 10 per cent has increased significantly over the last three decades.

Senior managers, mostly in business but also in government departments and state-owned enterprises, have benefited substantially. Surveys show that, between 2004 and 2010 alone, the average chief executive pay packet at our biggest companies rose by almost 80 per cent, to $1.5 million, and the number of chief executives paid more than $1 million rose from six to twenty-six.[81] One detailed study of chief executives' pay revealed that their salaries tended to rise much faster than either average salaries or returns to shareholders.[82] Less information exists on senior management incomes below the chief executive level, but we know that, for instance, three New Zealand companies – Fonterra, Telecom and Fletcher Building – now have between them forty-one executives on over $1 million each.[83]

As top incomes have risen, the rate of tax levied on those incomes has fallen. In the 1980s, the top tax rate was cut from 60 per cent to 33 per cent (the cut offset somewhat by the closing of a number of tax loopholes and the introduction of a fringe benefit tax); after rising to 39 per cent, the top rate is now once again at 33 per cent.[84] Income from capital gains (earned from selling assets such as property or shares) has remained almost entirely untaxed.

New Zealand does not have a strongly progressive tax system ('progressive' means that people pay proportionately more tax as their income increases). People on lower incomes pay nearly 30 per cent of their income in tax (in part because GST affects a larger proportion of their income); middle-income earners pay *less* tax, at around 25 per cent; and people earning $150,000 a year pay around 34 per cent.[85] If untaxed income from capital gains were taken into account, the actual tax rate of New Zealand's highest earners would reduce further – possibly to the point where it fell below that of the lowest-paid New Zealanders.[86] Most countries in the developed world tax capital gains; at present, New Zealand largely does not. The tax paid on New Zealand's highest incomes is currently less than in almost any other developed country.[87]

Accepting the great divide?

Income inequality in New Zealand rose sharply from the mid-1980s through to the mid-1990s. It then plateaued before falling slightly under Helen Clark's Labour Government, thanks largely to Working for Families,[88] but never recovered to its pre-1980s level. And this 'great divergence' in incomes has been accompanied by an apparent contradiction: as income gaps have increased, so has society's acceptance of them. Support in New Zealand for the idea that 'the government should reduce income gaps between the rich and the poor' has fallen from 50 per cent in 1999 to 40 per cent in 2009, while support for the rich paying more in tax fell from 71 per cent in 1992 to just over 50 per cent in 2009.[89]

These attitudes can perhaps make sense when viewed in the context of New Zealand's history of egalitarianism. The word 'fairness' has many inflections, and it is telling that a key phrase in New Zealand's history has not been 'a fair society', which might imply something about equality of incomes, but 'a fair go', which hints at being given a chance – and then being left to get on with it.

Reducing inequality may also have lost support because of its being associated with conformity. Pre-1980s New Zealand is often remembered as a relatively conformist country, in which equality was entwined with ideas of security and stability, and much that smacked of difference (whether challenges, dissent or unusual talent) was seen as a threat.[90] A more equal society is also sometimes seen as a more conformist one, and reducing inequality as equivalent to a limitation on talent or ability.[91] But this book argues that a society with less income inequality can in fact foster social mobility and opportunity. By providing a secure financial foundation and rewarding a wider range of occupations, it gives more people the confidence to take risks, express themselves and develop their talents.[92]

The challenge now

Income gaps in New Zealand, after steadying or declining over the last decade, are now widening again. From 2009 to 2011, incomes fell for everyone in the lower half of New Zealand's income ladder, and the number of people who struggle to cover the cost of everyday needs nearly doubled.[93] In contrast, incomes in the top 10 per cent have now rebounded from their small slump following the global financial crisis. Recent pay increases for chief executives and other top earners have, proportionally, significantly outpaced those of people on low and middle incomes.[94] On the Gini coefficient measure, income gaps in New Zealand are now the widest since detailed records began in 1982.[95]

The policy with the greatest recent effect on income inequality was the National Government's tax changes in 2008–10. These largely benefited the top 10 per cent,[96] giving $152 a week more to someone on $150,000 and just $16 a week to someone on $30,000.[97] Rather than reducing income gaps directly, the current government appears to be focused on equalising opportunities. The Treasury has warned against 'assuming [that] raising incomes alone will address social outcomes' and urged a focus instead on measures to enhance social mobility.[98] While the government has not responded directly to this paper, Finance Minister Bill English has said that he is comfortable with the level of income inequality in New Zealand, and even raised doubts about whether government could combat it, suggesting that goverments 'don't have the levers.'[99]

But if this chapter's history of inequality tells us anything, it is that governments do make a difference. Even within the constraints of globalisation they can influence how incomes are distributed. We as individuals have some control over inequality, too, through the public pressure we place on governments and in the way we deal with those around us. How we think about income gaps, and how we decide to address them, will do much to alter New Zealand's levels of inequality in the years to come.

In the middle

Kristine and Craig Absolum *live with their four children in Whanganui, having moved there from Auckland in 2008. Max Rashbrooke interviewed Kristine for this viewpoint.*

When the Absolum family moved to Whanganui five years ago to escape Auckland house prices, they didn't think they would end up relying on Working for Families tax credits to make ends meet. But that's what happened.

Although both Kristine Absolum and her husband Craig worked full time in Auckland – she in telesales, he as a baker – they still couldn't afford to buy a decent home. So they moved to Whanganui, bought a house for just $140,000 and settled in. Craig was working again as a baker, for Progressive Enterprises (the owners of Countdown), earning around $43,000 a year. Kristine did accounts for local businesses. While they had to feed four children aged between sixteen months and eleven years old, it seemed perfectly feasible on two incomes.

But then the global financial crisis hit Whanganui businesses hard, and Kristine was made redundant in early 2012, just after the birth of their fourth child. They would have had to manage on just Craig's $640 a week after tax, were it not for $320 a week in Working for Families tax credits; this lifts their annual family income up around the $60,000 mark. 'That, Working for Families, is the difference, that's what makes getting by possible', Kristine says. 'They talk about doing away with it for middle-income earners, and I think, oh my God, no.'

Even with Working for Families, the Absolum budget is tight. Out of their $960 a week, $320 goes on house-related items, such as the mortgage and rates. Their other fixed weekly costs include $35 for phone and broadband, $60 for power (their old, draughty house is too expensive to insulate), an $80 loan to repay their second car purchase, petrol at $70 and insurance of $30. (With Craig driving to work, Kristine finds a second car essential for the children's transport, shopping and other family activities.)

That leaves around $365, and once fruit and veges and meat ($80) and general supermarket shopping ($200) are deducted, there's just $85 a week left for everything else – most of which goes on the children. Family come first. Soccer, Scottish country dancing, school uniforms and fees eat up the cash pretty quickly. 'After that, we don't have a lot left over', Kristine says. 'We certainly don't get to go on fancy holidays.' Instead, they go camping, which they love – but even then, 'you have got to choose the campsites that are less expensive'.

For one of their children, they get a disability allowance of $40 a week. They also save $150 a month so that they will be able to help their two eldest children through university ('we did some forward planning when we were in a far better financial position'). They haven't been able to keep that up, however, for the two youngest.

Each week, Kristine says, 'We tightly budget to cover our food costs, and some weeks it's tough … We have three reasonable weeks, then one much tighter week. Absolutely, it is tight. It is very, very tight.' Does she feel they miss out as a result? 'I do feel there are definitely some things I'd like to do that we can't do. I'd love my kids to be doing swimming, but I can't afford it. Going to the movies is very rare. My son is going to go for his birthday, but that's a very rare treat.' Things like takeaways happen maybe once every three weeks. 'I'd also like to be able to see my family more often than we do. You have to save for ages to get up to Auckland.'

However careful they are, expenses are everywhere. While a community services card defrays the cost of doctors' visits, Craig's last one still cost $65, and 'that hurt – that particular week, that hurt'. Breakages and emergencies are an ever-present threat. Kristine worries a lot about how they would cope if one of the cars broke down. And if the roof leaks, 'I get up there and silicon it up, and hope that it sticks.'

The children know how tight money is, too. When one of her sons opened his presents last birthday, his first reaction was to ask how Craig and Kristine had been able to afford them. 'At ten years old, that shouldn't be your primary thought', Kristine says. 'It breaks my heart to hear that.'

She'd like to be working again, and certainly has the skills. Her work history includes accounts work, and a spell in the military, 'fixing aircraft'. But, as Kristine says, it's so tough to get a job when even big local employers like engineering firm Axiam are laying off staff and there can be 'hundreds' of applicants for each job. 'I love it how the government says, "Go and do this" … I really just wish someone would give them a reality check. It's not as easy as that.'

But even though she'd almost certainly get work in Auckland, Kristine doesn't regret the move to Whanganui. 'Being down here enables us to do so many more things for the children. We get a far better lifestyle here, with far more time together as a family.'

When it comes to inequality itself, she doesn't begrudge the rich all of their income, but says it's 'not necessarily to do with talent. Some of it's to do with a little bit of luck, some of it's to do with timing. Sometimes it doesn't matter what you do. It might not work out for different reasons.' So, how does it work out for the Absolums? Craig is a highly experienced, hard-working baker; he earns $640 a week. Fair pay and just reward … or perhaps not? As Kristine says, 'It's what they pay, that's the thing … There are jobs that pay more, but they aren't secure.'

Their experience over the last five years has also left the Absolums worrying about those even worse-off. 'We find it really hard to make ends meet, and we are considered low- to middle-income', Kristine says. 'How on earth do people on less than us manage? How on earth do they cope? It frightens me to think of just how tough some people must be doing it.'

Part Two
Issues and Debates

3 Inequality and the West

Robert Wade

> It is our job to glory in inequality and to see that talents and abilities are given vent and expression for the benefit of us all.
> *Prime Minister Margaret Thatcher*

> Poverty bothers me. Inequality does not. I just don't care.
> *Willem Buiter, Professor of Economics, London School of Economics, Financial Times, 2007*

The decades since the 1980s have seen elites around the world exercise an extraordinary ability to claim the fruits of economic growth for themselves. In this particular race, the United States has been the frontrunner. Between 1977 and 2007, the top 1 per cent of Americans gained 57 per cent of the increase in national income; from 2000 to 2007 the top 1 per cent gained 93 per cent of the increase.[1] In terms of wealth, the richest 1 per cent owned about 35 per cent of household and corporate wealth in 2006–7 (the latest year for which statistics are available).

The trend in the share of national income accruing to the top 1 per cent between 1913 and 2003 is shown in Figure 3.1. The top 1 per cent gained a rapidly increasing share over the 1920s to reach nearly 23 per cent by 1929, the eve of the Wall Street crash, then experienced a more or less continuous loss of share till the late 1970s. This was followed by an abrupt about-turn and a more or less continuous increase till the end of the series in 2006, when the share regained the level of 1929, thus paving the way for the second great crash.

Trends in other developed countries – especially in the Anglo-American world – have moved in the same direction. In Britain the average remuneration of chief executives at the country's hundred largest companies rose by about 40 per cent in 2010 – a year of close to zero GDP growth – to reach £4.2 million, or 145 times the median wage.

Indeed, the world total of High Net Worth Individuals (HNWIs), people with more than US$1 million of free cash, has surged since the great slump started in 2008. In 2010 the number exceeded the previous peak in 2007, even as governments of developed countries implemented

Figure 3.1 Share of top 1 per cent in US income, 1913–2006

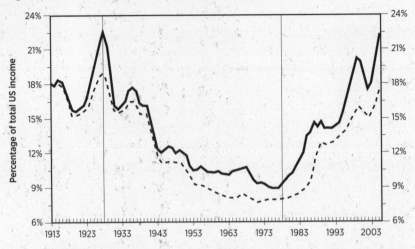

Note: The solid line represents personal income from all sources, including capital gains. The dotted line excludes capital gains.

Source: J. G. Palma, 'The Revenge of the Market on the Rentiers: Why Neo-Liberal Reports of the End of History Turned Out to be Premature', *Cambridge Journal of Economics*, 33, 4 (2009), p.836.

austerity budgets. Although most HNWIs are concentrated in the US, Japan and Germany (53 per cent of the world total live in those countries), the fastest increase in HNWI numbers is in Asia-Pacific countries, whose total exceeded Europe's for the first time ever in 2010.[2]

The growing number of very wealthy individuals fuels demand for 'passion' purchases, from Ferraris to diamonds, from art to fine wines. Prices in the international art market are so sensational as to give Sotheby's and Christies their highest profits in years. Reviewing recent eight-figure sales in both the art market and homes, an *International Herald Tribune* article concludes, 'for the 0.001 percent, life proceeds sweetly'.[3]

Yet even as big business and the top 1 per cent of the distribution captured the proceeds of rising prosperity throughout the 2000s, western political and intellectual circles continued to neglect the subject of vertical income inequality. The prevailing assumption has been that public action to curb top-level inequality is infeasible and illegitimate.

True, some politicians, driven by budget pressures and a need to placate the public sympathy evoked by the Occupy movement, did talk for a time about the desirability of higher taxes on the rich. President Obama endorsed the 'Buffett rule' that millionaires should not pay a lower rate of tax than their assistants; and the 'fiscal cliff' negotiations of December 2012 seem to have resulted in a congressional agreement to raise taxes on upper incomes by a little, as the price of big spending cuts. The British Conservative–Liberal Democrat coalition government floated the idea of a 'mansion tax' – a levy on all houses worth over £2 million – as a partial offset to its plans to bring down the top income tax rate. The French Socialist president proposed a 75 per cent marginal tax rate on top incomes (a method of taxation that aims to tax individuals based upon their earnings, rising as income increases).

But higher taxes on the rich everywhere run into fierce opposition, not just from the rich but also from politicians who depend on the rich for financing election campaigns. They and their intellectual supporters have tended to steer public debate along the track of 'Does individual X deserve his £1.4 million bonus?' Once on this track, issues of the society-wide structure of income distribution are safely bypassed.

Causes of income concentration

What then are the drivers of income concentration and the reasons for the lack of opposition to it?[4]

Concentration of financial power

In 1997, just before the start of the widespread financial crises of the late 1990s (including the East Asian, Latin American, Russian and Long-Term Capital Management crises), the value of financial transactions, such as the sales of stocks and bonds, was about fifteen times the world's annual gross product. Today, even in the hard times following the global financial crisis, the ratio is almost seventy.

The jump from fifteen to seventy times in a little more than a decade is part of a larger global concentration of corporate power over the 2000s. A recent analysis identifies a global 'super-entity' of 147 interlinked firms accounting for a high share of the world's corporate revenues. The super-entity is itself dominated by finance: *all* of the top fifty except one are financial firms.[5] The realm of finance completely dominates the realm of Gross Domestic Product (GDP) (the 'real economy').

Such concentration provides financial firms with the leverage to colonise the governments of nation states and shape public policy in line with their preferences, creating a ratchet such that the power of finance over public policy, both national and international, cannot now be much diminished, however much some politicians and activists may wish it to be so. To use the vernacular, high finance has governments by the short and curlies, nowhere more so than in the US and the UK, which house the major international financial centres.

Behind the concentration of financial power and the financial colonisation of many western governments lie the technologies of the

Figure 3.2 Share of US income deciles, 1947–2009

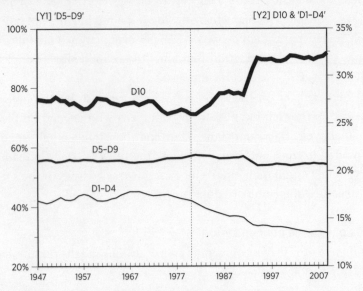

Note: D10 is the top decile of the population by income, D5–9 the middle 50 per cent, D1–4 the bottom 40 per cent.

Source: J.G. Palma, 'Homogeneous Middles vs. Heterogeneous Tails, and the End of the "Inverted-U": It's all about the Share of the Rich', *Development and Change*, 42, 1 (January 2011), p.105.

information revolution and the shift in the public policy paradigm towards 'deregulation' and maximising the scope for private profit-making. Many mainstream economists provide legitimacy for the shift in public policy by presenting 'the market system' as a mostly efficient and self-adjusting system; and by allowing the phrase, 'the market system', to obscure the key distinction between 'the market', composed of many competing producers, and 'giant corporations', which are able to set public policy in their own interests. Thus freed, corporates have driven the share of profits in US national income to record heights, and the share of wages to the lowest ever recorded. Progressive political movements wishing to tackle inequality face daunting gravitational forces.

Interests of the rich
In America over the 2000s, high-income households have been paying their lowest share of federal taxes in decades, and corporations frequently avoid paying any tax at all. In 2008, the most recent year available, the 400 highest-income tax filers paid only 18 per cent of their income in federal income taxes; in 2007 they paid just 17 per cent; and they pay little by way of payroll taxes or state and local taxes, which are major burdens on middle-income families. They pay so little because most of their income is classed as capital gains, *three-quarters* of which goes to the top 1 per

Table 3.1 Decile shares (per cent) of national income, US and average for 133 countries, 2009

	US	133 countries
D10	33	32
D5–9	55	52
D1–4	13	17

Source: J. G. Palma, 'Homogeneous Middles vs. Heterogeneous Tails, and the End of the "inverted-U": It's all about the Share of the Rich', *Development and Change*, 42, 1 (January 2011), p.104, table 1.

cent of income earners. The tax rate on capital gains is the lowest it has been since the 1920s. President George W. Bush rammed a tax cut on capital gains and another on dividends through Congress in 2003 on the wave of euphoria over the 'victory' in Iraq.[6] The Clinton administration, by contrast, was positively socialistic: during the first term the top 400 taxpayers paid close to 30 per cent of their income in federal taxes.

In Britain, meanwhile, the Labour Party government in the 2000s deliberately refused to stand up to people who through technically legal but morally reprehensible ruses ended up paying a minuscule amount of tax on their enormous wealth. Labour Chancellor Alistair Darling boasted that he wanted London to be a welcoming home for Russians, Chinese and Saudis, which meant low taxation and 'light-touch regulation'.[7]

But talk of 'the rich' or 'the top 1 per cent', although a convenient shorthand, obscures what has really been happening. In many western countries 'the rich' have been transforming themselves from an 'establishment' elite, concerned to foster the well-being of the whole society as a buttress to their own position (including via progressive taxes), to an 'oligarchic' elite, concerned to use public power to redistribute society's resources upwards to themselves (including via regressive taxes). This elite has acquired a vastly disproportionate influence in politics, civil service and media.

Interests of the middle classes
Surprisingly, the middle classes also acquiesce in income redistribution to the very top – but looking more closely at trends in income distribution helps explain why.

Figure 3.2 shows the shares in national income of US population deciles (each decile includes 10 per cent of the population), from 1947 to 2009. The share of people on the top rung (to use the metaphor from Chapter 2) rose sharply starting around 1980. The share of the middle 50 per cent of the population (people on rungs 5 to 9) remained fairly constant. The share of the bottom 40 per cent (people on rungs 1 to 4) fell steadily after 1980. So *the rising share of the top 10 per cent was more at the expense of the bottom*

40 per cent than the middle 50 per cent. What is more, this pattern is found in many other middle- and high-income countries (as Table 3.1 shows).

In addition, the effect of inequality on the middle and upper-middle classes has been disguised by their ability to increase their consumption faster than their (slowly increasing) incomes by borrowing – often from the financial resources available as wealth-holders at the top seek to multiply their assets. So the owners and managers of capital are happy as they keep labour costs down while sales increase, resulting in high rates of profit.

The middle and upper-middle classes also find the promise of tax cuts attractive, even if the cuts benefit the rich most of all. And the current generation of the middle classes has internalised the Reagan/Thatcher values of individualistic aspiration ('winners take all', 'let failures fail'). It expects to rely on its own efforts to get ahead – or at least, this is its self-image.[8]

Since fear of loss is a more powerful motivator than prospect of gain, talk of 'reducing inequality' prompts middle-class anxiety that the government may try to pull up those below them in the income hierarchy; this worries the middle classes more than those above them rising even further away. Better to let the rich keep their income than have tax-financed transfers boost those below them – all the more so when (as now) many in the middle classes see themselves on the edge of the abyss, loaded up with debt and worried about unemployment.

Conservative ideology and its easy links to 'non-negotiable' values
However, the concentration of corporate power and the interests of the rich and the middle classes cannot be the end of the story. Political ideologies and cognitive beliefs that justify the existing distribution of material conditions of living are *widely believed*, including by people who accept that they have no prospect of becoming rich.

Large parts of western electorates – not just the rich and middle classes – have accepted a conservative *vision of a moral society* in which the role of government is to encourage largely free, private markets, and to accept the income distribution that results from the operation of those markets (provided the government does not rig the markets in favour of its cronies). In this conservative worldview, government attempts to reduce income inequality, within some limits, only weaken the moral fibre of society by weakening the link between law-abiding effort and reward. Such a society produces adults lacking in self-discipline and self-reliance; it produces welfare scroungers.[9]

Contrary to the normal popular response to hard times, which is to demand more regulation and social insurance, this conservative worldview has surged in popular support since 2008. The Tea Party movement in the US, for example, highlights the so-called 'unholy alliance' of big business and big government as the defining issue of public policy, holding up the 'free market' as the moral alternative. Get government intervention out of the way, it says, and everyone deserving can climb the beanstalk, scramble through the hole in the sky, and arrive in the land of freedom, peace and prosperity. But visceral anti-government sentiment now goes far beyond conservative circles. 'You can trust the government to do the right thing most of the time' now elicits an affirmative reaction from only 10 per cent of American respondents, down from three-quarters in the mid-1950s.

For the public at large, these beliefs are ideological in the sense of having only a loose connection to daily life and to things we actually experience and can test for ourselves. Our belief in this narrative, then, is not based on *our* experience, but rather on the cultural stories we are told about the moral order of society, stories we accept at an emotional more than a deliberative level. The neoliberal narrative has a big emotional or rhetorical advantage over, for example, a Keynesian narrative – named for John Maynard Keynes, whose work provided intellectual justification for the 'mixed economy' and social democratic policies from the late 1930s to the 1970s.[10] Neoliberalism gains acceptance from its simpler emotional or metaphorical connection to a whole set of values that are 'non-negotiable', like freedom, individual initiative, personal responsibility, the level playing field, private property, democracy, efficiency and the good life. This mindset inclines people to think that, when ninety-five bones are hidden in a room into which are let a hundred dogs, the five who emerge without a bone must be deficient in skills and motivation.

In psychologist Daniel Kahneman's terms, conservative ideology has a powerful anchor in system 1 thought, the system of emotional, intuitive and quick thinking, in contrast to system 2 thinking, which is deliberative and slow.[11]

It is also buttressed by an active right-wing movement of wealthy thinktanks and financed advocates in other organisations, including political parties and university departments.[12] Media bias, meanwhile, is overwhelmingly in favour of the conservative worldview. The British newspaper-reading public, for example, is exposed to a foghorn of right-wing opinion. Over the 2000s the right-wing national newspapers accounted for about 75 per cent of sales, the non-right-wing ones (including the *Financial Times*), 25 per cent.

Economists' defence of inequality

Economists have defended inequality – or policy neglect of it – with two well-developed instrumental (not moral) arguments. The first stems from the conception of the market as a *coordination* mechanism, allocating scarce resources to competing ends.[13] Equilibrium prices in a competitive market produce an efficient allocation of resources. In particular, a competitive labour market produces the optimal income distribution, such that each factor of production earns the value of its marginal productivity. The relative remuneration of banker and builder must be fair, provided markets are competitive.

Extending this proposition from the model to the real world, mainstream (or neoclassical) economists tend to presume that any 'political' interference with market-determined income distribution has efficiency costs, just like any other interference with the price system (managed exchange rates, tariffs, credit subsidies, industrial policy); and that the efficiency costs of political interference in market-determined income distribution are typically large. The premise is that 'markets may be imperfect, but governments are even more imperfect'.

This argument has some way to go before it can even be called simplistic; yet it has commanded wide agreement in mainstream economics (led by neoclassical economists), because it fits so well with mathematically tractable models of competitive markets as the core institution of a moral and prosperous society. It resonates with the system 1 values (automatic, intuitive) inculcated during their professional training.

Economists' second instrumental justification for inequality is based on the conception of the market as a mechanism of *incentives* for the development of skills and innovation. The assumption is that individuals choose neither their occupations nor their balance between 'work' and 'leisure' on the basis of intrinsic satisfactions, but only on the basis of *extrinsic* material rewards. Only by allowing individuals to keep most of the market value they create will they be diligent and creative. Then their diligence and creativity will rebound to the benefit of the rest of the society, including the poor, through 'trickle-down'.

The neoclassical definition implies a larger conception of society as composed of rationally self-maximising individuals, with competition, conflict and zero-sum games as the dominant social processes. It treats altruism, community, cooperation and solidarity as merely instruments in the competition for whatever is scarce. And in terms of how it generates economic knowledge, it prioritises rigour, consistency and mathematics as cardinal virtues, marginalising meticulous observation of what people, businesses and governments actually do.

Economics education, especially in Anglo-American universities, is all about inculcating individualism-based constructs. Teaching of both the history of economic thought and comparative economic systems might expose students to other conceptions of economics. But both subjects largely disappeared from university syllabi as the Cold War wound down; and where taught, they still tend, as during the Cold War, to present the history of thought, and comparative economic systems, with the Anglo-American market system as the endpoint of history (which in turn justifies not giving the history or the comparison much attention).[14]

How can we prioritise inequality?

In recent decades, many of those who traditionally championed equality of outcomes have abandoned that cause. This was partly a tactical choice. In the words of Roger Liddle, one of the principal ideologues of the British New Labour Party:

> Several reasons were clearly important in Labour making this choice ... [First, a sense] that intellectually Thatcherite neoliberalism was triumphant, and that the post-war welfare state consensus had irretrievably broken down and could only be rebuilt on a basis that incentivised (and did not penalise) hard work at all levels of society.[15]

But it was not just a matter of tactics. Leading centre-left figures really did believe in a vision of a moral society close to that of conservatives, one in which 'the key to justice as fairness can be seen in terms of the procedural securing of *opportunities* rather than a substantive commitment to patterned relative *outcomes*' (emphasis added).[16]

But this is like fiddling while Rome burns – while income concentration soars. People of progressive political views need to try to build a consensus for a more equal society by challenging more actively the intellectual arguments of the inequality defenders and providing justification for pulling the switches in the other direction. Putting moral criteria aside, we can ask questions such as, is the present degree of income inequality necessary for good economic performance, is it efficient, and are its negative societal spillovers small? These questions take the debate onto the same terrain as the inequality champions, engaging them on their own terms.

Income concentration and economic performance

One popular argument of the inequality defenders, such as Margaret Thatcher and Tony Blair, is that sizeable top-level inequality (implicitly, more or less what we have today, including in the US) is necessary to generate the innovation, corporate management and productivity from which the whole population benefits.

This argument falls down at the first nudge. Comparing top-level inequality in six Anglo-American economies and eight continental European and Japanese economies, from 1913 to 2003, we find that in 1978 the income share of the top 1 per cent was roughly the same in the two sets of economies: around 5–8 per cent. Then it took off in the Anglo-American set to reach the range of 8–15 per cent by 2003 (the US in the lead, followed by the UK), while the share in the continental European and Japanese set remained fairly constant (5–8 per cent all the way through).[17]

However, while the Anglo-American economies became much more unequal at the top than the continental European and Japanese economies, their economic performance was not noticeably better (before the Eurozone crisis, of course). This suggests that economies can remain highly productive and innovative, like the northern Europeans, with much less concentration of material income and wealth at the top than in the Anglo-American type.

In short, one criterion by which inequality is too high is when income concentration (for example, the share of the top 1 per cent) lies above a threshold set by countries in the same income bracket that have equal or better performance in terms of growth, poverty reduction, skills and the like. By this criterion, top incomes in most Anglo-American countries are too high, in the sense of not being *necessary* for good national economic performance.

Inequality and incentives

The more specific version of the argument that sizeable top-level inequality is necessary to generate good economic performance operates at the level of microeconomic behaviour. It says that inequality is necessary to generate the innovation, corporate management and productivity from which the whole population benefits.[18]

The argument only has to be stated to be open to doubt. More plausibly, top-end income recipients in the Anglo-American countries would be equally productive even at Scandinavian levels of post-tax remuneration relative to the median, because their most important reward is not the income but the respect and power. Put another way, it is implausible that at Scandinavian levels of remuneration top-end income recipients would retire and play golf. Can it be seriously argued that without a more than 40 per cent increase in remuneration in one year, 2010, the chief executives of the hundred largest British companies would have steered their companies less productively, or that – had they decamped to Switzerland or Hong Kong in protest – their replacements would have done so?

Two empirical studies are relevant here. First, Claudia Goldin and Lawrence Katz studied the remuneration differentials in cohorts of Harvard graduates.[19] They found that around 1980 the differential between those who entered careers in finance and those who went into other professions (such as medicine, engineering and law) was more or less zero, while by the 2000s Harvard graduates working in finance received almost three times more than other Harvard graduates, controlling for factors such as grades in college, standardised scores on entry and year of graduation.

This is the short answer to why graduates in physics, engineering and maths headed into finance over the 1990s and 2000s. In 2007, on the eve of the financial crisis, 47 per cent of Harvard's graduating class entered consulting firms or the financial sector.[20]

Given the 'externalities' of this super-compensation in finance – including the formation of a class that dominates the democratic political system to its own advantage, and the draining away of bright graduates, also known as human capital, from the 'productive' (or non-financial) economy – there is a good case for curbing the size of the financial differential.

This case is underlined in the second empirical study. Daniel Kahneman discovered that the apparent success of financial high-fliers is generally a cognitive illusion. One kind of evidence came from his study of twenty-five wealth advisers over eight years. The success of their advice 'resembled what you would expect from a dice-rolling contest, not a game of skill', he reported. They could hardly be described as 'deserving rich'. Their riches were undeserved – that is, too big.[21]

Lower down the income hierarchy, the argument that incentives provided by high inequality motivate people to work hard overlooks the distinction between incentives and capacities. Those with low or specific skills may not be able to respond to the incentives to earn more. Indeed, hardly anyone can respond to the incentive of a million pound prize for winning the London Marathon.

Income concentration, aggregate demand and financial fragility

A third criterion for when inequality is too high relates to the link between inequality, aggregate demand (spending on goods and services) and financial fragility (economic malfunction more generally). Inequality above a certain level is *macroeconomically inefficient*, in that it raises the probability of financial crisis and economic slump. It does so through at least four mechanisms.[22]

First, above a certain level of inequality, economies tend to become 'debt-intensive'. The other side of income concentration at the top is stagnant or falling incomes lower down. One result is insufficient aggregate demand to utilise productive capacity, including the employment of the labour force. So a 'common interest' develops among firms, households, politicians and financial regulators to allow an explosion in private debt to fill the gap between (a) the demand supported by incomes, (b) the demand generated by aspirations to participate in the boom and (c) the demand needed to utilise productive capacity.

Second, above a certain level of inequality, developed economies tend to enter bubble dynamics. After the early 1990s the surge in income concentration unleashed a flood of global capital as those at the top hunted for ways to store and multiply their wealth. Bank assets (loans) soared, and bubbles erupted in housing, property, business and art; with a repeat after the early 2000s. The bursting of the house price bubble in the US, the UK, New Zealand, Iceland and many other western economies helped to turn an ordinary business cycle downturn around 2007 into the larger financial crash and ensuing slump.

Third, the huge returns to financial operations distort business incentives, channelling investment away from productive uses into redistributive uses like mergers and acquisitions, private equity funds, property and financial engineering (as in the case of Harvard graduates).

Fourth, and most fundamental, high concentrations of income and wealth propel 'state capture', such that finance comes increasingly to dominate the state apparatus and the democratic process more generally. In the post-war decades, before the surge in income concentration, 'establishment' elites recognised that their prosperity and privileges depended on the prosperity and social peace of the society at large; accordingly, they designed tax systems to meet widely accepted criteria of equity, and devoted a large part of public spending to public goods rather than redistributive goods (to themselves). Since the 1980s the dominant elites in many capitalist countries see less of a mutual interest in the well-being of their society, and use the levers of state power to sluice resources upwards. The dominance of monied interests in the United States has reached the point where the Supreme Court recently decided to grant the same 'freedom of speech' to corporations as to individuals, opening the floodgates to business purchase of politicians.

Today, the power of Wall Street and the City of London remains largely intact despite the financial crash and economic slump of the late 2000s. The initial effort at a 'Great Re-regulation' of finance has for the most part turned into the 'Great Escape' (as in the fate of the Dobbs-Frank Act and Volcker Rule in the US, and the Vickers Commission report in the UK).

Conclusion

The sharp increase in income concentration at the top of national income distributions over recent decades should have prompted a large body of social science research and public debate about the question: 'When are the rich too rich?' Instead, inequality is relegated because of the emotional and even deliberative (system 1 and system 2) acceptance of the idea that whatever distribution results from 'free markets' must be better than what results from 'government intervention' (beyond the limits of welfare transfers and tax exemptions for 'deserving poor'). This acceptance is bolstered by the belief that when the rich become richer everyone eventually benefits.

As outlined earlier, this free-market ideology resonates with 'non-negotiable' values like freedom, individual responsibility, efficiency and democracy, values embedded in the system 1 thinking of western cultures. In contrast, the more nuanced Keynesian policy paradigm has less resonance at the system 1 level; just as 'solidarity' has less resonance than 'freedom' in the thinking of those in the upper levels of the income distribution, who include most of those involved in the making and shaping of public policy. Even 'progressives' are much more comfortable worrying about 'poverty' than 'inequality', because the former is about helping 'others' while the latter comes close to questions about the appropriateness of the income of themselves and their peers.

Now, in the midst of a severe economic slump, minds (both system 2 and system 1) may be more open to inequality-challenging arguments than in the past – more open to understanding how the stagnation of income in most parts of the income distribution below the top contributed to a shortfall of aggregate demand, which was compensated by rising consumption on the back of easy credit, which paved the way for the crisis.

But the question remains: how to persuade political leaders and opinion-makers like the World Bank to focus on inequality as a problem, separate from poverty; and how to get it into not just their system 2 but also their system 1 thinking? The short answer is that, even if top-end incomes reach even higher levels of concentration, inequality will remain on the margins of public policy until radical changes are made in how political parties and candidates fund themselves, or until several more multi-country crashes have roiled the world economy, or, less likely, until there is mass revolt against oligarchic rule. In the meantime we should in the interests of accuracy refer not to 'democratic free market capitalism' but to 'plutocratic impunity capitalism'.

Don't let it get entrenched

Damian Christie *has presented numerous TV and radio programmes, including the politics show* Back Benches *and history programme* Hindsight*, both for TVNZ. He also runs a student media website, urs.net.nz.*

Inequality is an extremely important issue, for many reasons. There is, of course, a fundamental unfairness, sometimes, about who earns what. But what worries me most about inequality is when it gets entrenched.

I used to be a libertarian, and accepted the idea that if someone gets out there and earns money, it is entirely their money and other people are not entitled to take it. But over the years, I have started to see that things don't work that way. In particular, I've travelled overseas, and seen vast amounts of wealth held by individuals, wealth that had been in a certain family for generations. How could I marry that up with a libertarian philosophy arguing that people's wealth resulted solely from their own efforts? I now think that is unfair in some fundamental way.

I still hold to some of those libertarian beliefs. I don't object to people coming up with an idea and making a lot of money from it. That's basic capitalism, and that's as it should be. There must be incentives for people to work harder, and take risks, and try things out.

But I now see a lot of what could be called market failures – the market not rewarding all work fairly. In my own industry, the media world, there are inequalities. A magazine salesperson, even one who is quite inexperienced, will be very well paid if he or she is selling a lot of advertising. Yet the writer whose work appears on the same pages as those advertisements gets a standard rate of about 50c a word, and this rate has been the same for years now, no matter how good or experienced you are. The result is that top writers earn less than a junior sales person – yet you could ask: 'whose work is actually selling the magazine – the sales rep or the journalist?' This illustrates a general rule: whoever is closest to the money gets paid best, regardless of their relative contribution.

Of course, there are many examples of hard work reaping reward. The richest person I know is also one of the hardest workers I know, and can claim credit for much of his success. Very often he works right through the night. But at the same time, there are people who have become wealthy thanks to what can only be thought of as some strange accident. Property developers, for instance, can be worth hundreds of millions simply because they know how to play the game.

It's evident what happens if societies allow wealth to build up unchecked: centuries and centuries down the line, they are left with a small number of people owning all the property and the means of producing wealth. In New Zealand, entrenched inequality hasn't been an issue until relatively recently. But now it is starting to solidify and become more pronounced.

When inequality is entrenched, it becomes harder – or nearly impossible – for people to rise up out of difficult situations. The rich are so rich that they can virtually monopolise the key opportunities: the best schools, the connections, the other advantages. The property market embeds that inequality, especially in Auckland. Anyone earning $80,000 a year or less will struggle to buy a house in Auckland. For the rest, even ignoring the capital gains they can make, simply having a home creates an advantage, in terms of the kind of life – the security, the foundation – that it allows.

In contrast, I see some young people, particularly when I'm doing court reporting, who have been given a very tough start in life. They may not have helped themselves much, but the odds were stacked against them right from the start. Although it may sound awful, I sometimes think that there is nothing they have that will get them out of their situation, no matter how many chances they are given.

All this, I think, flies in the face of the idea of equal opportunities. Of course, we respect people who have come up from working-class roots in New Zealand, and we elect them regularly: just look at Paula Bennett, or John Key. But using those examples to argue that anyone can get ahead is to ignore the fact that there used to be more routes out of poverty: through free university education, through good-quality state housing and other means. That enabled much greater mobility than is the case now. Of course people still find routes through; of course there are exceptions. But a country isn't made of exceptions.

So what should we do about this? For a start, meaningful change won't be achieved by tinkering, or through a few more scholarship schemes. We need to look at things like death taxes or estate duties, to level out those entrenched inequalities. We need more ways of saying to people that if they are earning large amounts, it is partly because of their situation: what society has given to them, and the advantages they were born with. And we should try to get them to make a bigger contribution, whether it's through higher taxes or estate duties, or by creating more incentives to be philanthropic.

If there's one thing we should focus on, it's the next generation. Much of the answer lies with education and ensuring that children are brought up with the right opportunities. Education is the key – so regardless of whose responsibility we think it is, we need to ensure children are healthy, clothed and well-fed, so that the education sinks in. That will cost money, much more than we are spending now, but it's the only way we can stem the massive inequality of opportunity that's led us to where we are today.

4 The Cost of Inequality
Ganesh Nana

Economics sits at the heart of income inequality. Economic processes, structures and institutions are primary contributors to inequality, yet their role in its creation and maintenance is often unquestioned, and the impact of inequality is regarded as something that is the job of 'social agencies' to fix.

Economic analysis over recent decades has failed to grasp the threat posed by widening disparities within society. Even within the narrow confines of financial modelling, economists have missed the damage inequality does in the standard assessments of benefits and costs, and Gross Domestic Product (GDP) growth. More fundamentally, they have failed to see how inequality prevents us from maximising our well-being. Such a task in economic policy was always supposed to take priority over the generation of more income. But somehow these fundamental considerations, which have always been in the economists' textbook, have been overlooked in the current-day application of economics.

By limiting the opportunities for all to maximise their potential contributions to economy and society, inequality impacts on both the wealthy and the less fortunate. Inequality does not belong in the 'social problems' basket. Rather, it is an economic issue that imposes costs on all of us. We need to put it front and centre once more, and realise that inequality is, in essence, an albatross around our collective necks, a shackle that hobbles all of our options and opportunities.

The primacy of economic analysis
Rightly or wrongly, many decisions about the nation's ills are made using analysis from a supposedly 'economic' perspective. Almost any proposal can be killed with one lightning bolt – the claim that 'it would endanger our economic prospects' – which, in turn, is code for, 'We can't afford it.'

As the economist John Maynard Keynes once put it:

> the ideas of economists and political philosophers, both when they are right and when they are wrong, are more powerful than is commonly understood. Indeed the world is ruled by little else. Practical men, who believe themselves to be quite exempt

from any intellectual influences, are usually the slaves of some defunct economist.[1]

Because today's decision-making is heavily influenced by the claims of economic analysts, we all need to be literate in the language of modern economics. This will help us expose the all-too-frequent instances where economic analysis undertaken in today's world is devoid of the underpinnings that should be the foundation of the discipline.

The confusion of economics with financial analysis

Economics was supposed to be about people, the resources they possessed, the behaviour governing their decisions and actions about using those resources, and how such decisions might lead to better (or worse) outcomes. As a catch-all term for these outcomes, economics textbooks use the word 'utility'. We might, in today's world, more appropriately use the term 'well-being'.

Whatever the expression, or its definition, it was always clear that economics was about goals and objectives that were more than just narrow monetary gains.

But recently, economics has given way to narrow financial analysis focused on precisely those monetary gains. Economics may lack the evidential, factual database and undeniable truths that characterise a core science. But many practitioners pretend that it is one, using evidence to show spuriously accurate measurements of a given outcome, with equally beautiful equations tracking relationships that claim to explain or predict outcomes.

This misplaced desire for mathematical precision has led some economists to overlook the assumptions embedded in our theories: for instance, the assumption that people are self-interested individuals making choices based on good information and a rational decision-making process. Our focus on things that can be measured simply, like financial returns, has also sidelined more complex issues such as society's wider well-being. This dominance of financial analysis, claiming to be economic analysis, leaves outcomes being viewed (and measured) narrowly in terms of monetary costs and benefits.

So, what has this got to do with inequality? Well, it is fundamental. If you are led to believe that economic outcomes are to be solely focused on dollar signs – the total amount of income generated, regardless of how it is divided or what good it does – then inequality does not appear in your decision criteria. It's not in the vocabulary of the economic analyst. And

Figure 4.1 Relationship between economic analysis and social outcomes

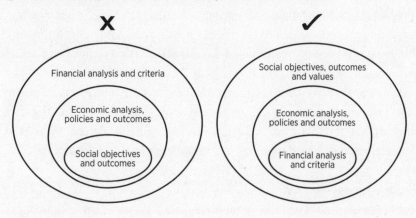

so the impacts on inequality of a given policy do not feature highly in the supposedly 'economic' analysis of its effects.

A standard example is the move to lower barriers to international trade. The textbook analysis shows there are 'winners and losers' to increased international trade. In simple terms, the winners are the consumers who can buy lower-priced products, while the losers are the workers employed in the domestic sectors who are now displaced, and the firms for whom they worked. A narrow analysis calculates that, where the value of the gains to the winners outweighs the value of the losses, the net gain to overall well-being makes the policy a good one. However, the analysis does not include the effect of the *distribution* of the losers, who may be from one community (or region), while the winners may be more widespread. This disparate impact, while positive in overall terms, may have the effect of increasing inequality – but that is not directly factored into the policy decision.[2]

There is an argument that policies to reduce inequality may adversely affect economic performance or outcomes. Not only is this incorrect in its own terms, as we will shortly see, but such an argument is false because it assumes that inequality measures are excluded in our definition of economic performance.

Economic analysis, after all, is about more than ensuring that the market mechanism works as depicted in the conventional textbook; the mechanism is not an end in itself. Economic analysis should always be a means to an end, where the end is defined more broadly, reflecting society's values and objectives (see Figure 4.1).

In other words, financial objectives are a subset of broader economic goals. These economic goals are, in turn, a subset of the comprehensive set of objectives and values that a society has determined. Financial considerations should be subservient to society's values, and not vice versa, as currently seems to be the case. An encouraging development is the Treasury's recently published Living Standards Framework,[3] which includes 'increasing equity' as one of its measures. This framework also makes clear that New Zealand needs to focus on more than just maximising GDP growth. Despite the development it is difficult to escape the conclusion that much of our decision-making remains driven by narrow financial analysis based on monetary measures of benefits and costs.

Reclaiming economics

Our first task is to wrest the economics discipline away from its financial disciples and their narrow concern with allocating resources solely to increase income, and return it to its foundations: allocating resources for maximum well-being (or, for the economist, utility). So we need to examine well-being (or utility), and show that inequality has a direct effect on it.

To do this, it is helpful to distinguish three types of inequality: inequality in income, inequality in wealth and inequality of opportunity. It is the interaction of these three species of inequality that is so damaging to our well-being.

Wealth can be defined as resources from which benefits can be gleaned. The 'benefits' might simply be income, but the definition of resources should be all-encompassing: land, inheritances, physical ability, skills, health, knowledge, whakapapa and more. Opportunity is more subjective, but should, at the least, include the ability to participate in and contribute to society's activities, including economic activities.

Undoubtedly, these terms are all inter-related, as Figure 4.2 indicates; so, where does one start? We could start with income. Wealth is, generally speaking, accumulated from income. Take, then, an individual who has landed a high-paying job. The income from this job would help that person accumulate wealth, in the form of, say, a home and being increasingly able to pay off the mortgage. The house could then provide the financial basis for opportunities to explore business ventures (for example, helping family members set up in business as building contractors).

Or, we could travel anti-clockwise around the diagram and suggest that the high-paying job itself could lead directly to opportunity, as the networks and experiences it generates directly open up other business ventures. Such opportunity can then lead to increased wealth in the form of a valued business venture that generates a stream of income.

Figure 4.2 The inter-relationships of income, wealth and opportunity

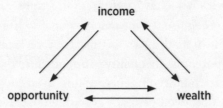

Or, we could start with wealth, which can be used to produce more income. For example, wealth in the form of a rental property generates rent. With such rental income, opportunities then open up for new ventures or, perhaps, investment in re-training or new skills. But wealth on its own can also open the doors of opportunity. As above, one could use the family home (perhaps inherited) as the financial basis for business – an asset against which to borrow that all-important first loan. Or it could be that the location of one's inherited home enables entry to better-resourced primary and secondary schools. In time, these opportunities can in turn generate income.

Finally, to close the circle, we could start with opportunity. Opportunities could be generated through winning a scholarship, or a place on an apprenticeship programme. With opportunities open, the income tap usually flows more smoothly (and perhaps faster), making wealth accumulation easier. And opportunity, in and of itself, may open the doors to wealth, from which income can be generated.

To look at this differently, from the negative perspective, we could say that an increasing disparity in the distribution of wealth will, if nothing else adjusts, accentuate income disparities. An increasing inequality of wealth will, likewise, accentuate inequalities in opportunities. And increasing levels of income inequality will perpetuate disparities in wealth, while disparities in opportunity will accentuate inequality in income as well as in wealth.

In this way, income inequalities damage our well-being (or utility) by creating unequal opportunities, which in turn limit the life chances of many. But because inequalities, if left unchecked, grow over time (especially as parents pass advantages and disadvantages on to their children), the damage to our well-being is compounded. This sets the scene for the reinforcement, or the perpetuation, of inequality in outcomes. More precisely, once a noticeable level of inequality becomes embedded in a society, a standard, market-led economy[4] will eventually (if not inevitably) lead to further increasing levels of inequality.

But this will only be seen as an issue of concern if the economist accepts that inequality is within society's definition of utility. And, as we noted earlier, we need to recognise that growing inequality has negative effects for the wealthy as well as the less fortunate. By reducing the ability of some to fulfil their potential, inequality of opportunity reduces the ability of the economy in its totality to generate improved income and wealth for all. This reduces the well-being of everyone in society. For example, inequality of opportunity leads inevitably to a workforce that is less skilled (and is thus less productive) than would otherwise be the case. If this workforce is unable to access educational opportunities, then it falls on business owners to provide that training, or to put up with less productive labour. Another example involves the costs of protecting both property and possessions in an unequal community. Whether these are insurance costs, private premium payments or taxpayer-funded police, justice and prison services, these expenses fall on the wealthy as well as the less fortunate.

While many economists are likely to keep on using monetary income and wealth as proxies for well-being (or utility), thinking about opportunity forces them to take a broader perspective. Identifying the impact of income and wealth on opportunity helps bring inequality under the gaze of the economist and within the ambit of economic analysis.

Of course, it could be argued that the damage to well-being is partly offset if inequality leads to greater growth that benefits us all. But, as we will shortly show, even on the narrow terms of pure monetary returns, inequality acts as a negative influence on growth, not a positive.

Strengthening the argument: inequality is inefficient

Here, we need to show that inequality can cause problems with our economic mechanisms and outcomes.

This task – making economics prioritise inequality – is easier if we can show that increasing inequality is an inefficient use of resources. After all, good economic analysis is founded on the desire to improve, preserve or protect the efficient use of resources. If an argument could be made that inequality and inefficiency go together, then there would be an even stronger case for the economist to become concerned about growing inequality or widening disparities.

In fact, this case is clear: there is a very real economic loss incurred by the existence of unemployed, under-employed, untrained, disenchanted, disconnected, disenfranchised and, indeed, disruptive resources. In other words, when people are deprived of the opportunity to achieve their full potential, we are ensuring that these members of society are not fully utilised. Resources are left idle and excluded. The existence (or, indeed, expansion) of such a group can, as a minimum, be seen as inefficient.

This is the cost of the lost opportunities; but there is also the cost of the ambulances at the bottom of the cliff. These are the additional resources that have been diverted away from wealth-enhancing activities and allocated towards picking up the pieces. Again, this cannot be considered an efficient use of our resources.

For example, take the cost of remedial education programmes. In a well-functioning society (with a similarly well-functioning economy), children would come to school ready for a good day's tuition (and play). Where they are not, schools' budgets are diverted to 'preparing the child to be school-ready'. By this we are not referring to the money that is well spent on all the programmes needed to cater for the wide range of children's abilities, interests and aptitudes. This is, rather, the money spent on 'catch-up' programmes such as numeracy and reading recovery, as well as specialist staff and teacher aides, not to mention the resources needed to cope with plain old behavioural and social interaction problems. Just imagine what could be done with these resources if they were re-diverted to improving, broadening, enhancing and invigorating the curriculum and the extra-curricular offerings for today's young. Just imagine what that could do for their opportunities for tomorrow.

Why do some economists overlook this inefficiency? One reason is the underlying assumptions of the microeconomic model in which economists have all been schooled.[5] Our training leads us to believe that a properly functioning market with minimal intervention will lead to an ideal allocation of resources because the market mechanism allows individuals to decide what to make and what to buy.

The model from which the conclusion derives remains a beautiful piece of analysis that is close to the hearts of most economists. The model depicts individuals as 'choosing' between many production and consumption options, with the market mechanism ensuring that our individual choices do indeed lead to the ideal allocation of resources.

But the inconvenient reality is that the model has many underlying assumptions, including a central one: that all resources are indeed fully employed. That is, the production and consumption options that we are choosing between are those arising from an economy where all resources are fully employed. The model assumes that there are no unemployed, under-employed or disconnected resources to be concerned about.[6]

If we can see past this assumption, then it is only a very short road that leads to the conclusion that where resources are not fully employed, the resulting allocation of them cannot really be seen to be efficient, let alone ideal.

Strengthening the argument further: inequality as a market failure

The argument that economists need to think about inequality is even stronger if we can show that inequality represents what is known as a market failure. A market failure – which just indicates that a simple market, with no or little government intervention, is failing to produce a desired outcome – should be a red light on the dashboard of any economic policy analyst. To all but the most theoretically pure, if such a market failure can be identified, even the most standard and conventional economic framework justifies a role for intervention, or remedial government action.

A market failure can arise when the income accruing to an individual or group does not reflect their resources (wealth, skills, contribution and effort). The textbook example is the existence of a monopoly. A monopoly can extort monopoly or above-normal profits (or income) in excess of those in more competitive activities. Such monopoly profits generate a sub-optimal outcome, in that consumers literally pay the price of this extortion.

Of course, a pure textbook monopoly does not exist in the real world.[7] But there are sectors where monopoly characteristics can be detected, sectors in which a limited number of firms supply a particular product or service. For example, New Zealand's electricity generation industry is dominated by four large players. Similarly, airport companies are, in general, alone in the provision of airport services in their area. In such sectors, it is the role of regulatory authorities (the Commerce Commission, for instance) to police the profits (or prices) of firms to ensure that consumers do not suffer the consequences of minimal competition.

Amongst others, Adam Smith warned that the use of market power by individuals or groups may need to be constrained:

> People of the same trade seldom meet together, even for merriment and diversion, but the conversation ends in a conspiracy against the public, or in some contrivance to raise prices … But though the law cannot hinder people of the same trade from sometimes assembling together, it ought to do nothing to facilitate such assemblies …[8]

So, how can inequality be a market failure? Or, at least, how can it contribute to a market failure? The relevant point here is the perpetuation of the inequalities in outcomes described earlier. The income accruing to certain groups in a society reflects not their self-acquired wealth, or skills, or contribution, or effort, but the advantages they have inherited. Where the income is noticeably in excess of what their wealth, skills, contribution or effort would warrant, then such returns are similar to monopoly profits. These above-normal incomes are evidence of a sub-optimal outcome, and are thus a justification for intervention.

As noted previously, a monopoly firm[9] is, or should be, properly regulated so that their monopoly profits are not excessive or made at the expense of consumers. Similarly, if some groups in society have more opportunity than others (due to the perpetuation of disparities), regulation is needed to make sure that the income they enjoy is not excessive or due to a fortuitous position that in itself arises from a perpetual increase in disparities in income, wealth and opportunity. In other words, the more fortunate people should enjoy an income in line with their effort, skills and contributions, but not be able to generate excessively large incomes at the expense of the less fortunate. In this case, the 'regulation' of unjustified inequality might take the form of measures to reduce excessive income, including higher taxes (as outlined below). It could also involve more measures that – like scholarships and apprenticeship programmes – can increase opportunities and stop the cycle of income and wealth disparities growing and perpetuating over years and then across generations.

A measure of the failure

We now need to gauge just how important is this market failure. Is it marginal enough to ignore, or is it undeniably large? To answer this question, it's helpful to think about the economic cost of unequal opportunities: the lost income that would have been generated had all resources been employed. Put differently, this is the income that could have been produced had the unemployed labour resource actually been employed. Of course, this risks reverting to the – rather narrow – use of money as a proxy for well-being; but an order of magnitude expressed in this way still helps us comprehend the size of the loss.

New Zealand's annual GDP of $208 billion, generated from 2.2 million people employed, suggests an average GDP per person employed of around $94,000 a year.[10] The cost of the lost opportunity of our unused resources, using the official figure of approximately 160,000 unemployed, is then around $15 billion. If we add in the additional 120,000 or so currently counted by Statistics New Zealand as 'jobless but not officially unemployed', then this lost opportunity cost heads towards $27 billion. That's large in anyone's book.

Some might argue that the unemployed resources will not be as efficient as the average resource already employed, and that we shouldn't use the average $94,000 figure. Of course, if they are not as efficient, then that inefficiency results, at least in part, from the failure of the market to open opportunities to this group. However, if for argument's sake we reduce the average GDP from these resources by half, the order of magnitude remains well over $10 billion. This number remains too large to ignore.

Another measure could be the lack of opportunity to engage fully in education. Take the number of New Zealanders without a Level 2 NCEA qualification, which is probably the minimum level of education required for full participation in a modern economy. Narrowing the argument to those aged between twenty and forty years old, this figure was around 264,000 according to the latest (2006) Census. This is in the order of about 10 per cent of those employed, and if they contributed as much to the economy as they would have done with a Level 2 NCEA qualification, we have roughly another $5 billion as the cost of this market failure.

Of course, spending on benefits and other ambulances at the bottom of the cliff are extraordinarily expensive and inefficient uses of resources (time, effort, skill, human endeavour, pure dollars), and could be added to these costs. And, again, these are only monetary measures of cost. They very likely underestimate the cost of the reduction in overall well-being (or utility), especially if we start to accumulate costs over time, as the impact of disparities in opportunity, income and wealth all perpetuate over generations.

What can we afford to do?

These arguments make a strong case for intervention to move the market towards a more efficient, and better, outcome. At the very least, we should do some practical things to minimise the costs arising from the market failures described above. So what are practical options either to reduce the disparities, halt perpetual increases or, at least, minimise the consequences of inequality?

If we had to pick just one thing to tackle, it might be the growing inequality that arises from people's difficulties in finding an adequate and affordable house. Housing is central in so many ways. It affects inequality in wealth, as a large proportion of New Zealanders' wealth is in their family home. It compounds inequality in income, as an inadequate amount of money remaining after housing costs then limits people's options. Family decisions around housing can also open or close many opportunities. They can limit or enhance access to good jobs (which are not often found near areas of affordable housing); to community facilities and infrastructure; and to schooling and broader education opportunities; and can affect people's ability to participate in and contribute to community activities and to develop networks.

The government needs to intervene in the market, and build low-cost, first-home houses. That the market is failing to provide adequate affordable housing to significant groups of the community is justification for this intervention. If these efforts divert[11] some resources from top-of-the-market property developments, that is to be accepted, because the gain in opportunities from reducing inequality will easily outweigh such a cost.

To reduce income inequality directly, we need a more progressive income tax system. (More welfare payments are not ideal, as they are only an ambulance at the bottom of the cliff, although in the reality of today's world they form part of a package to halt the broadening of income disparities.) A capital gains tax, of some form or another, could assist with housing inequality and reduce the widening of other wealth-related disparities. Inheritance rules, and estate and gift duty, are also vehicles to prevent wealth disparities from becoming overwhelming, and we need to think about how to use them more effectively.

Of course, no option or policy to mitigate these failures is perfect: some have side-effects, some can be gamed and some will be exploited by the unscrupulous. However, that can be said about almost all interventions, not to mention the market mechanism itself. It is the nature of human systems and societies that there will always be individuals who will attempt to exploit or bend rules to their benefit. This reinforces the need for effective policing and positive incentives for people to abide by the rules. Just as any sports match requires a set of rules, it also requires a set of judicial officials (such as referees and umpires) to enforce them. The notion of a self-regulating system is only valid if the system itself is not captured by particular players. The case for intervention cannot be invalidated by the claim that some will attempt to bend the rules. This just strengthens the argument for stronger policing.

Critics of a more progressive tax system often claim it discourages innovation and the entrepreneurial spirit; or that higher tax rates reduce people's desire to work, and so lower productivity and competitiveness.

Some critics go further still, arguing that such policies could see long-term emigration of the higher-earning skilled workforce and the prospect of capital flight if we regulate too tightly, or tax too highly.

Any case for intervention must address these concerns and place them in context. Investors take many aspects into their equations when considering expenditure decisions. While some investors will be swayed by short-term tax and subsidy inducements, for example, others will be more attracted to longer-term gains accrued from a more cohesive society and a well-trained, healthy and productive workforce. Similarly, the migration decisions of individuals will be influenced by a raft of factors, ranging from family or personal situations, climate, employment opportunities, commuting and transport considerations, crime and safety concerns, house prices, access and proximity to quality schools, health services, and sport and recreation facilities, not to mention wage and tax rates. To highlight only a narrow selection of these factors is to ignore the complexity of the many investment and migration decisions made by individuals and organisations.

Similarly, as with any case for intervention, concerns over emigration and capital flight must engage with the full complexity of inequality. For example, take the relationship between income tax and productivity or growth. A 2008 OECD report[12] found that corporate and top personal income taxes have a negative effect on productivity. However, a recent Institute of Taxation and Economic Policy study of the performance of forty-one states in the US over the past ten years found little relationship between income taxes and economic outcomes.[13] Such contrasts caution against easy dismissals or shallow engagements, just as it places burdens on those advocating intervention.

When we balance these arguments, we should also include in our calculations the potential gains from a cohesive (and inclusive) society where individuals are actively encouraged to pursue opportunities. Such a society and economy – one where the ambulance at the bottom of the cliff is neither so necessary nor so predominant – may indeed be an attraction to people and their funds.

The costs of doing nothing

We need to recognise that growing disparities in wealth, income and opportunity are an economic concern. There are very real costs to growing inequality, borne across the whole spectrum of society. These costs can be in the form of higher taxes for greater police and law-and-order efforts or higher insurance premia to secure property. Costs fall on having to operate businesses with a less trained or skilled workforce, while the impact of disaffected and disconnected individuals limits the potential that communities could otherwise achieve. All of these costs need to be weighed in the light of the broader concept of well-being, not the narrow definition of financial benefits and costs. These wider costs, these failures of opportunity, are too large to be ignored by economists. To those who prefer to avoid the issue by saying, 'We can't afford to do anything about inequality', there is a very simple retort: 'We can't afford not to.'

The value of support

Pete Bryant *is a member of the consumers group at the Downtown Community Ministry in Wellington, and was interviewed for this viewpoint by Max Rashbrooke.*

'I got told one day by a judge, when I was getting sentenced – the judge goes, "Well, Mr Bryant, society owes you nothing." I said, "Well, if society owes me nothing, I owe society nothing." The judge gave me six months for being smart.'

By the time the magistrate had delivered his message, rejection had been a recurring theme of Pete Bryant's life. When he was growing up in Rotorua in the 1960s, his violent, alcoholic father and largely absent mother often left Pete and his brothers desperate for food. One good source, he says, was the local Tip Top factory, 'which used to throw out all their defective bags of bread'.

Pete's father would attack his wife and beat his sons, and, on one of the rare occasions that he bought Christmas presents, subsequently broke them and burnt them on the fire because the children had opened them early. Pete's parents eventually sent him away to foster care. By this time, he had learnt a certain way of living: 'From as far back as I can remember, I learned how to do stealing. Back then it was living to survive, because our parents didn't give a shit about us.'

These messages imprinted in early childhood led to a life lived in institutions, on the street, at night shelters and in boarding houses. Spells of work were periodically interrupted by various crimes and their resulting prison stretches, including one for armed robbery in the 1990s. Drugs and alcohol also featured prominently in his life.

But being punished by the courts, and being told that society was not responsible for him, did little to break the cycle. That break came first from Pete himself, driven by his desire to look after a stepson from an earlier relationship. And like many people who have started to turn their life around, Pete can be withering in his contempt for those who have not yet done so. He stresses, over and over, the need for individuals to make the right decisions, to take responsibility for themselves.

At the same time he also acknowledges the support he has received from various organisations in Wellington, where he has lived for the last few years. Top of the list is the Downtown Community Ministry (DCM), which is funded largely by public donations, the Wellington City Council and the Ministry of Social Development to work with homeless and otherwise vulnerable people.

DCM staff, led by director Stephanie McIntyre, have helped Pete both in small ways, such as clothing grants, and with larger interventions around managing money and other life skills. The guidance DCM provides has been invaluable – and has created something akin to a caring family for the first time in Pete's life. 'If I end up having to fall back on them, they are there', he says. 'They are like a family. They have always been here for me. I don't need to feel abandoned like I did in the past.'

DCM manages his finances for him, getting his benefit transferred into its own bank account, then paying his bills and giving him the remainder to spend. It also provides food and other forms of support that have helped Pete look after his stepson. 'I have DCM to thank to a certain extent for that, because they have kept him down here in Wellington with me. They've given him food for school – we get a food parcel a week if we so choose.'

DCM has also provided part-time work. 'Steph [McIntyre] gave me a job here, and I have appreciated it', Pete says. 'Even though I have stuffed up a few times since I've been here, I have always stuck at it and tried to make it better.'

The city council, for its part, has rented Pete and his stepson a flat in Mt Cook – the first place he has ever had in his own name in his nearly fifty years of life. At a rent 70 per cent of the market rate, this flat gives Pete the foundations of a better life for him and his stepson. Various other forms of government support have provided at least a bare minimum income; he's been on the sickness benefit, the unemployment benefit and, most recently, the DPB.

Pete's story testifies that money spent on welfare and support is not money wasted; it is an investment in our future success. (And of course more funding for these services would enable them to support more people.) This investment changes lives of all kinds, including those marked by decades of extraordinary strain. In other words, support works – and pays a dividend – even where years of punishment have achieved very little.

For society as a whole, there is a purely financial payoff in reduced criminal justice, health and welfare costs. The payoff for Pete is a part-time cleaning job in central Wellington that he got at the start of 2013; just a few months later he had been made a supervisor. In one sense, the returns are modest: once he earns over $100 a week, his DPB gets cut by 30c for every dollar earned; and that, added to the standard tax rate, is the equivalent of a 40 per cent tax, and leaves him earning just $10 an hour in the hand.

But, as Pete says, 'The point is, is that it's work. And if I can show people that I'm a good worker … eventually word of mouth will get around and eventually I'll have heaps more work.' Ultimately, he'd like to be a full-time, self-employed cleaner. But whatever happens, it's been an astonishing journey, from night shelter to supervisor in just eight months. His life story is, as he himself puts it, 'a work in progress'.

5 What Kind of Equality Matters?

Jonathan Boston

The nature of the problem

Concerns about increased levels of inequality, especially income and wealth inequality, lie at the heart of this book.[1] The purpose of this chapter is to address some of the deeper philosophical and ethical questions that underpin these concerns. At least five types of questions deserve attention.

First, does equality matter and on what grounds can the quest for greater equality be justified? For instance, is more equality desirable as an end in itself or as a means to secure other important societal goals, or both?

Second, what kinds of equality are most significant? After all, there are many potential candidates – rights, opportunities, outcomes and so on – and many different 'spaces' in which equality might be pursued, such as education, employment, healthcare and political influence. Which of these candidates and spaces matter most, and why?

Third, how far should equality be pursued? Should we aim merely for somewhat less inequality than currently prevails, or should the objective be more ambitious – even absolute equality, in some cases? And regardless of the ultimate objective, how much equality can we practically achieve, especially given the huge differences in human talents and circumstances, not to mention financial constraints and the limits, certainly within liberal democracies, to the coercive powers of the state?

Fourth, what priority should be accorded to the goal of equality? In other words, where does equality rank in the scale of values relative, for example, to liberty, efficiency, family autonomy and so on?

Finally, whose responsibility is it to address unjustified inequalities? Does the responsibility lie primarily with the state or does it rest with local communities, the voluntary sector and private charity?

The purpose here is to shed light on some of these questions,[2] in particular, which of the various candidates for equality matter and which ones should be equalised, at least to some extent. The conclusion, in short, is that not all types of equality (or inequality) are of similar importance. Hence, the goal should not be to equalise *everything* to which the principle of equality could potentially be applied, nor to aim for perfect or absolute equality. Instead, the goal should be to equalise (or at least eliminate any gross inequalities with respect to) those dimensions of life that fundamentally affect a person's ability to enjoy their rights as citizens and participate as full, active and equal members of society. In practice, this means embracing an approach that is sometimes referred to as *specific egalitarianism* rather than *general egalitarianism*.

While achieving a high measure of equality is sometimes justified, more commonly we should be willing to settle for a modest movement towards greater equality. As the Nobel laureate Amartya Sen argues, our quest should not be for a perfectly just society, for this is impossible.[3] Rather, the goal should be to remove manifestly unjustified inequalities. In practice, this will typically involve choosing between realistic and feasible alternatives based on transparent, defensible criteria – or what Sen calls a process of 'realisation-focused comparisons'. From a policy perspective, this means taking a nuanced approach, pursuing multiple objectives, balancing a range of competing considerations, and making principled, evidence-informed judgements.

The different kinds of equality

The principle of equality is almost universally endorsed and has often been a rallying cry for political reform. Indeed, as Sen highlights, every contemporary theory of social justice places importance – if not overriding weight – on the idea of equality and advocates equalising *something*.[4] Virtually everyone, therefore, can be regarded as an *egalitarian* – at least in some sense. Yet the actual *kind* of equality that is championed varies greatly, as do the reasons why the favoured types of equality are deemed to be attractive. Hence, while equality is highly valued, there is huge disagreement about *why* equality matters and *what* precisely should be equalised.

Within the relevant philosophical literature, a wide range of variables, dimensions and personal attributes have been identified as important and thus potential candidates for equalisation. Amongst the most common candidates are: equal liberty, equal rights (or equality of *some* rights), equal political power or influence, equal capabilities, equal social status, equal access, equal opportunity (or equality of *some* opportunities), equal treatment (or equal legal and political treatment), equal holdings of primary goods, equal resources, equal outcomes (including equal income, wealth, utility, happiness, well-being, welfare, etc.), equal respect and concern, and assigning equal weight to every person's interests (or their utility gains and losses). While this list is not exhaustive, it captures most of the variables or attributes (or the domains in which equality can be applied) that are seen to be important by one or more of the major philosophical traditions.

Different schools of thought emphasise different kinds of equality. For instance, those who value human freedom most highly want to ensure that freedom is maximised and that all citizens enjoy equal liberty. They thus place less weight on other values, including those kinds of equality that might conflict with the maximisation of liberty or equal liberty for all. Similarly, there are different views about the social and economic costs of realising (or not realising) certain kinds of equality or achieving other goals. If the costs of achieving a particular kind of equality are thought to be high, there will be an understandable reluctance to endorse equality of this kind or to pursue it with vigour.

Given such differences, why is the principle of equality taken so seriously by so many? The answer, very simply, lies in the near-universal endorsement of the idea that human beings are equal in some fundamental respect or, at the very least, should be assumed to have equal moral value or equal dignity regardless of their ethnicity, gender, age and so forth. (The philosophical basis for such assumptions lies beyond the scope of this chapter.)

Assessing the different kinds of equality

What are the merits, then, of the different kinds of equality?

Equality before the law

Let us start with one of the most widely accepted principles: equality before the law (or what is sometimes called equal justice under the law). This principle means that everyone should be subject to the same laws and entitled to the equal protection of the law, irrespective of their socio-economic status, gender, ethnicity, religion and so forth. Hence, no one should be above the law and no one should receive special privileges. But it is one thing for all people to enjoy the equal protection of the law in a *formal* or technical sense, and quite another for this protection to be equally meaningful and *effective*. After all, access to the legal system in most countries can be extremely expensive. If a society has significant inequalities in income and wealth, citizens will not have an equal capacity to protect their rights. Because of this, many defenders of the principle of equality before the law argue that the state should provide significant financial assistance to those with limited resources so that all citizens have genuinely equal protection. (This distinction, between *formal* and *substantive* – or *effective* – ideas of equality, is discussed further below.)

Equal basic liberties
The principle of equality before the law is a subset of a broader egalitarian principle – the idea that all people should enjoy equal basic liberties or equal rights. This principle is both highly prized and widely supported. For instance, one of the leading political philosophers of the twentieth century, John Rawls, identified the principle of equal basic liberties as the first principle of justice in his landmark volume *A Theory of Justice*. As expressed by Rawls in a later book, *Political Liberalism*, every citizen ought to have 'an equal right to a fully adequate scheme of equal basic liberties which is compatible with a similar scheme of liberties for all'.[5] Societies should, in other words, seek to maximise the overall amount of liberty enjoyed by their citizens, consistent with each citizen having the right to equal personal liberty. Indeed, Rawls regarded basic liberties (such as civil and political rights like freedom of expression, conscience, religion, association and peaceful assembly) to be of such great importance that they should have absolute priority over all other considerations – including the demands of his second principle of justice, concerned with equalising certain general opportunities and ensuring that resources are allocated in an equitable manner. Under Rawls's approach, therefore, it would be unjustified to sacrifice even a small amount of liberty in order to realise other goals, such as poverty alleviation or longer life expectancy.

Rawls placed absolute priority on liberty not merely because it is useful (as are income and wealth), in determining a person's overall well-being and their capacity to pursue their 'life plan', but also because it is essential for protecting the private aspects of a person's life and for the practice of public reasoning through, for example, freedom of speech. Without extensive liberty, in other words, many critically important institutions, values and decision-making processes would be at risk. And without *equal* basic liberties, there could be extreme injustice, such as widespread and serious racial and gender discrimination. But while few question either the ideal of extensive liberty or the related principle of equal personal liberty, many scholars have raised doubts about whether Rawls's first principle of justice should have total priority over all other considerations. For instance, although basic civil and political rights are vitally important, a good case can be made that preventing hunger and malnutrition is equally, if not more, important. In some instances a minor or temporary infringement of a basic liberty may be justified if essential to minimise or prevent severe human harm, such as starvation.

But irrespective of the relative weight given to basic liberties, what are the conditions required for such liberties to be meaningful, effective and enjoyed equally by all citizens? Consider, for example, the conditions required for genuine *political* equality. For the democratic process to have integrity and legitimacy, citizens must be able to participate freely, fairly and effectively in decision-making, and have equal opportunities to exercise political influence.[6] Plainly, this entails more than simply the right to vote or for votes to carry an equal value. For instance, if disadvantaged citizens are not to be excluded from political life, they must have access to education, healthcare and social assistance. Likewise, if citizens are to have a fair opportunity to influence the democratic process, there must be appropriate controls on how political parties and election campaigns are funded. Otherwise, political equality will be materially compromised, with wealthy citizens and large corporates able to use their financial resources to exercise disproportionate political influence. To quote Rawls:

> If the public forum is to be free and open to all, and in continuous session, everyone should be able to make use of it ... The liberties protected by the principle of participation lose much of their value whenever those who have greater private means are permitted to use their advantages to control the course of public debate. For eventually these inequalities will enable those better situated to exercise a larger influence over the development of legislation. In due time they are likely to acquire a preponderant weight in settling social questions ...[7]

Fortunately, in New Zealand there is a multi-party commitment to the democratic ideal of political equality. As a result, there have been reasonably comprehensive and effective controls on electoral finance for many decades, including limits on the campaign spending of political parties, candidates and other participants in the political process. By contrast, in some democracies, like the US, there are much less extensive controls. Indeed, in 2010, in an important decision, the majority of the US Supreme Court declared that laws prohibiting or limiting corporate and union political expenditures were unconstitutional, thus enabling individuals and organisations to spend vast sums through so-called 'political action committees'. As the economist Joseph Stiglitz has persuasively argued, where the rich enjoy a disproportionate political influence, they will invariably use this influence to capture an even greater share of a nation's resources and entrench their wealth.[8] Hence, a genuine commitment to political equality needs policy measures to reduce the risk of, if not prevent, such outcomes.

In short, a plausible case can be made that if basic liberties are to be enjoyed equally and substantively, more is required than merely the absence of external constraints (often known as *negative* liberty). Citizens also need the means to use their rights fully and to participate effectively in the democratic process (known as *positive* liberty). This requires, as Amartya Sen has argued, looking carefully at whether people have the 'basic capabilities' to function as citizens and turn their resources into valuable activities and outcomes.[9] Such capabilities include good bodily health and bodily integrity; the capacity to think, imagine and reason; having the social bases of self-respect; being able to participate in meaningful relationships; and being able to contribute to public life. For such capabilities to be realised, and for people to enjoy the rights of citizenship, the state will need to redistribute resources to those who would otherwise be disadvantaged and excluded. Hence, there is a direct and undeniable link between the goal of equal civil and political rights and the distribution of income, wealth and other material resources. This is not to suggest that, to achieve equal basic liberties, the state must strictly equalise material resources across individuals, families or households; but equal basic liberties are certainly incompatible with high levels of poverty and massive social and economic inequalities.

Equality of opportunity
Much of what can be said about equal liberties can also be said about a closely related principle of social justice, namely equality of opportunity. While this principle finds wide support across the ideological spectrum, there is much disagreement about what it actually means, where it should be applied and how it should be achieved. Which particular opportunities matter? Should the goal be to equalise opportunities at or near the beginning of each person's life (the start of the 'race') or during the whole of a person's life (at all significant points during the 'race')? What are the best means to achieve greater equality of opportunity, and do they include positive discrimination – for instance to ensure equality of opportunity for disadvantaged ethnic minorities, such as Māori and Pacific peoples?

Broadly speaking, there are two main versions of the principle of equality of opportunity. Both apply especially to those seeking positions, roles and opportunities that confer certain advantages or benefits, such as public offices, educational or training positions, and job vacancies; and both relate to the distinction between *formal* and *substantive* kinds of equality.

The first version is often referred to as *formal* equality of opportunity or as the non-discrimination principle. Put simply, this requires no more than the absence or removal of *external* constraints that might prevent individuals using their gifts and talents. Under this approach, for instance, discrimination against individuals due to circumstances over which they have no control – such as their ethnicity or gender – is regarded as unfair. But while such an approach supports governmental efforts to prevent unjustified discrimination, it fails to address the unfairness arising from large inequalities in the distribution of natural endowments, such as intellectual abilities and physical skills, or economic resources acquired via inheritance or sheer luck.

For instance, members of disadvantaged ethnic minorities might not face overt discrimination when seeking work, but if they are poorly educated, or simply poor, they will certainly not enjoy the same employment opportunities as those who are well educated and affluent. In other words, there may be no racial barrier preventing them from applying for any of the available jobs, but without a fair chance to obtain the relevant skills and expertise, they will not be able to compete on an equal footing. They will not, therefore, enjoy genuine equality of opportunity. So while formal equality of opportunity is a necessary condition for the requirements of social justice to be properly satisfied, it is not sufficient. Arguably, for justice to prevail, equality of opportunity must be achieved in a *substantive* sense.

The practical implications of this, however, are potentially very demanding. Consider, for instance, the case of candidates applying for jobs. *Formal* equality of opportunity requires only that the applicants for the relevant positions are assessed on their merits and that the preferred candidate is selected on the basis of defensible criteria. But many otherwise highly capable people will be unable to apply for such jobs because they lack the relevant skills, expertise or qualifications, and this lack may be the direct result of limited opportunities earlier in their life due to childhood poverty or a poor quality education. In other words, despite their innate ability, they have not enjoyed a genuine opportunity to become appropriately skilled or qualified. If competitive disadvantages of this kind are to be reduced, there will need to be government intervention to minimise poverty and equalise educational opportunities.[10] This raises the question of how far a society can and should go in trying to overcome the inequalities associated with a child's accident of birth or other arbitrary factors over which a person has no control.

Rawls argued that the fundamental aim should be to achieve *fair equality of opportunity*. Under this approach, given any distribution of natural endowments, those who have the 'same level of talent and ability, and have the same willingness to use them, should have the same prospects of success regardless of their initial place in the social system' or family resources.[11] Yet satisfying such conditions would be challenging, to say the least. It would require, amongst other things, a very large redistribution of resources to less well-off families and communities, as well as policies to constrain the capacity of wealthier or highly motivated parents to use their financial resources or influence to secure 'improper' advantages for their children via the purchase of better quality education or through gifts and inheritance. Inevitably, such efforts would have significant implications for payments made within families, and would entail much higher levels of state interference in family decision-making. The extent to which such interference is accepted will clearly depend on the value placed on family autonomy, the nature of the constraints being considered, the likely effectiveness of such constraints, and the priority accorded to fair equality of opportunity. Even with comprehensive policy measures, however, it would be hard to offset or overcome the many arbitrary factors that affect a person's life and opportunities.

Moreover, equalising the chances of success – in employment or in other areas of human endeavour – among those of equal ability, drive and ambition would not address other large sources of unequal opportunities. These include those arising from the fact that not all worthwhile human activities and capacities are equally valued by society and from major disparities in genetic endowments. The latter disparities include differences in innate talents and abilities, as well as variations in levels of energy, ambition and effort (which in turn can contribute to substantial differences in *acquired* skills and abilities). In the interests of fairness, there are clearly grounds for seeking to mitigate the worst effects of such disparities. Yet it must be acknowledged that there are practical limits, for any given level of resources and technology, to how far this can be done: for instance, at present the impact of most major disabilities can be only partially mitigated. Concerted efforts to compensate fully for, or to override, the outcomes of such 'natural lotteries' could also generate major disincentives to work and impose large economic costs.

Realistically, then, the quest for substantive equality of opportunity, however ethically appealing, can be pursued only so far. This does not mean that concerted efforts, both public and private, to *move towards* such a goal are unjustified. On the contrary, they fully deserve our support. But a measure of realism is also required: not all disadvantages and disparities can be overcome. And beyond a certain point, the pursuit of substantive equality of opportunity is bound to conflict with other important moral values, such as family autonomy. So those seeking greater social justice must consider a range of issues, including: what level of equality of opportunity is sufficient or 'good enough', what measures to override the natural lottery of birth are justified, how can cases of gross injustice be addressed most effectively, and how can people be best equipped to function as free and equal citizens.

There is a further dimension to this issue, however, that deserves mention. A good case can be made that not all opportunities are of equal moral significance. Few people would argue, for instance, that all citizens should have an equal opportunity to travel into space or take their annual holidays in expensive overseas resorts. Against this, there are clearly some opportunities which matter a great deal. This is because they profoundly affect a person's well-being and life chances. Such opportunities, it can be argued, include access to all those goods and services that are essential for the satisfaction of basic human needs. Included in such a list would be 'specific' goods like food, clothing and shelter, but also important services such as education and healthcare. A good case can equally be made for including access to those opportunities that people need to participate fully in their society and enjoy a sense of belonging (see below). Critical in this regard are access to paid employment – that is, equal employment opportunities – and fair opportunities to exercise political influence (as argued earlier).

To illustrate briefly, the opportunity for people to participate in the labour market, using their gifts and skills in a productive and satisfying manner, is widely seen as essential in the quest for a more just society. To quote the 1988 Royal Commission on Social Policy in New Zealand:

> Work, both paid and unpaid, is central to well-being ... How work is distributed, the conditions under which it is performed and the significance attached to it have an impact on every other aspect of social policy ... The primary instrument for achieving a fair and just society must be economic and social policies designed to provide wide employment opportunities.[12]

Related to this, in countries which value democratic governance, the power relations in firms, especially large ones, are often altered so as to give employees more influence on how their companies are run or through stronger collective bargaining provisions. (These approaches are discussed in Chapter 13, 'The Rewards of Work'.)

The economist James Tobin, who advocated equalising opportunities to enable people to enjoy those *specific* goods and services that are essential for life and citizenship, referred to this approach as 'specific egalitarianism'.[13] This approach certainly has merit. The main challenge, however, is determining the precise range of goods and services to which the principle of equality of opportunity should apply, the quantity and quality of the goods that should be provided, and the relative priority that this objective should receive in the overall scheme of things. There are also significant practical issues over how best to pursue specific egalitarianism, especially given New Zealand's ethnic disparities and diverse family and household circumstances. For instance, does one try to equalise opportunities for households or individuals? What mix of universal and means-tested assistance should be adopted? Similarly, there is scope for debate over how far specific egalitarianism is compatible with large inequalities of income or wealth. Overall, however, a commitment to specific egalitarianism implies restricting wealthy individuals (to the extent that this is feasible) from purchasing privileged access to designated goods and services.

Equal outcomes
A rather more controversial proposition is the idea that societies should seek to equalise certain specified outcomes. Again, there are many different views on which outcomes should be equalised. For some, material or economic outcomes, such as income or wealth, are critically important; while for others, more abstract outcomes, such as health, happiness and well-being, figure more prominently. A particular outcome, such as income, may be emphasised because it is needed to achieve other desirable ends, such as health and happiness; or because it is sufficiently important that, if possible, everyone should be able to enjoy the same amount of it. But whatever the case for equalising outcomes and whatever the selected candidate for equalisation, various problems arise.

To start with, there are major conceptual, methodological and practical problems. Suppose, for instance, that the aim is to equalise income: does this mean that we should focus on the incomes of individuals, families or households? Likewise, should the goal be to equalise incomes across society on a continuous basis – that is, at every point in time – or over the course of individuals' lifetimes, or at some particularly crucial stage in their lifecycle, such as early childhood? And regardless of the answer, how exactly is such a goal to be achieved? Numerous implementation problems are bound to arise: the great variability of annual incomes, the complexities of measurement and the practical challenges of redistribution, to name but a few. Similar challenges are likely if other outcomes – such as wealth, welfare, well-being or happiness – are chosen instead. Indeed, in some cases the conceptual, measurement and practical difficulties will be even greater. How, for instance, should states of happiness be measured and compared, and how could levels of happiness be equalised?

To compound these problems, efforts to equalise certain outcomes may well be inconsistent with other important principles. Take again the issue of income. Equalising each person's income will inevitably conflict with the principle that resources should be allocated, at least in part, on the basis of need. After all, one person – for instance, a seriously disabled person – may require greater assistance than another. Giving every person, or every family, the same income will result in some people having far more than they need (or want), while others experience severe hardship.

Similarly, a plausible case can be made that some inequalities in income are deserved, and thus morally justified. Rewarding people for their effort, contribution or merit may be socially just. A person who makes a huge effort to achieve some particular task is arguably more deserving than someone of equal natural abilities who decides to make absolutely no effort at all. This assumes that individuals enjoy some autonomy and that their behaviour is not completely dictated by their genetic inheritance or social circumstances. After all, to reward (or penalise) people for matters over which they have no control would be unfair. To be sure, there is scope for debate over the extent to which individuals are genuinely free and able to influence their destiny; but to argue that freedom is an utter sham or that individuals have absolutely no control over the effort they expend on a particular task would be to challenge the ethical foundations upon which most modern institutions operate, not least the criminal justice system.

A further problem with the goal of equalising income, wealth or well-being is that the measures required are likely to impose major economic costs or have other detrimental consequences. For instance, attempts to equalise incomes may damage work incentives and reduce risk-taking, investment and entrepreneurial activity. Over time, this is likely to result in a slower rate of economic growth, higher unemployment and poorer social outcomes. Additionally, the quest for income equality could well damage important social institutions and practices, including the accumulation of capital and inheritances. Tolerating a certain measure of income inequality, therefore, may be the price of ensuring that everyone is better off over the longer term.

This is not to suggest, however, that massive inequalities in income or wealth are economically and socially advantageous, or that the redistribution of income from the non-poor to the poor is unjustified. Rejecting absolute income equality does not mean that *any* level of inequality is morally acceptable. Likewise, while the New Zealand Treasury may be correct to argue, as it has recently done, that there is 'no definable "right" level of inequality',[14] this does not imply that all potential distributions of income or wealth are equally justified. There are two critical considerations here.

First, there is a strong and widely accepted ethical imperative to minimise human hardship and deprivation. So wherever a society has moved beyond mere subsistence and enjoys a reasonable surplus of goods and services, there is a compelling case for the state to provide a robust and adequate safety net. The broad aim should be to ensure that everyone's basic needs are satisfied and that all citizens have the opportunity to participate as full and equal members of their society. To quote the Report of the Royal Commission on Social Security in New Zealand in 1972:

> The community is responsible for giving dependent people a standard of living consistent with human dignity and approaching that enjoyed by the majority, irrespective of the cause of dependency.[15]

Likewise, the Commission argued that the objective of social assistance should be:

> to ensure, within the limitations which may be imposed by physical or other disabilities, that everyone is able to enjoy a standard of living much like the rest of the community, and thus able to feel a sense of participation and belonging to the community.[16]

Second, as argued elsewhere in this book, countries with relatively high income inequality often perform worse on a host of social and economic indicators than those with less inequality.[17] The evidence suggests that more unequal societies tend to have poorer outcomes in relation to life expectancy, infant mortality, mental illness, teenage pregnancies, homicides, imprisonment rates and educational performance. In other words, high income inequality is associated with greater *inequalities* in certain outcomes, such as education and health outcomes, as well as a larger average amount of social ills, such as imprisonment rates and the spread of preventable diseases. These things tend to afflict those at the bottom of the income distribution ladder in wholly disproportionate ways. A related problem is that societies with high levels of income inequality tend to have lower levels of social mobility than do more egalitarian nations. This means that those at the bottom are more likely to get trapped in relative poverty with inter-generational inequalities becoming more entrenched. Not only does this reduce the opportunities enjoyed by the poor, but persistent and chronic poverty has more adverse consequences than transitory periods of poverty. This is damaging for both the individuals directly affected and the wider society. For such reasons, there is a good case for using a range of policies, including tax and social assistance programmes, to moderate the degree of income inequality, and especially to ensure that the extent and duration of poverty are minimised.

Social equality

One final kind of equality deserves mention: the equalisation of social status. According to the political philosopher David Miller, social equality or equality of status involves 'a society in which people regard and treat one another as equals, and together form a single community without divisions of social class'.[18] Such a society would have minimal social differentiation or social distance between people, and would be devoid of privilege. Otherwise, people may feel stigmatised or have their self-respect undermined because of their particular 'station' in life. Closely linked in the ideal of social equality are notions of fellowship, solidarity, social cohesion and social inclusion. As Miller argues, social equality requires equal citizenship rights, including civil, political and welfare rights; sharing a common life, including the absence of segregation based on ethnicity, religion or other social distinctions (especially in relation to public institutions such as schools and hospitals); and the avoidance of socially divisive differences in material resources. After all, social equality is impossible if people lead radically separate lives – for instance, in terms of where they live, work, socialise, shop and play – because of massive income or wealth inequalities.

Relevant here is the idea of 'complex equality' advanced by the political philosopher Michael Walzer.[19] According to Walzer, social goods – such as education, income and public recognition – ought to be allocated in different, non-cumulative ways, so that 'having more of good X gives a person no particular advantage in the competition for good Y'.[20] To quote Walzer:

> In formal terms, complex equality means that no citizen's standing in one sphere or with regard to one social good can be undercut by his standing in some other sphere, with regard to some other good. Thus, citizen X may be chosen over citizen Y for political office, and then the two of them will be unequal in the sphere of politics. But

they will not be unequal generally so long as X's office gives him no advantage over Y in any other sphere – superior medical care, access to better schools for his children, entrepreneurial opportunities, and so on.[21]

To realise complex equality, Walzer argues that a system of 'blocked exchanges' is required. Under this approach, goods obtained in one sphere cannot be exchanged for goods in another. For instance, as previously discussed, those with substantial financial resources should not be permitted to deploy these resources to 'buy' votes or influence in the political arena. Where such exchanges are not blocked, equality of status and condition will be hard to achieve. Instead, social goods will accrue in a cumulative manner to the same people. Inevitably, such people will be privileged and seen to be privileged. To compound matters, social inequality of this kind may well become inter-generational, thus entrenching privilege over long periods of time.

Blocking exchanges between various spheres will often have merit. But it will not always be feasible. Hence, we need to focus on those exchanges that are most likely to undermine social justice and which are also open to policy interventions, such as education, healthcare, housing, political finance, and so on.

One final point: the quest for equality between people implies that inter-personal comparisons, or relative measures, matter. Avoiding excessive disparities in individuals' social circumstances and opportunities is important, not merely because such disparities may be unjust, but also because they can have damaging implications for self-esteem, societal relationships and social outcomes. But while relative measures clearly matter for a variety of reasons, so does a person's *actual* well-being, or welfare, happiness, and so on. To suggest otherwise would imply, as Joseph Raz has pointed out, that:

> ... the happiness of a person does not matter except if there are other happy people. Nor is there any reason to avoid harming or hurting a person except on the ground that there are others who are unharmed and unhurt.[22]

So while a good case can be made for being concerned about a person's well-being in relation to other people's well-being, their actual objective circumstances matter – independently of their relative circumstances.

Conclusions

As highlighted in this chapter, there is almost universal acceptance that equality matters. Yet there is no consensus on what *kind* of equality should be championed. Even amongst those who concur on what should be equalised, there is often disagreement about what such equalisation actually means in practice, how much of this particular kind of equality is necessary or sufficient, how such equality can best be achieved, and what specific policy trade-offs are justified.

Yet several conclusions can be drawn. First, there are multiple dimensions in which equality matters, some of which are closely linked. Not all dimensions or types of equality, however, are of the same importance. Hence, the goal should not be to equalise *everything* to which the principle of equality could be applied; nor should perfect equality necessarily be the goal.

Second, the achievement of *formal* equality – in the sense of formal legal equality or formal equality of opportunity – is vitally important. But while a necessary condition for social justice, formal equality is not sufficient. If social justice is to be achieved, there must also be *substantive* or *effective* equality. This implies that people need more than a formal right to equal justice or equal liberty; they also need the means and capability to ensure that this right can be acted on. Hence, anyone pursuing equal basic liberties must give attention to human capabilities and to the distribution of income and wealth. One cannot, in other words, proclaim the virtues of equal basic liberties and remain indifferent to the capacity (or otherwise) of individuals to protect their rights or enjoy their liberties. Advocacy of equal liberty implies an ethical commitment to ensuring that all citizens have the financial and other means to realise the values inherent in the notion of equal liberty. Only governments have the resources to ensure that all citizens are able to enjoy their rights and liberties in a substantive sense.

Third, there are other principles of equality that also deserve serious attention, such as equality of opportunity and social equality. Giving weight to these kinds of equality has major implications for the distribution and use of material resources within a society. As argued above, if equality of opportunity is to be pursued, certainly in a substantive sense, then considerable efforts must be made to ensure that those born into socio-economically disadvantaged families are not deprived of the education, employment, healthcare and other significant opportunities that are inevitably enjoyed by those born into better-off families. This implies not merely the provision of a comprehensive and adequate social safety net, but also active governmental measures to offset the hardships, burdens and difficulties that are often associated with poorer families. Aspirations of equality of opportunity and social equality also have implications for the extent to which wealthier citizens are allowed to use their resources to purchase political influence and social privileges. Indeed, a strong commitment to substantive equality of opportunity raises important questions about how far these large inequalities of income and wealth should be tolerated.

Fourth, and related to this, while equality (of various kinds) matters, it is not the only thing that matters. There are many other values, including various non-egalitarian principles of social justice, that warrant attention. These include the provision of rewards for effort, merit or contribution; the related issue of ensuring that there are adequate incentives to encourage creativity, enterprise and innovation; and the desirability of protecting important social institutions, such as the family. Some of these goals conflict with certain egalitarian principles. Various trade-offs are thus unavoidable. But this does not justify a quick readiness to sacrifice equality in the pursuit of other goals, or giving overriding priority to the dictates of the market. Conversely, the quest for greater equality (of various kinds) should not trump all other considerations.

Although absolute equality and perfect justice are unobtainable, we should not abandon all efforts to secure *greater* equality or a fuller measure of justice. Likewise, while there may never be complete agreement on the *right* distribution of income and wealth within a particular society, this does not imply that all possible distributions are equally justifiable. On the contrary, there are many reasons for favouring a relatively egalitarian distribution of resources. Not only will this help ensure that all citizens are able to enjoy their basic rights and liberties, it will also lead to greater equality of opportunity and a stronger sense of social equality. As a result, there is likely to be higher social mobility, thereby increasing the extent to which citizens share a common life together and their capacity to develop their gifts and capabilities. Overall, this is likely to enhance the common good, building greater prosperity and fostering a more cohesive, harmonious and stable democracy.

What are the policy implications of this analysis? In New Zealand, given the substantial increase in income inequality since the early 1980s, the marked ethnic disparities that are evident in many areas of policy, and the significant poverty experienced by many low-income households (especially those with children), a strong case can be made for placing more emphasis over the coming years on redistributive policies, particularly those designed to reduce poverty.[23] This will require a mix of both income redistribution and in-kind transfers, and both universal and targeted services. The precise nature of this mix needs careful attention. In particular, consideration must be given to the most cost-effective ways of enhancing individuals' capabilities and equalising those opportunities which are most important for citizens to lead worthwhile and fulfilling lives – lives which, in Amartya Sen's terms, they have reason to value. This requires us not only to give equality a relatively high priority, but also to pursue those forms of equality that really matter. Achieving greater *specific* egalitarianism, in other words, is a noble objective and should be one of the foremost goals of any society which treasures the pursuit of justice.

Income, not budgeting, is the issue

Tamara Baddeley is a home care worker in Wellington. A member of the Service and Food Workers Union, she has also been a spokesperson for the Living Wage campaign. Max Rashbrooke interviewed Tamara for this viewpoint.

It's sometimes said that those on low incomes need to manage their money better, but you can't tell Tamara Baddeley anything about budgeting. Once the essentials are paid for, she has $10 a day to look after herself and her nineteen-year-old daughter.

Baddeley's job is to care for people in their own homes when they can't do it themselves. Her patients range in age between sixty-five and ninety-eight. Some simply struggle to do their own housework. But others have dementia, or need help throughout the day. One of Baddeley's patients has to be hoisted into the shower, showered and dressed, then hoisted back into a wheelchair and pushed into the dining room for morning tea. Baddeley returns at midday to help him with lunch and a toilet break, and again in the evening to get him into bed. Some of the other people she looks after have had strokes and are 'totally reliant' on the help they get, Baddeley says.

On top of this physically and emotionally gruelling work, she often gives patients their medicine, and is trained in stoma care. She also acts as a kind of counsellor – 'they talk to you about it, their illness' – and as the 'eyes and ears' of the health service, alerting doctors and hospitals when people's conditions worsen.

Baddeley works up to twelve hours in a shift, seeing six to ten patients a day in Wellington's southern suburbs. For this she gets paid $14.80 an hour. Such low pay makes her feel 'undervalued and unappreciated'. It reflects government underfunding of health services, the workforce's lack of power, and the fact that work carried out by women has historically been underpaid – and undervalued. As Baddeley puts it: 'We are doing similar work to registered nurses but we are not getting paid for it. We are not getting recognised for it.'

The pay is also unpredictable, as Baddeley's workload changes from fortnight to fortnight, depending on how many patients she is asked to see. This makes budgeting even more difficult. But on average, she works around thirty-seven hours a week, which gives her an income of about $490 after tax (with a petrol allowance included).

Now that her daughter is nineteen and studying to be a mechanic, they no longer get any Working for Families payments. If her daughter qualifies for a student allowance, it will do little more than cover her travel costs, course expenses and a tiny bit of spending money.

Baddeley's budget breaks down as follows:

Income	Weekly
Pay (after tax)	$490
Expenses	
Rent	$200
Phone	$25
Power/gas	$25
Car running costs	$25
Life insurance	$15
Petrol	$50
Supermarket shop	$75
Milk/bread etc	$15
Cellphone	$10
Total	**$440**
For everything else	$50

She has just $50 a week – less than $10 a day – to cover everything else that two people need: shoes, clothes, doctors' visits, birthday presents and so on. It's nowhere near enough for week-by-week living, let alone dealing with emergencies. 'Heaven help you if your car breaks down', Baddeley says. And of course saving for the future is out of the question.

Strict budgeting is simply a part of her life. 'You become very good at budgeting through necessity, not choice', Baddeley says. Her parents help out with meat parcels, and she gets jobs such as car repairs done, wherever possible, by mates – at mate's rates. She can't remember the last time she bought clothes at full price, and, even though she loves books, almost always buys them second-hand or borrows them from the library. She and her daughter have takeaways maybe once a month. She doesn't smoke, and only very occasionally drinks.

As far as entertainment goes, they last went to the movies four years ago when she won tickets off the radio, and they haven't had a holiday – beyond trips to see her parents in Taupo – for six years. They certainly don't have Sky, so if her rugby-mad daughter wants to watch a Hurricanes game, they have to go to the local clubrooms and buy a $4 jug of lemonade to last them through the evening.

'It's budgeting, it's buying only "own brands" at the supermarket, it's buying only exactly what we need', Baddeley says. 'I have been doing it for twenty years. I can't do it any better than I do now.'

For this, and other reasons, Baddeley is supporting the Living Wage campaign, led by community groups, churches and unions, for workers to be paid an hourly rate of $18.40, rather than the minimum wage of $13.75 (see Chapter 11). So what would she do with that extra money? 'Well', she says, 'I'd like to be able to know that if I wanted to go to the movies at the weekend, I could actually do it and enjoy it, and not have to figure out what's going to be cut to let me do that. Or I'd like to be able to plan for a real holiday and go somewhere where you're not relying on someone's hospitality. Or not panic when the car goes for a warrant. Or go to the clubrooms and actually buy a beer rather than a jug of lemonade for four dollars.'

'Or', she says finally, 'maybe I could cut back and not have to work Sunday, and be able to go away for a weekend.' And, perhaps, be able to relax the budgeting just a little.

Part Three
Consequences

6 Only One Deck

Karlo Mila

> And my Father used to say:
> Oh we came to this land of plenty
> and we came to this land of hope ...
> *Pauly Fuemana of the Otara Millionaires Club*
> *('Land of Plenty')*[1]

Pauly Fuemana's lyrics epitomise the migrant dreams of the people from the Pacific[2] who came to Aotearoa/New Zealand in search of a land of milk and honey ... and 'plenty'. Yet, like other people struggling in New Zealand, they have encountered an unequal society and have often been confronted with a dream deferred and an economic landscape of ever-rising milk prices and unaffordable basic household items.

Pacific migrants have typically started at the bottom rungs of the income ladder. During multiple recessions and aggressive structural reform, they have frequently been the first to be let go. This has left more than half of Pacific children up to the age of seventeen in New Zealand growing up deprived of basic needs, such as having sufficient clothing and footwear, adequate sleeping arrangements, a healthy diet and good nutrition, and access to affordable healthcare.[3] This represents a challenging dynamic for a diverse, young community with a big stake in New Zealand's future: by 2026, Pacific peoples will make up 10 per cent of the country's population.[4]

Sadly, Pacific peoples[5] are an almost 'textbook' example of an ethnic minority experiencing significant and enduring income inequality: indeed, a Pacific person living in New Zealand is 2.6 times more likely than the average person to be living in hardship.[6] But how did this happen? What is the state of play right now? What does this mean for our future? And finally, what can we do about it? While some answers can be attempted here, in truth we will progress only if we are all willing to tackle these problems collectively and to look bravely and honestly at the visible signs of privilege in this country.

Pacific in relation to Māori

Although Pacific peoples often have a similar 'on the ground' inequality profile to Māori,[7] and although many Pacific nations have experienced colonisation, in New Zealand those of us from Pacific islands and nations are not dwelling on land and resources that our families once used to own and govern. The wealth and industry critical to New Zealand's prosperity were not once in our hands. Nor has legislation developed by the settler colony sought to dispossess us further, minimised our opportunities, treated us differently or, for the most part, stripped us of sovereignty. We are positioned very differently to Māori in this respect: in New Zealand, Pacific peoples are part of society that is categorised by some as 'tauiwi', that is, we are non-indigenous settlers in this land.

Article Three of the Treaty of Waitangi states that Māori, as citizens of New Zealand, should have the same rights and privileges as British subjects. Yet, if we view rights and privileges as extending to such things as having the same life expectancy and improving levels of infant survival, enjoying the same health status, earning similar incomes, experiencing comparable living standards, and so on, we can clearly see that these rights and privileges have never been fully realised by Māori. And it is clear that Pacific migrants too have never enjoyed the same rights and privileges as those experienced by other New Zealanders.

So citizenship and core beliefs about what it means to be a citizen lie at the heart of concerns about embedded inequalities for Pacific peoples – rather than a dishonoured treaty. When Pacific ethnicity is statistically associated with being two-and-a-half times more likely to be deprived, and when half of Pacific children grow up in poverty without having their basic needs met, it is immediately apparent that equal access to the rights, privileges and freedoms supposedly afforded by being born into a civilised western society are somehow systematically denied. Pacific children born in this country nominally and technically have the right to be educated to a level that gives them the freedom to realise their career aspirations; the right to work hard to achieve their dreams; and the right to live healthy, full, long lives. But the fact is that they do not actually have ease of access to these rights. Pacific children growing up in New Zealand deserve to be free from the deeply ingrained societal inequalities, irretrievably tied to ethnic origin, which can constrain and damage their well-being and achievement.

A personal perspective

> I am the seed of the migrant dream
> the daughter who is supposed to fill the promise
> hope heavy on my shoulders
> I stand on the broken back of physical labour
> knowing the new dawn has been raided
> and milk and honey is linked to obesity and diabetes
> and our hearts are drowning in buckets of povi masima[8]

This is part of a poem I wrote at the turn of the century, when I was working as an organiser for the Service and Food Workers Union. I have never been dispassionate about inequality, even as I have watched my own circumstances change across my lifetime. I was born in New Zealand. My father was a Tongan migrant who could not read or write, but learned a trade and worked hard to further his dreams for his daughters. My Pākehā mother was university-educated, but had spent some time as a sole parent and a working mother, and understood the barriers that might be in the way of her brown daughters (who were from the wrong side of town) and their aspirations. My middle-class mother worked hard to show us how to manoeuvre and bypass barriers of prejudice, and my father pumped us full of his dreams that New Zealand was the land of opportunity.

So I am perhaps living proof that inequality is not the final word in what is possible for young Pacific peoples. Both my partner (who is Tongan) and I have PhDs, despite coming from relatively deprived backgrounds and attending low-decile schools in struggling suburbs. But it is not the case that we 'pulled ourselves up by our bootstraps' while our peers succumbed to lazier days getting stoned and playing video games somewhere in South Auckland. It was not that simple, or individual. We were both the recipients of more than one affirmative action scholarship, and were both supported by enabling families with very high expectations. We were buoyed by teachers and mentors who supported and believed in us; sometimes we were housed and homed by these people who went an extra mile for us. We were the 'lucky ones' who were able to overcome failures and setbacks at university level (which we were far from prepared for) and we were able to soldier on until, as we looked at the fairly normal abilities of those around us, we began to feel just as entitled to our privileges and developed the confidence to cut it in any crowd. This did not happen overnight. A lot of people and policies were committed to our success, including the government departments and the corporates that sponsored us.

All the people I know who are in a similar boat feel a calling to spend their careers giving back in various ways, and this includes tackling the challenge of enduring inequality. Whatever your personal achievements, when you belong to an ethnic community that frequently finds itself on the hard edges of economic, educational and employment disparities, the stakes are always high, and success cannot be measured purely on individual terms. Talk of inequality is about the bread and butter of people we know and love, or the lack of it. Inequality means watching people close to you – extended family, community networks, neighbours and friends – who are persistently struggling, in challenging circumstances, to try to maintain their dignity, to keep their households afloat, to do their best for their children and to make good decisions by weighing up the constrained range of choices on offer to them.

I use the word 'constrained' quite deliberately, because although there is a notion that everyone in this country enjoys a full range of free choices, in fact many have to deal with what academics call 'default choice'.[9] People with limited resources are forced to 'choose' less than optimum options by default, through lack of knowledge, resources, time, local facilities or power. It is what happens when you can't afford a car and all the shops within a walking radius sell cheap liquor, pokies, five different types of deep fried food, and no fruit and vegetables. It is what happens when the schools around you serve up an accent to your five-year-old so that he sounds like Jake the Muss from *Once Were Warriors* and learns not to make eye contact with adults, rather than numeracy and literacy. It is what happens when he comes home and asks you why he has a black face. It is what happens when you don't feel safe walking down your streets unless you have gang protection, and four out of five of the older boys, brothers and cousins you admire, are already finding that this is the only sphere in which they shine, where they are respected, accepted and recognised as powerful and productive.

It is what happens when the real banks won't lend you money and the loan sharks are wooing you, cheap bait for bad debt. And when no one you know actually owns their own house, or knows what a PhD is, or has plans for their future. And most of your time is spent making sure that you can get food on the table and that the power won't get cut off; and you know there is no money for extras like Saturday sport for your talented kids because you can't afford boots or fees, no swimming lessons, and no class photos, and no Lucky Book club books; and your children already know that there are things in life that are beyond their reach, that are not for them, and they are already feeling it in ways that make them burn inside. This is not about options: this is about making the best of bad situations, and survival. (As I have said, I am not dispassionate about inequality, and will not pretend to be so.) How do these children present themselves creditably to our society without the shame and stigma of identifiable poverty, further compounded by ethnically marked bodies? How do they ward off the pain of shame and humiliation? How do they grow up feeling good about themselves and society, and hopeful for their futures? How do they avoid failure in a society that has already become complacent (and sometimes dismissive) about systemic disadvantage, and has already associated it with personal failings, bad families, individual lack of capacity or cultural stereotypes? How do they free themselves from these prejudices, resist internalising them and realise opportunities for mobility up a steep social gradient?

Pacific ethnic inequality: how did we get here?

As the Australian academic John Connell has put it, 'Migration is largely a response to real and perceived inequalities in socio-economic opportunities, within and between states.'[10] This is a useful way to think about the historical and material conditions of the last centuries and how they have led to large flows of labour migration across the globe. The rapid growth of the Pacific population in New Zealand was stimulated by a vast labour shortage in the late 1960s and early 1970s, when Pacific peoples were targeted and encouraged to come and fill unskilled and low-skilled jobs in expanding manufacturing industries.[11] Well-established 'chains' of migration brought them to New Zealand in unprecedented numbers to be employed within a narrow range of industrial sectors.[12] 'In most cases these immigrants did the jobs Pākehā New Zealanders no longer wished to do or had been educated beyond: shift work, factory work, assembly line production, processing, cleaning, work involving long hours in unpleasant conditions.'[13] While migration and work of this kind provided a way of advancing wealth, position and prestige for Pacific migrants, many, if not most, hoped for better for their children than the factory floors.[14] Yet those who migrated from the Pacific to fill these jobs came from countries that did not have a tertiary qualification system, and they entered a society that was not only already unequal but also had clear ideas about where Pacific migrants would be positioned.

Because of the limited opportunities for permanent entry into New Zealand for Pacific peoples, many came as temporary visitors and overstayed their permits.[15] It is said that this practice was tolerated by the state and encouraged by employers, as long as they needed low-skilled labour in manufacturing.[16] But in 1973–74, an oil crisis changed the nature of the global economy and New Zealand faced a recession. Unemployment rose from 0.1 per cent to 5.6 per cent, and the secondary industries, where the majority of Pacific workers were concentrated, were hit hardest.[17] Jobs, once plentiful, became scarce. Two of the responses to the economic downturn – the loss of jobs and the competition for scarce resources – were to 'racialise' workers from the Pacific.[18] The government's approach shifted, and it embarked on an 'overstayers' campaign' in 1974–1976, in which Pacific peoples were targeted as illegal immigrants in New Zealand and were seen to be threatening the right of 'New Zealanders' to jobs.[19] This campaign included the notorious 'dawn raids' and a policy of arresting 'anyone that did not look like a New Zealander' on the streets (thus requiring Polynesians to carry passports at all times).[20] As Graeme Lay writes: 'Xenophobic feelings were fomented by the National Government during the latter half of that decade and the word 'Islander' came to assume a pejorative aspect.'[21]

The recession was followed by a period, 1984–92, of intense restructuring that had significant and negative repercussions for Pacific peoples.[22] Manufacturing industries had relied on tariffs to protect them from competitive imports, and the removal of these tariffs resulted in massive job losses among Māori and Pacific peoples especially.[23] Hundreds of thousands of jobs were lost in the primary and secondary sectors where raw materials were manufactured into goods; the simultaneous growth in the tertiary sector required technological, professional and business skills, or capital, which most Pacific workers did not have.[24] In the late 1980s, Pacific peoples were more likely to be participating in the labour market compared to the total population, but by the mid-1990s they were more likely to be unemployed.[25] Within a decade, the unemployment rate of Pacific peoples had risen from 6 per cent to 29 per cent,[26] and their participation in the labour market has never fully recovered.[27] 'Last on, first off', with the fewest transferable skills, Pacific peoples were a disposable and politically expedient labour force now surplus to the requirements of a shrinking job market.

There were two obvious responses to this industrial collapse and the increasingly negative and racialised treatment of Pacific workers. One was to leave: during the early 1990s there were net losses of people back to Pacific homelands.[28] The other response was to retrain so as to be less vulnerable to recession and structural reform. In 1986, more than half of Pacific peoples had no qualifications whatsoever, but within fifteen years, two-thirds had gained a qualification, demonstrating a decisive shift in

Figure 6.1 Unemployment rates for Pacific peoples and the total New Zealand population

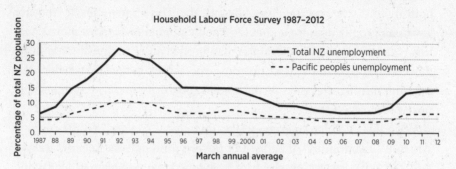

Source: Statistics New Zealand, Household Labour Force Survey, licensed by Statistics NZ for re-use under the Creative Commons Attribution 3.0 New Zealand Licence.

the Pacific labour market and a widespread community effort to up-skill, retrain and achieve educationally. But despite these factors, and this huge effort by a people to regroup, to find ways to achieve, and to succeed in the New Zealand education system, in 2012 Pacific peoples still had much higher rates of unemployment than the total New Zealand population and remained concentrated in unskilled or semi-skilled jobs.[29]

Figure 6.1 is a good indicator of how unemployment has affected Pacific peoples over more than two decades. It shows they are still vulnerable to economic fluctuations, and when the job market shrinks, as it did during the recent global financial crisis, Pacific peoples take a disproportionate hit.

In other words, inequality does not happen overnight and attempts to become equal do not have fast effects either. If we want to account for how Pacific people have come to be at the sharp end of the inequality spectrum, we need to understand the context of labour migration, and New Zealand's economic and political climates, which changed from golden weather to a declining labour market and the end of the warm welcome (such as it was).

Pacific ethnic inequality: what's happening now?

> Every time I look around (Every time I look around)
> Every time I look around
> It's in my face
> *Pauly Fuemana of the Otara Millionaires Club ('How Bizarre')*[30]

When we take a snapshot of the Pacific population right now, a number of things stand out. First, our youth: we have the youngest population of all ethnic groups in New Zealand; almost half our people are under the age of twenty.[31] (Indeed, some economists argue that this younger age structure may be an important explanation for Pacific people's lower net household worth and to a lesser degree their lower incomes.)[32] Another key demographic feature is that the Pacific population is now more likely to have been born in New Zealand than in the Pacific nations.[33] This shifts the cultural dynamics from not only the issues facing first-generation migrants but also the issues facing second and third generations exclusively raised in New Zealand.

What does it mean to grow up Pacific in New Zealand? Of the roughly 200,000[34] children living below the poverty line in New Zealand, one in four (44,120) are Pacific children.[35] Seventy-two per cent of all Pacific peoples live in the most deprived neighbourhoods (deciles 8, 9, 10) in New Zealand, and only 7 per cent live in the wealthiest neighbourhoods (deciles 1, 2, 3).[36] Forty per cent of Pacific children live in poverty.[37] Socio-economic disadvantage, if not significant poverty, is thus a defining characteristic of most Pacific families in New Zealand. The high concentration of the Pacific population clustered in overcrowded,[38] substandard housing in low-income neighbourhoods is one of the most significant challenges facing the Pacific population – especially since poor health is one of the consequences. A recent study of infectious diseases and New Zealand hospital admissions showed that in 2004–8, once the ages of the different populations were accounted for, Pacific peoples were 2.4 times more likely to be admitted than European and other groups. Michael Baker and his team of researchers 'noted clear ethnic and social inequalities in infectious disease risk', and concluded that 'inequalities have increased substantially in the past 20 years, particularly for Māori and Pacific peoples in the most deprived quintile'.[39]

Beyond health, there are wider problems with this concentration of disadvantage. People not only need to be able to cope with their own poverty and disadvantage, but also with the poverty and disadvantage of their neighbours.[40] Overseas research has pointed to the problems of migrant communities being clustered in low-income, heavily urbanised areas: 'The creation of concentrated low income neighbourhoods has had social consequences for the people who live in these locales, and particularly for the young people who form their expectations from the world they see around them.'[41] In New Zealand, one-third of the Pacific population lives in the area that, before Auckland's 'supercity' was created, was known as Manukau City.[42] There, every ward has the lowest level of community resilience possible and the highest community need.[43] Local council surveys show that fewer than half of Manukau City residents feel a sense of pride in the way their city looks and feels[44] – the lowest ranking of all cities surveyed. More than one in four Pacific female high school students feel unsafe in their neighbourhoods.[45] A quarter of all students in Manukau City leave school without achieving credits for basic numeracy and literacy.[46]

Concentrations of disadvantage in health, housing and opportunity feed into educational issues. Right from the very beginning, at the early childhood level, Pacific children have the lowest rate of participation, with fewer than four out of ten Pacific children aged two to four enrolled in early childhood education, and only half of all four-year-olds enrolled.[47] In compulsory schooling, less than a third (30 per cent) of Pacific students leave with university entrance compared to 48 per cent for non-Pacific students.[48] Young Pacific people, then, disproportionately become classified as NEETs – an acronym for 'not in employment, education or training' – where ethnic inequalities are well established.[49]

These young people have to contend with the hardest lesson that the labour market has to teach: that the ability to supply labour does not mean that you are in demand. This group has been described as 'the lost generation': bright, eager – and unwanted; and no groups are as unwanted as Pacific and Māori young people. A multi-country study of labour market discrimination that included New Zealand noted 'persistent discrimination in all twelve countries studied' and 'institutional racism and cultural discrimination', adding that 'those who get the "short stick" will continue to face poor prospects for full economic inclusion and justice'.[50] Even when Pacific young people make it into university or polytechnics, their completion rates are 40 per cent compared to 58 per cent for the total population.[51] This has improved over the years, but not enough to reduce embedded ethnic inequality. Rising hopes, greater expectations and improved educational qualifications have also had to come to grips with shrinking opportunities, global recession and 'persistent discrimination' in the labour market.[52]

Conclusions: what does it mean for our future?

> I've got some questions in my mind that definitely need some answers right now, cause I gotta know, got all the pieces to the puzzle but can't seem to make it fit, so I'm lost, tell me where to go.
> *Smashproof featuring Gin Wigmore ('Brother')*[53]

The Pacific population has the highest growth rate of any ethnic group, with 38 per cent of the population under the age of fifteen.[54] Young Pacific peoples represent significant arteries in New Zealand's future lifeline.

We can't afford to exclude them from participating in a vision of New Zealand's economic future. But if almost a fifth of all our young people can't even get their feet on the first rung of the career ladder, that must be exactly what we're doing.

US president Harry Truman once said, 'It's a recession when your neighbor loses his job; it's a depression when you lose yours.' When young Māori and Pacific people lose theirs, it seems it's called an underclass.[55] The fastest way to create an underclass is for New Zealand's leadership to divide society into worthy taxpayers and those who are unworthy. But working within a deficit paradigm that constructs young Pacific peoples as part of the 'South Auckland problem', or as an 'underclass' or the 'brown tail' of New Zealand, does a disservice to this generation and all it has to offer us collectively. There are plenty of other, and better, narratives out there, as this chapter has shown.

Even as I write, I am confronted with what novelist Chimamanda Adichie calls 'the danger of a single story'. The angle of inequality and disparity is not wide enough or flexible enough to capture and accurately reflect the lived experiences of an entire ethnic group. Every community has its own bell curve. We Pacific peoples have our own elites, high-fliers and traditional hierarchies, as well as our well-educated 'up and comers' and rising voices. Inequality, deficit and disadvantage do not constitute the sum total of our experience here in New Zealand. We laugh, we live, we achieve, we work, we fall in love, we shop, we play sport, we enjoy music, we make art, we create and we participate in society in all sorts of ways. Like everyone else, we make the best or worst of what we have, depending on our circumstances, the resources and supports we have at our disposal and our state of mind at any given moment.

We, as a community, are also asking why we experience enduring inequality in this country and what we can do about it. At least part of the solution seems to lie in the innovative and 'onto it' answers we create and our collective experience of achievement against the odds. But in the end, our fate is determined not by talent and achievement alone, but by the conditions of society, and whether they are conducive to all people participating in equal ways, or whether they are set up to maintain privilege, create social distance between the 'haves' and 'have nots', and render some parts of society an unwelcome burden. So the task of tackling our collective problems, which are so strongly associated with entrenched inequality, cannot be left in the hands of those who do not benefit from change, who have no compassion or love for those who are suffering from the status quo. As Eva Perón once said, 'When the rich think about the poor, they have poor ideas.' What is certain is that we must address the 'default choices' and the constrained opportunities on offer to children who are growing up in communities of concentrated disadvantage. We have to counter what that concentration of deprivation does to people, their health, their educational opportunities, and their hopes and dreams and aspirations. But even so, no answer we find should ever be seen as an adequate trade-off for the ability to keep on asking challenging questions, or a reason to forget the ultimate migrant dream of all of us thriving, instead of some of us barely surviving.

There is a well-known Samoan proverb, 'O le fogava'a e tasi', which states simply that, on the boat in which we all journey, there is 'only one deck'. Here in New Zealand, we are all on that one deck together. The poverty and pain of some parts of society are always going to be felt by others, no matter how much white flight we have, how many private schools we set up, how many gated communities we build. There is only one deck. We are in this together, whether by investing collectively in the health of the people who will be our future workforce, or by meeting the cost of educating a society so that its members can participate in ways that are not predetermined by decile number, ethnic background or geographical location. These are the real issues we face as we move into the twenty-first century. More than half of the Pacific population is now born in New Zealand. We are part of the mix of modern day Aotearoa, here to stay, sharing in the fate of the nation and making up a growing share of the human capital that will take us into the centuries to come. We have only got one deck.

A divided Auckland?

Chris Harris *is a researcher, planner and consultant based in Auckland, and is writing a book on the city's transport issues.*

Auckland's 'big joined-up problems', as the sociologist David Craig once put it, are 'affordable housing, transport, [and] inequality and ghettoization'. Auckland may be one of the most multicultural cities in the world, but it is also one of the most divided. The Whau River to the west, and the bodies of water either side of the Otahuhu portage, act as a kind of moat, with an increasingly gentrified North Shore and the central isthmus on one side, and relatively poorer communities south and west on the other.

Transport investments (and non-investments) have reinforced this natural moat. For nearly nine kilometres on the western side of the Whau River, no bridge has ever been built to connect south to north, despite endless talk. Until recently, motorway bridges across the Whau River and Henderson Creek sat unwidened for over fifty years, even as West Auckland developed beyond them. And there are other bottlenecks. At Mount Wellington, the six-lane motorway northbound from Otahuhu necks down to four lanes, before widening again to six lanes further north, with traffic from Pakuranga connected north of the restriction. Such bottlenecks help to keep the poorer populations of west and south Auckland behind the 'moat'.

Ironically, this situation is compounded by transport decisions that shifted the predominantly Māori and Pacific communities out of the centre in the first place. In the late 1960s, the Māori and Pacific population of Auckland was heavily concentrated in areas such as Grey Lynn, Freemans Bay, Herne Bay and Ponsonby. Much of this population was displaced by the construction of what is the largest downtown motorway junction in Australasia, alongside a council-driven urban renewal programme. New communities were forged by this construction – communities on the edge of town, out of sight and out of mind.

This need not have happened. Other cities have managed without a major central motorway junction: Adelaide has none, while those of Perth and Brisbane are far less obtrusive than Auckland's. And despite its size, our central motorway junction can still only cope with traffic from inner-suburban Auckland and the North Shore. So once the Auckland Harbour Bridge was widened to eight lanes in 1969 (benefiting well-heeled North Shore residents), there was no way that other bridges and roads from the south and west could be widened, or in some cases built at all.

One alternative to this unfolding disaster would have been to invest in the rapid rail scheme advocated by long-serving Auckland City mayor Dove-Myer Robinson. This would have improved access to the west and south without bringing excessive volumes of traffic into the inner city. The other alternative would have been to 'double up' (add more lanes) to the motorway network. By the 1970s the government's motorway plans for Auckland had grown to include additional motorways across Meola Reef from the north, from Henderson to the west, and up Dominion Road from the south. But even contemplating such a move was a sign of desperation: those roads were never going to happen.

By failing either to build rapid rail or (less sensibly) double up the motorway network, transport planners failed the west and the south. The suburbanisation of these areas proceeded on the assumption that problems of accessibility would be solved – but they were not. A kind of social contract between the state and the people of these areas was broken.

The consequences of this breach have been far-reaching. Poorer populations have become isolated from the opportunities offered by good jobs, which are mostly in areas they cannot reach because the transport to get there is non-existent, too crowded or too expensive. They are confined instead to the shrinking pool of low-paid, blue-collar jobs that are within easy reach. Residents of higher-income areas, meanwhile, have consistently had their transport options improved.

South and west Auckland are logical places to build the affordable housing that the city desperately needs. But there is little point building in these areas without better transport links to the central city (thereby bridging the 'moat'). The result today is constrained house building, with a bias in favour of building high-priced houses on the North Shore. The transport system, supposedly set up to relieve congestion and support suburban expansion, has actually blocked Auckland's natural growth corridor to the south. This limited supply of affordable housing helps drive house prices sky-high.

Building rapid rail on the existing corridors south of the Auckland Harbour Bridge could have created an effectively unending string of satellite towns at least as far as Mercer; while also developing lower-density suburbs off to the side (at Karaka, for example) with park-and-ride systems. But without rapid rail and other public investment, anything south of Mount Wellington is now perceived by some Aucklanders who could afford to live there as 'crime-ridden and too far from the CBD' or lacking in the right sorts of schools and middle-class peer groups.[1]

It is not too late to fix some of these problems. A proper rapid rail system (including a downtown tunnel to speed access from the west and keep the trains moving) would repair part of the broken social contract with west and south Auckland, and be a pragmatic investment in a viable future for the whole city.

Of course, using public transport (including rapid rail systems) has to be affordable as well. When a Radio New Zealand Insight documentary team talked to Naenae College pupils on a trip to Te Papa museum on Wellington's waterfront, they discovered that most of these young people had never made the trip from their Lower Hutt neighbourhood into downtown

Wellington before.[2] The school's principal attributed this in part to their families' 'lack of resources'.

The affordability of public transport will be a factor in Auckland also. Tickets across existing and future public transport systems need to be within the price range of people on low incomes. Any loss in fare receipts per passenger would be offset by: increased patronage; greater social cohesion; reduced traffic congestion; and savings in road building (fewer new roads would be needed). There would also be potential gains in land value, as the planned towns along the rapid rail network could be developed with a reasonable expectation that sections would sell.

In a city with Auckland's traffic problems, cheap and uncongested public transport would build strong connections between the centre city, more affluent suburbs, and areas now perceived by some as 'crime-ridden and too far from the CBD'.

In other words, if we are to remedy David Craig's 'big joined-up problems', and do more to connect a divided Auckland, a major investment in public transport systems remains the key – just as the neglect of public transport has aggravated these problems in the first place.

7 Building Inequality

Philippa Howden-Chapman, Sarah Bierre and
Chris Cunningham

In Aotearoa/New Zealand, as in most developed countries, we spend much of our time indoors, so the quality of the houses and flats we live in has an important but largely unrecognised impact on our lives. Houses are a costly commodity, usually the largest financial asset most families own or rent. But beyond the financial costs, housing has a fundamental effect on people's sense of belonging, the communities they live in and, most basically, their health.

Unlike the more advanced countries in the developed world, New Zealand seems to have lost sight of the principle that housing is a key part of our social and physical infrastructure, with important public, as well as private, benefits. As a result, many of our buildings are of poor quality – they often leak, and are damp and cold.

What this failure means is that differences in housing are a huge part of inequality in New Zealand, in terms of both wealth and health. These differences are the result of historical factors (in particular, Māori have often been excluded from proactive housing policies) and ongoing structural problems (there are, for example, great divisions between those who own their house and those who rent). Only with a significantly different set of policies will we be able to address these divides.

A history of unequal homes
Many of New Zealand's first colonial settlers wanted to found a society premised on widespread property ownership. But as early as 1863, observers were complaining about slum landlordism in New Zealand, and the inability and unwillingness of governments to intervene to improve housing conditions.

These problems arose because in some ways colonisation in New Zealand was a mix of progressive impulses and standard economic constraints. It was based on a public–private partnership, with the privately run New Zealand Company driving the project, the government a reluctant legislator, and Māori notions of kaitiakitanga (guardianship) increasingly shunted aside, as land for colonial development became both commodified and scarce. The Wellington Town Belt, for example, is largely a legacy of the New Zealand Company's proposition that physically defining the urban limits would enable family 'small-holdings' to be close enough to the city to provide not only decent housing but also labour for economic development. In Wellington also 'one-tenth' of the land purchased by the New Zealand Company was set aside to be leased out on behalf of Māori, supposedly for their benefit. Even this minimal obligation was largely unfulfilled – 'patchy at best' was the phrase used in the Waitangi Tribunal's 2003 report.[1] The case of the 'Wellington Tenths' exemplifies a history of neglect of Māori needs that has continued to the present day.

But more consistently (at least for Pākehā), the state has long recognised that it has a role in helping people obtain the housing they need. Indeed, an emphasis on moral values has characterised much New Zealand housing policy. During the evolution of New Zealand into a liberal welfare state, providing and maintaining decent homes for families and whānau have been considered important policy roles. The state has intervened through various direct and indirect regulations and financial assistance to builders or private individuals, through loans, tax exemptions or cheap credit.[2]

The colonial provincial governments, for example, were responsible for building the fencible cottages for retired soldiers from England and Ireland, who agreed to act as militia. The First Liberal Government built houses for white-collar workers living along the commuter tram and rail lines. The First Labour Government, working with Fletcher Construction as well as other companies from 1935, set up public–private partnerships deliberately designed as a state intervention to stimulate the economy by constructing thousands of state houses. These state houses were built not only in new suburbs, but wherever workers and their families were needed to construct hydro-electric dams, or provide social services, as teachers, doctors and nurses.[3]

This building programme transformed the quality of New Zealand housing in many ways. Not only did it provide high quality, affordable houses for those who needed them, it also set the standard for other housing: the building specifications used for state housing became the norm for the whole industry until at least the 1960s. The state house building programme also paved the way for other, substandard houses to be demolished.

Post-war governments – both National and Labour – continued to make concerted efforts to improve state housing,[4] as well as implementing policies to support home ownership, 'a form of tenure increasingly embedded in the national psyche after World War One'.[5] In addition, the government gave below market rate 3 per cent loans, and supported the capitalisation of the universal family benefit, allowing people to turn a stream of anticipated benefit payments into a lump sum that could be used as a deposit on a house. Both policies contributed to rising levels of home ownership in New Zealand.

However, Māori were initially excluded from these initiatives and were often left in very poor quality housing. Evidence of this comes from the reports of medical officers and other officials in local authorities, who were (and still are today) expected to oversee the quality of housing. A 1941 letter from the Palmerston North Medical Officer of Health, Duncan Cook, to the Director-General of Health raised concerns about the lack of action taken since 1933 on crowded housing conditions among Māori living in Tangoio:

> Further to my memorandum on the above subject of the 15th August, 1933, I have to report that little improvement in living conditions has been achieved.
>
> Following a recent epidemic of pneumonic influenza the Health Inspector reports that certain Natives are still living in overcrowded conditions and suggests that the sale of sixteen of the huts by the Native Department to Natives be expedited with the view to improving the overcrowded conditions.
>
> I suggest, therefore, that you write the Native Department again painting [sic] out our apprehensions with respect to the health of this community and request that if possible some active programme be put into effect.[6]

In the same year, the wife of a Māori man overseas fighting in the Second World War wrote to the Director-General of Health, requesting help in getting a government house so that she could keep her 'family warm in the winter'.[7] The Director-General acknowledged her letter, but stated: 'Although it seems doubtful as to whether anything can be done for you in regard to a house, I am forwarding a copy of your letter to the Native Department who will communicate with you further.' There is no evidence in the file as to whether the woman and her children were able to move into a government house.

Access to the benefits provided by government housing policies was restricted by judgements about who was 'deserving' and who was not, as well as related conflicts between government departments. Before the Second World War, Māori had been excluded from mainstream housing assistance on the basis that their needs would be met by the underfunded

Native Department. It was not until the mid-1950s that Māori were able to apply for State Advances loans,[8] and then only if they were:

> ... considered to be 'living in a European manner' (i.e. not rural), 'if the personal factor is satisfactory' (i.e. meeting standards normally expected of a reasonable member of the community), and 'if the security offered is in an area acceptable to the corporation' (i.e. urban, in a Pākehā area, with private single-holder title).[9]

Māori living conditions were, consequently, a cause for concern. A post-war Parliamentary Select Committee heard evidence of the appalling housing conditions facing Māori in many rural areas, such as the Hokianga. People were often crowded into houses that might lack basic amenities, including electricity. Concern about poor housing was expressed in a combined submission from doctors and engineers:

> ... people who marry are unable to obtain decent housing, but are allowed to erect and live in shacks made up of old materials which the Maori can readily obtain. The materials include bags of nikau and any sundry junk, and as the size of the shack depends on the quantity of materials available and the ingenuity of the builder, it usually takes the shape of a lean-to with one to three small rooms devoid of satisfactory ventilation and sanitary arrangements.[10]

Poor though much rural housing was, Māori encountered even more problematic issues with housing as they increasingly moved into urban areas after the war to seek broader openings and greater educational opportunities for their children. As anthropologist Joan Metge pointed out, inequalities in income were translated into inequalities in housing – and thus health:

> The acute housing shortage and the high price demanded for accommodation have forced the majority of Maoris to congregate in the poorer parts of most towns, where overcowding and inadequate sanitary arrangements endanger their health and standards of living.[11]

Underlying this urban residential segregation were racial attitudes as well as economics, as the writer and critic Bill Pearson pointed out in a 1960 book review:

> Many pakehas are willing to accept Maoris as equals only if they conform to European values and standards, while other pakehas may

deride them for attempting to act otherwise than they are expected to. Many pakehas, too, are unable to distinguish between the enforced segregation of a minority and segregation that is desired by them: thus, some pakehas, in the name of an abstract equality will advocate the abolition of the four Maori seats and the Maori schools at the same time as they are complacent about the exclusion of Maoris from the more desirable suburbs.[12]

It was not until after the Second World War that discriminatory treatment by government agencies became less evident, and greater efforts were made to meet Māori housing needs. In his 1943 booklet *The Price of Citizenship*, Sir Apirana Ngata had drawn attention to the connection between Māori participation in the war and their future role in helping to shape the country.[13] The Department of Māori Affairs, which oversaw a growth in Māori housing initiatives, was established at the end of 1947 out of the former Native Department and in recognition of the need to house and support Māori returned servicemen. The government had agreed that Māori and Pākehā soldiers should be treated equally, and under pressure from the Māori War Effort Organisation, the department started to put together a housing arm from about 1943.[14] There was a debate about whether Māori houses would be built to the same standards as those of Pākehā, but the Rehabilitation Department was insistent that they should. Returning servicemen sharpened the focus on equality.

In 1943 the government decided that ceilings for Māori housing loans could be lifted; the fifteen-year repayment term was extended to twenty-five years; and in 1945 the government agreed to a 25 per cent subsidy for any house built by the department. This decision gave financial equity to many Māori who were unable to provide deposits to raise mortgages. Māori Affairs expanded their housing portfolio during the 1950s, from an annual number of 365 in 1949–50 to 550 in 1957–58.[15] By 1962–63 the department's Māori housing programme was at its peak, making 1,098 houses available, while the State Advances Corporation was providing a further 328 loans and 311 state rentals for Māori. These initiatives were part of a general trend towards improving outcomes for Māori, whose incomes were catching up with those of Pākehā throughout the post-war period until around 1987 (see Chapter 10). But these initiatives, while valuable, never fully redressed the effects of Māori dispossession. As a result, Māori home ownership continued – and continues today – to lag behind that of Pākehā, with damaging consequences.

How housing helps create rising inequality

Policies to encourage home ownership continued into the 1980s. In fact, it is easy to forget the extent to which the state assisted many households into housing in the decades before that, when the state rather than banks financed most home mortgages.[16] Indeed, for Māori 86 per cent of money for home mortgages through this period came from government through the Housing Corporation or Māori Affairs.[17]

However, an economic recession in the early 1980s and an ideological shift led to the financial industry being deregulated from 1984 onwards. Private banks became the main source of housing finance. They lent more money but at commercial interest rates and this led to increased house prices and interest rates.[18] After 1991, the incoming National Government sold the government mortgage portfolio to the banking sector; the government was now responsible for less than 4 per cent of all new home lending.[19] Although state house building had continued through the 1980s, this reduction in state financing coincided with a reduction both in building and other forms of housing support. The government ignored the call to increase the supply of affordable housing, and indeed sold off state houses. Its preference was for market-led solutions, as part of a decisive move away from the provision of state housing.

This shift from state to market provision created a growing gap between those who owned houses and those who did not. The increasing consumer price inflation of the 1970s and 1980s, combined with rising real mortgage interest rates of the 1980s onwards, made it more difficult for those who were renting to buy houses, adding to the value of home ownership.[20] Those owning property prior to the housing boom of the 1970s and the later housing price bubble between 2000 and 2007 benefited through capital gains, amplified because New Zealand is one of the few countries in the OECD without a capital gains tax. First home buyers, meanwhile, faced high indebtedness, inflated house prices and, at times, high mortgage rates. A so-called group of 'intermediate renters' burgeoned:[21] people excluded from home ownership because of the high cost of housing and their inability to accumulate a deposit.[22]

Those in state houses and others on low incomes, meanwhile, had to contend with state housing rents being raised to market levels. An accommodation supplement was introduced to assist with rent payment,[23] but this supplement was not always able to cover the cost of the rent increases and left some tenants unable to meet their rent payments.[24] (Market rents were subsequently abolished by Helen Clark's Labour Government.) These changes were part of a wider restructuring of social

Figure 7.1 Housing tenure in New Zealand, 1916 to 2006

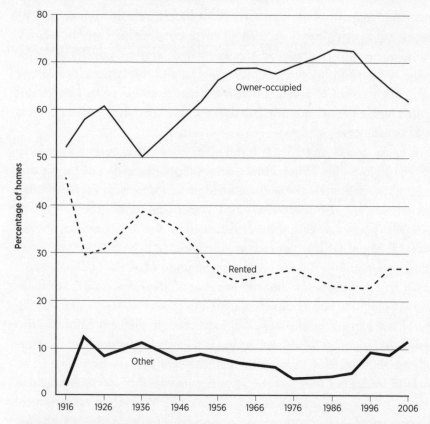

Note: The data source for the graph is in the 2006 Census. The category 'other' represents households that have not specified their household status in the Census, or those who are not renters or owners, such as people who live in houses provided with their job.

Source: Ben Schrader. 'Housing and government – A property-owning democracy', Te Ara – the Encyclopedia of New Zealand, updated 4 Deccember 2012, http://www.teara.govt.nz/en/graph/32431/housing-tenure. Creative Commons Attribution: Non-Commercial 3.0 New Zealand Licence.

policy which, combined with rapidly rising unemployment (up to nearly 11 per cent), radically exacerbated the gap between rich and poor – and between those who already owned houses and those who rented. Severe housing need and crowding increased, with a corresponding increase in infectious diseases, particularly in children.[25]

There was, unsurprisingly, a steep decline in home ownership from the beginning of the 1990s, and a steady increase in the number of households dependent on the private rental market.

Home ownership peaked in the late 1980s and early 1990s (see Figure 7.1), when around three-quarters of private dwellings were owner-occupied. Since then, home ownership has fallen to around 65 per cent nationally. The number of people on one income, unable to purchase a lower-quartile-priced house at standard lending criteria, has more than doubled since 1996.[26] Whereas the median house cost just twice the median income in 1980, it now costs 5.3 times the median income.[27] As the cost of housing has risen without corresponding increases in salaries, home ownership has become significantly delayed or unachievable for many on low and middle incomes, especially in the larger cities. Those most likely to suffer greatest housing stress continue to be households with a single parent (usually female), a single income, beneficiaries and aged pensioners.[28]

Because Māori and Pacific households have often been poorer than Pākehā households, these trends have simply exacerbated the historic inequalities in home ownership outlined earlier. Māori and Pacific-headed households are also more likely to face serious housing need.[29] Levels of Māori home ownership have plateaued at about 37 per cent (below national levels), with 55 per cent of Māori renting or boarding: at the same time, expectations of home ownership amongst Māori are falling. A 2011 study reported that only about 50 per cent of Māori in rental households were planning to buy a house (compared to about two-thirds in 1995).[30]

A large part of the problem is the decrease in 'housing affordability'. Using this common measure, housing is regarded as 'affordable' if people or households spend no more than 30 per cent of disposable income on housing; at higher percentages, 'housing affordability' decreases.[31] From the early 1990s onwards, people in the lowest fifth of income earners spent 40 per cent of their disposable income on housing, while those in the top fifth paid less than 20 per cent.[32] While housing affordability improved a little after the 2000s housing bubble burst, unaffordability remains a key driver of household crowding and in extreme cases homelessness.

Another factor in housing access is that Māori continue to be more likely than Europeans to report racial discrimination when buying or renting a house. Successive covert studies of discrimination in the private rental market have confirmed racial discrimination by private landlords.[33] A comparison of the 2003 and 2006 New Zealand Health Surveys found that, whether buying or renting, Māori were still up to fourteen times more likely to report being treated unfairly because of their ethnicity than were Europeans.[34] This discrimination, particularly in the private rental market, constricts the availability and choice of low-income housing for Māori and Pacific families.

When people cannot obtain affordable, high quality housing, they are forced to live in a variety of inadequate situations. Most concerningly, recent research has shown that thousands of children are experiencing severe housing deprivation (or homelessness),[35] officially defined as lack of access to minimally adequate housing.³⁶ These children are living in situations with no security, little privacy and, in some cases, not even basic amenities. At least one in every hundred New Zealand children younger than fifteen years has been found to be severely housing deprived in 2006, most of them living in overcrowded houses with extended family.³⁷

Our terrible housing conditions

Rising house prices relative to incomes has meant many tenants can no longer choose to become owner-occupiers. These tenants are disadvantaged over time by not being able to buy a home, while owner-occupiers are accumulating an asset, which gives a return in the form of untaxed housing services. Tenants are not only likely to be increasingly financially worse off by not having any investment in a house, but the houses they rent are more likely to be in poorer condition than owner-occupied housing.³⁸

Our housing standards were essentially set by the Housing Improvement Regulations of 1947; extraordinarily, these still apply today.³⁹ Two-thirds of our current housing stock was built before insulation standards for new buildings were introduced in 1977 after the first oil shock.⁴⁰ And even these very minimal regulations of existing dwellings have been poorly enforced; local councils cite a number of reasons for their inaction, such as few alternatives for occupants of poor housing, a lack of resources and unclear legislation.

Light-handed building regulation from the 1990s onwards has not improved matters; modern buildings are thus likely to have their own set of quality issues, alongside those manifested in older buildings.⁴¹ Inadequate regulation and enforcement of housing standards, coupled with high rates of deferred maintenance,⁴² have led to serious problems in the quality of New Zealand's housing stock overall. Older rental accommodation is in the poorest condition; over 50 per cent of renters reported one or more major problems with their dwelling compared to 28 per cent of owner occupiers.⁴³ Over two-thirds of children living in poverty (defined as living in households earning less than 60 per cent of median income) live in rental housing; half of these are in private rental housing.⁴⁴ Perhaps unsurprisingly, New Zealand is seen internationally as having notably poor housing standards – a genuine outlier in the developed world.

One of the effects and likely causes of poor housing quality is that New Zealand, compared with other developed countries, has one of the highest rates of residential mobility. In the period before 2008, almost twice as many New Zealanders (19 per cent) as British people (10.6 per cent) moved each year.[45] At the 2006 Census, the usual period since last moving for households was 3.7 years; but households that owned their dwelling tended to be more settled (6.3 years), while tenants were more mobile (2 years). This turnover is so high because renters often move in order to improve the quality of their housing and the health of their children.[46] This can lead to a number of social and medical disadvantages, as enrolment in primary health organisations and local schools is set up on the basis of residential stability. In some areas there is an under-supply of midwives and places in primary health organisations, so that children requiring regular immunisations, or people with chronic illnesses such as diabetes that require close monitoring, miss out on the healthcare they need. Children moving often from one school to another can also find it difficult to form close relationships with teachers and classmates, and may not access the remedial educational support they might need. (See Viewpoint 12.)

Poor housing leads to poor health
New Zealand has appalling rates of what are normally considered Third World diseases, especially among children: meningococcal disease, rheumatic fever, cellulitis, bronchielectesis and childhood pneumonia.[47] Other developed countries have significantly reduced or virtually eliminated these diseases, but in the two decades after 1989, the New Zealand rate of admissions to public hospitals for infectious disease increased strikingly by 51 per cent – equivalent to 17,000 additional hospitalisations. The risk of admissions for infectious diseases was more common among people with Māori and Pacific ethnicities and those living in areas of relatively high poverty.

This shocking record is directly connected to our substandard housing. Poor housing causes ill-health, particularly in children and older people, who spend up to 90 per cent of their time indoors.[48] Housing quality also has a cumulative impact on children's development.[49] Young children are particularly vulnerable to exposure to (for example) lead from paint or water, asbestos, mould, microbes or pesticides – all more common in older houses.[50]

Many other factors are also at play. Younger and older people are especially susceptible to cold, damp, mouldy and polluted indoor environments. Their thermo-regulatory systems are less robust, and their lungs are more sensitive to cold indoor temperatures and inflammatory pollutants such as second-hand tobacco and particles of nitrogen and carbon from unflued gas heaters. In addition, moist indoor air is harder to heat, and cold, damp air promotes both mould growth and the survival of viruses. Relatively cold and hot temperatures also stress the human immune system. The typical household heating pattern in New Zealand is to warm only one room of the house, so people cluster together in that room to socialise and in some cases to sleep communally. This environment makes the transmission of viruses and bacteria more likely, particularly from adults to children.

Overcrowding also plays a major role in spreading disease – and again, it principally affects those unable to get better housing. Results from the 2008 General Social Survey found that people in rented housing (16 per cent) were twice as likely to experience discrimination as those in owner-occupied housing (8 per cent). People in one-parent families with dependent children (16 per cent) and unemployed people (19 per cent) had higher than average rates of discrimination.[51] With this discrimination forcing them into low-quality housing, and combined with growing income inequality and a trend to lower home ownership, it is no surprise that there are many low-income households trying to lower the rent per person by increasing household crowding.[52] Nor is it a surprise that the proportions exposed to household crowding (one or more bedrooms short) in 2006 were 42.6 per cent for Pacific peoples, 22.8 per cent for Māori and 4.7 per cent for European/Other.[53] And when families sleep together in a single room over winter – a kind of functional or 'adaptive' crowding that cannot be gauged from Census data – the true level of household crowding may be even greater than estimated.

Crowded houses are likely to include a reasonably high proportion of smokers, increasing exposure to passive smoke for others in these houses. Overall, overcrowding increases the spread of close-contact infectious diseases, which are passed from person to person. Respiratory infections such as childhood pneumonia and infectious diseases such as rheumatic fever and meningococcal disease are almost unknown in other developed countries.[54] These infectious diseases make the largest contribution to hospital admissions; they represented a fifth (20.5 per cent) of all acute admissions in 1989–93 and over 25 per cent in 2004–8. Māori and Pacific peoples experienced the highest rates of hospitalisation for infectious diseases, with their rates typically more than two times higher than those experienced by Europeans – and their rates are rising more rapidly.[55] This evidence suggests that household crowding is probably making a major contribution to the very high infectious disease burden in New Zealand.

Building greater equality

The quality of housing creates different pathways that accentuate social and class differences in New Zealand. Historical policies have left Māori and Pacific families living disproportionately in low-income households. Meanwhile, the reduced government involvement in the supply of housing, the privatisation of housing finance and a recent under-supply of housing have all contributed to a general rise in inequalities in access to housing and housing-linked wealth.[56]

People on low incomes are more likely to live in older housing, which is often in poor condition. Rental housing, which is largely unregulated, is liable to be in poorer condition than owner-occupied dwellings, and Māori and Pacific peoples are more prone to be discriminated against when seeking to rent better quality rental housing. Poor housing leads to poor health, or aggravates already poor health. In contrast, where historical circumstances and family background work to people's advantage, they are more likely to be able to afford good quality housing – and to pass that advantage on to their children. In all these ways, inequality in housing creates other equally serious inequalities, and damages the health and lives of many of the poorest families.

To address the great divide between those who own and rent houses, New Zealand urgently needs to increase the supply of low cost, high quality housing. There are strong grounds for learning from the original post-war pattern of mixed communities, where children of those who rent and those who own their own houses go to the same local schools and play in the same local sports teams. We need more developments with a mix of social housing, privately rented houses and owner-occupied homes. But we cannot rely on private developers, who clearly have provided little affordable housing in recent decades: we need to augment their supply with central and local government house building.

Given that the large majority of New Zealanders live in urban areas and that increasingly extreme weather events are likely to have a greater effect on poorer communities, these housing developments should be of high quality, compact and close to reliable public transport. Government should reconsider a version of the State Advances mortgages as well as working with private banks to ensure preferential rates for first home buyers. It should also reconsider the advantageous aspects of the old Department of Māori Affairs loans, which included a maintenance contract as part of the mortgage. This would help to ensure that New Zealanders are less likely to put off maintenance on their houses as a way to reduce their expenses.

Finally, for those who are going to continue to be in the rental housing market, it is essential that New Zealand lift the quantity and quality of new social houses. The inadequate nature of housing regulation needs to be revisited, not only for new but also for existing housing, so that we bring our housing stock up to international standards. Given how important housing is as national infrastructure, the government needs to implement a warrant of fitness for rental properties. A warrant of fitness would enable prospective tenants to have some measure of the quality of the property and how it could affect their health, as well as giving them some idea of how energy efficient the house or flat is, so that it is known how much it is going to cost to heat the house adequately.[57] This was one of the key recommendations in the recent Children's Commissioner's Expert Advisory Group report on tackling child poverty; another was a recommendation for more social house building.

Improving the quality of our housing is one of the best and simplest ways to prevent disease, especially among children. That we do not invest more in it is extraordinary. Robust New Zealand community trials have shown that retrofitting insulation into existing houses and installing effective heaters is a cost-effective way of improving the health of the occupants; the benefits substantially outweighed the costs.[58] When these policies were rolled out nationwide, an evaluation concluded that the benefits outweighed the costs by almost five to one (the evaluation included gains from reducing avoidable deaths).[59] Moreover, the recent Healthy Housing Programme, formerly operated by Housing New Zealand, found that when state houses were extensively refurbished and joint efforts were made by housing officers and visiting nurses to improve families' living conditions and healthcare, hospital admissions for children fell by two-thirds.[60]

In short, resurrecting government policies to encourage home ownership and house maintenance, increasing the stock of affordable and social housing, and the establishment of standards for all rental houses would make a huge difference to bridging the great divide between the 'haves' and the 'have nots' in New Zealand.

Rebuilding divisions?

Mary Richardson is the executive director of the Christchurch Methodist Mission, and was interviewed for this viewpoint by Max Rashbrooke.

'It seems astonishing that when solutions were proposed to rebuild Christchurch, poverty and inequality were not something deemed worthy of repair,' says Mary Richardson. 'The rebuilding of Christchurch offered us an opportunity to create a better city – for the entire community, rich and poor.' Instead, it is being rebuilt in a way that she fears will exacerbate pre-existing inequalities.

Studies on post-disaster responses show that the well-off recover faster than the worse-off, Richardson says.[1] Poor households' economic and material losses, while less in absolute terms than those of the rich, can be devastating; these households never fully regain their pre-impact levels, and this increases their vulnerability to future events. People who under normal circumstances 'get by' can fall into poverty. 'We know that a disaster can widen the gap between rich and poor. Recovery is not neutral.'

Given that warning, Richardson adds, the city should have been 'entirely focused on ensuring we didn't exacerbate the disparities'. The first priority should have been attending to people's basic needs so as to reduce the disaster's psychological and emotional impact – and high on that list of 'basic need' would be housing and community institutions. But two-and-a-half years after the first earthquake hit, there has been 'no meaningful house building at all', only fraught insurance and EQC processes. As a result, there is a severe shortage of homes, and rents are escalating.

The rebuild, Richardson says, could also have directed its attention to the suburbs, especially those hardest hit by the earthquakes. Instead, it has focused on the city centre and commercial interests. The rebuild could have invested in training and job creation right from the outset. Instead, much of the labour will be imported while youth unemployment remains high. Now Christchurch is 'in danger of becoming two cities: one for people with great opportunity, and one for people stuck in permanent poverty'.

The divide started, she says, with the recovery planning process, which overrode local democracy. Shutting out the voices of the city's most vulnerable, it favoured instead the interests of large investors and businesses. The resulting city-centre plan is based on big commercial ventures: a convention centre, a stadium, a performing arts centre, large hotels and high-end shops. Its limited size keeps property prices high for pre-existing landowners. 'And it is largely made up of spaces which you have to have discretionary income to enjoy. It's not very inclusive of those who are struggling.'

But that, she says, is hardly surprising, given the models that the Christchurch

Central Development Unit sought to emulate. International inspiration came from places such as the Solidere redevelopment of Beirut's Central District and the Lower Manhattan Development Corporation, both notable for creating 'striking disparities and capital accumulation by a few'. Rich national and international investors have dominated these developments and created 'a pervasive politics of exclusion'. Both have been criticised for their lack of transparency and accountability to the public.

In Beirut, Solidere helped displace the city centre's original inhabitants, who were never able to return; the city became a gleaming centre surrounded by neglected slums. In Manhattan, those most in need – the low- and middle-income earners and the unemployed – were left without assistance or representation, while the corporation was given the power to make decisions with 'minimum democratic oversight and with maximum legal circumvention'.

Richardson fears a similar result in Christchurch: 'When you build a city where everything has a price associated with it, some people just can't participate. Those who we work with – people struggling to get by, people on the margins of society – won't be a part of it.'

The alternative is to build a city in which everyone feels welcome, and in which all people matter, including those who lack economic resources. That implies, first of all, taking a much harder look at the problems of suffering, poverty, exclusion, unfairness, and injustice. 'It is time we were attentive not just to all the bright and dazzling things, but also the dark and difficult things.' It also requires us to acknowledge a mutual regard for each other – 'the idea that we are our brothers' and sisters' keepers, and that ultimately, our humanity depends on everyone's humanity.'

Richardson adds: 'We won't prosper long if we favour only the prosperous, because the success of our economy depends not just on the size of our GDP but on the reach of our prosperity.' In spatial terms, this implies a Christchurch in which planning reflects community concerns about jobs and housing; a Christchurch with ample social housing, even in the CBD; a Christchurch in which small businesses as well as large can flourish; a Christchurch rich in public spaces, with parks, libraries and galleries. It does not imply a place that reflects, in its planning and building decisions, an increasingly divided city.

More broadly, extending prosperity's reach would ensure: 'That economic recovery means the economic recovery of families and households not just businesses; that every single person willing to work can get job training that leads to a job, and earn a living wage that can pay the bills; and that there is a safety net for those who lack adequate income or a network of family support'.

In short, this would be a city with a more equal society, a city where, Richardson says, everyone could live with dignity and respect – 'a city that reflects the values, care and commitment of ordinary New Zealanders'.

8 Crime, Imprisonment and Poverty

Kim Workman and Tracey McIntosh

Despite the media's relentless focus on crime and violence, New Zealand's crime rate has fallen significantly in the last twenty years.[1] Yet the number of people in our prisons has more than doubled in that same period.[2]

This is a major failure in the way we run our country and a colossal waste of talent and lives. Our incarceration rates – among the highest in the developed world – make us an international outlier, and represent, in the words of Finance Minister Bill English, 'a moral and fiscal failure'.[3] Nor can the rates be explained as the application of good policy, because, as this chapter illustrates, there is ample evidence that imprisoning people does little to prevent crime or reduce reoffending.

Indeed, our imprisonment statistics are devastating; devastating for victims of crime and other forms of social harm; devastating for individuals; devastating for families; devastating for communities; devastating for the loss of human potential; and devastating for the rupture that crime causes, sometime across generations.

So why, if crime rates are dropping, do we have so many people in prison? One could argue that it is not because New Zealand society is becoming more criminal but rather because we have an increasingly divided society. In any society with large income gaps, trust and empathy between different groups tend to diminish, and those in power become increasingly concerned to punish, rather than help, those who offend. In such a society, people in certain communities, especially ethnic minorities, are more likely to be stigmatised, blamed and punished for their supposed failings – creating a reinforcing spiral of poverty and offending that weakens us all. This chapter sets out the damage that this approach does, and how we might turn it around.

Stories and myths

Crime and punishment statistics always tell a story. There is a tendency to think that the story is a simple one. It often assumes that criminal and victim can always be classified into separate and distinct categories. The story of punishment is similarly simplified. It is largely seen as a reasoned and rational societal response to unacceptable behaviour; although perhaps overly lenient for some. The fact that a criminal justice system may produce discriminatory outcomes is rarely considered. Issues of over-representation of particular groups become so much part of the dominant story that they are normalised and naturalised and again rarely interrogated. In reality, the stories are far more complex. Tony Paine, the chief executive of Victim Support, an organisation that meets the needs of around 70,000 victims annually, puts it this way:

> It is very easy to talk about victims and offenders as if they were two quite separate groups (both demographically and morally). Of course the world is not that black and white. The New Zealand Crime and Safety Survey[4] tells us that 50% of all victimizations are experienced by only 6% of New Zealanders and that the social and demographic indicators that identify those who are most likely to be victimized are identical to the markers for those likely to be offenders. The life stories and cultural contexts that weave victims and offenders together (often within the same person) make any artificial separation between offenders and victims just that: an artifice that oversimplifies our complex world.[5]

The prison population reflects this fact, as most inmates have experienced severe poverty and have higher victimisation rates that the general population.[6] They are also typically young: over 50 per cent of inmates are between the ages of sixteen and thirty-four.[7] As a National Health Committee report noted:

> Although there have been changes in the constitution of the prison population, those who are incarcerated continue to represent the most marginalised, culturally censored, socio-economically disadvantaged and 'powerless' of society. The majority of prisoners of any country, including New Zealand, are those that come from a context already shaped by social exclusion. Among other things, they are likely to be from an ethnic minority, have limited education and a history of instability, unemployment or underemployment, substandard diet and housing conditions, and inferior medical access. Their health reflects this disadvantage and like them, tends to be poor.[8]

These sets of characteristics may lead to a marked and stigmatised marginalisation, in which deprivation due to social, economic and political factors is entrenched and far-reaching.

The prison population is also 94 per cent male. However, the number of women in prison – especially young Māori women – is growing much faster than the number of men, and we need to be mindful of this and the implications of rising female imprisonment for family and community.[9]

Less crime, more people in prisons

Our prison population has skyrocketed in recent decades, rising from 91 per 100,000 people in 1987 to 199 per 100,000 by 2011.[10] (If we disaggregate the data, we find that New Zealand's Māori imprisonment rate is 700 per 100,000.) While this national figure is still dwarfed by that of the USA, which has a current rate of 750 per 100,000, New Zealand has moved well beyond the western bloc countries with which it has been traditionally compared. This could be a symptom of a high rate of crime – except that we have witnessed a steady decline in the crime rate in recent years.[11]

While inequality and poverty have increased significantly in recent decades, reported crime has declined, from 475,154 recorded offences in 1995–96, to 394,522 offences in 2011–12. This is a drop in the crime rate over this sixteen-year period from 1,281.7 recorded offences per 10,000 people to 891.0 per 10,000.[12] Crime rates have been falling in many other countries as well, for a variety of reasons. Local factors behind the drop include the lower proportion of those aged fifteen to twenty-four in the population, and a change in police behaviour. The last three years in particular have seen a shift from a 'zero tolerance' approach and an emphasis on control and suppression, to a range of strategies aimed at keeping both adults and young people out of the court system. That includes diversion of youth offenders, pre-charge warnings for adult offenders and positive engagement with high-crime communities. But regardless of the reasons for this reduction, it is difficult to argue that New Zealand is one of the most dangerous countries in the world, as our imprisonment rates would suggest.

Since our bulging prisons cannot be accounted for by higher crime rates, some would argue that they reflect a necessary social response to crime: that imprisonment is a deterrent to committing crime and a way of preventing people from reoffending. However, prisons fail the evidence test on both these counts. Most studies find little evidence that the threat of imprisonment deters people from crime, especially in communities where 'mass imprisonment' (discussed in detail later) is the norm, and prison carries little stigma.[13] In particular, more severe punishment – long jail terms, as opposed to suspended sentences, for example – has been shown to exert no deterrent effect. Prison is also an obvious failure when it comes to rehabilitation. According to the Department of Corrections, in 2010, 61.9 per cent of prisoners reoffended within two years of release – up from 55.4 per cent in 2005. Prisons can in fact retard the rehabilitation process, because they expose first-time inmates to more hardened criminals, and because excluding people from society may only reinforce the problems that led to their original offending. So while prison is clearly necessary for offenders who are currently beyond rehabilitation and who would otherwise pose a danger to society, for many offenders it is totally ineffective.

In these circumstances, imprisonment becomes 'normalised' and incarceration becomes one more contributor to social dysfunction, weakening communities and reducing the social capital and social solidarity that are the bedrock forces preventing crime.[14] An additional effect of such 'normalisation' is that the prospect of prison loses much of its supposed deterrent effect – becoming, instead, an inconvenient expectation, a 'fact of life' or even, on some accounts, a 'rite of passage'.[15]

Poverty and crime

Looking at the wider issues, we have to ask: what causes crime in the first place? To answer that question, thinking about *who* goes to prison gives us some basis to argue that poverty is a significant part of the problem. Too many prisoners have experienced considerable social harm and have gone on to perpetuate and perpetrate social harm on others. The cost to society is enormous.

Most people who live with considerable financial constraint make strong contributions to family and community. Offending is not a characteristic of their lives. Yet research and practice suggests that there are strong links between crime and poverty. Official crime rates are always more elevated in poorer communities, on both sides of the coin: victimisation rates are higher amongst the poor, and the poor are more likely to be arrested and convicted for offences. And, of course, social statistics in New Zealand strongly suggest that poverty is racialised: Māori and Pacific peoples experience ongoing, disproportionate levels of poverty.[16]

It remains difficult to describe comprehensively the prime mechanism that links poverty to crime.[17] But there is a range of drivers. For young people who have grown up in violent communities, where constant physical self-defence is the only means of survival, acts of violence are an ingrained and apparently logical response to threats and challenges. For others, especially people with low self-esteem and limited work skills – and in areas where there are few jobs available – crime represents one of the few relevant sources of income and status. Children growing up in poorer households may be more vulnerable to some forms of maltreatment, which they then recycle, as learned behaviour, in their own parenting. They also experience transience, because their parents shift home in search of decent housing or work, which makes it hard for children to form lasting bonds; and they may not receive enough love and attention from overworked and chronically stressed parents.[18]

Children and youth who have experienced a number of deprivations, unmet needs and damaging life experiences are at high risk of adult offending. Children on that trajectory will show conduct disorder and frequent defiance of authority. When schools respond punitively, the children will truant, become vulnerable to substance abuse, and link with others like themselves in gangs, in order to support each other's anti-social behaviour. As they age, their behavioural disorders and criminal lifestyle may become increasingly entrenched and more difficult to change. As a consequence, their prospects for rehabilitation become progressively lower.[19]

As the Dunedin life-course study of over 1,000 New Zealanders (and other research) shows, people from low socio-economic backgrounds are three times more likely to commit crime than those from wealthy families.[20] Unless one espouses the repugnant belief that those people are inherently less 'good' than others, we must accept that growing up in poverty does damage individuals in ways that are not under their control and may predispose them to commit crime.

However, the main problem New Zealand faces is not growing crime but a rising prison population. What role does inequality play in this problem? There is, unfortunately, no research on the links between inequality and imprisonment looking specifically at New Zealand, but international research points to a strong connection between the two. One answer is found in the work of John Pratt, a New Zealander and a leading international criminologist, who has mapped the trend towards more punitive forms of punishment. This, he argues, reflects populist and political sentiments that align with the rhetoric of getting 'tough on crime'.[21] His work shows that prison populations have risen in much of the western world and that particular sectors of those populations are more likely than others to find themselves in prison than others. In short, changes in the levels of social support to marginalised communities, and the increased penalisation of the social welfare system, contribute to increased vulnerability in marginalised communities. Such communities struggle to marshal their 'social capital', develop shared norms and values, and build relationships of trust.[22]

American legal academic David Garland, meanwhile, has argued that in recent years the forms, functions and significance of punishment in modern society reach well beyond its ability to 'reduce reoffending' or 'preserve public safety'. The way that prisons are run and the values that underlie their management communicate meaning about the nation's attitude to power, authority, legitimacy, morality and society.[23] They are part of growing opposition to policies that appear to benefit the 'undeserving poor', increased cynicism about welfare, and growing support for more aggressive controls for an underclass that is perceived to be disorderly, drug-prone, violent and dangerous.

This approach is evident in New Zealand, where punishment increasingly extends beyond prisons. The communities that most offenders come from have experienced a reduction in primary healthcare services, increased evictions from and ineligibility for social housing,[24] increased levels of unemployment,[25] a decline in the level of welfare support,[26] the introduction of 'workfare',[27] and increased pressure to 'behave' without any commensurate provision of support.[28] In addition, reviews are planned into the way government responds to child abuse and neglect,[29] and there is talk of a review of the youth justice system. In both cases, the indications are for 'tougher' measures to be taken.

Communities that are already marginalised and vulnerable are then punished more stringently by a criminal justice system responding to the 'tough-on-crime' desires of a more unequal society. Countries with narrower income gaps tend to make greater use of short sentences or alternatives to prison, in part because they are more trusting and cohesive, and therefore more likely to see offenders as being worthy of good treatment and rehabilitation. In contrast, New Zealand's criminal and corrections policies reflect a structural move towards, and a popular enthusiasm for, punishment – especially in the way that prisons are used. This is a logical consequence of an increasingly unequal society in which the desire to punish, rather than rehabilitate, prevails. It is hardly surprising, then, that international evidence shows that countries with wide income inequalities tend to have more people in prison than more equal countries.[30]

Prison practice

This structural move towards a more punitive society can be seen at work in the New Zealand criminal justice system over the last two decades. Alternatives to custody have been seen as too soft and as rewarding the criminals, despite the multiple failures of incarceration. Imprisonment has become more punitive and more security-minded. Prisoners have become less eligible for such privileges as release to work and family visits, and more likely to be described in official reports as culpable, deserving of punishment and sometimes dangerous. They are no longer individuals who could potentially be reintegrated but risks to be carefully managed.[31] Prisoners become objects rather than subjects.

The government's Reducing Crime and Reoffending Result Action Plan (which increases both investment in offender rehabilitation and the focus on addressing the drivers of crime) has failed to unravel the impact of all the criminal justice legislation introduced since 2002. This failure has increased the extent to which offenders and prisoners are punished.

Moreover, there has been a concerted effort to increase the level of punitiveness within the prison system, even beyond the basic punishment imposed by the loss of a person's freedom. This is in line with international experience, which shows that more humane approaches are more common in more equal societies, while unequal countries tend towards harsher treatment.[32]

Tough on criminals – tough on communities of crime

New Zealand's increasingly punitive approach to imprisonment affects some communities disproportionately, and there is ample evidence that many Māori communities in particular are being devastated by imprisonment. As one report in 2010 observed:

- Māori were four to five times more likely to be apprehended, prosecuted and convicted than their non-Māori counterparts
- Māori were also seven-and-a-half times more likely to be given a custodial sentence
- Māori were eleven times more likely to be remanded in custody awaiting trial
- Māori women were five-and-a-half times more likely to be apprehended and ten times more likely to receive a custodial sentence than New Zealand European women

- Māori men were four times more likely to be apprehended and seven times more likely to receive a custodial sentence than their New Zealand European equivalents.[33]

In general, Māori are being imprisoned at a rate six times that of non-Māori. For Māori males born in 1975, it is estimated that 22 per cent had a Corrections-managed sentence before their twentieth birthday, and 44 per cent had a Corrections-managed sentence by the age of thirty-five.[34] It is worth noting that Māori are over-represented in this way not just because they come from marginalised communities but also because they are specifically discriminated against. Human Rights Commission research shows that, for the *same* behaviour, Māori are more likely to be arrested, prosecuted and convicted than Pākehā. As the Māori Party co-leader Pita Sharples put it, 'There are societal attitudes and prejudices about Māori and crime. This leads to an increase in profiling by police, which in turn frames the application of discretion used and ultimately increases the arrest rates for Māori.'[35]

The term 'mass imprisonment' describes a situation where imprisonment rates are far higher than the comparative and historical norm, and fall disproportionately on particular (often racial) groups, so that the effects cease to be explicable in terms of individual offending and involve whole communities. Mass imprisonment 'implies a self-sustaining cycle of increased incarceration, reaching across generations'.[36] In this situation,

> Imprisonment becomes part of the socialization process. Every family, every householder, every individual in these neighbourhoods has direct personal knowledge of the prison – through a spouse, a child, a parent, a neighbour, a friend. Imprisonment ceases to be a fate of a few criminal individuals and becomes a shaping institution for whole sectors of the population.[37]

We can identify 'Māori mass imprisonment' as one of the problems facing our country today. This level of engagement with the criminal justice system creates an experience and knowledge of the system that has substantial impact on Māori whānau. For many Māori youth caught up in the system for the first time, their experience and knowledge of sanctions and confinement well pre-date their own engagement. And the impact of punishment (particularly incarceration) is not limited to the individual who is sanctioned. Rather, there are collateral effects and consequences that spread from the individual outwards, damaging and rupturing social relationships and connections. The damage can persist through time, generating long-lasting and potentially inter-generational effects.

One of the clearest examples of this is the impact of imprisonment on families. Individual incarceration is a collective experience.[38] The 2010 National Health Committee report notes that the families of prisoners tend to be among the poorest in society, and that imprisonment affects communities as well as families:

> [T]he most vulnerable communities are more susceptible to the cycle of imprisonment. High imprisonment rates can erode the stability and cohesion of the whole community. The large proportion of Māori in New Zealand prisons means the impacts of imprisonment fall disproportionately on Māori whānau and communities, and results in many living on the verge of crisis.[39]

Criminologists Dina Rose and Todd Clear have found that there may be a 'tipping point' in certain communities, so that crime increases once incarceration reaches a certain level.[40] As they put it:

> [H]igh rates of imprisonment break down the social and family bonds that guide individuals away from crime, remove adults who would otherwise nurture children, deprive communities of income, reduce future income potential, and engender a deep resentment toward the legal system. As a result, as communities become less capable of managing social order through family or social groups, crime rates go up.[41]

Ways forward

To reduce our prison population, we will ultimately need to embrace equality both inside and outside the justice system. In other words, a wider commitment to reducing income inequalities would logically be complemented by more egalitarian forms of justice. These alternative models, based around support not punishment, would emphasise the fairness and compassion that are at the heart of egalitarianism. Restorative justice, for instance, is a voluntary process in which those affected by wrongdoing are brought together to hear each other and thus acknowledge the harm done, identify needs and obligations, and decide how to deal with them. As opposed to traditional rehabilitative programmes, which are in some senses 'done to' offenders, in restorative justice the offender is

... the author of his own readmission to civil society. Entirely in accordance with the emphasis on personal responsibility and individual rationality so central to neo-liberal philosophy, restorative justice may plausibly be seen as an attempt to revive rehabilitation for a new political era.[42]

A recent Ministry of Justice report showed that restorative justice conferences reduced reoffending by 20 per cent. A further report, based on a conservative average reduction in reoffending of only 10 per cent (rather than 20 per cent), estimates that 1,500 restorative justice conferences would generate $5,100 per conference in public sector benefits, thanks to their potential to reduce criminal activity. The police would need to make fewer arrests, the Department of Corrections would have fewer prisoners and ACC would have fewer claims for injuries caused by crime.[43]

Another promising intervention is therapeutic jurisprudence, which focuses on the law's distinct impact on emotional life and psychological well-being. It recognises that the law itself may function as a therapeutic agent. Using the insights of the social sciences, it examines the effects of rules of law, legal procedure and the specific roles of legal actors, including counsel and judges, on the psychological well-being of people affected by the law.[44] The thinking behind therapeutic jurisprudence is increasingly being applied in the design of social policy responses to anti-social behaviours in areas such as youth justice and domestic violence.

This approach has also resulted in the development of specialist courts, such as drug courts and mental health courts. One 2006 study showed drug courts in the United States and Canada had reduced crime rates by between 8 and 26 per cent.[45] A 2008 report on the drug court in New South Wales found offenders were 38 per cent less likely to be reconvicted of a drug offence, and 17 per cent less likely to be reconvicted of any offence. About 80 per cent of criminal offending in New Zealand happens under the influence of alcohol or drugs, but the justice system typically orders treatment only as or after a sentence is imposed.[46]

A third alternative model, based on so-called justice reinvestment policies, can directly address inequalities in the system. The justice reinvestment model involves identifying the amount of financial and non-financial resources consumed by the justice system and considering whether those resources can be distributed more effectively, in order to provide a better social dividend to communities and the wider public.[47] In the words of Andrew Coyle, a British academic and former prison governor:

There is an increasing awareness that the criminal justice system on its own cannot effectively help former offenders to be reintegrated into their former neighbourhoods. There has to be a parallel reorganisation of resources to make resettlement a primary objective. Policy makers are beginning to recognise that successful resettlement depends on the presence of strong civil institutions. As the justice reinvestment movement begins to point to the end [of] an excessive dependence on criminal justice, it may also hold the promise of a deeper, systemic reform – one that is rooted in a deepening recognition that the resolution of issues of public safety need to engage every institution in civil society. These will include health and housing, workforce development, family and social welfare.[48]

A better way to make prison policy

Recently, there has been a greater willingness on the part of politicians, the media and – it seems – the general public to look at 'what works' and to accept that the emphasis in recent years on harsher punishment and longer incarceration has not in fact worked. The government's Reducing Crime and Reoffending Result Action Plan has changed the focus of the criminal justice discussion from 'what should be done' to 'how'. Ongoing discussions have taken the justice sector beyond a blind commitment to traditional approaches, and towards a more adventurous exploration of recent developments worldwide in offender transformation and prisoner reintegration.

In the long term, the aims of criminal policy should be defined so that they accord with the aims of general social policy. That would include introducing cost-benefit analysis into criminal political thinking – in the widest possible sense, including also non-material costs for offenders and victims. Criminal justice policy also needs to pay greater heed to its effect on Māori. The Waitangi Tribunal's recent report *Ko Aotearoa Tēnei* proposes solutions to inequalities that are based on a fundamental shift in attitude and approach by the government:

> Unless it is accepted that New Zealand has two founding cultures, not one; unless Māori culture and identity are valued in everything government says and does; and unless they are welcomed into the very centre of the way we do things in this country, nothing will change. Māori will continue to be perceived, and know they are perceived, as an alien and resented minority, a problem to be managed with

a seemingly endless stream of taxpayer-funding programmes, but never solved.[49]

Fortunately, the problem of crime and punishment is not an intractable one. Our present situation is part of our social landscape, not our natural one. Inequalities wreak havoc for all members of society, not just those who live in conditions of scarcity and deprivation; but a more equal society will deliver greater levels of social justice and, in turn, have a positive impact on the criminal justice system.

The state as parent and warden: Stan's story

Stan Coster ('Dokta'), **Tracey McIntosh** and **Ian Lambie** *are involved in a collaborative project that is looking at institutionalised life in New Zealand, focusing on Stan's experiences and insights. This viewpoint results from interviews conducted by Tracey with Stan.*

In April 1969, soon after the death of his mother, Stan and his four siblings were placed by Child Welfare on preventive supervision with a local family in Hastings. Later in the same year they were removed on warrant as being 'indigent' and made wards of the state.

These were not the first hardships that Stan had experienced, but rather the culmination of a largely difficult and deprived early childhood. Well before his birth, the family had come to the attention of Child Welfare and other agencies. Agents of the state have remained a feature of his life, and as Stan remarks, 'The state has written my life and made me the person I am.'

Stan remembers his mother as a good mother who struggled with the day-to-day trials of bringing up a young family with scarce resources, and a serious illness that saw her spend long periods of time in hospital. His father left the family in the early 1960s at a time when his mother was already dealing with poor health.

During this period, social welfare reports document concerns that the children were being inadequately parented. The school they were attending noted that while the children were well behaved, they often arrived at school unkempt and seemingly undernourished. In the years prior to her death, his mother entered into a relationship with another man and violence became a regular feature of Stan's life both as a victim and a spectator. Difficult family relationships were intensified by overcrowding: the family lived in a one-bedroom house while they waited for a state home to become available.

After the death of Stan's mother, the children moved from foster home to foster home. As Stan recalls, 'In the beginning we were placed in foster homes in pairs, and then they just placed us separately.' In the years immediately after her death, Stan's life was characterised by constant change. Official welfare reports of the time testify to several different homes and schools. In less than one year he had been moved five times in three different regional areas. He was placed in both private foster care and children's homes.

His memories of this time are bleak, and he saw and suffered abuse and felt that he was in a constant state of rejection. Psychological reports from this time saw him as an emotionally damaged teenager, vulnerable to bullying, shy and sometimes impulsive, although also a talented rugby player. There were indications that he could resort to violence if frustrated or angry. His resistance to further victimisation probably characterised his later life outcomes. For Stan, violence became a rational response to his environment. As he got older, he says, he realised that spontaneous acts of violence or disproportionate reactions to incidents built him a reputation that meant he was less likely to be bullied or targeted.

The years until he turned fifteen continued to be framed by constant movement within the foster home system. During this period he started to be picked up for successive minor infractions: petty theft, truancy, running away and drinking issues. Days after his fifteenth birthday, having been involved in a number of offences, he was admitted to Epuni Boys' Home, which reinforced an emerging criminalised identity. At Epuni, Stan's education in things criminal expanded significantly, and fighting became a much greater part of the way he engaged with the world.

On being released from Epuni he briefly lived with his father. During this period he appeared before the court on a number of occasions on car conversion and related charges. In 1976, after been convicted on some of these charges, he was sent to Waikeria Borstal and was subsequently discharged from Social Welfare care. The role of the state as parent had concluded and the role of prison warden emerged in its place.

By this time Stan was a quiet, sometimes violent, often unstable young man. His gang affiliations were also an element of his identity. 'The Mongrel Mob was always a part of my life. Family members were in the Mob, so it has never been a gang in my eyes; it was just whānau.' Reflecting on his life, Stan feels that much of his path was determined from the beginning: 'I had no way out, and my life got worse as the years went on.' While he wanted to join the army, his criminal convictions made this unlikely, and so later on his gang membership became his 'poor man's army'.

The twenty years that followed his time at Waikeria Borstal were spent largely in residential confinement or imprisonment. Short periods were spent on the outside but he returned time and again to prison, sometimes for relatively minor offences and breaches, and sometimes for more serious offences. While Stan agrees that he was thoroughly institutionalised and knew the intimate workings of the prison system, he remained a challenging prisoner within the structure.

During his last long term in prison, he resolved to make changes to his life so that he could remain on the outside. He engaged in programmes and focused largely on self-directed ways of healing. He has now been out of prison for over ten years and has been involved in a number of programmes aimed at helping young people find other pathways. Still, his story is not a redemptive one; it is his life and it remains a bare one. He recognises that things could have been different for him if opportunity rather than deprivation had been his constant companion. Stan ultimately offers this insight into his life: 'I have spent most of my life within four walls, having created my own reality. I am a product of the system.'

9 Schools and Inequality

Cathy Wylie

Inequality and poverty are amongst the greatest challenges for New Zealand's education system. There is a problem, first, of deep poverty. A substantial number of families in New Zealand often cannot earn enough to provide what their children need. In 2008, 19 per cent of our children and young people were living in families that have to economise on essential items, including food and healthcare – families living in vulnerable circumstances with constant financial stress.[1] Hardship rates were even higher for Māori and Pacific children and young people (32 and 40 per cent respectively).[2]

Income inequality presents another major challenge for schools. Deprivation affects learning, and inequality has wider impacts also. When housing costs lead to socially segregated communities, schools situated in low-income areas have difficulty drawing on a full range of knowledge, skills, networks and opportunities to support their students, in and out of classrooms. In turn, that makes it harder for these schools to improve their students' educational achievement levels; thus students' opportunities and their ability to contribute later to social and economic well-being are limited. Income inequality makes it less likely that New Zealand can make the most of its young potential.

Education can, of course, have a significant role in countering inequality and fostering opportunity. International analysis suggests that providing good quality education in every school, regardless of local income levels, offers one of the surest ways of deflecting the impacts of income inequality at the personal and social levels.[3] Schools can and do make a difference for students from poor homes – if the schools themselves are well supported. But our education system often leaves the schools serving these students hamstrung. Instead of countering inequality, our system too frequently reinforces it.

How does poverty affect school learning?

Children from low-income homes often start school on a less stable platform than others. They have had fewer opportunities to develop the knowledge and skills that schools build on and extend,[4] often including less experience of good quality early childhood education.⁵ Their early development is more likely to have been affected by poor nutrition and health.

Research undertaken in 1999–2000 provides valuable information about what is happening to New Zealand children. At that time, five-year-olds starting school in decile 1 schools (schools with the greatest concentration of children from low-income homes) had average early reading scores that were almost half those of their peers starting school in decile 7–10 schools. Maths scores were on average a third below those of these peers.⁶

Children in poverty often live in conditions that hinder their ability to learn. With low incomes, their parents may find it impossible to feed them adequately or keep them healthy, both in their early years and their schooling years. Clothes or shoes for school may be unaffordable; likewise, books and computers, paints, musical instruments or sports gear may be outside the family budget. Public libraries are free (and most offer internet access) but they are often out of reach without a bus fare. Parents who are stressed from the daily challenge of making ends meet will be less able to give children the interaction that helps them develop. Working long hours, holding down two jobs, and inflexible work places are all features of life on a low income – all militate against parental engagement with a child's school, limiting parent–teacher interaction.

Parents want their children to succeed – to have opportunities, to learn, to grow. But for those who come from a background of hardship, it is often a lot harder to support success. Parents who did not, for example, gain much from their own school experience may not connect so readily with their children's learning activities, or be able to support and extend these at home. Enjoyment of reading is a keystone to learning, and to an expanding knowledge of the world; reading and playing with words, patterns and symbols are all important if children are to make the most of their formal education.⁷ Parents who are not called on to communicate with others in their work, or who are isolated through lack of work, are less likely to be comfortable discussing things with children or encouraging them to become confident communicators and thinkers. Stress and uncertainty that accompany hardship can make it harder for parents to convey optimism that effort is worthwhile, that one's actions can achieve desired goals.

These parents may not be able to give school attendance the priority it needs, particularly when school is associated with costs that are hard to meet, or when children have other responsibilities (such as the care of younger siblings or grandparents). Regular attendance at school can also be eroded by poor health, which is much more likely to occur among low-income families living in overcrowded or low-quality housing.[8]

Poverty also affects housing stability and therefore the stability of school enrolment. Low-decile schools have much higher student turnover rates than others, often because poorer parents have to shift house when they cannot afford rents. For example, 42 per cent of low-decile primary schools had student turnover rates of 20 per cent or more, according to the 1999 New Zealand Council for Educational Research national survey; only 7 per cent of high-decile primary schools came into this category.[9] When children have a stable enrolment in a school, teachers can develop good relationships with students and their families, both of which are important to successful learning.

There is, of course, no inevitable path from poverty to low educational achievement. But poverty does make it much harder for students to make the most of school, particularly where it is coupled with low parental education levels. Early experiences of poverty, even when family incomes later rise, show some persistent associations with lower educational performance levels.[10] For example, the longitudinal Competent Learners study found in 2002/03 that only 27 per cent of fourteen-year-olds who had lived in low-income homes (measured when they were five years old) had reading comprehension scores at the median level – even though many of their families had increased their incomes over the period. In comparison, 50 per cent of fourteen-year-olds whose homes were medium-income when they were close to starting school, and 74 per cent of those whose homes were high-income had scores at the median level.[11] So the work of schools serving children from poor homes would be much more effective if their families' living standards, pay levels and work conditions were also addressed.

The challenges for schools in low-income areas

New Zealand's *average* scores on the reading, maths and science international PISA tests are good. But we also have a much wider *gap* between our best and worst performers than other high-ranking countries such as Finland, Canada or South Korea. Compared to these countries, New Zealand's schools are confronted by:

- A much higher proportion of school-related differences (up to two-thirds) shaped by differences in the socio-economic intake of our schools (when looking at fifteen-year-old students' scores on the PISA tests across countries that have average PISA scores similar to ours).

- A wider spread of results because our poorest (and wealthiest) children are more concentrated at either end of the spectrum than in other highly ranked countries.
- Poor children having less opportunity to attend schools with a more even social mix (that offer better support for children's learning) than disadvantaged students in other high-performing countries.

This last challenge reflects New Zealand's policy emphasis on parental choice, coupled with stand-alone, self-managing schools that compete for students.[12] Such an emphasis has left many low-decile schools (serving low-income communities) smaller than they were and less able to attract their community's higher-performing students, who migrate to higher-decile schools.[13]

Low-decile schools face more issues than do other schools, particularly in attracting and retaining experienced teachers. Even in the current economic downturn, 20 per cent of decile 1–2 secondary school principals had difficulty finding suitable teachers in 2012, a difficulty faced by only 3 per cent of their decile 9–10 secondary school peers. Low-decile schools also have greater difficulty with student attendance and behaviour. In 2012, 76 per cent of decile 1–2 secondary school teachers experienced some serious student disruption in their classes, compared with 59 per cent of decile 9–10 secondary school teachers.[14] Student attendance and behaviour issues are compounded specifically by the *concentration* of children from poor homes: if these children were more evenly spread among schools, there would be a lower level of disruption to learning overall. (Once again, the effects of structural inequality can be plainly seen.) Unsurprisingly, secondary teachers in low-decile schools suffer more from burnout (they score 31.8 on a scale measuring indicators of work-related burnout, compared with 24.2 for their high-decile school colleagues).[15] Although there are many dedicated teachers in low-decile schools, the intensity of this work can be draining.

Low-decile schools do receive some additional support. The KidsCan charitable organisation currently assists 43,000 students in 201 schools, providing shoes, raincoats and food; another 21,000 students in 105 schools are on the waiting list. School breakfasts provided in low-decile schools by Fonterra and Sanitarium are being extended, supported by government funding. Low-decile schools now get more government support for strategies to deal with student behaviour and attendance, through schemes that put social workers in schools and through school nurses. Priority is also given to low-decile schools for the Ministry of Education's

Positive Behaviour for Learning initiatives – evidence-based programmes that foster positive behaviour, social skills and self-management among students. Low-decile schools also receive somewhat more government funding per student. But, important though this funding is, it usually does not stretch far enough to provide all the additional learning opportunities that students from poor homes need. As an example, digital learning is more likely to occur in high-decile than low-decile schools.[16]

Additional government funding per student still leaves many low-decile schools with less money to use for student learning than high-decile schools, which can tap additional funding through donations from parents, fundraising and (mainly at secondary level) attracting international fee-paying students. A 2012 comparison of the total income of five decile 1 and five decile 10 primary schools found that the decile 10 schools had about $1,100 more to spend per student each year than the decile 1 schools.[17] The decile 1 schools' income per student amounted to about $7,518 per student; the decile 10 schools', about $8,653. Yet one US study estimated that students from poor homes needed 40 per cent to 100 per cent more funding per student to provide equitable learning opportunities.[18]

Countering poverty in primary schools

Educational responses to poverty have to work within a system that makes schools responsible for their own management and development. This autonomy was brought into being with Tomorrow's Schools in 1989, and it has come at a cost:

- In our self-managing schools environment, it is up to individual schools to find and employ teachers, and there is no systematic support to ensure that low-decile schools can recruit teachers of the calibre they need.
- Government funding to support new professional learning can be intermittent and piecemeal. Lack of continuity presents challenges for sustained responses to the impact of poverty.
- In the absence of systematic ways for schools to learn from and be supported by others, promising ideas are often untested or unshared, and struggling schools have too often been left to fend for themselves.

The schools most affected by this isolation, predictably, are those already grappling with the problems of inequality and poverty – that is, our lowest decile schools.

Gaps in resources are likely to make it harder for schools to close gaps in scores. For example, over the period 2008–11, 31 per cent of students in decile 1–2 schools achieved a maths score at the fifth stanine level (around average) or higher on the national PAT maths test, compared with 60 per cent of students in decile 5–6 schools, and 78 per cent of students at decile 9–10 schools.[19] The figures are similar for the PAT reading comprehension test.

To close the gaps in educational performance, students in low-decile primary schools need to learn at a faster rate than their peers in higher-decile schools – a big ask for both students and teachers. Of course, how much difference teachers can make is a vexed issue, and hard to measure definitively. But it is safe to say that schools can and do make a real difference in the education of children from poor communities. The 'gaps in results' between low-decile and other schools are being addressed in a number of ways, with success in some cases. However, it is also important to acknowledge that schools cannot do this on their own; schools cannot counteract by themselves the impact of poverty and inequality.

To 'close the gaps' in students' performance, outside assistance in low-decile schools is often needed. Recently, seven South Auckland primary schools spent three years working with Auckland University researchers who had strong knowledge of different teaching strategies. They examined with the teachers how student achievement patterns related to the strategies used with different students. From insights gained in this process, teachers were able to use more nuanced and targeted strategies. And in these schools, the percentage of students achieving at the national average level rose from 39 per cent to 59 per cent. More students were achieving above the national average than before – an increase from less than 1 per cent to 10 per cent (still less than the 23 per cent who achieved at this level nationally).[20]

Educationalist Stuart McNaughton, who led the researchers working with these schools, describes himself as a 'cautious optimist' about what schools serving low-income areas can achieve with students from poor homes, if they are well supported. But he thinks that 'substantial and enduring gains' are not possible unless what occurs in schools is augmented by what occurs out of schools.[21] For that reason, his next research programme will focus on what is called the 'summer learning loss'. When students from poor homes return to school after the summer break, they have often lost ground or remained at the same level they were at the previous year. But their peers from more advantaged homes have continued to make learning gains through the holidays, because of the way their time was spent.

'If we knew then what we know now!', as one long-serving principal put it in 2011, looking at the results from his low-decile school over the last decade. 'What we know now' reflects a new way of framing teaching, so that it connects strongly with individual students' needs. Previously, this principal had looked at teacher planning and student work separately; now he and his curriculum leaders focused on what students actually learnt from particular lessons, and how their learning related to goals for that lesson. These goals were shared with students so they knew what they were working towards. That brought more energy into the learning, and student achievement improved.

At another low-decile school, Māori and Pacific students made several years' mathematics progress in just one year when their two teachers worked with an external researcher-teacher educator to try a new approach. This was based on the Ministry-funded Best Evidence Syntheses of research findings about how student outcomes can be improved.[22] Again, student energy was better harnessed because students were made more aware of the goals for their learning, and how to achieve them through more focused strategies. Students were empowered to become more confident learners. Processes of learning became more enjoyable both in their own right, and because students could see real gains.

Two of the strengths of New Zealand primary education have been an emphasis on the individuality of each student, and a flexible curriculum. This has been sharpened in recent years by more timely and informative student assessments being developed for schools. The revised New Zealand Curriculum now emphasises the importance of teachers working together to evaluate how their strategies are working. Teachers are probing assessment results and other evidence of student learning to decide on the priority for each student, and reviewing the outcomes of their teaching for students.

In one low-decile, multicultural school, the principal reported on these new processes. Without using any additional funding or support, she was able to speak of 'remarkable' achievements:

> We've got professional learning communities that share professional reading and data. Everyone focuses on four students in their class, one has to be someone who's struggling, and they bring their data [about the children's performance], they talk about their programme,

decide what their next steps for that student are, and then in two weeks they have to come back and report on what they had done and how that's gone. Our achievement data this first half of the year has improved remarkably. It's about giving teachers the time and the strategies and the framework to look at what they're doing in a way that is non-threatening, inside a secure and supported environment. Even our weakest teachers are doing remarkably better.[23]

There are, in short, some great things happening in New Zealand primary schools to counter the impacts of inequality and poverty. But these changes are still occurring unevenly, depending significantly on networks of individual school leaders and teachers. Many low-decile primary schools lack the knowledge and support they need to provide more focused learning for their students, and these schools do not reach the starting point for results that narrow the gap between students from poor homes and the national average. And once a programme of professional support from outside a school comes to an end, it is harder for these schools to continue building on what they have gained. The national Numeracy Development Programme, which ran in the decade to 2009 and reached most schools, saw students' mathematics knowledge and skill improve over the course of the programme. But after the programme ended, and schools were no longer supported with knowledgeable facilitators, low-decile schools often struggled because they lacked strong mathematics teachers who could support other teachers. Higher staff turnover and a greater reliance on beginning teachers in those low-decile schools also make it harder to build or sustain the kind of strong school culture and teaching practice that helped narrow the gaps.

Much has been learnt over the last decade, but much more is needed. The principal who wished he had been able to better serve his past students – 'if we knew then what we know now!' – was struggling to understand the plateau his teachers and students had reached, the reasons for it and what they could try next. For while student performance had improved, his school needed to keep improving if the students were to reach and keep apace of the national average. The plateau he identified was not unique to his school. While low-decile schools are being given priority in the new professional development funded by the Ministry of Education, there appears to be less knowledge-building and sharing occurring. Such work needs national-level, deliberate and continuing support: but our policy environment is not one that strongly supports such ongoing connections.[24]

Countering poverty in secondary schools

In secondary schools, it is the introduction of NCEA (in 2002) that has made the most difference to the achievements of students from poorer homes.

NCEA Level 2 is an important stepping-stone to further education and employment. As the Ministry of Education warns, 'future educational and job prospects will be limited for those who leave school without NCEA Level 2'.[25] But NCEA achievement varies markedly in relation to the socio-economic area served by a school. Fifty-seven per cent of those who left decile 1–2 schools in 2011 succeeded in gaining NCEA Level 2 qualifications or equivalent. That rate of success was 15 percentage points below the 72 per cent of school-leavers from decile 5–6 schools and 32 percentage points below the 87 per cent of school-leavers from decile 9–10 schools.

However, NCEA removed some of the artificial constraints on the proportion of students who could leave school with a qualification. And this made a powerful difference in what teachers could provide in order to engage students with learning. Previously, the proportion of students who left school without a qualification had barely shifted since 1989, despite a lot of effort on the part of individual teachers. The NCEA framework opened up new opportunities. The framework is built upon curriculum-based 'standards', with each standard describing what a student needs to know, or what they must be able to achieve, in order to meet the standard. When a student meets a standard they gain credits towards national qualifications. Students are much more aware of what they are aiming for, and what it will take to get there. There is more alignment between what happens in classes and what students are assessed on, and more opportunity for school-based assessments. The qualification, being made up of credits from different standards, allows more customisation to individual students, their strengths and interests.

Over time, success rates with NCEA have improved markedly, particularly in low-decile schools. These schools have been working hard. They pay more attention now to individual students' accumulation of credits to ensure they are on track to get a qualification. The Starpath Project (research aimed at addressing educational inequality in New Zealand) has shown low-decile schools that they need to ensure that individual students wanting to access university have credits in the standards that universities set as their criteria for entrance.[26]

Low-decile schools also seek to offer their students courses that will attract attendance and effort because they are relevant. For example, Northland College, a small decile 1 school in a rural area, increased its

NCEA Level 1 success rate (of Year 11 students participating in NCEA) from 11 per cent in 2004 to 65 per cent in 2009, and to 78 per cent in 2011 (higher than the 58 per cent success rate for decile 1 Year 11 students participating in NCEA nationally). The school set goals for each student, and teachers undertook concerted professional development so they could make the most of the new qualifications framework. In addition, the school focused on improving literacy and numeracy in Years 9 and 10, as a foundation. Shrewdly, it also offered 'trades academies', courses that would appeal to students who might otherwise have found school of little purpose, and made them conditional on students gaining NCEA Level 1.[27]

NCEA allows students to tackle standards when they are ready, rather than having to do them at a given school level or age. This is another policy change that has helped low-decile schools improve their students' educational achievement. Staying on till Year 13 enabled another 12 per cent of students in decile 1–3 schools to gain NCEA Level 2 in 2011.[28] It also meant a slight closing of the gap with higher decile schools. Looking at students gaining NCEA Level 2 in Year 12 (the year most students tackle it) decile 1–3 school students have success rates 16 percentage points below their decile 4–7 peers, and 28 percentage points below their decile 8–10 peers. If those who gain NCEA Level 2 in Year 13 are included, the gaps closed somewhat to 12 percentage points and 21 percentage points respectively.

But while individual low-decile secondary schools get priority for some Ministry of Education support, the much-needed systematic support, along with knowledge-building and knowledge-sharing, generally remains lacking.

Gaps in education policy

Education policy in New Zealand recognises that schools serving low-income communities need more government resourcing and support. Over the past decade, quite a few of these schools have been able to improve the learning and achievement of many of their students. Their ability to do so has been dependent on their access to well-founded professional development, new frameworks for qualifications, more useful assessments, and research-based knowledge. It has also depended on being able both to attract and retain teachers with expertise. To make progress, these schools have needed the commitment of teachers and principals, *and* good educational infrastructure and policy: all of this is beyond the control of any school on its own. But the infrastructure we have been able to offer our schools has not been systematic. Not all low-decile schools receive the support they need, nor do they have all the expertise they need within the school. Low-decile schools continue to be over-represented among schools that face the greatest challenges with issues of school leadership and governance.

New Zealand's education policy struggles with the consequences of schools being left to stand alone and compete, presenting choices for parents that can be constrained by their place on the income ladder. This policy approach makes it harder for schools to work together, to share and build useful knowledge, and offer new programmes. It also makes it difficult to provide children from poor homes with schools that have an even social mix. This could be tackled by ensuring that social housing is available in more areas. It could also be tackled within education by making access to schools a matter of ballot rather than location.

Balloting to access schools is an unlikely policy option. But increased social mixes in schools could be achieved by moving to a district-wide approach to defining enrolment zones, rather than continuing to use enrolment zones that schools largely defined for themselves in the 1990s. This approach would improve the achievement of students from poor homes, without diminishing the achievement of students from middle-income homes. Other options for education policy to increase social mixes could include: setting the levels of parent donations; reserving 20 per cent of all school places for students from poor homes; and funding low-decile schools to provide innovative programmes that will also attract students from middle- and high-income families (in what is known as the 'magnet' school approach).

New Zealand's high rate of income inequality contributes to the isolation of students from poor homes, and the depth of the challenge for low-decile schools. It is not a challenge they should face by themselves alone, school by school. Education has made some progress recently in closing the gaps between students from poor homes and others. But we will need, at the least, a much better infrastructure for schools, more even social mixes at schools, and new ways for schools to work together if we are to keep making some gains.

So, what school did *you* go to?

Asher Emanuel *is studying law and English literature at Victoria University. He attended Auckland's Saint Kentigern College on a scholarship, and graduated with the NZQA Premier and Top Scholar awards.*

The events and chances of early life – especially the school years – have consequences so significant that they rapidly winnow out the so-called winners from the losers. Even at my early stage of life, I see the effects of this inequality.

There are many young people far more personally qualified to discuss this issue than I. While all too many of my peers suffered the violence of poverty and inequality, my parents always had work and could pay their bills. So the very fact that my words appear here, and not those of a peer less privileged, is telling enough. But even if I cannot speak personally about the harm done by inequality, I can comment on the damage it does to us all – even among the relatively young.

It strikes me that by adulthood most people have settled into their rung on the economic ladder, subject perhaps to small movements as luck would have it, but rarely experiencing a significant change of station. Time has sorted those who will have from those who will not have.

It is all too easy to rationalise this state of affairs, to fall back on the comfortable narratives of merit and exceptionalism, the familiar adjectives: hard-working, talented, deserving. And for a long time I believed that New Zealand had achieved a functioning meritocracy: that we rise and fall on the qualities of our character.

But to believe that skill and effort are the primary factors in individual success requires that we also believe that entire sections of our community are less talented, less hard-working and less deserving of success than their peers. That is a leap I cannot make. To me meritocracy seems increasingly a myth, one built upon a wilful blindness about the forces that actually do more to form our economic destinies. It feels like a rationalisation, one that allows the prosperous to abrogate any sense of duty to those less fortunate.

With this in mind, when I look at my own story, I do not see a triumph of will and perseverance. I see a life in which the caprice of luck is as much the protagonist as I am. Each of the factors that have led me to this point – relative wealth, education, incidental opportunities and connections – is due more to good fortune than my own actions. Since I did not work for these things, my claim to deserve or be worthy of them is less than just. It is even less just if this state of affairs is translated into a substantially unequal distribution of wealth.

As time draws me and my generation closer to that divergence of prosperity, I see first-hand the processes of luck and caprice working everywhere. These processes determine not just who has the greatest real opportunities – the best education, in particular – but also who bears the greatest *markers* of success. These latter are too often used as proxies for actual assessments of a person's merit, substitutes for that more difficult enquiry.

Promised as the great equaliser, our education system is instead for many the beginning of these slow processes of divergence. Alongside our public schools are private schools for which many parents are willing to spend over $15,000 a year, half the national median income for a single person, which suggests they see some added advantage in private education.

I doubt that these schools provide a better education, if education, in the truest sense of the word, means a fuller understanding of life, one that enables young people to make their own independent way in the world. Often, it is simply in drilling their students to pass exams that these schools excel. (I should know: I went to one.) But they nonetheless possess vast resources that their public counterparts do not. Among these are the obvious: the extracurricular activities, the additional tutoring for scholarship candidates and, in many cases, the scholarships to help graduates finance their tertiary education. These alone assist their students to achieve certain goals, such as university entrance, and they clearly belie the claim that we all have equal opportunities from the beginning of our lives.

But even beyond that, the resource that does not appear explicitly in prospectuses or billboard advertisements is the mark of class and wealth that such schools give their students. Whenever I fill out a form applying for an internship or the like, I am asked which school I attended, alongside and sometimes as a replacement for information about my performance at school. Questions like these show a deference to superficial marks of class that masquerade as, instead of actually being, a measure of capacity or skill.

These disparities are not limited to private schools: a number of public schools have cultivated the same markers of class. This creates a further, geographical, divergence. When houses cost more because they are in the 'right' zone for a certain school, moving into that zone becomes prohibitively expensive for many. House prices are then a barrier akin to private fees: those not born into the right zone miss out.

So from the age of five, and for thirteen-odd years hence, we are classified and sorted not simply as we might hope by our individual effort and achievement, but by the name of the school that we attend.

Of course that individual effort is a factor: but even that is subject to social forces. To take just one example, children in low-income families suffer disproportionately from preventable diseases, largely as a result of poor quality housing. Their ill-health in turn limits their attendance and their ability to concentrate in class, thus reinforcing the existing inequalities between them and their more fortunate peers.

And so my friends and I have been, and will continue to be, slowly sorted, not by dint of our innate merits, but by factors that ought to be irrelevant: the community in which we were born, the wealth of our parents, the housing and schools in our neighbourhood. In this way are my peers slowly winnowed away from the pack and left behind.

This system is in large part a legacy of our parents' generation, who, it seems to me, adopted the language of meritocracy as a means by which to numb the pain of large inequalities. But my generation is beginning to see the damage it has done, and to recognise how easily any one of us might have been left behind. I do not think we will repeat the same mistakes.

10 Inequality and Māori

Evan Te Ahu Poata-Smith

Inequality between Māori and non-Māori has been an enduring feature of New Zealand society. But in recent decades, it has coincided with another unwelcome development: the growth of income gaps within Māori communities.

These inequalities stem from the general social and economic position of Māori in New Zealand society, but also from the policies pursued by both Labour and National governments from 1984–99 and largely retained, although modified and softened, by Labour-led governments from 1999–2008. Despite the overwhelming evidence that these policies substantially increased inequality, as detailed in this chapter, they have been revived and extended by National-led governments since 2008.

This raises controversial questions about the current direction of Māori economic and social development. Who is currently benefiting, and who is not? To what extent do current ideas about Māori development empower some groups of Māori, while disenfranchising or marginalising others?

The end of the golden weather

The position of Māori in New Zealand society springs first of all from two distinct, although interlocking, processes: the alienation of land and resources through European colonisation; and the later Māori labour migration, required to provide a workforce for an emerging capitalist society.[1]

Increasingly dispossessed of their economic base over the century that followed the signing of the Treaty of Waitangi, Māori were forced to rely increasingly on wage labour to meet their basic needs. As the New Zealand economy expanded after the Second World War, industry became centralised in the larger cities, especially the greater region of Auckland. Rural unemployment was high, and Māori migrated in large numbers to the urban centres. The Māori population, meantime, was growing fast – much faster than the economic base (land and resources) remaining in Māori ownership could sustain. An increasing Māori population and its redistribution to urban areas, where Māori were likely to encounter limited employment opportunities, poor housing and overcrowding, were matters for discussion even by conservative academics concerned about the threat to New Zealand's social cohesion.[2]

The vast majority of Māori families were incorporated into the working class and into the lower levels of segmented labour markets; they were concentrated in blue-collar occupations such as in the freezing works, on the waterside, in construction and transport, and as coalminers and railway workers. These occupations often had long hours, low pay, and difficult and unpleasant working conditions. The limited opportunities for economic advancement were reinforced by discrimination in hiring and promotion practices. In his research in the 1950s, James Ritchie confirmed what many Māori already knew: that such discrimination was 'endemic in the social context of both town and country'.[3] In the 1960s, a visiting American Fulbright scholar, David Ausubel, highlighted the emergence of 'an urban Māori proletariat' as well as the existence of widespread anti-Māori prejudice and flagrant forms of discrimination.[4]

The relative economic prosperity of the post-Second World War period may have encouraged an impression of social tranquillity and harmony, but the reality was that the prosperity generated by the long boom did not accrue to everyone equally.[5] Indeed, the assimilative ideology of 'one nation, one people' that dominated official state policy with respect to Māori, and the prevailing view at the time that New Zealand possessed the most harmonious 'race relations' in the world, concealed the harsh social and economic reality for the majority of Māori migrants to urban areas. Māori found themselves crammed into inadequate housing and concentrated in specific neighbourhoods and in particular regions of cities. In this context, economist Bill Sutch warned of the development of 'a miniature Harlem' in Auckland and to a lesser extent in Wellington.[6]

In 1961, J.K. Hunn's landmark report on the Department of Māori Affairs[7] demonstrated the systemic failure of the assimilation policies that had governed 'indigenous affairs' in New Zealand since the nineteenth century.[8] The Hunn Report found that even in a time of economic expansion and growing labour shortages, Māori did not necessarily share the benefits: 'It is a paradox that, while New Zealand's industrial development is handicapped by a shortage of manpower, there are pockets of under-employment among able-bodied Maoris and the unemployment rate for Maoris is higher than for Europeans.'[9]

During the 'long boom' (as this period of prosperity was known), Māori social and economic inequalities were viewed largely as a technical and temporary problem that would be resolved once Māori families were fully integrated into the labour force of an expanding capitalist economy. After all, with economic growth occurring in advanced capitalist countries at such a scale that output would double every sixteen years, each generation could expect to be roughly twice as well-off as its parents and four times as well-off as its grandparents.[10]

But the belief that the benefits of a booming economy would trickle down to Māori families – thus eliminating the inequalities that existed between Māori and Pākehā – was shattered as the New Zealand economy entered a prolonged period of economic and political crises by the early 1970s. A country that prided itself on good 'race relations' and an absence of class inequality was confronted by unavoidable evidence of Māori economic, cultural and social deprivation. A formidable Māori protest movement arose as part of a generalised upsurge in struggle on a global scale. This movement was characterised by unprecedented levels of class struggle, and the emergence of a wide range of social movements that challenged the complacency of mid-twentieth century New Zealand.[11]

The dramatic upsurge in Māori protest and discontent, intensified by the prolonged economic stagnation and rising unemployment from 1974 onwards, forced successive governments to respond to the evidence that many Māori occupied a relatively impoverished and peripheral place in New Zealand society. Numerous studies confirmed that Māori continued to experience disproportionately poor educational outcomes, high levels of unemployment, low income levels, ill-health and hence lower life expectancy, higher rates of imprisonment, low rates of home ownership and high rates of state dependency.[12] The existence of such dramatic inequalities, between Māori and Pākehā New Zealanders in particular, combined with the systemic failure of the state to ameliorate or transcend these inequalities, made Māori challenges to the legitimacy of the state all the more potent and forceful.

The state also faced an economic crisis that severely limited its ability to defuse this growing crisis of political legitimacy. Declining profitability, inadequate levels of investment, minimal productivity growth, economic stagnation, the historically low terms of trade, and high levels of public and private debt were classic symptoms of an economic crisis.[13] This prolonged crisis profoundly shaped the basic direction and orientation of New Zealand politics from 1974.

Enduring inequalities

If Māori entered the 1980s far behind non-Māori communities in terms of income, wealth and access to basic services, they were to fall even further behind in following decades. This was in large part because successive governments since 1984 implemented a neoliberal political agenda. Indeed, the period 1984–99 represents a major turning point in New Zealand politics, as the Fourth Labour Government, from 1984–90, embarked on a systematic programme of restructuring, an approach continued under National governments from 1990–99.

This restructuring brought increasing hardship and poverty for many New Zealanders. People across the country faced falling real incomes, inter-generational unemployment, cuts to benefit levels, and deteriorating employment conditions and job security.[14] The restructuring had a disproportionate and sustained impact on working-class Māori families. Ranking New Zealand households[15] from the poorest 20 per cent (quintile 1) to the richest 20 per cent (quintile 5) consistently shows households with a Māori adult as disproportionately represented amongst those in the first three quintiles, and significantly under-represented amongst those on high incomes. This is significant because, from the collapse of the long boom in 1974, and up to the year 2001, the real incomes of the bottom 60 per cent of New Zealanders declined, while the wealthiest 20 per cent of the population increased their incomes substantially.[16] As a result, the growing levels of income inequality during the 1980s and 1990s adversely affected Māori more than Pākehā.

The removal of industry subsidies and import tariffs also hit hardest those blue-collar occupational industries in which Māori and Pacific peoples were concentrated. These industries shed labour in order to compete more profitably on the world market. This trend was compounded by the restructuring of the New Zealand economy since the mid-1970s, which had seen the importance of the financial (or banking) sector of the economy grow dramatically relative to the industrial and commercial sectors. This had dramatic implications for the employment prospects of working-class Māori, given the relatively youthful nature of the Māori labour force together with its lower educational attainment and its higher concentration in blue-collar industries and occupations.

Māori unemployment also increased dramatically. From 1988, the Māori unemployment rate rose sharply, from 13.5 per cent in March 1988 to a high of 27.3 per cent by March 1992. By 1998, a report commissioned by Te Puni Kōkiri noted that, despite improvements for Māori in some areas, overall the gaps had either remained the same or widened.[17]

Closing the gaps?
Between 1999 and 2008, Labour-led coalition governments made a fundamental commitment to reducing the gaps between rich and poor,

and to increasing social cohesion. In his budget speech in 2000, the Minister of Finance, Michael Cullen, announced a series of initiatives to close the 'divisive and debilitating gaps that have opened up throughout New Zealand Society'.[18] The government, Cullen argued, was committed to closing the 'most urgent and visible gaps' that existed between Māori and Pacific peoples and other New Zealanders.[19] However, initiatives designed specifically for Māori generated ongoing political controversy, amidst claims that Māori were receiving privileged treatment through special access to resources and a range of targeted programmes.[20] The political backlash was such that the 'closing the gaps' catch-phrase was abandoned only a year into the Labour–Alliance coalition's term. The policies initially put in place around the 'closing the gaps' strategy were subsequently realigned under the 'reducing inequalities' policy framework that encompassed a range of social and economic initiatives.[21]

Then, in the 2004 budget, the Labour-led government unveiled Working for Families, a package ostensibly designed to help low-income families by providing financial support and overcoming barriers to finding paid work. This flagship welfare initiative represented a significant concession after years in which government systematically eroded workers' rights, dismantled support for low-income families, and neglected child and family poverty. But it is important to recognise that these small but significant concessions were shaped by the political and economic character of the period. From 1984–99, the costs of the welfare state were increasingly incompatible with the need to restore levels of profitability in the economy, which required curbing state expenditure and the costs associated with state intervention in the market place. In contrast, the Fifth Labour Government and its coalition partners were aided by the cyclical economic upswing from 1999–2007, which reduced pressure on the government to continue the programme of neoliberal restructuring.[22]

In the context of this cyclical economic recovery, income inequality declined slightly in the period 2001–7, reflecting a reduction in unemployment and the impact of Working for Families.[23] Nevertheless, many New Zealand families (including a disproportionate number of Māori families) were not in a position to take advantage of these policy concessions. Because the reforms only targeted those who were actively participating in the labour market, they largely excluded families reliant on income support, such as those whose primary focus was caring for children, the sick or the elderly, or those who were themselves living with illnesses and disabilities. Statistics from the Ministry of Social Development for April 2006 revealed that 93,423 Māori children and 137,857 non-Māori children were excluded from the benefits of the Working for Families initiative on that basis. This represented 45.9 per cent of all Māori children, 29.6 per cent of Pacific children and 12.3 per cent of Pākehā children.[24]

In addition, beneficiaries gained very little from Working for Families. For many, the increases in family support in 2005 were largely offset by losses in core benefits and special benefits that saved the government around $237 million.[25] Since poverty has become entrenched amongst sole-parent and benefit-dependent Māori and Pacific families, and because a disproportionate number of the poorest children are Māori, this policy did little to ameliorate some long-established inequalities.

Not surprisingly then, the Ministry of Social Development's *Social Report 2006* showed that Māori had fallen further behind Pākehā on a range of key measures, despite the 'closing the gaps' policies.[26] While the report showed that Māori had improved in absolute terms on all measures for which data were available, the relative gaps between Māori and Pākehā had widened in many cases. The only measure going back to 1986 that showed a very marginal closing of the gap was unemployment; according to the report, Māori unemployment was 3.3 times the Pākehā rate, compared to 3.4 times the rate in 1986.

Despite a number of important concessions and an apparent softening of the hardline approach to economic management, overall economic policy was still driven by a tight monetary policy aimed at maintaining 0–3 per cent inflation, and a 'medium-term' objective to maintain substantial budget surpluses. Because the Labour-led governments of 1999–2008 remained firmly entrenched in a vision of the liberating power of the market place and globalisation, their concessions never fully compensated for the repressive anti-working-class policies of the post-1984 governments.

Although the cyclical recovery ended, and was replaced by the most severe global financial crisis and economic slowdown since the Great Depression, National-led governments from 2008 have remained fixated on fiscal austerity, regardless of the social cost. The twin objectives of returning to budget surpluses by 2014–15, and bringing government debt down to 20 per cent of GDP by 2020,[27] are being funded by 'restraining the growth in core Crown expenses'. As Finance Minister Bill English has noted: 'The Government's return to surplus will require continuing control of the long-term drivers of costs in areas such as welfare, health, education and law and order.'[28] This builds on the fiscal austerity measures in Budget 2011, including cuts to KiwiSaver, Working for Families, student loans and the core public service.[29]

This commitment to continued neoliberal policy reform and fiscal austerity will exacerbate the impact of the global recession and entrench levels of inequality in New Zealand society. It is already widely acknowledged that these policies, both internationally and in New Zealand, have substantially increased inequality.[30] In 2010–11, inequality increased significantly, as incomes rose in the top third of the population and fell for everyone else.[31] Once again, Māori will be disproportionately affected: in fact, Māori unemployment rates have risen significantly. The unemployment rate for Māori was 13.3 per cent in the year to March 2012 – up from 7.9 per cent just five years earlier.[32] On a different measure, 17.6 per cent of Māori males and 27.5 per cent of Māori females were classified as not being in employment, education or training, compared with 11.5 per cent of all males and 14.6 per cent of all females in this age group.[33]

Emerging inequalities

One of the features of recent decades has been the growth of inequality and social polarisation within Māori communities. While Māori have been disproportionately represented in the bottom 60 per cent of households, household economic surveys from 1982 to 1996 show that Māori have also been consistently represented in the top 40 per cent.[34] The growing social inequalities in New Zealand society have not affected all Māori equally: a minority have directly benefited from the fiscal agenda that was implemented from 1984 onwards.

The surveys reveal that households with Māori adults were more evenly spread across income groups in the 1980s than in later years.[35] From the late 1980s to 1994, the proportion of households with Māori adults in the lowest fifth rose to 37 per cent (58,500 households). At the other end of the distribution, the proportion of households with a Māori adult in the top fifth dropped from 13 per cent in 1988 to 8 per cent in 1992, then rose to a high of 16 per cent in 1996, returning to 13 per cent in 1998.[36] The fact that a small proportion of Māori households is located in the top fifth of all households is significant. While the vast majority of households have lost disposable income over time, the households in the top fifth have improved their absolute and relative position significantly.[37]

Wealth is yet more unevenly distributed than income.[38] The 2003–4 Survey of Family, Income and Employment shows a very skewed distribution of wealth, measured as 'net worth': those in the top tenth hold 50 per cent of the total wealth.[39] Table 10.1 shows the wealth distribution between major ethnic groups. In a perfectly symmetrical distribution, the mean – the average wealth per person – would be the same as the

Table 10.1 Wealth distribution between major ethnic groups

	Population %	Total Net Worth %	Mean $	Median $	Mean/Median Ratio
European	83	92.7	178,400	86,900	2.1
Māori	10.4	4.3	65,800	18,000	3.6
Pacific peoples	4.9	1.3	41,400	6,700	6.2
Asian	6.4	3.8	95,600	21,000	4.6
Other	1.9	1.2	100,200	19,000	5.3

Note: The classification of ethnic groups is based on total responses to the question on ethnicity in the Survey of Family, Income and Employment (SoFIE) conducted in 2003/04; this is the reason the figures exceed 100 per cent.

Source: Cheung, *Wealth Disparities in New Zealand*, 2007, p.10.

median, measured as the amount of wealth held by the middle person in the distribution. When the mean is much greater than the median, it shows there are abnormally large numbers of wealthy people 'pulling up' the mean, and that wealth is unequally distributed. As the table clearly indicates, the distribution of wealth for Europeans is significantly unequal (the mean is twice the median) while the distribution for Māori is even more unequal.

In short, both income and wealth have accrued unevenly among Māori. This raises a central question: how should we evaluate 'Māori development'? It also raises a further question: who is currently benefiting and who is not? This process has not taken place on a level playing field. In recent years, the field has been sharply tilted in favour of those representing tribal corporations and Māori business interests. They have been able to exert a disproportionate influence over the formation of the Treaty of Waitangi settlement framework – and the scope of Māori development. Since this group has interests in the profitability of tribal commercial ventures or private Māori-owned businesses (or both), its members benefit from a general policy package that helps them achieve those profits: low rates of corporate tax, minimal state intervention in the market place, reductions in compliance costs and so forth.

This has significant implications for understanding Māori development. Those Māori representing tribal corporations and commercial interests benefited from the significant reduction in corporate tax rates. Yet these tax cuts were funded through large cuts in welfare expenditure and the commercialisation of health, housing and education – all of which have impacted severely on Māori households located in the bottom 60 per cent of income earners (whose real income declined significantly through much of the restructuring period). So, while those Māori representing tribal corporations and commercial interests have directly benefited from the economic policies of successive governments, the vast majority of Māori families have borne the brunt of the economic restructuring.

Indeed, one of the critical developments in New Zealand politics since 1984 has been the way the state has relied on representatives of iwi to sell the idea of Māori capitalist development. Māori businesses and commercial interests have been cultivated by successive governments in an attempt to set the parameters of an acceptable strategy for Māori development, while marginalising more far-reaching alternatives. Even though this locks Māori self-determination into a free-market, capitalist economic framework, the strategy has been effective because it appeals to those Māori business interests whose profitability has been enhanced by the restructurings of the 1980s and 1990s.

During this period representatives of commercially restructured iwi authorities were able to position themselves as the principal Māori authorities, and thus negotiate the Treaty of Waitangi settlement framework and the agenda for Māori economic development.[40] In the absence of alternative representative structures, and with the move to the direct negotiation of Treaty claims in the 1990s, iwi authorities were left in a privileged position to negotiate directly with the government over particular claims, and to link purely commercial deals to the settlement of those claims under the Treaty of Waitangi.

Despite this, Māori development has always been contested. The adoption of neoliberal strategies for managing iwi assets and resources has never been particularly popular amongst Māori communities at the flax roots. In fact there have been profound levels of discontent, for instance, with the use of corporate models for the management and distribution of Treaty settlement assets. There are concerns about the commercialisation of Māori culture, the insecurity of tribal assets for future generations, and governance and internal tribal democracy.[41]

In the last decade, debates about Māori economic and social development have occurred amidst a political backlash against programmes targeting Māori communities and the Treaty of Waitangi settlement process. Despite unequivocal evidence that growing levels of inequality have more adversely affected Māori than Pākehā, some sections of the public believe that Māori are, in fact, a privileged minority, benefiting from special access to resources and targeted initiatives. Since 2004 some prominent politicians have generated popularist support for the idea that indigenous claims relating to partnership and sovereignty are undermining harmonious 'race relations'. They have called for a comprehensive review of programmes that target Māori, and an examination of legislative references to the principles of the Treaty of Waitangi, both of which are said to undermine the principle of 'one law for all'.[42]

It is important to make a number of points. First, iwi leaders have long been the target of racist double standards and cultural marginalisation. In many situations, this has intensified in the context of the Treaty settlement process, which some have pejoratively referred to as the indigenous 'grievance industry'. This trivialises Māori experiences in a way that seeks to place the onus for Māori material deprivation on iwi, hapū and urban Māori communities. In this narrative, the violent history of colonisation, the systematic dispossession of Māori land and resources, racism, and the assumption of European cultural supremacy miraculously disappear. Yet all have been powerful forces in shaping the lives of many Māori.

Secondly, while it is true that the Māori commercial asset base grew significantly from the mid-1980s,[43] the wealth of iwi corporates is often overstated. In reality, iwi have limited capacity to deal with significant intergenerational inequality. Even if all iwi beneficiaries were the recipients of an equal share of tribal wealth, the impact on income inequality as a whole would be marginal. The scale of inequality in New Zealand is such that it would take a substantial redistribution of society's resources (most of which are tied up in private ownership) to make a difference. For this is a country in which the top 10 per cent of the population owns over half (51.8 per cent) of total net worth, and the bottom 50 per cent collectively owns a mere 5.2 per cent: changing this distribution would require a transformation of society itself.

Finally, 'scapegoating' has a long history in New Zealand politics. It diverts attention from the impact of the 1980s and 1990s restructuring, which widened and entrenched inequality while directly benefiting a small proportion of the population; and it diverts attention from the failures of recent Labour-led governments to reverse systematically the dramatic decline in living standards that most New Zealand families experienced during the 1990s. It also diverts attention from the impact of the current National-led government's renewed enthusiasm for financial austerity. An examination of the real roots of privilege, wealth and power has, for the moment, been deflected. Indeed, the people who stand to benefit from the extension of current policies make up the small minority of privileged New Zealanders who have accrued considerable wealth under a pro-market, pro-business agenda fuelled principally by cuts to state spending on education, health and social welfare.

Conclusion

References to the Treaty of Waitangi in legislation, and the state's recognition of historical grievances, both represent significant concessions after years of concerted struggle by Māori to combat the inequalities and racism that have underpinned New Zealand society. But these concessions have not compensated for policies that, since 1984, have dramatically widened social and economic inequalities.

Many Māori have been, and continue to be, critical of the Treaty of Waitangi settlement process and of the iwi governance structures created by that process. There is also much criticism of the lack of any significant trickle-down to tribal beneficiaries and Māori communities more generally. This is not to suggest that tribal corporate executives and Māori entrepreneurs are not in any sense committed to the improvement of the economic and social position of Māori. But their strategies for tribal development have so far been confined to the commercial framework of market capitalism.

The uncritical adoption of pro-market policies and corporate models for managing Treaty settlements only tends to institutionalise the inequalities of wealth and political power that exist within Māori communities and between Māori and non-Māori. For the vast majority of Māori families, any attempt to achieve self-determination within a system based on inequality and class exploitation is ultimately contradictory. Real change will require us to challenge the logic of the market, rather than extend its influence.

Back to the Māori future?

Anake Goodall was formerly the chief executive officer of Te Rūnanga o Ngāi Tahu and a key negotiator for the Ngāi Tahu Treaty Settlement in the 1990s. He now works as a social entrepreneur and independent director.

At the creation

It is interesting to speculate on the vision that the Māori leadership of the nineteenth century had in mind as they signed the Treaty of Waitangi. What did they envisage a co-created Aotearoa/New Zealand (and their role in that nation-building exercise) would look like?

A genuine blending of the Māori worldview, with its dynamic, community-grounded customs and values held in a frame of reciprocal responsibility to each other and the natural world, and the equally dynamic western model, with its technologies and capital market economy and systems of management, would have been a heady mix indeed.

We do enjoy, fortunately, a unique national approach to life, one that shapes our view of both each other and the external world. But the merger has been a largely one-sided affair, with the indigenous instinct being overwhelmed by the globally dominant western frame. It has taken a long time for Māori to tack their way back into the contemporary field, and the relatively impressive progress of late is still tentative and fragile.

Simultaneous with this Māori return to the mainstream, the foundations of the western development model are being shaken, and hard. From massive instability in financial markets through widespread civil protest across the globe to the ever-lengthening shadow of climate change, the underlying assumptions of the global orthodoxy are being called into question.

The Māori collectives now arriving back on the scene are playing by rules inherited by others, the received wisdom of the majority. While they do have distinctive indigenous icons, it often seems their traditional values – their true North Star – are unnecessarily left at the boardroom door as the price of entry.

But this time of great change could be a chance to revisit the co-creation opportunity that was passed up in the mid-1800s. And the confluence of burgeoning Māori capacity, international market turmoil, and the pressing need to identify new ways forward means, this time around, the emerging Māori institutions might even show us the way.

A gradual return to form

During the past three decades Māori collectives – in the form of land trusts, re-emergent iwi authorities and new pan-Māori ownership structures – have begun to reassert themselves.

They are uniquely embedded in their communities, combining in single entities the interests of shareholders and stakeholders, citizens and investors and social agents, and – most fundamentally – close family members. They are microcosms of wider society, having to represent, and then reconcile, the demands of these multiple interests. And these tensions are being navigated in a context of significant inter-generational poverty. But from modest beginnings, these entities are gently rousing the sleeping capital in their midst. Building on their modest legacy assets and more recent Treaty settlements, they are now collectively responsible for marshalling some $40 billion of financial capital.

These assets are, however, often being deployed in an unthinking 'me too' fashion, mimicking the activities, values and measures of success of the western, single-dimension, profit-maximising model. Where does the welfare of Tangaroa feature in the decisions by pan-Māori fishing entities to undertake bottom-trawling techniques that destroy seabed ecosystems? How are the core human values of whanaungatanga and manaakitanga reflected in the poor working conditions of the foreign crews utilised by these same companies?

What do we make of tribal authorities selling land assets returned to them in the Treaty settlement process as token recognition of ancestral lands lost last century? Can we see evidence of these groups using their increased financial capacity to, over time, repatriate historic pā sites, or increase their quota holdings in culturally important fish species, or reclaim other icons of their proud histories?

What are we to make of the inevitable defence that each decision not to exercise these newly available options 'increases the bottom line' and 'ensures maximisation of shareholder return'?

We might well ask whose frame of reference and whose values are being used in this family of emerging 'me too' organisations. We might also wonder if these single-focus, profit-maximising outcomes are consistent with the vision held by the Māori signatories to the Treaty, or the tribal leadership's vision across the long intervening generations.

The seduction of pragmatism

Of course, we must not assume simple answers to these complex questions. After six or more generations of dispossession, not only from one's assets but also from the experience of managing them, it takes time to re-establish institutions, and to build the human capital required to run them. And it takes time to rebuild reputation and trust, with external parties and with internal stakeholders alike.

Neither can we take away from some very creditable early results. Early mover Ngāi Tahu has already distributed more to its constituents than it received in its 1998 settlement. Meanwhile, net funds under management have increased nearly threefold to approximately $600 million in 2012. As well as funding environmental restoration, education, cultural revitalisation, economic development and community infrastructure programmes, the iwi has established subsidised savings accounts to bolster tertiary education, home ownership and retirement income for its members. These are potentially game-changing interventions in communities of considerable need, and should be celebrated. And perhaps it is fair enough, and only rational, that these newly energised entities should start by emulating the models of others with which they are now familiar.

In other words, for the Māori collectives reclaiming their seat at decision-making tables across the country, hard-headed pragmatism has served their communities well in recent times. Their people have survived, albeit across a wide spectrum of 'well-being'. Wearing the clothes of the majority, they have increasingly found their way in the new world. They are reconnecting with their own attenuated membership, regaining their voice in regional and national affairs, and quietly reshaping their worlds in their own image.

Adopting the outsiders' recipe has worked, at least as measured by the widely accepted standards of capital accumulation and financial returns. And we are seeing a steadily increasing flow of resources through these organisations back to their stakeholder communities. There is already much to celebrate; and it is still early days.

Yet these organisations carry out the same business activities as their non-Māori peers, measure themselves by the same standards, and in many ways are indistinguishable from them. They tend not to explore and celebrate, or exploit for advantage, the unique cultural differences they have at their disposal. Too often they treat such traditional instincts as value-destroying, and therefore to be denied.

And so the hard questions remain. What, if anything, is uniquely Māori about these institutions or the way they operate or make their investment and distribution decisions? What, if any, activities do these organisations deliberately avoid as a result of their unique ownership base?

If Māori merely mimic the dominant models of our time, won't they reap exactly the same unsatisfactory harvest for their communities? Won't they contribute to ever-lengthening dole queues, as labour continues to be displaced by financial capital, even though their own members are already over-represented in those same queues?

Won't the future of their descendants, ironically, become even more captive to the decisions of remote policy-makers, central bankers and international agreements negotiated without their input? Won't they be exacerbating climate change, the irreversible degradation of natural ecosystems and the destruction of the realms of their own departmental gods?

Won't they themselves be fuelling the very inequality that is considered by many to be directly responsible for a litany of Māori misery, including increased rates of imprisonment, obesity, teen pregnancy and suicide?

It seems strange, and more than a little disquieting, that Māori might want to use their recently reclaimed voice and scarce financial capital to purchase more of these negative outcomes, and especially when the adequacy and sustainability of the current economic orthodoxy is now in such serious doubt.

The confluence of old and new

Ideas have their purpose, in their time, and then we need to leave them behind. Ka pū te ruha, ka hao te rangatahi: the old net is cast aside, and the new net goes fishing.

We can understand how the values, philosophies and worldview of Māori were sidelined by the onslaught of nineteenth-century settler society. We can see why the new has been adopted and the old put to one side.

But the model that supplanted the traditional Māori worldview some two centuries ago is no longer looking sustainable, or a welcoming path to a collectively better future. The world no longer enjoys 'business as usual', and may never do so again. Increasing climate variability now appears to be an indisputable fact. We have unprecedented disruption in global financial markets. We are beginning to hit natural resource constraints, whether in the form of Peak Oil, Peak Water or a burgeoning world population that is already straining global food systems. We are also seeing civic unrest across the globe from Occupy Wall Street to Idle No More to protests over a range of civil society concerns and rising anger amongst the '99 per cent'.

Each of these world-changing forces threatens to further divide us into 'have' and 'have-not' camps. So where is the independent Māori institutional voice at this time? Where are the investments by Māori entities in alternative models, rooted in community, that might genuinely be described as being 'of the people, by the people, for the people'?

These questions are a reminder that a traditional worldview, where the health of the planet and its ecosystems comes before the rights of people to benefit individually from the commons, may have much to offer in these troubled times.

Perhaps there is again considerable value in a framework that recognises other living beings, including plants, animals and fish, as familial relations who share a reciprocal responsibility for each other's welfare. Perhaps a community model that assumes a collective responsibility for the welfare of all its members, and then conducts itself accordingly, might help restore trust and community cohesion, and return meaning to both aspects of 'civil society'.

Perhaps the traditional gift economy, with its wide, unconditional distribution of seasonal bounty and the associated, reciprocal obligations to pay it forward, might again have its place, in a world that needs to move from a paradigm of perpetual growth to one of sufficiency. Perhaps all those past insights could be grafted back onto the Māori institutional rootstock that is now taking hold and beginning to flourish.

This could only be done by Māori organisations themselves, as the keepers of both the old and new elements of this potential hybrid. These are of course the same organisations that have been contradictorily successful by copying increasingly unstable foreign models and by subordinating their own unique needs and values to the desire to be in the mainstream.

To achieve this step-change would ask a great deal of these new entities, many of which have only existed for a short decade or two. And it is much to ask of a new leadership, especially when it is only just beginning to enjoy contemporary 'success'. Genuine leadership requires considerable courage and remains a lonely business.

Back to the drawing board?
There has been precious little research into the alternative governance, management and distribution models that might provide a more natural 'cultural fit' for Māori and their inter-generational outlook.

To date, Māori organisations have not developed barter economies or 'crowd-sourced' funding vehicles, or established their own credit unions. Nor have they adopted localised food production and distribution systems. Nor have they created urban gardens, community-owned renewable electricity generation or communal housing developments in urban areas.

When instituted elsewhere, these initiatives succeed on a platform of local community connectedness, relationships, reciprocity and active generosity; all being strong characteristics of Māori society. So it is surprising that these ideas, which are being adopted and adapted everywhere from Pakistan to New York City, have been so little explored by Māori collectives, especially given their potential to reduce the burdens of poverty and inequality borne so disproportionately by their own constituents.

It is hard to put down the seduction of that which works, at least until it patently no longer does. It is always with great reluctance that we walk away from familiar current practice and habit. Such is the downside of the stickiness that is collective 'culture'. But just as earthquakes make possible new relationships and ways of doing things that could not be envisaged before the event, so too do broader societal challenges offer the opportunity – and pressing need – for new ways of doing things. The rules are changing, fast, and irrevocably. And the continued payoff for mimicry is doubtful at best.

We now have a unique opportunity to try, once again, to co-create aspects of our society. We could (re)turn the dial just a little more towards environmental consciousness and responsibility, a little more towards a collective, shared responsibility for each other.

To find this place, Māori institutions will have to lead the way. It is their deep cultural instincts that are being called upon to ground our communities. It is their investment capital that is still fluid enough to be shifted easily into new patterns and relationships. It is their ties that bind us most effectively, to the land and to each other. And it is their human capital that will disproportionately carry the burden of straddling the two worlds and weaving them together. We need the unique perspective, capacities and potential of these Māori institutions to help us all create the path forwards; and they in turn deserve our unreserved support as we explore these uncharted waters together.

The first European settlers arrived in the Otago harbour in the early 1800s. They were ill-equipped to survive the conditions, let alone feed themselves. Local Ngāi Tahu provided them with fish and other foods, and shelter, to get them through the first winter and give them time to get established in that new environment. Maybe it is time for our newly minted Māori institutions to reclaim that old discarded net and use it creatively to provide for all of us again; but with the benefits being enjoyed more equally this time round.

Part Four
Looking Ahead

11 Reducing Inequality
Paul Barber

The costs of income inequality are clear: they are measured in the diseased lungs of children, in the lives wasted behind bars, in the stress and despair of those battling mental illness, and even in the gated communities sheltering the rich. Those who work on the frontline, like Pam Waugh from the Salvation Army, see the human price of excessive inequality every day and have no doubt about the need to narrow the widening gaps.

> No matter how frugal these families are, parents face the tough choices of paying the rent – often eating up 70 per cent or more of the household budget – or feed the family for the week, pay school costs or the power … If food wins over rent, then they face eviction and homelessness, and this is what we are seeing daily.[1]

The destructive effect that inequality has on people's lives, as documented in the Vulnerability Report series from the New Zealand Council of Christian Social Services (NZCCSS), can be seen in testimonies such as this one, from Nettie Holm of Te Whanau Putahi:

> I live and work in a poor community in NZ. I am daily reminded how much the gap between the 'rich' and the 'poor' is growing. I see and hear of all the options available to my friends' families; in contrast, I sit with my friends in this community and recognise the huge disparity. For the latter, choice is severely limited! Choice is a luxury when it comes to healthy food, school trips/camps/electives, engagement in sports teams or music tuition. When there is simply not enough money these luxuries are beyond reach. What does this do to a parent who wants the best for their child?[2]

The economic cost of child poverty alone is up to $8 billion a year,[3] in increased health and justice spending, and wasted potential – without even considering the intangible damage to children's hearts and minds. Large income gaps counteract many of our best-intentioned policies to overcome poverty. Charity breakfasts for children from poor families, for example, must be one part of a much broader and coordinated response to the systemic poverty that blights New Zealand. Likewise our focus on teacher training, when much research shows that a major influence on children's educational achievement is their home environment. If we do not also address income inequality in our society, these problems will only get worse.

The social service agencies that make up the NZCCSS (where I work) act not out of ideology, but because we constantly see real suffering, and because we know that we must not walk past on the other side of the road while people suffer.[4] That is the literal meaning of the word 'compassion': to 'suffer with' others. We recognise ourselves in the struggles and misfortunes of others, and know that 'There but for the grace of God go I.'

The purpose of this chapter is to consider how we might look toward a more equal society, with better outcomes for the poor but better outcomes for people in middle and high income groups as well. As Karlo Mila states in Chapter 6, we have only got one deck – income inequality affects us all. Looking hard at what reducing inequality actually means, the challenges in obtaining a consensus, and acknowledging the complexity of the task, allows us to take the first steps towards a happier, healthier and more cohesive society.

A more equal society

What, then, is the alternative? It is a more equal society: one that reduces the income gap between the poorest and the wealthiest in our country; one in which all citizens are genuinely able to participate; one in which the rewards of work are fairly shared. It is a society that includes and enables, rather than excluding and disabling. Underpinning this vision is a set of strong values and principles – among them fairness, equity, justice, human rights, and enlightened self-interest. These values come from a rich variety of sources, including our faith traditions, human rights thinking, tikanga Māori and Pacific cultures. A deep belief in empathy and reciprocity is the moral basis of the world's faith traditions. The principle 'What you wish done to yourself, do to others' is found in various forms across the world faiths. It can be applied to our social and economic relations.[5] Māori traditions of reciprocity and sharing embody this same sense of deep interrelatedness, recognising our mutual interdependence.

The word 'fair' is so widely used and is so deep in our subconscious that its meaning is hard to pin down. Fair price, fair share, fair play, fair deal – these words are about how we 'regulate relations among people who are in conflict or rivalry or opposition in some way. They are about both the way we deal with one another and the results of those dealings.'[6] In other words, fairness is about processes *and* outcomes. As a society, New Zealand has a history of recognising that fair process needs also to deliver a fair outcome, and that this is not always guaranteed. The history of the Treaty relationship shows the challenges of practising fairness. Māori have struggled over many, many years to have their culture and their experience fairly reflected in the process of negotiating and settling Treaty claims. At the same time, some non-Māori have seen modern Treaty settlements and compensation as somehow unfairly giving advantage to Māori. What may be perceived as fair from within Pākehā culture may well be experienced as deeply unfair by Māori. Finding a deeper meaning for fairness therefore involves a sharing of responsibilities and benefits, pursuit of the common good and protection of human rights.[7]

People tend to share an understanding of the 'procedural' dimension of fairness, that it requires honesty, candour and openness. We think of it as a way of working between people with differing ideas of right and wrong without predetermining what the end outcome might be.[8] Central also to understanding fairness is the idea of reward for talent, contribution or effort. For example it seems 'only fair' that those who have worked hard or studied for a long time should be rewarded for their effort and ability. Thus there will be unequal outcomes for people who have differing skills, work ethics or levels of contribution, and this is in fact 'fair enough'.

In this way of thinking, unequal outcomes can be fair, if the process creating those outcomes is perceived as fair by those involved and by the wider society. But in some situations we end up questioning whether either the process or the outcome was fair. For example, the enormous pay packages of some New Zealand company executives are outcomes that appear to many to be in excess of a fair reward for skill or effort. Are the processes for setting executive pay then really 'fair'? Even if the process is broadly 'fair', the question remains, how much difference in outcome is acceptable and still 'fair enough'?

A 'fair' process also has to acknowledge that people start the 'process' from different positions. This affects our response to 'unfair' situations such as disability, discrimination or disadvantages of birth. It has come to be accepted that people with disabilities are entitled to additional assistance so that they may have a 'fair chance' to participate fully in society. In this case, the extra share of resources they receive is widely accepted as 'fair'. The challenge for our society is to determine what level of resources is 'fair' in order for those who are disadvantaged by circumstances out of their control to have a 'fair chance', and to decide how actually to distribute those resources.

Understanding fairness involves empathy, as a society or community, as well as individually. It involves the 'capacity to recognise and at least to some extent share another's situation, feelings or motives'.[9] Without this quality of empathy, the notion of fairness loses much of its moral meaning. If the notion of fairness is not combined with empathy, then it can quickly turn into a kind of callous indifference towards the impact of events and social action on others.

These ideas of fairness were powerfully articulated twenty years ago by New Zealand church leaders calling for a 'fairer society'.[10] They argued for:

- Fairness in our dealings with other people
- Fairness in the way responsibilities are shared
- Fairness in the distribution of income, wealth and power in our society
- Fairness in the social, economic and political structures we have created
- Fairness in the operation of those structures so that they enable all citizens to be active and productive participants in the life of society.

Reaffirming these principles in 2011, church leaders stated:

> We see the responsibility of the State as providing for a just sharing of society's wealth and resources for all its citizens. This includes: adequate income for everyone, fair taxation policies, access to good health care, affordable housing, and living sustainably. These are not privileges but part of the common heritage of humanity. Social welfare is part of a greater picture of social, economic and environmental priorities and decisions about spending. Caring for others makes us better people and strengthens our community.[11]

This moral commitment to caring for each other is one many can share, whether our values come from a religious tradition or not.

On a more pragmatic level, we are all deeply connected with one another, and the suffering and well-being of others affects us. As Part 3 indicates, high inequality is a cost to society. Enlightened self-interest, therefore, tells us that a fairer society is one in which everyone does better – not just those at the bottom. Research suggests that more equal societies have better outcomes across the board. Greater equality means more trust, stronger communities and greater social cohesion; stress, aggravation and disorder are lower for everyone. Everyone's health is better; all children get to learn in more focused, less disruptive classrooms; and general quality of life improves.[12] In other words, increasing the well-being of others enhances everyone's well-being.

A better society is also one in which government, businesses, communities and families all invest in the children of that society, who, as its most vulnerable members, suffer the most from rapidly rising inequality. In particular, Māori and Pacific peoples are hugely and disproportionately affected by inequality – yet it is the young, rapidly growing Māori and Pacific populations that are central to New Zealand's future. The choice to reduce the gaps between rich and poor is an investment in those young people now growing up – and an investment that will benefit the whole nation.

A fairer society will therefore be stronger for all, and geared towards a better future. In many ways, it would resemble the vision of the late Paul Callaghan, who wanted to make New Zealand 'a place where talent wants to live'. Because more equal societies are healthier, more cohesive and generally more pleasant places to live, he argued, they generate a virtuous cycle, attracting talented people whose talent in turn enhances those societies. 'If we care for our environment and create a just, equitable and creative society', Callaghan said, 'then we can attract the best in the world.'[13]

This is not, then, a nostalgic vision of a bygone 'golden age'. Many changes of the last thirty years (such as the resurgence of Māori culture) have made New Zealand a more diverse, open and confident society. But we need to advance those achievements while also unwinding the enormous damage that inequality has done.

What is a low level of inequality?

Although we are arguing for a *more* equal society, few want a totally equal one. Some people will always earn more or less than others depending on their ability, hard work and contribution to society. The question is then, what level of income inequality is reasonable and achieves the best outcomes for everyone in this country? What level of inequality will deliver the best combination of social and economic innovation and development, while reducing social harm? And what can New Zealand practically achieve?

There is no easy answer to those questions and we must be careful as we look for solutions. Acknowledging the contradictory social attitudes discussed in Chapter 1, the first step must be to establish the social and political will to address income inequality. With this momentum established, reducing New Zealand's income gaps to the levels of the developed world's most equal societies is a reasonable target. Holding inequality at this level represents a good balance in the modern, globalised world, allowing countries such as the Czech Republic, Austria and the Scandinavian nations to achieve excellent healthcare and well-being while also having dynamic and open economies.

In the 1980s, New Zealand had roughly the same level of inequality that those countries do now, and at that time our richest 10 per cent of households had average incomes around five times higher than the average of the poorest 10 per cent. Currently the top 10 per cent have on average *nine times* the income of the poorest 10 per cent, so it is a feasible goal to return to that five-to-one ratio from our current level.[14] Since New Zealand has achieved this level of equality in the past and other modern, progressive countries are achieving it today, it is not an unrealistic ambition.

Reducing inequality: the counter-arguments

The first argument, so often heard throughout the global recession, is: 'We need to get the economy right, then we can afford to look after our health and social well-being.' The best way to get people out of poverty and reduce the income gap, it is argued, is to grow the economy, generating more jobs and higher incomes.

Economic growth is of course important (at environmentally sustainable levels), incorporating more jobs, higher productivity and better incomes for lower paid workers. But it is not true that investment has to follow growth: in fact, the secret of some of the world's most successful societies is that they did it the other way around. For example, Norway began its social investment programmes – including paid maternity leave and gender quotas – long before the country became rich. As Norway's Director-General of the Ministry of Children, Equality and Social Inclusion, Arni Hole, put it: 'We started to really develop the welfare state in 1966 – that started long before we found oil in the North Sea.'[15]

Although public finances have suffered in the global financial crisis, New Zealand's government debt is one of the lowest in the developed world: it is not a reason to stop investing in social infrastructure. While it is true that New Zealand has high levels of private debt run up by households and businesses (and this is a significant concern), it is not in itself a reason to reduce government borrowing.[16] The sooner the government makes those investments in social infrastructure, the sooner the country and the population reap the rewards of the long-term growth they will generate.

Another common argument is that the rich should not be asked to contribute more, because they already pay more than their 'fair share' in taxes. The top 10 per cent paid 42 per cent of all income tax in 2010;[17] that is because they get a disproportionately large share (34 per cent) of all income. Given that progressive tax rates mean they should be paying a much greater percentage of their income than others (reflecting the much greater profit they have made from our common investment in roads, healthcare, education and other services), the 42 per cent figure probably reflects some tax avoidance among the wealthy. Data from Inland Revenue show that many top earners don't even pay the top tax rate and some avoid paying what they should.[18]

As Chapter 2 argued, if (currently untaxed) capital gains are accounted for, the rich may well pay a *smaller* share of their income in tax than those on low incomes do. They also pay less in tax than they would overseas. In New Zealand, high-income earners pay just 21.6 per cent of their total earnings in income tax. They would pay much more – between 26 and 34 per cent – in Australia, the United States, Canada, Ireland and the United Kingdom.[19] In New Zealand the top tax rate has been halved since the mid-1980s, while other forms of tax for the wealthy, such as estate duty and gift duty, have been abolished. On any terms (comparative or absolute) it is hard to see top-earners as hard-done-by in today's New Zealand. It is equally hard to argue that they should not contribute more, by way of tax, to the common good.

A related argument is that, if we reduce income gaps, the most talented people will leave New Zealand. As Paul Callaghan pointed out, more equal societies are also attractive to talent; this is also reflected in the Global Creativity Index.[20] History shows too that such migrations rarely, in fact, occur: Scandinavian societies have high tax rates, and yet retain plenty of millionaires, despite having low-tax countries nearby. Most importantly, perhaps, we have for too long been overly worried about the actions of a small handful of people. Research on the salaries executives receive in New Zealand shows that their pay has increased much faster than the performance of their companies would seem to justify.[21] In contrast, international evidence suggests that more egalitarian companies, which give staff greater say over how business is done, outperform their competitors, by using ideas from all employees.[22] New Zealand needs to become a country that draws on the talent, hard work and ingenuity of our whole workforce.

The final argument is about 'freedom'. It is sometimes claimed that promoting equality means reducing freedom – the freedom of high earners to spend their income as they choose. Yet, beyond a certain point, very large incomes do little to purchase 'freedom'; reductions in these incomes through (for example) increased taxes, would not significantly reduce choice or freedom for the people concerned. At the other end of the scale, increasing incomes (through, for example, improved pay or welfare benefits) greatly increases choice and opportunity for poorer households. Affording a better education, a warmer house, good food, or adequate healthcare – all these allow for a fuller participation in society. And they represent a significantly greater 'freedom' for poorer households. A more equal society, therefore, increases some freedoms without materially limiting others.

The task ahead – can we do it?
The hardest question is a practical one: can New Zealand in fact tackle inequality? Very few developed nations have been able to halt the last two decades of rising inequality, so what hope for a small country whose political and economic interests are closely tied up with global trade, and which is subject to the whims of international financial markets?

The task will not be easy. There are many challenges, notably the 'hollowing out' of our domestic labour market through the global competition for cheap labour, and the perceived potential for capital flight. In a global economy, manufacturing, in particular, will go wherever labour is cheapest, environmental costs most easily transferred and taxes lower. So it is likely that more such jobs will be outsourced offshore, depriving New Zealand of a traditional employment route out of poverty. Meanwhile, the ever-increasing demand for IT-related and other degree-level jobs will continue to drive certain salaries higher, creating an increasingly polarised (and hollowed-out) workforce. Despite the economic benefits of greater equality, the spectre of 'capital flight' – investors withdrawing their money from the country – is often used to oppose policies that would reduce inequality. Vested interests that benefit from high inequality will inevitably mount a vigorous lobby against some policies that seek to reduce inequality. Both domestic and international investors, they will argue, would be reluctant to invest in New Zealand if they felt their future returns would be reduced through higher labour costs or taxes. Credit downgrades from international credit agencies are a similar threat. In both cases, it is argued that jobs would be lost and economic growth reduced if government focuses on a reduction in inequality rather than an increase in productivity.

These economic challenges can to some extent be overcome or minimised. As Chapter 13 suggests, there are ways we can build a manufacturing base in this country and at the same time retain high-quality, high-paying jobs. Building our reserves of capital would help counter capital flight, and other more equal countries have maintained the highest possible credit ratings. The other benefits of investing in this country (such as a well-educated workforce, low corruption and minimal bureaucracy) would be enhanced by the social and economic stability and cohesion that greater equality brings with it.

A more serious obstacle to the realisation of greater equality is the fact that almost thirty years of rapid social and economic change have left their marks in our social attitudes. Surveys of New Zealand values and attitudes have shown that people consistently underestimate the size of the gap between rich and poor; they also indicate that New Zealanders have become more accepting of greater income differences.[23] The majority of people surveyed also believe that people are in need because of laziness and lack of willpower rather than because society treats them unfairly.

Despite these attitudes, an underlying sense of fairness remains. Most people think that income differences in this country are too large and that it is the government's responsibility to reduce the growing gap between rich and poor. They are also willing to pay more taxes for health services, education, pensions, job training, and assistance for the unemployed and those on lower incomes.[24] A political opinion poll taken in July 2012 indicated that inequality and a growing sense of 'us and them' were among the top five political issues that needed addressing at the next election.[25] Other surveys taken after the global financial crisis show increased support for income redistribution.[26]

This sense of fairness reflects one aspect of our national character. The other aspect is a widely shared belief in the importance of self-reliance and the responsibility of people to look after themselves. The path to reducing inequality will involve working out ways as a society to balance these twin forces of individual self-interest and a desire for fairness.[27] As the economist Joseph Stiglitz has said: 'Paying attention to everyone's self-interest – in other words to the common welfare – is in fact a pre-condition for one's own ultimate well-being … It isn't just good for the soul; it's good for business.'[28]

There is also growing concern about inequality from those who describe themselves as conservatives. American commentator David Frumm puts it this way: 'Equality in itself never can or should be a conservative goal. But inequality taken to extremes can overwhelm conservative ideals of self-reliance, limited government and national unity. It can delegitimise commerce and business and invite destructive protectionism and overregulation. Inequality, in short, is a conservative issue too.'[29] New Zealand Shareholders' Association member Des Hunt, commenting on high executive pay, puts it more directly: 'I'm a capitalist but I'm disgusted. I'm a member of the Institute of Directors, but I'm so embarrassed. The people at the bottom are struggling, and people at the top are getting too much. Capitalism can only survive if everybody is sharing some of the benefits.'[30]

Work done in the United Kingdom on how to change people's attitudes suggests that people are more willing to support policies based on 'proportionate universalism', in which most people receive some benefit but the greatest benefit is directed towards the more disadvantaged.[31] An income support payment for families with dependent children, as recommended by New Zealand's Expert Advisory Group on Solutions to Child Poverty, is an example of this kind of policy. Every child from birth to age five would be eligible regardless of family income, but payments would reduce as the child ages and be targeted based on family income from age six.[32]

A culture of restraint

Reducing inequality will need a commitment from us all to contribute to creating a culture of restraint. Restraint is a way of making voluntary moral choices to reduce income gaps, and involves social persuasion and changing values. It is about individuals, organisations and communities choosing to preserve and build on the country's essential social fabric. It is a place where classic conservative values of stability and social cohesion meet the social democratic values of equality and fairness.

Showing restraint involves working to change attitudes to inequality; this will involve drawing on our cultural, spiritual and social strengths as a country. We need to work to reduce acceptance of the growing divide. We can all help influence business, local and central government and other organisations to restrain unwarranted pay growth in their highest paid roles and to raise pay and conditions for employees on the lowest and middle incomes. We can do this whether we are outside (through lobbying and public campaigns) or inside these businesses and organisations.

In our open and democratic society, there are many opportunities for individuals and groups to participate as active citizens. District health boards, local councils and regional authorities as well as our Parliament are accessible: information is publicly available and decision-making processes are open for input. One consequence of growing inequality is a loss of political and civic engagement for those at the bottom. The shift to greater restraint will need individuals and groups to find ways to re-engage and demand accountability from those making decisions affecting them.

Steps on the path to reducing inequality

So how can New Zealand tackle the country's rapidly rising income inequality? As the contributors in this book have indicated, it's not easy. And this section closes with Linda Tuhiwai Smith's 'call for concepts', a broad call for the deep consideration that will bring to the table the concepts we really need to tackle inequality.

Our response must be a shared process including leadership from Māori and Pacific communities and producing results that work for everyone. Māori and Pacific communities are New Zealand's fastest-growing and youngest populations, but our current employment, education and welfare systems are not serving them well. The deep and diverse Pacific cultures need to have their spaces and ways of working respected and nurtured, so that their young people can feel that they are at home in our society.

As a first step, there are three key areas where action can be taken now that would make a difference. These are actions that involve government – thus a political will; they also depend on organisations, businesses and people. They are:

1. Getting more people into well paid jobs
2. Improving people's ability, once they are in work, to be well paid
3. Narrowing income gaps through the tax and benefit system.

The following three chapters suggest some of these immediate steps, and ask questions about the long-term strategies for reducing income inequality. Chapter 12 is about improving vocational education so as to give more people the chance of getting skilled, well-paid, rewarding jobs. These ideas, which reflect the need for greater mobility and opportunity as well as income, complement those set out in Chapter 9 on primary and high school education. Chapter 13 looks at how the workplace could be reshaped to deliver a fairer return on everyone's work, and how we can build the kind of high-performing companies that will succeed in the world economy. As Chapter 14 sets out, government policies can help reduce the impact of the failures of the market, redistributing income and wealth through a fairer tax and social welfare system.

These three chapters can tell only part of the story. In particular, they place a lot of importance on the world of paid work. People outside the paid workforce make enormous contributions to our society as parents, caregivers, volunteers and mentors. Wider discussion of possible solutions will need to consider how to ensure people not in paid employment receive an adequate income (such as proposals for a universal basic income).

Tackling inequality will require action on a range of social and political measures that extend beyond this book. Regulation and legislation, for example, to limit excesses and extremes of behaviour in economic relationships may need to be examined. Excessive inequality is a product of market failure, and we need regulatory oversight that ensures well-functioning markets and a robust safety net to help people who are left behind by the market.[33]

Public services, such as housing, education and health services, also strongly affect social inequality. When free to use, they are an inherently egalitarian service open to all, and make up a large but invisible part of the 'wages' of the lowest paid. A more equal future will need careful consideration of the role of public services; in particular, it will need far more investment in housing.

Reducing inequality may also need us to consider moving, quite literally, closer together. Today, many New Zealanders see less of different groups in society, so their sympathy for them dwindles, they acquiesce to measures that widen income gaps further, and then they see even less of different groups ... and so on into a negative spiral.[34] To break that cycle may require, among other things, considering policies that will help people to understand each other's lives better, including a focus on building affordable and social housing in amongst market-driven private housing, and funding for transport schemes that reduce the isolation of some low-income communities.

The connection between reducing inequality and protecting the environment also needs to be examined. There is international evidence that addressing inequality and overcoming local and global environmental challenges are closely related, but there is more work to be done to understand the impacts in New Zealand.[35]

'What is measured is what matters' – what we choose to research reflects our priorities as a country. We need to do more research into inequality in New Zealand and its effects. Underfunding of research means that basic measures of inequality that are taken for granted in other countries – especially around social mobility and the proportion of tax paid by different groups – are simply not available. We could also make more use of alternative measures of people's economic contributions, for example, the social return on investment (SROI) model mentioned in Chapter 1.

What you can do

Inequality is ultimately an issue for us all, which is why many of the actions outlined in the following chapters need to be coordinated by government in some form. An emerging mandate for government can be seen in shifting public opinion towards tackling inequality. Opinion polls show that the issue is in people's minds like never before,[36] while an ever-increasing number of reports, both here and internationally, are highlighting the issue.

However, people wanting to create a more equal New Zealand should not wait for government action. The social change that is required in our country can be driven as much by what happens in our own civil society as it is by what happens in Parliament or Treasury.

Taking part in the Living Wage movement is one example of how to help reduce inequality. A 'living wage' differs from a minimum wage in that it provides the income necessary for the basic necessities of life, enabling workers to live with dignity and to participate as active citizens in society. Organisations are encouraged by the movement to adopt a living wage voluntarily. A high-profile Living Wage campaign – based on highly successful British and American equivalents – is already being run here by churches, trade unions and community groups.[37] Researchers have identified a living wage for New Zealand of $18.40 per hour (to support a family of four on one-and-a-half full-time salaries), which is well in excess of the minimum wage in 2013 of $13.75.[38] The living wage does not depend on government regulation: businesses and organisations can implement it at any time. And the positive impact of introducing a living wage for employees, businesses and local communities has been demonstrated in London, and is strongly supported by London's Conservative mayor, Boris Johnson.

Throughout New Zealand groups and networks are researching and developing other initiatives such as cooperative banking, complementary currencies, establishing a commission to investigate ways to moderate high pay in this country, and other actions. The NZCCSS *Closer Together Whakatata Mai – reducing inequalities* programme is part of this work and seeks to support networking with others who are concerned about how to respond to inequality.

Shared futures

Turning around the trends of nearly three decades will not be easy, but the need for action is urgent. Inequality is like extra weight: easy to put it on, harder to get it off. But as this book makes clear, inequality is not driven solely by huge, impersonal, international factors. It is a direct result of choices New Zealand has made and therefore can be unwound if we choose to take the path to reducing inequality.

Despite the inequalities now dividing us, New Zealand is truly fortunate to enjoy a level of economic wealth and social stability that gives us real choices as a nation. Allowing income disparities to remain or grow further will ultimately drag down the well-being of us all. We can instead choose a better path, towards the happier and more cohesive country that a more equal New Zealand will be.

On generosity and restraint

Kate Frykberg is the chair of Philanthropy New Zealand and an executive director of a private philanthropic foundation. She writes in a personal capacity.

Money is an awkward subject, and inequality is an uncomfortable one. If we are fortunate enough to be financially secure, what do we feel when we think about inequality? Denial? ('I'm not really very wealthy ...') Defensiveness? ('I worked hard to get where I am today ...') Confusion? ('Well, I know it is a problem but I am not really sure what I can do – I like my nice house and don't plan to give that up – so really it is easier to just not think about it at all ...')

But we do need to think about inequality. As discussed elsewhere in this book, a large gap between rich and poor is not good for anyone. While it obviously hurts those in poverty, it can also pose a threat to people with money. An investment manager I know put it starkly: would you prefer a 99 per cent tax rate or civil war? And although much of the response to inequality must be collective, there are things we can do as individuals, especially if we are lucky enough to live comfortably.

These questions have been relevant in my own life. My husband Dave Moskovitz and I were fortunate enough to catch the internet wave of the mid-1990s. Thanks to Dave's geeky foresight, we started an internet company called The Web Limited in the flat above our garage in 1995, registering New Zealand's three-hundred-and-second domain name. Our first foray, an attempt at an online computer shop, was an idea before its time, and failed; however, we moved into internet development and established ourselves in the Wellington market, particularly with corporate and government clients.

In 2002 we sold our company to KPMG Consulting and moved out of this line of work. Although the sale was a small one in that time of major mergers and acquisitions, we suddenly found ourselves mortgage free in a nice house, with some money left over. Then what? What else did we really need? What did we want to do with our modest surplus?

Our response, and one that is open to many of us, has been to give. And yet giving raises its own questions. How much should we give? And how can we give in a way that addresses inequality rather than perpetuating it?

When deciding how much to give, it may be helpful to think about giving as a proportion of your income. Personally, I think that the number of zeros after the number is not important: it is the generosity that counts. And on this basis, the generosity of, say, a new immigrant who works on the minimum wage but still sends money back to family in their country of origin dwarfs the generosity of most of us involved in philanthropy. (In fact, the *How New Zealanders Give* research bears this out: people on lower incomes are generally more generous, in relative terms, than those on higher incomes.¹) Setting a target proportion of income can be helpful: 5 per cent or more is often suggested as a guideline. While this might be unachievable for some and too low a bar for others, it is helpful as a starting point and easy to budget for.

Deciding *how* to address inequality through giving can be more of a challenge. One of the best definitions of philanthropy is 'addressing the causes that made philanthropy necessary in the first place'. If we are all born equal but not all born with equal opportunities, then giving in a way that supports equality of opportunity makes sense. Support for people to get into affordable housing, succeed in education, get work and be a good parent can all be 'circuit breakers' in the cycle of disadvantage.

Giving our time and being actively involved with organisations working to address disadvantage is also helpful; while research is good, there is nothing like seeing things first-hand. Look also for organisations with a philosophy of 'do with' rather than 'doing to', as supporting families and communities to support themselves usually works better than a simple hand-out. For a more detailed discussion of these issues, Philanthropy New Zealand's home-grown model for giving, 'Feel, Think, Act', is a useful place to start.²

For Dave and I, giving is woven into how we do things. When we sold our business, we split the money into three parts: the first for traditional investment to fund retirement and our kids' tertiary fees, the second to provide seed funding for start-up companies and social enterprises, and the third to create a small charitable trust that provides four or five grants a year. Dave spends most of his time working with entrepreneurs and start-up companies, while I work in philanthropy in paid and voluntary roles.

The task of being generous towards others is also helped by practising restraint in one's own life (see Chapter 11). But it's not easy to decide 'how much is enough', or to stick to it. Restraint is not a fun idea, it doesn't come naturally to most of us, and it has to fight against a barrage of messages to buy, consume, get ahead. Happiness, whispers the marketing hype, is no further than our next purchase, be it lipstick or an Audi. We know that isn't true, yet we succumb anyway.

So how much is enough? 'Want', says the novelist Barbara Kingsolver, 'is a thing that unfurls unbidden like fungus, opening large upon itself, stopless, filling the sky. But needs, from one day to the next, are few enough to fit in a bucket, with room enough left to rattle like brittle brush in a dry wind.'³ But true though this is, few of us are Mother Teresa types, willing to give up our comforts and reduce our standard of living. An easier approach, therefore, might be simply trying to avoid increasing our consumption and wealth beyond where we are currently. Deciding to give away your next pay rise and avoiding excessive consumerism are small and achievable examples of restraint.

The bottom line? There are no silver bullets for addressing income gaps. But it is an issue that all of us, especially those who are financially comfortable, need to consider. And there are actions we can take. Being generous with our time and money, and practising a little restraint in our lifestyle and consumption, can be small but important steps towards addressing inequality.

12 Education and Skills

Paul Dalziel

> Skills have become the global currency of the 21st century. Without proper investment in skills, people languish on the margins of society, technological progress does not translate into economic growth, and countries can no longer compete in an increasingly knowledge-based global society.[1]

Tackling New Zealand's inequality crisis will require action across the full public policy spectrum, including new steps to help the workplace and the welfare state deliver a narrower spread of incomes (as Chapters 13 and 14 show). As the OECD quotation at the head of this chapter highlights, the importance of 'proper investment in skills', not just for individual citizens but for the economic well-being of the whole country, is a key policy area. We no longer live in a world where developed countries can sustain unskilled but reasonably well-paid jobs; most of those jobs have disappeared to lower-waged countries, particularly after tariffs and other barriers to international trade were dismantled in New Zealand and elsewhere during the 1980s and 1990s.

This reality has two implications. First, as examined in the surrounding chapters, we need systems to ensure that all citizens are supported during, after and outside of employment. Second, we need to make sure that the focus of our education systems (primary, secondary and tertiary; academic and vocational) is to help young people develop their abilities and acquire skills that together will help reduce inequality in New Zealand. This second issue is the subject of this chapter.

Thinking about skilled jobs, it is useful to distinguish three levels of skills. The first level concerns the core accomplishments of reading, writing, oral communication, numeracy and learning ('language, literacy and numeracy'). New Zealand has devoted considerable effort to raising these skill levels in recent years.[2] The second level involves what Australian policy advisors call 'employability skills', which are 'the non-technical skills and knowledge necessary for effective participation in the workforce'.[3] The Australians group these employability skills into three skills clusters: navigating the world of work, interacting with others and getting the work done; plus three enabling factors: workplace support, culture and values, and external factors. The importance of these skills is a key reason why all employers are now demanding 'skilled workers'. The third level of skills involves technical or discipline-specific skills. The future demand for these types of skills is difficult to predict, since rapidly developing technologies, changes in consumer preferences and the economic forces of globalisation continuously alter what counts as skills in New Zealand jobs. Two generations ago, my maternal grandfather was a master printer in Dunedin, but the typesetting and other capabilities he learned during his apprenticeship would not find skilled employment for a young person today. On the other hand, digital animation and related skills currently required on an industrial scale at Weta Digital were unimaginable until relatively recently.

The rapid changes in demand for particular technical or discipline-specific skills is one of the key reasons why 'navigating the world of work' is the first employability skill in the Australian framework. This is also important for employers, as the OECD quotation at the head of the chapter recognises. The worst outcome is when local citizens find themselves trapped in low-wage jobs because they do not have 'the right skills', at the same time as local firms are constrained in their ability to grow (or need to spend thousands of dollars on overseas recruitment) because they can't find 'the right skilled workers'. There is evidence that this is exactly the situation we face in New Zealand, and that a skills mismatch is contributing significantly to the country's inequality crisis.

Evidence for skills mismatch in New Zealand

The Ministry of Business, Innovation and Employment maintains a long-term skill shortage list and an immediate skill shortage list for potential migrants.[4] There are stringent conditions for occupations to be included on these lists. For an occupation to be on the immediate list, there must be confirmed evidence of a shortage of the relevant skills in specific geographic regions. The long-term list includes only occupations with a base salary of at least $45,000, and there must be an ongoing and sustained shortage of people with appropriate skills, both globally and across all geographic regions in New Zealand. Despite these stringent requirements, large numbers of occupations exist on both lists. In September 2012, for example, there were 128 occupations on the long-term list and 101 different occupations on the immediate list, or 229 occupations in total.

This problem takes on another dimension when we look at Table 12.1, which uses 2006 Census data to show the incomes of people aged thirty-

Table 12.1 Distribution of total personal incomes of the New Zealand usually resident population aged 35–39 years, by ethnic group, 2006 (percentage)

	European	Māori	Pacific	Asian	Other	All
$20,000 or less	36.2%	49.2%	47.3%	53.3%	54.9%	39.5%
$20,001–$40,000	32.6%	34.9%	39.7%	28.4%	24.8%	32.8%
$40,001 or more	31.2%	16.0%	12.9%	18.3%	20.4%	27.7%

Note: The first five columns do not include responses that decline to identify their ethnicity. Where a person reported more than one ethnic group, they are counted in each applicable group.

Source: Statistics New Zealand Census of Population and Dwellings, 2006. Licensed by Statistics NZ for re-use under the Creative Commons Attribution 3.0 New Zealand Licence.

five to thirty-nine. In this age group, people are typically well advanced in building career paths that will strongly influence future income; they will also probably have completed secondary and perhaps tertiary qualifications. In 2006, the statutory minimum wage was $9.50 an hour, so that working 40 hours a week for 52 weeks at that rate would have earned someone just under $20,000. The first row of the table shows that nearly 40 per cent of all people in the thirty-five to thirty-nine age band reported *less* total personal income than this benchmark figure. The proportion was higher still – around 50 per cent – for Māori, Pacific, Asian and 'Other' ethnic groups.

A large number of occupations have immediate and long-term skill shortages at the same time that nearly 40 per cent of those aged thirty-five to thirty-nine have income levels that are no higher than those of a full-time *minimum-wage* job, despite more than two decades of accumulated education and experience since they turned fifteen. These statistics point to major problems in New Zealand's skill formation system, but they also suggest ways to reduce inequality and improve the country's economic performance. We need to do much better at helping learners develop skills that fit the demands of employment in occupations with skill shortages.

In this context, it is worth recognising the importance of employees with trades skills equivalent to a Level 4 qualification on the New Zealand Qualifications Framework. The 2006 Census, for example, recorded that more than 200,000 technicians and trades workers – 11 per cent of the employed workforce – were in occupations generally requiring Level 4 qualifications. Another 67,413 people were employed in occupations generally requiring this level of qualification in community and personal services, in clerical and administrative work, and in sales.

Table 12.2 Top 20 occupations requiring a Level 4 qualification ranked by number of employees, 2006

Occupation	Number of employees
Motor Mechanic (General)	14,388
Electrician (General)	13,491
Chef	12,909
Carpenter	11,397
Secretary (General)	11,397
Personal Assistant	8,997
Painting Trades Worker	8,940
Hairdresser	8,769
Fitter (General)	7,335
Cook	6,198
Plumber (General)	6,153
Real Estate Agent	5,769
Printing Machinist	5,202
Gardener (General)	5,037
Hotel Service Manager	4,866
Property Manager	4,545
Real Estate Representative	4,461
Baker	4,182
Defence Force Member – Other Ranks	4,179
Sheetmetal Trades Worker	3,903

Source: Statistics New Zealand Census of Population and Dwellings, 2006. Licensed by Statistics NZ for re-use under the Creative Commons Attribution 3.0 New Zealand Licence.

The ability of the education system to develop Level 4 skills for these occupations is critical for improving economic performance and reducing inequality. These occupations represent core skilled jobs for 'middle New Zealand', as can be seen from the list in Table 12.2 of the top twenty occupations requiring a Level 4 qualification. Attaining Level 4 skills for these occupations is therefore a pathway towards higher income for a large section of the labour force; and the quality of these workers' skills contributes towards higher productivity in key sectors of the national economy. At the same time, if more New Zealanders can move into these jobs, the resulting reduction in the number of unqualified people in the labour force will tend to raise wages for 'unskilled' labour.

What should the education system do?

There is no suggestion that the education system can solve the inequality challenge *on its own*. Inequality is entrenched in all five pillars of New Zealand's welfare state – employment, income, housing, health and education. This creates a self-reinforcing cycle of disadvantage: without good employment, it is difficult to earn good income; without good income, it is difficult to obtain good housing; without good housing, it is difficult to maintain good health; without good health, it is difficult to achieve good education; and without good education, it is difficult to gain good employment.[5] Nevertheless, the fundamental point remains: a key component in any successful, multi-pronged approach to reducing inequality in New Zealand will be to ensure that the country's education system is well-equipped to boost skills for all its diverse learners.

So how do we ensure that all young people are able to construct learning and employment pathways in which they are rewarded for developing and using valued labour market skills? I was a member of a multi-disciplinary research team that, from July 2006 to September 2012, explored such questions under the heading of 'education employment linkages'.[6] My part of the research identified a framework resting on what I term 'the four D's of education and skills formation':[7] *discovery*, *discipline*, *display* and *diversity*. The framework argues that we need to increase opportunities for secondary school learners to *discover* their talents, to *discipline* these discovered talents through study, and to *display* those disciplined talents with the right qualifications, taking into account the wide *diversity* of talented young people in our education system.

Education policy in New Zealand is currently dominated by a focus on raising participation and completion rates in secondary and tertiary institutions. This focus addresses two of the four D's – *discipline* and *display* – by aiming to increase the number of citizens with higher levels of qualifications. The policy does not address *discovery* and *diversity*; yet a substantial body of evidence argues that inequality of opportunities for young New Zealanders is driven by systemic weaknesses in these two elements within New Zealand's education system. This was highlighted by the Secretary for Education at the time, Lesley Longstone, when she wrote in the foreword to the *Ministry of Education Annual Report 2012*:

> … the system is still under-performing for Māori learners and Pasifika learners, and learners from communities with significant social and economic challenges. While our education system continues to under-perform for these learners, we are not entitled to call ourselves world-class. In the current economic and fiscal climate, we need to make sure we are not wasting a single opportunity to generate knowledge, skills, creativity and confidence in New Zealand's young people and its workforce.

Longstone's concern was supported by a synthesis of material from fifteen national evaluations and reports of good practice in the previous four years by the Education Review Office. That synthesis was very critical of poor secondary school responsiveness to diversity:

> Too many of our most vulnerable students, especially in secondary schools, are the unlucky recipients of a curriculum that is fragmented and bears no relationship to their cultural backgrounds or to contexts that have relevance and meaning for them. The curriculum they experience takes no account of their strengths, interests or next steps.[8]

The need to improve learning outcomes for Māori and Pacific students in New Zealand's education system is universally recognised as urgent.[9] In addition, there is some recognition that stronger support is needed throughout the education system for learners who discover they have a relatively high ability to excel in what are traditionally called the 'trades skills'. Promising moves to provide extra support include: vocational pathways that map out relevant learning progressions; tertiary high schools and trades academies that improve links between high schools and tertiary institutions; and the review of industry training currently underway. But more could be done, as is well illustrated by the example of Australia's strategy for 'green skills'. The chapter concludes with an overview of these initiatives.

Vocational pathways
Mark Oldershaw, the chief executive of the Industry Training Federation, has observed that New Zealand's 'senior secondary school programme is heavily structured around the "pathway" to university [so that] the 70 per cent of students who don't go to university are not given the same clarity as to what they need to do to get on a pathway to further training and work'.[10] The historical reasons for this situation are easy to understand.

For three decades following the end of the Second World War, the New Zealand economy produced full employment for anyone wanting a job (although the era's social expectation for married women *not* to want paid employment must be acknowledged). The school leaving age was fifteen, and the national examinations sat by most students around that age (School Certificate) effectively acted as a drafting gate for academic progress by maintaining each year a 50 per cent failure rate. Thus, young people without academic interests would typically fail School Certificate and leave school at fifteen to find employment, further assisted by a tightly regulated apprenticeship system and protected points of entry into the labour market (such as nursing in public hospitals or employment in railways workshops).[11] Students who continued to the sixth form were almost all preparing for University Entrance examinations at the end of that year, so the senior secondary school programme was naturally structured around that route to university.

The economic reforms after 1984 marked a turning point with the closure of protected pathways for youth employment in the public sector; the apprenticeship system was abolished in 1991; the industry training schemes introduced after 1992 turned out to have a bias against younger people (at least until the introduction of Modern Apprenticeships in 2000); the school leaving age was raised from fifteen to sixteen in 1993; Level 1 of NCEA replaced School Certificate in 2002; and New Zealand came to develop one of the highest youth unemployment rates in the OECD.[12] This means that more young people are now staying at school longer, but the education system in New Zealand has responded only slowly to this more diverse range of learners in its senior secondary schools.

This gradual response can be seen in how the NCEA, for example, has allowed the introduction of a wide range of 'industry-based' unit standards so that secondary schools have been able to broaden their offerings to allow more students to discover, discipline and display their abilities in areas outside the traditional 'curriculum-based' achievement standards. It is worth noting, however, that students in these latter subjects can strive to have their results endorsed as 'achieved with merit' or 'achieved with excellence', but this is not possible for the industry-based unit standards (which are simply 'achieved' or 'not achieved'). Thus, the education system still does not encourage young people studying industry-based subjects to discover if they have meritorious or excellent abilities in these skill areas, and those who do have these advanced abilities are not able to display excellent performance through their NCEA qualification.

A recent development with huge potential is the design of 'vocational pathways' for inclusion in NCEA qualifications as part of the government's wider Youth Guarantee policy.[13] Vocational Pathways is a joint initiative between the Ministry of Education, the Industry Training Federation and individual industry training organisations (ITOs). It has created 'work and study maps' of pathways into five groups of skilled occupations: construction and infrastructure, manufacturing and technology, primary industries, service industries, and social and community services. Currently there are five groups but more are possible. Each pathway includes a set of curriculum-based and industry-based assessment standards that are recommended by the sector as reflecting skills, knowledge and competencies valued in the relevant industries. Students who achieve sixty Level 2 credits from the recommended standards (including a minimum of twenty credits from the specific sector-related standards), as well as the NCEA Level 1 literacy and numeracy requirement, will have their NCEA endorsed with the relevant vocational pathway.

These vocational pathways are designed to be used by employers and educators as well as learners. They clearly fit the 'discover, discipline and display' model advocated in this chapter. As students progress in their secondary school studies, they are able to use the maps not only to determine where their discovered strengths and interests might be taking them in terms of employment opportunities, but also to choose further credits that will discipline those strengths to develop skills that have been credibly identified as valuable. If successful, the learners' qualifications will convey to potential employers in their chosen industry that they have completed a coherent programme of foundation studies relevant to the sector, and so are well prepared for employment and further study (including, in some cases, at university level).

The gap between school and ongoing education
One of the greatest problems in the New Zealand education system is student disengagement. Leading the charge to address this problem is Stuart Middleton at the Manukau Institute of Technology (MIT).[14] Middleton recognises that young people are now staying longer in school, but he has also shown that this is accompanied by much higher levels of disengagement: *physical disengagement*, when students drop out of education completely; *virtual disengagement*, if they are physically present but not learning; or *unintended disengagement*, if they are learning but not developing relevant skills. His solution to this worldwide reality was to develop individual and flexible learning pathways for learners, and to found the Centre for Studies in Multiple Pathways as a resource hub for this modern approach.

To create multiple pathways for diverse learners, we need to break down the traditionally sharp division between secondary schools and tertiary institutions, as well as barriers between education in institutions and training in employment. Consequently, MIT established New Zealand's first blended School of Secondary-Tertiary Studies in 2010. This was followed by government funding for twenty-one trades academies launched around the country in 2011 and 2012 on the basis of partnerships between schools, tertiary institutions, ITOs and employers.

Some of these academies are based entirely in schools, some require a mix of attendance at school and at a tertiary institution, and a small number (including the Manukau initiative) are based entirely at a tertiary institution.

The underlying principle is to engage learners by providing each person with an individually designed learning programme, which allows them to move towards completing an NCEA Level 2 qualification while simultaneously achieving credits towards a nationally transferable trades-based qualification. Each programme combines practical hands-on learning in a tertiary environment with appropriate theoretical material studied in a secondary school environment. Participating students are able to understand and experience the relevance of their learning to their career aspirations; this in turn motivates effort and offers tangible benefits for success. Another feature is that the programmes take secondary school education for trades skills very seriously. These courses are not second-rate options designed as a cheap solution for failing learners; rather, they encourage the pursuit of excellence as occurs in academic study, an important step towards putting industry training on the same footing as other parts of the education system.

This policy is still in its early days and is operating on a relatively small scale; nevertheless, the initial indications are that its programmes can raise educational achievement among students who might otherwise disengage from learning. But for it to be wholly successful, there must be employment opportunities for graduates. The expectation is that programmes will be responsive to business and economic needs, but to put this expectation into practice there must be good information on evolving skill demands in industry. This issue has bedevilled industry training policy for a long time, as the next section discusses.

The review of industry training

In July 2011, the government launched a review of industry training 'to consider the extent to which the industry training system delivers the skills to maximise the productive potential of New Zealand industries and the employment and earnings of people in the workforce'.[15] Within the review, one issue is particularly important: leadership on skills training. Individual ITOs currently provide leadership within their industry, but the government review is proposing to take that responsibility from them. ITOs would still be able to contribute to skills leadership, but the intention is that industry groups would work directly with the Ministry of Business, Innovation and Employment and the Tertiary Education Commission to communicate industry skill needs.

The question of who is anointed by government to exercise leadership in determining industry skill needs has been a vexed one over the last fifteen years.[16] The Regional Partnerships Programme introduced in 2000 included funding for economic development agencies to prepare three-yearly economic development strategies, which typically included a regional skills gap analysis. The ITOs were given their current leadership role in a change to the Industry Training Act made in 2001. Under the government's Skills Action Plan launched in May 2002, the Department of Labour set up its Job Vacancy Monitoring Programme to analyse existing and emerging skill shortages. In 2006, the Regional Facilitation programme required institutes of technology and polytechnics to prepare high-level statements of regional tertiary education needs, gaps and priorities based on widespread consultation on the social, cultural and economic characteristics of their respective regions.

Two submissions to the government review by the Council of Trade Unions argue for an alternative to this disjointed history of skills leadership. Rather, leadership in industry training requires the full participation of government, the education sector, business and unions:[17]

> The CTU believes that there is room for consolidation of expertise and advice around the leadership function. It is too disaggregated at the moment. There could be much greater cohesion around a model for skills leadership that can really drive change and responsiveness. It can include how to attract people to industries, emerging trends, and so forth – but also to drive more of an action plan for each ITO.

To allow such a consolidation to take place the parties will need to pool resources. A first step has been taken by the creation of a joint working party on vocational education and training, set up by the ITOs, to build and support an effective vocational education system. But it is only a first step.

Green growth and green skills
As a final point, it is worth looking at a more ambitious approach being carried out just across the Tasman. Internationally, policy advisors are concerned that technologies to reduce energy consumption and carbon emissions will not be taken up quickly if tradespeople do not have the technical skills needed to advise customers or install and maintain new equipment. In New Zealand, three high-level reports on green growth either fail to mention 'skills training' entirely or omit any discussion of the role of trades training in boosting green skills.[18] These omissions are in

striking contrast to policy in Australia, where the federal government has invested millions of dollars to upgrade the ability of TAFE institutes (the equivalent of New Zealand's institutes of technology and polytechnics) to offer training in industry-defined green skills.[19] Examples include purpose-built training facilities such as the Sustainable Hydraulic Trade Centre at the Sydney Institute, the Irrigation Training Facility at the Northern Sydney Institute, and the Macarthur Building Industry Skills Centre at the South Western Sydney Institute.

In December 2009, the Australian federal and state governments also signed a formal Green Skills Agreement 'to build the capacity of the vocational education and training (VET) sector to deliver the skills for sustainability required in the workplace and to enable individuals, businesses and communities to adjust to and prosper in a sustainable, low-carbon economy'.[20] This agreement was supported by a new and broadly representative Green Skills Agreement Implementation Group (including members from the Australian Chamber of Commerce and Industry, the Australian Council of Trade Unions, tertiary educators, state governments and the federal government) and a budget of AU$5.3 million over four years. It has already resulted in all the training packages supervised by Australia's eleven industry skills councils being revised to include skills for sustainability.

Conclusion: investing in skills

The Australian example of investing in green skills illustrates what is possible in an education system explicitly designed to support what the OECD terms 'proper investment in skills'. There are initiatives currently taking place to improve New Zealand's system for skills formation in the trades, but greater effort in education policy is needed to build on those initiatives and ensure equality of opportunities for young people in our secondary schools to discover, discipline and display their diverse talents. Equality of opportunity in skills formation by young people will go a long way towards sustaining greater equality of incomes among the country's adult population.

Just so many obstacles

Kelly Belcher *has worked as a security guard, prison officer and cleaner. She has been an articulate spokesperson in the press on issues around low pay. Kelly lives in south Auckland with her two children, and was interviewed for this viewpoint by Max Rashbrooke.*

Are there equal opportunities in New Zealand? Not according to Kelly Belcher.

Kelly is thirty-four, a sole mother of two, and lives in Papakura in south Auckland. She has always been determined, in her words, 'not to be that stereotypical single mother'.

Since the age of twenty Kelly has been working, as a security guard and as a prison officer, among other jobs. She was living in Manurewa, and in a relationship, but she and her partner split up after she had Dillan in 2004 and Tayla in 2006. The next year she went to work full time at the Aotearoa Credit Union – and it was then that the obstacles began to mount up.

For a start, there was her rental house, which was damp (like so many other New Zealand homes, as Chapter 7 sets out), and had broken water drains leaking into it. 'The Telecom linesman had never seen a house like it – his socks were damp just from walking on the carpet.' But Work and Income NZ wouldn't advance her the bond she needed to get another place, so she ended up taking the home owner to the Tenancy Tribunal (and winning).

Around this time, her daughter Tayla developed bronchiolitis and a chronic ear infection. But for years the health system delivered poor care, while Tayla continued to get ear infections (as many as nine a winter). In 2011, Kelly finally took Tayla to a specialist who was so angry at the health system's incompetence that she insisted the local district health board should pay for a private operation.

Kelly moved the family out of their damp house in 2008, but working full time with two children remained exhausting. The day started at 4:50 a.m., so she could feed and change the children, deal with any illnesses, take them to daycare and then get to work; she didn't go to bed until 11 or 12 at night. 'I had no downtime, only weekends. I used to love Saturday mornings, because I didn't have to rush. I'd put the babies in bed with me. I'd be thoroughly and utterly worn out.'

In retrospect, she says, the lack of a family support network made being in full-time work untenable. 'I went back to work because I thought it was going to make things better. That was the biggest mistake I made. It just wasn't sustainable.'

The need for time off to look after Tayla meant Kelly had to quit her job in 2010. By this time, she was 'completely burnt out', and a severe drug allergy had inflamed the tissue in her heart and lungs. 'There was such a host of things going on', Kelly says, 'that I think my body just said, "Bugger you". I was just not caring for myself. I spent – and still spend – money on the children rather than on me.' A year later, the drug allergies were still cropping up, one of them so bad that ambulance staff said she looked 'like I'd had a chemical burn'.

In 2011, Kelly returned to work, this time as a part-time cleaner. For the rest of that year, she worked twenty-four hours each weekend, for $13.50 an hour. Once she started working, Kelly came off the DPB (providing around $15,300 a year) on the basis that her cleaner's wage would be topped up by Working for Families to $22,500 a year. But Inland Revenue miscalculated, and underpaid her by $150 a week. Ultimately, she was given $4,000 in backdated payments, but only after a 'nightmare' battle and multiple pleas to Work and Income NZ and Inland Revenue, all of which left her wondering, as she put it, 'Why do I have to beg?' Later, she discovered she'd also been eligible for a new employment transition grant, worth hundreds of dollars.

In late 2011 Kelly enrolled in a pre-degree health course at the Manukau Institute of Technology, as the first step towards working in children's emergency medicine. While working twenty-four hours a week and looking after the children, she got excellent grades.

In 2012 Kelly started a paramedicine degree at AUT. Meanwhile she had moved from Manurewa to Papakura in search of affordable rent, but kept her children at the same school so as to not damage their education. 'I don't do myself any favours', she says. 'But they have always had the same daycare, they have always had the same school. I didn't get that as a child.'

The result was that, lacking a car, they'd all take a train and a bus to Manurewa, then Kelly would get another bus to the AUT campus in Manukau City, before reversing the trip each afternoon: 'I spent two hours a day travelling each way, and if we missed a connection, that would ruin my day.' Her only rest was on Friday nights, as the children stayed with their father at weekends.

In 2012, the health system let her down again, when several doctors refused to take seriously her complaints of having severe facial pain. It was only after months of repeat visits that she had an operation – which revealed big chunks of broken cartilage in her nose.

It is difficult to describe Kelly's opportunities as equal when they are viewed against these barriers. The stress of fighting the system almost every day can drain you of all your energy, Kelly says. 'You feel hopeless. It gets so depressing. I don't do crying – I get mad! – but even so, it's so tiring to have to complain all the time.'

There's also the constant and dispiriting shortage of money, even when you have work. With the cleaning job she 'ran at a negative. I wasn't on a benefit, not getting my full entitlement, had to pay transport, and there was no provision for me to save, so nothing to fall back on if I had a lean week. I was better off on the DPB, cash in hand, because I didn't have to pay for travel, which was over $100 a week.'

While she believes, in general, that people should be 'productive' and look for work, the support provided is 'woefully inadequate'. Kelly would like to see no childcare fees for people earning under $25,000 a year, as a start, and improved before- and after-school care for older children 'to help working parents keep it together'.

Things are improving for Kelly and her two children. She's once again working at the credit union, twenty hours a week on a better wage, and has resumed her studies at AUT. Now that she's getting her entitlements, she has been able to buy a second-hand car, which has transformed her daily commute. And, after years of trying, she has a Housing New Zealand flat.

But recent advances don't make up for the struggle of the last few years. Ultimately, Kelly says: 'I have tried to better myself, but essentially I have been really kicked in the teeth for it ... There's just so many obstacles.'

13 The Rewards of Work

Nigel Haworth

Most New Zealanders must work for forty years or more. Few are independently wealthy, able to choose if and when they work. For most, their wage or salary is the sole opportunity for decent housing, an adequate diet, appropriate clothing, a good education, necessary healthcare, leisure activities and a rewarding retirement. Their lives, and their happiness, rely heavily on their access to, and rewards from, work. They depend on the economy to do two things: generate enough wealth for a reasonable standard of living for all New Zealanders, and then share that wealth fairly. Moreover, they want to contribute positively to that wealth creation. Creating that well-functioning economy relies on many things, including better skills training, as the previous chapter shows. But we cannot achieve a more prosperous economy in which all benefit fairly without reshaping our workplaces to make them more democratic and, consequently, more productive.

They take the high road, New Zealand takes the low road
Unfortunately, for the last three decades we have been doing badly on both counts: generating wealth and sharing it fairly. The last thirty years have seen a marked shift in power and rewards away from ordinary workers to owners and managers. This has come about because the former have had their bargaining power weakened, as trade unions have been attacked by legislation while, despite their protestations to the contrary, companies, company owners and their managers face few constraints on their ability to perform in one of the easiest economies in the world in which to do business.

As Council of Trade Unions economist Bill Rosenberg argues, there has been a long-term trend that has changed the balance in the economy between income to employees and returns to employers and investors. Until 1993, employees received a greater (though rapidly falling) share of the economy's output than capital did. From 1994 until 2006 the position was reversed. Since 2006, the position has been less clear, with both shares hovering around the 50 per cent level.

Figure 13.1 Income: how it is shared

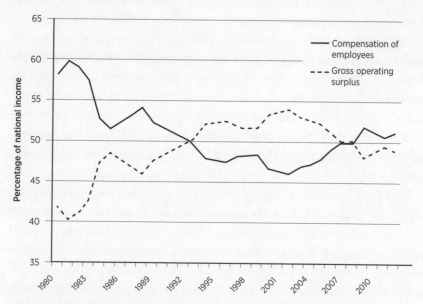

Source: New Zealand Council of Trade Unions (NZCTU), based on Statistics New Zealand National Accounts Data. This work is based on Statistics New Zealand's data which are licensed by Statistics NZ for re-use under the Creative Commons Attribution 3.0 New Zealand Licence.

Contrary to the arguments presented in the 1980s and 1990s during that extraordinary period of economic reform, this shift in power has not driven strong growth and improved productivity.[1] Once, New Zealand enjoyed one of the world's best standards of living, but in recent decades we have fallen further and further behind other developed countries, and we are now twenty-first out of thirty-four OECD countries when it comes to income per person. Our productivity performance is equally poor.

The reason we are doing so badly is that our policy-makers, and most of our investors, have chosen what is internationally known as the 'low road' to growth. The dominant business model has focused largely on controlling and cutting costs, on the basis that this would, eventually, lead to greater economic growth. Levels of government intervention and regulation have been kept low, and, above all, most employers have preferred to use a 'low-wage' model in tune with the 'low-road' approach to growth, a choice consciously supported by employment legislation in the 1990s and again since 2008. The result has been a weak economy, stuck in the 'low' end of the economic performance spectrum. Large numbers of low-paid, low-skilled workers are, for the most part, involved in the production and export of basic, low-value commodities; or in an underperforming and unloved manufacturing sector; or in a service sector marked by low skills, low levels of training and low pay. In addition, the low level of input that most staff experience in their company's decision-making means their ideas, talent and innovation often lie unrecognised and unused.

Fortunately, there is an alternative to the 'low road', often called the 'high road' to growth. For example, if our government were more willing to help shape growth, we would have better levels of innovation and technology investment, our companies would develop improved management skills, and we would have highly paid, highly skilled workers. We know that such shifts in strategic direction across an entire economy are possible, for other economies have done so successfully – Singapore and Finland, among others – and often from quite different initial circumstances.

That shift requires change in two key areas: collective bargaining and workplace organisation. Both require changed thinking among policy-makers, employers and trade unions. Without such change, which would generate fairer as well as greater incomes, other measures to reduce inequality in New Zealand will founder, because of the importance of work to household income. Of course, as the next chapter argues, redistribution as a result of government measures remains important. But it is equally important that workplaces deliver a narrower spread of incomes in the first place. The 'high road' to growth is the only option that can deliver both a better paid workforce and a stronger economy.

Wider economic settings

Before we can start reshaping the workplace, however, our companies have to be operating in the right environment. There are two important aspects of wider economic policy that must be revised if a high-income, high-performance labour market is to emerge in New Zealand. The first is our general policy setting for growth; the second is the specific settings needed for wage-driven, high-performance development.

In the last thirty years, New Zealand's core economic objective – and the sole focus of the Reserve Bank – has been to keep inflation low. While this approach has had some benefits, an emerging consensus argues that an unremitting focus on inflation is neither necessary nor desirable, and that multiple targets may be managed.

Above all, we need to place employment creation at the centre of economic policy-making, as the G20 has recently done. This is not simply a sensible policy setting. A key fear since the 2008 global financial crisis has been 'jobless growth', in which whatever 'bounce back' is achieved will be job-poor. This has occurred, for example, in the US, where corporate profits have recovered to their pre-2008 high but unemployment has barely decreased.

We must make sure that our wider economic settings renew our traditional commitment to full employment as both a political and economic goal. That goal was central to economic policy-making from the 1930s to the 1970s, but was lost in the 1980s economic reforms. Today, once again, we should not accept the view of employment as a contingent, arbitrary and simply 'nice to have' outcome of supposedly more important economic processes (see Chapter 4).

When it comes to more specific policy settings, a similar challenge to economic orthodoxy emerges in the growing debate around wage-led growth. As in New Zealand, the share of economic growth going to wages and salaries has been declining internationally since the 1980s. The causes of that decline are, variously, the impacts of globalisation and of the power of financial sectors, the decline in welfare provision, and the reduction in the power of trade unions to push salaries up. These changes have been driven by a philosophy that assumes that we must first generate economic growth, and then wages may be able to rise (although in practice wages for many people under this model have moved little).

Many now believe that it works the other way around, as we shall discuss later in relation to wage-led growth approaches.[2] In this view, salary and wage rises contribute to increased growth, because – to put it simply – better-paid employees work smarter, are more productive, generate more profits and higher wages, and consume and save more. Measures to support a fairer share for salary earners would include, among others, an explicit focus on full employment as a policy, effective minimum wage policies, legislation for stronger unions and improved collective bargaining, restrictions on financial speculation, restructuring of the finance sector, curbs on excessive executive pay and improved corporate governance.[3]

Changing our wider economic settings, therefore, could place employment creation in better-skilled, higher-productivity jobs at the centre of economic policy, rather than on the margins as an optional outcome. This, for New Zealand, would be a vital shift in policy-setting for, since the reform period of the 1980s, employment creation has been a secondary concern for policy-makers, in an economy with strong tendencies to take for granted the low-pay, low-skill, low-productivity 'low road' to competitiveness. The result, as above, has been low pay, fragmented training opportunity, loss of skill overseas, increased casualisation, a patchy employment record, and a recurring demand from employers to reduce further the wages and conditions of their staff. (One is tempted to ask these policy-makers: at what level of pay will the current model turn round a poor productivity, wage and training performance in the manner promised since the 1980s?)

Aside from wage-led growth, other much-needed big-picture economic changes include the creation of a stable currency, a resuscitation of manufacturing, investment in research and development (R&D), and a renewed emphasis on skills and training.

We need concerted measures that will stabilise exchange rates for our exporters and give those exporters confidence to invest in capital, innovation and training. There are many tools available, including orthodox strategies, such as reducing interest rates; and others from international experience, such as stronger controls over the financial sector, and taxes on financial transactions that are designed to reduce currency speculation. These policies may allow New Zealand to manage downwards our soaring exchange rates, which currently cripple our export sector. Currency stabilisation is neither easy nor a 'magic bullet', but other small (and large) economies – Singapore, Brazil, Switzerland and Hong Kong, for instance – have sought to 'sterilise' their currencies against speculative pressures that do long-term harm to the productive sector.

Our ailing manufacturing sector has halved in size in the last thirty years and this trend needs to be reversed. It is not only clear that the manufacturing sector is good for employment (creating 2.7 jobs elsewhere in the economy for each manufacturing job), as well as boosting skill levels, trade success and innovation; it is also clear that the importance of manufacturing in the global economy is growing, and that successful economies will require strong, modern manufacturing sectors.[4] This is the lesson, for example, of Germany's *mittelstand* – its small and medium-sized manufacturing sector – which has been so successful in recent years.

We need measures to improve a lamentable savings record and to divert capital from property into productive investment and R&D. Measures such as a capital gains tax on second homes, and increased government spending on R&D, may help to reduce the negative impact of the paucity of New Zealand's savings and R&D investment record.

As Chapter 12 outlines, we need added urgency in our training and development practices, some reform of skills training organisations, more apprenticeships and better management training. Our lack of high-quality management is increasingly understood to be a brake on the economy's performance. So much more can be done to prepare employees, managers and companies to perform better.

Improved productivity and high-performance workplaces

With the right wider economic settings, we could set about reorganising our workplaces – and, in particular, adopting what are known as high-performance work systems. In broad terms, high-performance workplaces are ones in which all employees are encouraged to be highly productive, thus generating greater profits and improved wages through measures that give them greater input into how their work is done and the company is run. The key to effective high performance is the empowerment of the workforce, such that they 'own' the process and the outcomes of high performance.

Important in this concept of 'ownership' is the notion of 'voice' – the ability of staff to participate fully and freely in the decisions that affect their daily working lives. This can extend to measures such as including a staff representative on company boards or on the committees that set executive pay. A true high-performance model tackles head-on the issue of workplace democracy and the sustained commercial advantages that result when workers have an independent and legitimate voice in decision-making. In contrast, partial high-performance systems that do not give staff more control over their workplace tend not to work well. Trade unions thus play a key role in these programmes. In many workplaces, it is only through an independent body, such as a union, that staff feel comfortable and respected when discussing improvements to their workplace. And because staff exert more control over their work environment, they tend to have more say in the distribution of rewards between employers and employees, and tend to gain higher salaries and wages, thus significantly reducing inequality at work.

In summary, high-performance models involve:

- increased use of technology (and the consequent drive to improve technology by means of more R&D)
- higher-skilled labour and empowered workforces
- flatter management structures and reduced dependence on crude managerial authority
- transformed work organisation
- better wages and conditions.

These systems have been shown to work elsewhere, given the right support from management, workforces and governments. In some economies, such as Germany, industrial democracy arrangements – such as worker-elected board members – have been at the heart of their economic success since the early 1950s. The European Union has actively promoted such models since 1994, and they can be found in many other cases, such as the John Lewis Partnership in the UK and in the Mondragon Cooperative system in Spain. And although EU-type works councils and worker directors are not a feature of New Zealand's business world, we possess examples of high performance success here. Fisher & Paykel and Fonterra are often quoted as important examples, but there are many other manufacturing and service delivery operations, in both the public and private spheres, that engage in high-performance activities, ranging from elementary productivity improvement tools to more sophisticated, organisation-wide change agendas.[5]

Viewpoint 13, following this chapter, shows how this approach can work in New Zealand companies. In the public sector, meanwhile, a high-performance scheme at Tauranga hospital has significantly cut the incidence of missed appointments, thus delivering significant cost savings and efficiencies in the use of hospital resources, simply by empowering staff to tackle the problem.

More generally, the evidence from New Zealand of the benefits of high-performance approaches is significant. They include:

- motivated staff, with greater job security and higher wages, who are able to participate in the decisions that affect them
- greater job satisfaction and more opportunities for personal and career development in a positive and satisfying workplace
- increased confidence, trust and openness in work relationships
- the ability to work through change and conflict constructively
- improved employee relations and reduced workplace conflict and tension
- improvements in work processes and service delivery
- easier staff recruitment and increased staff retention rates
- shared ownership of business outcomes and results and better business performance and long-term viability.

As the list suggests, high-performance behaviours will not only support improved productivity, and, therefore, improved competitiveness, but will also push and pull New Zealand along the 'high road' to improved skills, improved wages and an improved standard of living for the whole country.

This list also echoes the international evidence that high-engagement companies – ones that give their staff a greater say in how the firm is run – tend to outperform their competitors.[6] Those firms are drawing on the full range of ideas and abilities present in their workforce; and their engaged and empowered workers tend to be more motivated and more productive than their counterparts.

Yet, despite these international successes, high performance approaches remain muted in New Zealand for various reasons:

- our employment relations traditions that, post-1991, increasingly shut trade unions out of the workplace, denuding most human resource managers of any experience in using a complex, collaborative workplace model
- poor management capability and a fear of loss of managerial authority
- an emphasis on short-term financial gains, rather than on long-term, more sophisticated outcomes
- a post-1980s preference for a 'low-road', low-wage model
- the small size of many of our organisations, and the consequent lack of sophistication in human resource techniques and experience
- a much-weakened manufacturing base.

Overcoming such entrenched practices and conditions may require both stick and carrot. The carrot approach might well take up more generally the example of the current government's successful High Performance Working Initiative. This involves companies and high-performance consultants being supported by government to develop their own high-performance models. This strategy could easily be used more widely.

The stick approach, meanwhile, involves reforming our employment relations system, as outlined below.

The New Zealand employment relations system

Our employment relations system has not been configured to support high employment, higher wages or high performance for a generation or more. The current plan seems to involve driving down wages further, be it by changes to the minimum wage (as in the case of a lower youth rate) or in the introduction of the ninety-day measure (which promotes short-term, casualised employment using the pretext of easier access to employment for the unemployed). At present, neither government nor employers seem likely to break with this tradition. How then ought the employment relations system be configured for high performance and higher wages?

We can take the case of Singapore in the late 1970s as an interesting starting point. As management academics David Wan and Chin Huat Ong put it:

The government spearheaded an economic restructuring initiative in the late 1970s with a three-year corrective wage policy to phase out labor-intensive and low-technology industries. Wages were to be increased annually by about 20% across the board from 1979 to 1981.[7]

What Singapore did was simply price out of the economy many firms in the low-road, low-wage model. By decree, it drove up wages to force companies to innovate and invest in higher-technology, higher-productivity niches. Singapore did what the wage-led growth model preaches today. Its prime minister, Lee Kuan Yew, had no time for the vagaries of the free market, nor for many features of democracy that are important to New Zealanders. He needed major economic change and he needed it urgently. However, his political and economic policy approach would not be acceptable, if adopted wholesale, in New Zealand. So how can *we* achieve a system that raises wages?

One approach is the 'compact', 'accommodation' or 'partnership' model. This is the Scandinavian or Northern European approach, the model at the heart of Social Dialogue in the European Union and a model that harks back to post-1935 New Zealand. It involves the key parties – government, employers and unions – meeting regularly to decide on policies for training and development, investment, wage-setting and welfare policy (and so on), so that all parties give up something short term to receive, if the arrangement works, more in the medium or long term. Thus, for example, unions might accept planned wage growth, or agree to significant changes in work practices, in return for 'voice' in national economic policy-setting and in company decision-making; employers might accept, for example, the exercise of that 'voice' in return for improved government-supported R&D and investment in new technology, or a more active role in training provision. In New Zealand, this is a model that would have to be sustainable through the electoral cycle, as it is a decades-long process, and would require considerable strengthening of the trade union movement, such that workers were fairly and independently represented in the arrangements. One cannot underestimate the importance for sustainable high performance and partnership-based success of shifts in behaviour – of employers, employees and political parties – that take decades to bed in. This may well be *the* political challenge that faces New Zealand.

A second approach is more controversial. It reflects in principle both the wage-led growth model (see below) and aspects of the Singaporean experience (wherein unequivocal pressure is imposed to make change happen). In New Zealand, this could come only from government or a reinvigorated union movement (or a combination of both) seeking to put us on the high road to growth. Whilst there are some progressive employers in New Zealand, notably those supporting the Living Wage campaign, there is no evidence that employers have any broad-based desire for a sea-change in the current model; indeed, Business New Zealand and other business organisations tend to call for 'more of the same'. We must accept that the only probable driver of that sea-change will be a combination of government and workforce pressure to reverse the trend towards the low road to growth. Employers will have to face renewed wage pressure from trade unions that will chivvy them into higher-productivity and high-performance behaviours.

Most employers will, of course, reject this approach, bewailing the increased costs that will accrue to them, and threatening dire consequences for employment. Such arguments are to be expected, yet in some cases they are exaggerated. Take, for example the minimum wage.[8] Orthodox economists would have it that there is a damaging trade-off between jobs and minimum wage protection. But recent debate has questioned this orthodoxy, suggesting that minimum wage provisions may not only boost employment – as better-paid people work smarter, are more productive, and generate bigger profits and more job opportunity – but also diminish income inequality, reduce the dispersion of income and help some particularly disadvantaged sections of the labour force.[9]

A 'wages-push' or 'wage-led' approach in a high-performance-based model, by its nature, would change the structure of the labour force. For example, there would be a move from lower-skilled to higher-skilled positions. Training requirements would have to change accordingly. Both employers and employees would have to be open to new systems of work organisation and workplace decision-making. And the change might well, for example, also place great pressure on the welfare system as structural adjustments in the labour market worked their way through. Yet these are costs that must be accepted if we are to gain the high road to growth. Certainly, as the years roll by, and our employers operate in an economy universally reported to be amongst the most business-friendly in the world, the ever-more apparent lack of movement towards the high road suggests that a radical, game-changing approach is needed. Moreover, some of the best contemporary thinking about high-performance practices in our workplaces resides in trade unions such as the Public Service Association, the Dairy Workers Union, and the Engineering, Printing and Manufacturing Union – all organisations that could contribute significantly to improve overall economic performance if their message were heard more widely.

What practically might be done? An obvious approach is for governments, seeking to promote a long-term commitment to high-road growth through the electoral cycle, to adopt openly and comprehensively a wage-led growth model, as described above. As the economists Marc Lavoie and Engelbert Stockhammer put it:

> There is an alternative to neoliberalism. Indeed there needs to be an alternative to Neo-liberal policies, because the export-growth model is of limited use and generates global imbalances, while the model based on debt-led consumption is unsustainable ... A wage-led growth strategy would combine pro-labour distributional social and labour market policies, along with a proper regulation of the financial sector, including a reduction in the income claims of top management, most surely those in financial sectors, as well as a reduction in the claims of those collecting interest and dividend payments.[10]

This approach couples the macroeconomic settings discussed at the beginning of this chapter with explicit measures in law to rebuild strong, modern and effective trade unions as both a driver of high performance and as a firm check on the fair distribution of returns to high performance. In this approach, legislation to support a stronger, modern trade union presence is an essential part of improved economic performance.

The platform of labour protections

The final part of a 'high-road' approach to growth is to ensure that all workers are well protected. A strong platform of labour force protections – minimum wages, health and safety provision, protection of vulnerable workers, and so on – is essential for a high-performance, high-wage economy. We should support such a platform for a variety of reasons. The first is a moral imperative. For many in New Zealand, the hallmark of a decent society is its care of the vulnerable. This is simply what a decent society does. Second, it is politically sensible, as we see in cases where poverty and declining economic fortunes reach breaking point. The coherence of a country rests on the commitment to and of its citizens. If those citizens experience eroded material well-being, that commitment will fray. Violence and disorder are often the result. Third, the economic alternative to these minimum standards is an even more exaggerated 'race to the bottom', in which, as we noted before, wages and conditions are cut, and further cut, until, the orthodoxy suggests, growth takes off. But, again, just how low, for instance, must 'market-driven' wages go below the current minimum wage before the 'bounce back' predicted by economic orthodoxy? And how long must we see those lower wages in place before that 'bounce back' takes place? Are we, as a community, prepared to tolerate the wages and conditions that an end to a minimum standards platform might deliver?

In a low-wage economy, a minimum standards platform is often the only, albeit minimal, protection of the most vulnerable in the labour market against ever-greater inequality and despair. It must be preserved. We should also remember the 1988 Royal Commission on Social Policy's recommendation that the minimum wage be indexed at two-thirds of the average adult wage. For many, it is not simply a question of a minimum wage, but of a 'living wage' or, as the United Nations set out in its 1948 Universal Declaration of Human Rights: 'Everyone who works has the right to just and favorable remuneration ensuring for himself and his family an existence worthy of human dignity.'

A question of models

The societies and economic models that have consistently sought to address market failures and inequality, in and out of the labour market, have been universally social democratic in perspective. So it was that the great Scandinavian accommodations of the 1930s were formed. The New Deal emerged similarly in the US, as did our own post-1935 model. Even when governments of the right were in power, they adopted many of the key tenets of that social democratic model, as we saw, for example, in Germany's Chancellor Adenauer in the 1950s, or New Zealand's Robert Muldoon.

One possible driver of a new social and economic accommodation might be a renewed global crisis. A sea-change where the intensity of economic crisis compels a broad range of social partners, including business, government and unions, to agree to a national development approach. Or can we conceive of such a compact being constructed in New Zealand under the auspices of MMP, in which the system's tendency towards the centre promotes just such an accommodation? What is clear is that, if we are to achieve both growth and greater equality through better labour-market practices, a consensus is needed that encompasses economic policy-setting, wage-led growth, high-performance practices and a stronger voice for workers.

A collaborative approach

DSK Engineering *is one of ten firms taking part in the Hawke's Bay section of the government's High Performance Working Initiative. Max Rashbrooke conducted the interviews for this viewpoint.*

Hawke's Bay engineering firm DSK Engineering (DSK) is already seeing the benefits of a collaborative approach to working more efficiently – and thus boosting growth.

The firm is one of ten local businesses involved in the government's High Performance Working Initiative, in which business improvements are created as much by staff as they are by managers. Employing over fifty staff, DSK engineers steel- and aluminium-based products for the wine, food-processing and robotics industries in New Zealand and overseas. One of its larger jobs was decommissioning a Wattie's bottled sauce plant in Australia and re-installing it in Hastings.

Under the high performance initiative, staff from across the company took a long, hard look at how they were working, and where time, effort and money were being wasted. They found plenty of examples. At the most basic level, workshops were badly organised and cluttered, making it hard to work efficiently. In the words of general engineer Wayne Masterton, 'When we first started, we were [working] in a tight corner and everything was a bit of a mess. It was a bit disorganised.'

Poor planning and divisions between teams meant that handovers weren't being done properly, jobs had to be reworked because engineers didn't have the information they needed, and materials often arrived late, delaying work and wasting time and money. A lack of quality assurance checks on design drawings meant mistakes were not readily identified at a point where they could be easily and cheaply fixed.

While none of these problems may seem especially large or complex to solve, put together they have 'huge' effects on company productivity, says Glenn Manahi, the lead consultant on the Hawke's Bay programme. And that matters for the country as a whole. Since New Zealand firms cannot compete with overseas companies on labour costs or economies of scale, they have to operate at maximum efficiency, and where possible mimic other companies' advanced production techniques, if they are to survive on the global stage.

At DSK, the changes have been significant. The firm has shifted equipment so there is less double-handling and clutter, allowing the materials to move logically from one operation to the next. Workshops have been reorganised to make work more streamlined and efficient. 'Having everyone working together in sync … it becomes a bit more of a production line', Masterton says. The implications for the firm's productivity, and its ability to handle more work, are obvious. In addition, every job now has a 'kick-off meeting', says DSK founder Shane Kerrisk, 'so everyone who is going to be on the job is included. We run through the scope of the work, and they know what materials are ordered, when things need to happen, the key performance indicators. And again when the job is finished, there's a wash-up.'

Throughout the programme, staff have been equal partners in identifying and solving problems, and have regular, ongoing input into finding new improvements. 'It's changed the culture of the workplace', Kerrisk says. In contrast, other company improvement programmes have focused on managers, 'and they didn't have such buy-in because they were done without involving staff from the start'.

For DSK, the rewards have been significant. The company has already taken on one extra full-time worker, and is expanding its business. Masterton works on building mobile wind machines – 'like a big fan on wheels' – which help fruit and vegetable growers and vineyards prevent frost from settling on their crops. DSK has already sold machines, at $30,000–40,000 each, in Germany, and has had orders from Canadian buyers and interest from the US. At the same time, Air New Zealand is trialling their use as a new way to de-ice aircraft – 'this could be a whole new industry on its own', Masterton says. If these machines start 'really taking off',

he adds, they might even need their own dedicated workshop. Either way, Kerrisk says, 'It's definitely helped the company. It's prepared us to take on work and [to] know that the work can be done efficiently. And if you can do it efficiently, you can afford to charge a little bit less, and win the work [more often].'

As the firm has benefited, so too have staff. As an engineering firm, Kerrisk says, 'we are probably more susceptible than most to the brain drain. There are a lot of very large projects happening across the ditch, and our engineers are sought after.' And if the company isn't organised, 'and is allowing stuff to go out the door that you maybe aren't proud of, people are having to take backward steps all the time … They tend to get frustrated and they lose drive, and that can have a really bad effect on the business.'

In contrast, Manahi says, high-performance companies are good for staff morale. 'There's a lot more collegiality', he adds. 'At some businesses [in the programme], attendance has picked up. There are not so many issues with people being engaged. They want to come to work.' And because staff are better informed, they feel they have more to offer. 'Once they have all the information in mind, they can actually contribute at a higher level … The ideas just seemed to flow really beautifully.' Even at the workshop level, Manahi says, 'Staff themselves are starting to own the layout … they start to control those processes, and because they are controlling [them], they get greater efficiency out of it, just by managing those basic tasks.'

While those directly involved are, understandably, somewhat guarded about the programme's immediate impact on pay rates, Manahi says it 'has to put staff in a better position to have a conversation [about pay]'. He cites a 2012 Ernst & Young report which showed that $13 billion is wasted in New Zealand each year in unproductive work.[1] If staff are contributing to reducing that waste, he says, 'it certainly opens a conversation about rewards and recognition'.

14 A Better Welfare System

Mike O'Brien

Inequality of income is an inherent part of a market economy. Put simply, the use of money both as an incentive and as a reward results in some people receiving more than others. These differences are associated not only with the distribution of income and wealth, but are also (and more significantly) indicative of the ways in which people make judgements about the social and ethical values associated with both the distribution and accumulation of income and wealth in our society.

As this book has illustrated, there are, broadly speaking, two arguments for improving the outcomes that a simple market delivers. First, market outcomes are determined by the power of individual and group actors, and that balance of power can be altered; we argue here that there are sound reasons for shifting this balance of power in favour of the lower paid and unpaid. Second, even a market with a fairer balance of power than New Zealand has today will still lead to unfair outcomes that we may, as a society, want to adjust. The first argument has been explored in the previous chapter, which tackled the inequality delivered *within* the market. This chapter is concerned with giving concrete shape to the second argument: how to adjust the balance of power and reduce income inequality *through* direct government activities such as taxes, benefits and other financial payments. (Public services such as health and education have a critical role in reducing inequality overall, because poorer people rely on these services more than the wealthy; this chapter, however, focuses on the impact on inequality of income distribution, whether through work or welfare.[1])

In exploring this second argument, we need to answer three fundamental questions:

- First, what is a fair distribution of income so that all New Zealanders have a decent standard of living and a chance to support themselves and their children?
- Second, if income is to be distributed differently from the basic market allocation, how should the levels of benefit payments be set and how should they be funded?

- Third, why is poverty an issue that needs to be addressed in any society in which it is present, and why should we attempt, as a society, to reduce it?

A different approach to welfare

A decent welfare system would have two objectives: to help people back into work, where feasible; and to ensure people can still participate in society even when not in work.[2] Sadly, New Zealand's current approach to welfare is largely punitive. Sanctions are of course necessary to manage a welfare system effectively (just as tax avoidance measures are part of a good tax system). However, there is overwhelming evidence that punitive measures do not incentivise beneficiaries into the workforce. The truth is that most people, beneficiaries or not, *want* to work.[3] Much more effective as a means of encouraging beneficiaries into the workplace are measures such as: access to quality, effective education or skill development; access to appropriate, dependable employment; and access to mental health and addiction services. Educational and employment failure features prominently in the life histories of many beneficiaries; this takes time and skilled resources to reverse. Many have health issues that may always need support. Parents of young children may not have access to suitable childcare, and appropriate part-time work may not be available. These are realities in the lives of beneficiaries that frame their ability to move from welfare to work. A comprehensive, sustained and adequately resourced approach is needed to develop effective pathways from 'benefit' to 'work'.

International approaches to welfare in recent years have emphasised social inclusion and social investment,[4] frameworks that are the very opposite of the limited and punitive approach now prevalent in New Zealand. These international approaches are more comprehensive than ours, and focus on grappling with changing social and demographic issues, especially in relation to women's economic participation. However, the international experience and reviews are very clear that social investment approaches can be effective only if they include, and indeed are premised upon, reducing inequalities and poverty; too often in New Zealand, this has not been the experience or the outcome.[5] In other words, they must reduce the causes of social inequality as well as address the immediate needs it creates in society.

Much is said about welfare dependency, and how people can become trapped. However, beneficiaries also can – and do – take significant initiatives to improve their circumstances. Supporting this through a more flexible benefit system that worked *with* (not against) the realities of life on a benefit, and worked *with* the actualities of today's workplace, would see beneficiaries more readily taking up work where it was available. For example, a more flexible approach to the interface between income from benefits and from work would allow people to move more readily between work and care as personal and employment circumstances changed. Such an approach would reflect both the precarious nature of much work currently available and (again, as an example) the evolving patterns of family responsibility as children grow up.

In New Zealand today, moving between benefits and work is highly complicated, due to the complexity of tax rates, benefit abatements (the process by which benefits are reduced as earnings increase), and the nature of casual work. The benefit system assumes that people are either working *or* on a benefit, but this is often not the case. Casual work (short-term contracts, hourly rates, part-time jobs) can change almost weekly; the pathway to work for many beneficiaries will involve juggling shifting casual work alongside household management, children, and illness.

The current welfare system is a complex mix of benefit payments, supporting payments (such as the accommodation supplement and childcare assistance) and Working for Families payments. For beneficiaries, moving into work may well mean low paid, part-time or casual jobs – a step into work, but not a sufficient income. Yet navigating through the complexity of benefits and abatements, supplements and Working for Families, may present insuperable obstacles. Even giving the right advice can offer challenges for officials faced with this complexity. As a result, some beneficiaries do not claim or receive the assistance to which they are entitled.

As economist Susan St John has argued, there is no clear, simple rationale for benefit reductions.[6] A sole parent can earn up to $100 a week before income is reduced, and after that the benefit is reduced by 30 cents in the dollar, while for unemployment beneficiaries the reduction is 70 cents in the dollar for earnings over $80. In addition, beneficiaries pay tax on their earnings from work. The complexity is made worse for those receiving the accommodation supplement and childcare assistance, where the reduction in the level of assistance depends on income other than from a benefit. For example, for the accommodation supplement, assistance is reduced by 25 cents in the dollar once a beneficiary is no longer eligible for the unemployment benefit because of earnings.[7] The combination of reduced benefit payment (or reduced tax credits), loss of assistance such as childcare and accommodation supplement, and taxation can mean that beneficiaries gain very little from taking up paid work.

The case for improved benefit payments

People who cannot find work have a right to an income that allows them to participate in society. Unfortunately, New Zealand's current welfare payments – including benefits, tax credits and superannuation – are insufficient for too many people in this country, especially for households with dependent children.

Before benefits were cut in 1991, the unemployment benefit was $143.57 – equivalent to over 40 per cent of the average wage. In 1991 it was cut to $129.81 and has only increased with inflation since then, and is now $205 per week; maintained at the pre-1991 levels it would be around $228. The domestic purposes benefit (DPB) was also cut significantly in 1991. It is worth noting that, in the period when benefits were more generous (the 1970s and 1980s), fewer people relied on them, both in absolute and relative terms. Despite the supposed incentive effect of the 1991 benefit cuts forcing people into work, numbers on the unemployment benefit boomed in the 1990s. This suggests that benefit numbers have more to do with the availability of work than the level of the benefit – and it can be noted that unemployment was relatively low in the 1970s and 1980s.

As average wages have increased since the benefit cuts, beneficiaries have fallen further and further behind the rest of the population in net income, becoming increasingly excluded from mainstream society. Figure 14.1 shows how 'net average earnings' (the amount the average worker makes each week, after tax) have risen steadily in recent decades (even after adjusting for inflation), widening the gap between workers and beneficiaries. The graph also shows that while beneficiaries with children got a boost from Working for Families in the mid-2000s, those without have not had any increase in real terms since the 1991 benefit cuts.

Figure 14.1, which shows the widening gap between beneficiaries and salary-earners, would be even starker if it included the in-work tax credit (IWTC) for those in paid work with dependent children. Children do not receive the support provided by the IWTC if their parents are getting a benefit (or if they fail to meet the work requirements of twenty hours per week for a sole parent and thirty hours for a couple). The Child Poverty Action Group (CPAG) has argued that this is discriminatory, because it prevents some children with equal or greater needs from getting the support available to others. A case taken by CPAG is currently before the Court of Appeal.

Not only are benefits lower than they once were, and lower relative to wage earners: they are also inadequate for day-to-day living. The current

Figure 14.1 The widening gap: benefits and average wages, 1980–2010

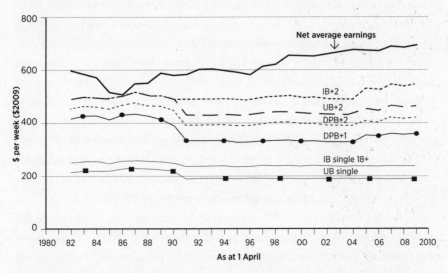

Note: IB+2: Invalid's benefit for parent with 2 children; UB+2: Unemployment benefit, 2 children; DPB+2: DPB, 2 children; DPB+1: DPB, 1 child; IB single 18+: Invalid's benefit; UB single: Unemployment benefit.

Source: Bryan Perry, *Household Incomes in New Zealand: Trends in Indicators of Inequality and Hardship 1982 to 2011*, Ministry of Social Development, Wellington, 2012, p.62.

single benefit rate for someone over twenty-five is $204.96 plus between $45 and $145 depending on the cost of their housing and the region where they live. What does this mean in terms of a standard of living? A case study from the Suzanne Aubert Compassion Centre illustrates how a beneficiary, 'Mike', gets $280 a week including the accommodation supplement, but pays $160 a week rent even in a subsidised council flat. After his other fixed costs, including power, he has just $48 a week, or $7 a day. This $48 has to cover food, transport, clothing and any other costs, and is $20 less than the weekly cost of food alone calculated by the University of Otago Cost of Food Survey for an adult living in Wellington.[8]

Benefits should instead be set at a level that would allow recipients to participate in New Zealand society and to have a sense of inclusion in that society. Each person has a vital stake in society and a role to play in it, which involves both rights and responsibilities. No citizen, by definition, should be an outsider since each person is part of the social fabric. If any individuals or groups are treated as outsiders, then the social fabric is immediately torn, which has the double effect of destroying shared responsibility and diminishing social connections and networks. Measures that work towards fairer income distribution can only create stronger and healthier communities.

There is now a vast body of evidence about the economic effects of poverty on children, both when they are young and in their later adult lives.[9] Children in poverty – currently estimated to be 270,000,[10] the majority in households receiving a benefit – have been the major casualties of the growing inequality and poverty in New Zealand over the last twenty-five years. Anne Salmond has commented that an ageing society that does not provide adequately for its children is consumed by a death wish.[11] Poverty also blights the lives of adults and makes our communities weaker. If, as a society, we were as wasteful in relation to agricultural resources as we are of our human resources, there would be a national outcry and demand for urgent action.

The argument for helping children is very strong for two reasons. First, children are rarely able to change their own circumstances but are largely dependent on what happens to the adults caring for them. Second, they are vulnerable because of their developmental processes and immaturity, and are disadvantaged if society does not provide for them adequately so they can realise their potential. In later years, it is hard for them to reverse negative experiences and lack of early learning and self-regard.

There is a strong link between parental circumstances and children's outcomes.[12] Children's well-being is too important to be left to luck, dependent on the circumstance of parents. While parents and families have the primary responsibility for their children, the well-being of future generations is a concern for society as a whole. Children's futures are critical to the social and economic well-being of any society: we all benefit from children doing well and, therefore, have a responsibility to help build those futures. Ensuring that all children have the best possible opportunities to develop their skills and talents is not only a moral obligation that many see and share, but also a commitment that is in the best interests of society. To adapt the common expression, it takes a society to help raise a child. Societies that recognise this wider shared responsibility are more effective in providing well for all children.

How high should benefits be?

Consider, for a moment, our provision for those over the age of sixty-five. New Zealanders have, over recent years, voted in governments that support the principle of retired people having an income and standard of living that ensures they are above the poverty line. We have agreed, collectively, that this is a responsibility that we all share. We want older people to live in dignity, not be reliant on individual acts of charity or their family, and have the opportunity to participate in society.

Table 14.1 Benefit rates in New Zealand, 2012

	NZ superannuation[13]	Unemployment benefit	Invalid's benefit	DPB, 1 child
Single adult (over 25)	$348.92	$204.96	$256.19	$293.58
Couple (where both qualify for the relevant benefit)	$536.80	$341.60	$426.98 (couple, dependent child)	

Source: Ministry of Social Development, Benefit Rates at April 2012, http://www.msd.govt.nz/documents/about-msd-and-our-work/newsroom/media-releases/2012/benefit-rates-table-april-2012.pdf (accessed 20 May 2013).

The same principles are not extended to beneficiaries. It is argued that, as working-age adults, beneficiaries are responsible for their own situation, and could act to change that. Significantly, and rightly, we do not condemn older people if they have insufficient income as a result of not providing for their retirement needs during their working years. Superannuation is paid to all over sixty-five without any moral judgements being made about their histories and circumstances. It might be argued that superannuitants have contributed financially over their working life, but the pension is paid irrespective of financial contribution, including, rightly, to those who have been out of the paid workforce for significant periods. Those who have been sick, unemployed or carers at home are all equally entitled to New Zealand superannuation.

As noted, basic benefit rates have not changed in real terms since the cuts in 1991. While superannuation payments cannot, by law, fall below two-thirds of the average net wage, there is no such formula applied to benefit rates. It is not just coincidence that the rates of poverty among older people are much lower than they are for families with children. Superannuation has been a very important factor in keeping those rates low.

Table 14.1 compares the weekly amounts after tax for: New Zealand superannuation and the unemployment benefit (payments for dependent children not included), the invalid's benefit and the DPB (payments for one dependent child included). As is evident, superannuation is significantly more generous than the other benefits.

This is not to argue that payments for superannuitants are too high; the evidence suggests that those living only on New Zealand superannuation (with no other income) are close to or below the poverty line. Rather, the figures highlight the inadequacy of other benefit rates. These have remained low partly because there is no embedded yardstick (such as the average wage) to use as a basis for adjusting those rates on a regular basis.

Should, then, we treat benefit rates as we do national superannuation? There certainly is a compelling argument for a closer relationship between the two rates if the goal is to reduce poverty and create a more equal society. That is, we should ensure the benefit does not fall below some set percentage of average earnings. An increase in benefits would improve the lives of the country's most impoverished people and strengthen their sense of inclusion in New Zealand society, improving beneficiaries' living standards and contributing to a stronger, more cohesive society. Improving benefits would significantly reduce poverty and would lift many children above the poverty line. It would also boost spending in the poorest communities and their businesses.

What would be the cost of these changes? In broad terms, Susan St John has calculated that extending the IWTC to beneficiary children would cost approximately $450 million a year, while a nominal 10 per cent increase in benefits would cost about another $450 million, based on current benefit costs.[14] Such an increase would still leave a significant gap between benefits and pensions and between benefits and low-wage jobs. Many readers will need little convincing that increasing benefit rates would make a positive contribution to the society we live in – yet others will have counter-arguments that form the basis of the next section. In conclusion here, however, it has to be noted that many of the arguments for *improving* incomes (for example, reducing taxes) are based on financial reward as an incentive for changing the behaviour of the higher paid, while *reducing* incomes is seen as providing the same incentive for the poorest!

Tackling the counter-arguments

Against the idea of increasing benefits – and the support for those who receive them – are a number of arguments. The first is that a significant increase in benefits would act as a disincentive for people to seek paid work and would encourage them to remain on a benefit. While this may be valid for a very small group, the available evidence is that the work ethic is strong among beneficiaries.[15] The indirect New Zealand evidence does not support arguments about a lack of motivation to undertake paid work; for example, benefit numbers fell when jobs were more readily available a few years ago (unemployment was just 3.8 per cent in late 2007),[16] and hundreds of people queue up every time, for example, a supermarket is opened, even though supermarkets often provide low-paid, insecure jobs.[17]

Contrary to popular opinion, there is no link between more generous welfare payments and increased time on benefits. Rather, as the Norwegian sociologist Thomas Lorentzen notes, the length of time people stay on welfare is shortest in countries where welfare support is most generous. 'Generous levels of assistance and support ... do not result in permanent poverty trap and extended stays on welfare.'[18] Why is this? The answer is in the paragraph above: people typically take jobs when there are jobs available. More generous benefits also encourage risk-taking by allowing people, for instance, to start up a new business, safe in the knowledge that if things do not work out, they will not end up in poverty. The vital issue is the supply of work, *not* the motives of beneficiaries. To take a simple illustration reflecting the effects of job availability: 97,111 people were receiving the DPB and 39,029 receiving the unemployment benefit in 2007. The comparative numbers in 2011 were 114,039 and 70,090 respectively.[19] The change simply reflects that more jobs were available in 2007 and beneficiaries took up those jobs. They were motivated to work because work was available.

A second claim is that there is plenty of work out there for beneficiaries who want it. But in November 2012 there were 175,000 unemployed people competing for jobs and a further 113,300 seeking further hours. The employed workforce at that time fell by 8,000 compared with the previous quarter. In addition, many jobs do not fit with beneficiaries' personal/caring commitments and with issues arising from their health requirements. For example, a person with a chronic mental illness may be able to work for a period of time or for parts of the week, but will then have occasions when they are unable to work because of that illness. This is not easy for employers to manage, and requires a flexible benefit system that enables the beneficiary to work as health permits and supports employers to meet their obligations.

A third opinion or belief is that benefit levels are, in fact, adequate, and problems arise only because beneficiaries spend unwisely and are unable to budget. All the available evidence, nationally and internationally, points to the same conclusion, namely that the poor and beneficiaries are among the best budgeters, because they have to be to survive. (The story of 'Mike', above, also made this point.) Data from the Household Economic Survey show, for example, that the lowest household income group spend a smaller percentage of their income on alcohol, tobacco and drugs than do those in the highest income group – contrary to popular belief that people are poor because they waste their money on alcohol and cigarettes.[20]

Paying for it all
Even if the case is made for raising incomes at the lowest level, how would increased benefits and more 'back to work' training be paid for: that is, how

does the country 'afford it'? 'Affordability' is a question of priorities and allocation of resources, a much more complicated matter than whether there is money 'in the bank'. Rather, 'affordability' in the context of the national economy incorporates two interlinked elements: where does the money come from (who pays), and what priorities and values determine how the money is to be allocated?

This brings us onto the tax system (the question of 'where does the money comes from'). As Chapter 2 sets out, New Zealand's tax system has become less redistributive over the last twenty-five years. Tax rates for the highest incomes have been halved, while the flat rate GST has hit low-income groups hardest. Political scientist Rob Salmond's analysis shows that, for the highest income group, 41 per cent of their income is spent on activities that attract GST, while for the lowest-income groups almost all of their income is spent on GST-liable activities.[21] In other words, tax changes over the last two decades have been an important contributor to the greater inequality experienced in New Zealand society over that time. As a result, and combined with the 1991 benefit cuts, New Zealand does significantly less to redistribute income and wealth than many other countries. Reducing income taxes also reduces the income the government has for meeting social purposes. The impact (and the cost) of reducing public services falls most heavily on the poorest, who rely most upon these services.

As Salmond has shown, on an international scale New Zealand is not a highly taxed country – our top earners would pay significantly more tax in any comparable country – so extra taxation would not impose an undue burden on New Zealand. There is a range of options available for increasing taxation, including reversing the tax cuts of 2010. The greatest advantage of these cuts – over 40 per cent – went to the highest income earners.[22] Tax income, overall, was reduced by $4.5 billion annually, balanced by a GST increase which fell heavily on those on lower incomes. The Council of Trade Unions has argued that we could instead have a 38 per cent rate on income more than approximately twice the average wage ($100,000), and a 45 per cent rate on income more than approximately three times the average wage ($150,000). This would align us with Australia's top tax rate of 45 per cent.

Increasing taxes for higher income earners would require extra measures to clamp down on tax avoidance, but this is an essential requirement of any tax system. Although not simple, tackling tax avoidance can be done through measures such as giving Inland Revenue extra resources, and tightening up the rules for the way trusts are used. After all, most developed countries have large gaps between their tax rates for different kinds of income, much larger than in New Zealand, yet manage to gather large amounts of tax revenue (that is, minimise tax avoidance).[23]

We could also broaden the reach of the system by targeting other kinds of income and wealth that are currently untaxed. The most obvious option here is a capital gains tax, which would raise approximately $2.5 billion a year, if it was set at 15 per cent and excluded the family home. As the economist Gareth Morgan has suggested, another option is to introduce an asset tax that would levy a fixed charge on people's assets every year.[24] Alternatively, we could do more to tax inherited wealth. New Zealand is extremely unusual among developed countries in not taxing inheritances, despite its potential for levelling out the playing field among those children lucky enough to inherit wealth and those who do not.[25] Or we could introduce other taxes that are difficult to avoid, like the 'stamp duty' that British citizens pay each time they sell a house.

As a more general point, it needs to be reiterated that fiscal measures (such as the tax system) are not simply or indeed primarily about money: they are about society's goals, values and priorities. The tax system collects monies and distributes the revenue thus collected, but neither collection nor distribution is 'value-neutral'. Both processes reflect decisions, made by society as a whole, about what is deemed important and what is not. There are currently strong arguments for increasing taxes on the more affluent, both because they are better able to afford those taxes and because that is part of their contribution to a society in which they live and work. The general argument of this book is that we all (including the wealthy) benefit from a less impoverished society – and that the wealthy are in a position to make a significant contribution to this 'better society'. It is a tenet of this book also that a fairer society would be a 'better society', and that fairness must be a key part in decisions we make about distributing incomes.

Looking to the future

A more equal society would ensure that all New Zealand families have sufficient income to give their children the experiences and opportunities they need to maximise their development and fulfil their potential.[26] This means increased benefit payments; but, fundamentally, investment in children's well-being needs to be central to all policy-making, especially in such key areas as health, education and housing. One simple example that would make a significant difference for children in low-income households is home insulation, which has been shown to have a marked impact on the health of children and, consequently, their school attendance and educational achievements. Reducing children's inequalities requires long-term commitment and sustained investment to produce these sorts of results. However, as this chapter demonstrates, reducing children's inequalities (perhaps more than in any other area of society) benefits everybody and those benefits are immediate and future-proofed.

The Children's Commissioner's Expert Advisory Group on Solutions to Child Poverty has recommended, amongst other things, that the government develop a 'food in schools' strategy to ensure that all children have adequate nutrition, supporting their health and learning. It has also recommended a form of universal benefit to provide better support for children, especially the youngest. This will not, in itself, eliminate child poverty, but it is a significant recognition of the importance we place on supporting children in New Zealand. A more equal society would also end the discrimination against children in beneficiary households that is held in place by the current work requirement for eligibility to the IWTC, as discussed above. Even these small steps, practical and immediate, would reduce the impact of poverty on New Zealand's children. More is needed – much more – before we have a society in which greater equality allows young people to grow to their full potential, able to meet the challenges of the twenty-first century with the capabilities they will need. Our children are our future, and as a society we are failing them. Taking the first steps, right now, would at least get us going in the right direction.

Unconditional basic income

Gareth Morgan and Susan Guthrie are the authors of The Big Kahuna, *a 2011 book that makes the case for an unconditional basic income in New Zealand.*

The decision to target income support using means-testing and other screening criteria has underpinned welfare policy in New Zealand since the nineteenth century. When income support became available for those of working age in 1938 in response to the Great Depression, targeting lay at its core.

But life has changed considerably since 1938. For a start, family life is far more fluid, and we can no longer assume that two parents provide financial and other support for their children. Nor can we assume that the skills that people acquire in their youth will be sufficient to guarantee them well-paid and secure work until retirement. And the opportunities people now have to hide their income from means-testing regimes were unheard of seventy years ago.

Because the world is a different place, targeting income support to working-age people nowadays comes with a host of serious problems. People are becoming trapped into relying on government income support because, in targeted systems, support has to be withdrawn as people start working or low-paid workers earn more. In many cases, the earnings from work are not enough to compensate for the benefits that are withdrawn. This problem of 'poverty traps' is part and parcel of targeted benefits systems.

Moreover, workers are likely to need to retrain throughout their working lives, missing out on income in the process, but the welfare system can't accommodate that reality. Circumstances now vary so greatly from one family to the next that a 'one-size-fits-all' solution creates obvious inequities, and more and more complex policies have become necessary. As a result, the direct costs of just administering the tax and benefits system are over $800 million a year.

A final problem is that there is an inherent bias in targeted regimes towards ever-lower levels of support for those in need. Targeted regimes create an underclass stigmatised by their need to receive support. Over time the willingness of the community to provide support fades as they come to believe they have less and less in common with the underclass of 'beneficiaries'. Pockets of severe poverty are the consequence.

Fortunately, it is possible to design a system to support people of working age that doesn't have these problems – although it does require a radically different mindset.

We can take our cue from New Zealand superannuation, which provides an *unconditional payment* to anyone aged sixty-five or over. New Zealand superannuation delivers recipients a level of well-being that is exceptionally high by international standards. In addition, roughly one in five of this age group continues to work and receive wages. As they are not penalised for doing so, the scheme works alongside self-interest and encourages independence. New Zealand Super is also very low cost to administer and comply with – a one-off check of the birth certificate and it's sorted – and there is no stigma attached to receiving it.

An unconditional payment to all working-age New Zealanders, regardless of their income or status, would provide each one with continual support through the various financial ups and downs of modern life. It would reflect the need for people continually to retrain, their uncertain and changeable parenting roles, and their other caregiver responsibilities.

Making the payment unconditional would remove the stigma attached to those who rely on it because of poor health or for other reasons. They would no longer be identified by the system. This would foster more connected and tolerant communities, and, the evidence shows, would ultimately translate into a more successful economy.

Critics of such a scheme would no doubt point to the 'madness' of giving income to millionaires and others who don't need it. But because of complex modern family structures and financial innovations, even our current targeted welfare system provides income to the well-off, while denying support to some of those who are most in need.

Others might claim that such a scheme could encourage nationwide sloth. This seems unlikely, given that work would be more rewarding than at present, because the payment would not – as benefits are – be reduced as people start to work more hours. And if the payment was set at a level just sufficient to maintain a reasonable level of health, the lifestyle afforded would be very modest – far too modest for most to maintain. An unconditional scheme would also provide funds for retraining to many people who, under current rules, would not be able to do so – thus making our workforce more productive, not less.

Such a welfare system must be accompanied by a tax system that taxes all income and all benefits from wealth – cash and non-cash – equally. Otherwise effective redistribution will not be achieved, as those with high levels of wealth will receive income support that exceeds what they pay in tax. The key is to recognise that wealth in the modern economy produces immediate benefits that do not take the form of cash: capital gains on property and services from owner-occupied homes are two clear examples. The reward from each of these can be easily measured and taxed accordingly. Such a tax system need not have progressive tax rates to be redistributive, a flat income tax rate will suffice. This further lowers the administrative costs of the redistribution and improves incentives to work.

To illustrate how such a policy could be funded, we have to make assumptions about what flat tax rate would be adopted. From that flows an affordable level of unconditional welfare payment for those of working age. There are, of course, numerous possible tax and welfare payments pairings. For example, a flat tax rate of 33 per cent would fund an unconditional payment of $11,000 after tax per adult, roughly the same as the current single person unemployment benefit. Underpinning this is the assumption that all assets, including housing, give their owners an annual income worth 6 per cent of their value, and that this income is taxed at the flat tax rate.

In 1938 it was clear to politicians and the public that the system they had was broken. Today, the world has continued to move on, and we need once again to realise that what we have just won't do. Fortunately, the option of combining unconditional income support to all adults with taxing all the benefits of wealth offers an exciting alternative to a permanently damaged system.

15　The Future is Now

Linda Tuhiwai Smith

New Zealand has no excuse for the systemic inequalities that have become entrenched and given moral legitimacy over the last twenty-five years. It makes no sense. If inequality is not addressed and instead becomes more stubbornly inter-generational, marked by race, region and the realities of poverty, then we as a nation have failed ourselves. The future, in one sense, is now. It is not an abstract, theoretical or even visionary picture of what the world may be like in fifty years or a hundred years. It is, rather, the potential we hold now, as a society. The future is what we choose to develop as well as what we choose to ignore. It is in our decisions and actions, our values and relationships, our language and mind-sets. There is no accidental future for society.

In this chapter, I try to be thoughtful about the future by reframing current public discourses and ways of thinking about inequality, poverty and privilege, as a strategy for opening up different kinds of talk, research, policy responses and social strategies. This approach is based on my scepticism of the current context and political paradigms to foster new talk and new responses. It is also based on scepticism about evidence-based public policy as the principal means by which issues of inequality are addressed by the state. Evidence is only powerful if the powerful accept its 'truth'. In this case the truth is that inequalities in a small nation like New Zealand are not only widening but also deepening, and this profile of inequality will have long-term consequences for society. Evidence can speak to a 'truth', but power is about defining what truth is real and what truth can be ignored. Some may argue that this is simply a perspective, a point of view or an ideological position. Those with power can determine what is truth and what is nonsense. Evidence needs compelling stories, the game-changing examples that move the status quo. Compelling stories need new language that moves people to act collectively and with will. Action takes courage and persistence, and needs to be focused on solutions rather than moralistic rhetoric.

Rising poverty, raising poverty

Talking about inequality, and especially about poverty, is a difficult conversation for New Zealanders. 'We' don't like to talk about it, or 'we' don't want to be told about it, or 'we' don't want to be reminded of it. In other words, poverty as described by the 'activists' does not really exist. 'We' do not like activists, especially those with an academic bent because 'we' do not like academics either. To take talkback radio as an example, the conversation is one with limited discursive and analytical strategies. Poverty appears to be defined in popular discourse as the result of dumb decisions made by stupid and irresponsible people. It is the fault of poor people that they are poor. 'We' do not like the way poor people talk; 'we' want them to 'get over it' and 'move on'.

At the same time, good hard-working people are made poor by the closing down of businesses, actions presumably based on good business decisions by very clever people who accept the realities of the market economy. A good worker and provider for others one day can, the next day, be redefined in popular and political discourse as a poorly skilled unemployed person, responsible for their own impoverished circumstances. The outcome of business closures is still attributed by default to those who have worked in that business. It is their fault because they were not sufficiently efficient, cheap or flexible enough to learn new skills. 'We' want them to pick themselves up, move families and households, and just get another job. 'We' want people to be grateful. The hegemony of neoliberalism has closed minds and conversations. Problem solved: *real* poverty does not exist in New Zealand except where people have chosen to be poor. 'We' do not have real poverty like those developing countries where poverty is somehow more authentic and worthy of our charity. According to these closed minds, 'our' people choose to be poor and deserve to be poor. This means there is no inequality – just smart people and dumb people. In addressing inequality in New Zealand we have to raise poverty, to understand that poverty has direct impacts on society, not simply because we pay for it but because we will keep paying for it over time. Deep poverty is not a temporary event.

The 'refusals'

We live in a time of refusals. A time in which public and political discourse around inequality, poverty and race is shaped by a refusal to see, to acknowledge, to act. That is:

A refusal to see poverty, racism, discrimination and marginalisation
A refusal to acknowledge a problem of widening disparities
A refusal to act systemically in addressing systemic problems.

These refusals make it impossible to 'name' an issue, to define it and convince others to care about it. We rely on celebrities to help us see because when we see the celebrity we see the things their glamour casts light upon. We depend on public figures to tell us what issues to act on, and which to ignore. Ultimately, it is only outrage, fuelling our courage, that makes us act beyond these refusals.

The wider the disparities the easier it is for those in positions of privilege to expand and maintain distance from those at the very margins of society, the easier it is to dehumanise them and assign them to a range of negative categories. It is much easier to assume what people are thinking and analyse their motivations when they are far away, as we are free to invent their characters, predict their behaviours, and determine their needs and how best their needs can be met. We expect them to behave normally (like 'normal people') but know they will not, so we second-guess them and blame them when things don't improve. It is also easy to see the 'plight' of the poor as an exercise requiring either punishment or charity, neither of which resolves the problem of inequality. In a contemporary version of Marie Antoinette's saying 'let them eat cake', solutions to poverty are often cynically designed programmes, funded on recycled resources from previous programmes closed down for lack of outcomes. This is not a recent phenomenon; we have experienced many cycles of programmes that prepare the unemployed with more work skills, computer literacy, work readiness and interview skills, as if somehow their skill development will create jobs where none exist. How convenient it is that with each cycle of government policy, memory of what has happened before in communities is obliterated, and capacity that was established before in provider organisations is dismantled.

How do we raise awareness and informed debate about inequality, about the widening gap between rich and poor, and about the devastating impact of poverty? One way, in my view, is to break out of the paradigm and talk about poverty in different ways, highlighting the range of poverties afflicting New Zealand. It is one thing to talk about poverty in terms of income levels, deprivation indices and disparities that are easily linked to educational under-achievement, literacy problems, skills deficits, crime, benefit fraud and brown people (meaning Māori and Pacific peoples). It is easy to align those hoary bogeys with poverty and material deprivation, and to come up with the justification that poverty is the fault of the poor and that society owes them nothing.

Pleasuring privilege

One way to think about extreme disadvantage is to contrast the privileges that accumulate to those who have extreme advantages. The privileged can assume their privilege has to be sustained and constantly 'pleasured'. There are three ways this pleasuring works: firstly, privilege has to be constantly acknowledged as 'well deserved' and as making a positive contribution to society; secondly, it has to be compensated for if attention and resources are shifted to the disadvantaged; and thirdly, it has to be rewarded with disproportionate influence in the formation of policy. More research attention should go on privilege and the multiple and cumulative opportunities and gains that are accorded to privilege that require no additional effort, talent or skill. As Chapter 2 notes, we need to know far more about wealth, starting with the most basic facts of its existence.

This 'structural privilege' gives entitlements, choice and opportunities for sustaining the privileged. The privileged, it would seem, are also very needy. They are articulate at expressing their needs and what they think the rest of society needs. The privileged can assume an authority to speak and to expect a response. This is not saying that individuals in this group are not humble, hard-working or deserving of every material comfort they have. It is saying that with material wealth flows a range of expected and unexpected benefits and opportunities within and beyond a single generation. These benefits can be known as social and cultural capital, but privilege is about power as much as it is about capital. With education, doors are opened, but without education, one can only knock at a door and hope it is answered. For the privileged, there simply are no doors.

Privilege is not what individuals choose. It is simply what happens as wealth and health are accumulated and banked for the future. Individuals may choose different life courses but the point is that, regardless of their choice, they can assume that opportunities will always be available to them. Privileged people have inherent access to good service, good advice, social networks and even good political representation. They get to speak to power as an equal rather than as a supplicant. They know that public servants are actually their servants.

Dismantling the 'master's house'

Feminist scholar Audre Lorde famously stated that 'The master's tools will never dismantle the master's house.'[1] The concept can be applied here in terms of the questions we need to ask of the relationship between structural inequality, structured poverties and privileges, and the core institutions of the state that are supposedly designed to address entrenched inequality, to protect the vulnerable and provide for citizens. We have invested deeply in our institutions and expend huge resources trying to make them work. They largely work for most of society. They do not work for all. Our institutions are also constantly reforming in response to global challenges, new technology and social change. The challenge is not just providing more choices for those best positioned to maximise their choices, but ensuring better and enhanced opportunities for those with limited opportunity to make genuine self-empowering choices.

As an educator I argue that, for both the individual and the family, education provides the most significant social pathway out of poverty and inequality. But this is to assume that education itself is not the production house of inequality, the place where the materially poor become even more impoverished, psychologically, emotionally and intellectually. It is not that anyone is trying to deny children educational success; there are, to the contrary, strong commitments within the educational system to ensuring all New Zealand children achieve at school. But, despite so much energy going into that effort, success remains elusive for a great many of our children. We need to look deeply at our systems and genuinely question their usefulness in resolving inequalities.

In Aotearoa/New Zealand, we like putting people in prison to punish, to exclude and to further alienate them from their deeds and responsibilities, and we have become more inclined to do so as inequality has risen (see Chapter 8). It is, supposedly, for everyone else's protection. But society is not protected. Prisons create prisoners. If not radically rehabilitated, then prisoners remain prisoners within society, as do their families. Having lots of prisons does not make a safe society, just a society that locks up people who then have to be dealt with later when they are returned to society. The prison industrial complex is as much a product of the neoliberal vision of society as inequalities. Yes, we have dangerous people who ought to be locked up, but we also create dangerous people who then need to be locked up.

Gifting the next generation

The rising generations of Māori and Pacific youth provide one opportunity to change the future if their access to that future is implemented now. In terms of the youthfulness of the Māori and Pacific populations and the ageing Pākehā population, this rising generation will form a significant part of the working and decision-making population (Pacific peoples, as Karlo Mila noted in Chapter 6, have the youngest of all New Zealand's populations.) Their aspirations, their values and their decisions will influence New Zealand's future. This demographic profile has been described as the demographic dividend, gift or collateral.[2] I call it a gift of hospitality, not in the sense of actively extending hospitality but as a gift of themselves. They will serve. How well they are prepared to exercise generosity and hospitality is up to what we do now.

In the years 1999–2001 I carried out research with young people across New Zealand between the ages of fourteen to eighteen.[3] It was the turn of the twenty-first century. Over the course of a year, we held a series of focus groups with young people from diverse backgrounds; we then conducted youth tribunals in four different regions in which young people were invited to present submissions to a panel of about six adults from different backgrounds. The research identified an interesting generation of young people, strongly connected to their place, their local communities and regional identities, and globally engaged. Their sense of local place, region or iwi was, as to be expected, highly informed. The skateboarders had views about what the local council was or was not allowing them to do; Māori youth knew their iwi contexts; and many youth knew that their future would take them away from where they had been brought up. Some individual presenters gave highly nuanced ethnographic accounts of their neighbourhoods, main street or landscape that showed they understood much more about the complexity of society than they may have been given credit for. More importantly, they probably had, through schooling, more conceptual tools for dealing with diversity than their parents' generation. Most were, as one might expect, hopeful, with high aspirations of their future adulthood, proud of their identities, articulate, opinionated and informed. Others, however, were aware already of where they were missing out, anxious about their future prospects, and suspicious of the world. This generation – people who were in their late adolescence at the beginning of the twenty-first century and the children some were then beginning to produce – can be seen as forming what has been referred to as the demographic gift, the generation that will support the nation going forward. This generation has enough to contend with without the deep divisions caused by inter-generational inequality.

The challenge of engaging the non-engaged
Education plays a crucial role in enabling social participation and providing pathways out of inequality and poverty (see Chapters 9 and

12). The big question sociologists ask is whether education leads to social participation and transformation or simply reproduces existing relations of power. Different governments have clearly had a focus on literacy and numeracy, the building blocks of education. But this focus on its own is insufficient without parallel labour market, social and economic policies. Poor people are not dumb people; they can read the contradictions of policies and the false hopes of political rhetoric and employ their own resistance strategies.

What does it mean to give up hope? In another project I met people in a community who were engaged to support their local schools. My role was to help them shape a school and community vision for education. The first attempt, conducted with parents, was an abject failure; parents' expectations of their local schools had dropped so low that they hoped only for schools to help teach their children to read. The second effort at community envisioning involved the children and the result was dramatically different; the community's children were much more able to express their hopes and dreams for the future. The project happened some time ago, but I remember to this day my own deep sadness at what it means to lose hope, to have no hope at all. The parents I was talking to, at that time, were in their twenties. The communities were rural and predominantly Māori. What does it mean to have given up on the systems that are intended to nurture aspirations, to provide the skills and wherewithal to be engaged in society?

I recall driving back to Auckland in my outrage, and asking my Vice-Chancellor Dr John Hood to officially 'adopt' those schools and communities. The university, I argued passionately, should be doing more than we were at the time to ensure our resources were being ploughed back into communities. By resources, I meant cultural and intellectual capital, as much as technical and educative. At the time, the university was grappling with its social responsibilities, and this little outburst may or may not have been helpful. I felt better having said it, but only temporarily, as the problem of hopelessness has not diminished. Graham Smith, the current head of Te Whare Wānanga o Awanuiārangi and a well-known Māori educator, has since referred to the challenge of providing a '360° community intervention' that goes beyond schooling to community development with national facilitation through better policy frameworks, and initiatives that work across health, economic development, employment, education and capacity-building.[4]

The current Whānau Ora programme attempts to coordinate some of the efforts of government through collaboration among service providers.

This initiative has value but is challenged by being essentially the same model that has resulted previously in people falling through the cracks and staying in the fissures of an unequal society. In other words, coordinating existing programmes might squeeze more out of the programmes through efficiency gains, but does not transform them. Some attempts have been made by providers to propose genuine alternative models that leverage off community strengths and use iwi-based frameworks, but many of these have not been funded. Providers are also shaped in ways that implicate them in the problem: they survive on contracts and have little infrastructure to re-imagine themselves. The key problem is embedded in the contracting paradigm, and the focus on short-term gains of individual clients rather than systemic change of the conditions that foster inequalities.

A call for imaginative excellence

In his book called *Radical Hope*, philosopher Jonathan Lear questions how society makes ethical decisions in the face of cultural devastation. He asks for *imaginative excellence* and a definition of courage that *calls for concepts* that help us *face up to reality*.[5] The question needs asking of our society now. Do we live in a time of imaginative excellence? Deep social divisions that overwhelm and immerse generations become entrenched for the privileged as much as for the poor. It locks in a set of relationships that come to determine and shape everything about that society: its sense of security, its own engagement with the world, its directions and accomplishments.

If we are prepared to face up to the reality of inequality, then the next step is how we *call for concepts*. Clearly, there are already individuals, community groups and agencies willing to 'intervene' and help fix the problem; they have been trying to fix the problem for a number of years. The *call for concepts*, however, requires us to do more work before rushing in to fix anything. It urges us to understand not only the empirical reality of inequality but the cultural devastation that inequality also represents. Whānau Ora does recognise the significance of cultural strengths in its approach, but Lear's idea of cultural devastation is about the whole of a society not just the groups that are identified and targeted as the problem of poverty. Inequality is a 'whole-of-society' problem and is not the problem of the poor. Imaginative excellence is how we as a society transcend our current paradigms and strive for a whole-of-society transformation.

Glossary

Accommodation supplement: Weekly financial support provided by the New Zealand government to help people pay their rent, board or mortgage.

Aggregate demand: The amount that households, companies and governments wish to spend on goods and services, given the level of prices; in other words, how much demand there is for the economy's products.

All-in tax rate: The average rate of tax incurred by an individual who faces national income taxes, local income taxes and flat rate 'payroll' taxes designed to fund social services. In most countries, the all-in tax rate is much higher than the simple income tax rate. New Zealand is rare in that much income is subject to just one rate of tax.

Anglo-American countries: Refers to English-speaking predominantly Euro-ethnic countries, notably the United States, United Kingdom, Canada, Australia, Ireland and New Zealand.

Assimilative ideology: The belief in the integration of minorities into a society that involves assimilation on terms that submerge the identity of the minority ethnic groups, obliging their members to conform to the majority culture.

Capital flight: The situation where financial assets denominated in a country's currency are rapidly sold due to an adverse event or belief relating to that country's economy.

Capital gains: The financial gain from the appreciation of asset prices. Such gains are subject to taxation in New Zealand only when received by businesses that trade in such assets, and when realised through their sale.

Complex equality: The idea that an advantage in one sphere, such as having a higher income, should not translate into other spheres, for instance by buying political influence.

Credit rating: An evaluation by an international rating agency of the credit worthiness of a government or corporation. A sovereign credit rating downgrade increases the theoretical risk that a government may default on its debt servicing. Such a default typically leads to an increase in the interest rates it must pay in the future.

Credit subsidies: Schemes in which government effectively subsidises borrowing by reducing the rates of interest that eligible borrowers are required to pay.

Currency stabilisation: Action taken to reduce excessive movement in the exchange rate of a country's currency. This can offset speculative buying or selling of assets denominated in that currency.

Decile: A group or section representing one-tenth of any given population. Decile divisions are commonly applied to individual, household or community incomes. Community income divisions are used to make socio-economic classifications of schools.

Default choice: An option that represents the action or outcome that will prevail unless an alternative choice is made. Our tendency to inertia means that, in most cases, the default choice will be the most common choice.

Demographic: An attribute of a population or sub-population relating to age, gender, ethnicity or other characteristic.

Discourse: A formal discussion about a particular topic or theme.

Disposable income: The entitlement to goods and services that people have after payment of taxes and receipt of benefits. See also 'Market income'.

Domestic purposes benefit (DPB): A weekly payment made by the New Zealand government to sole parents with one or more dependent children, or in some cases to other carers and to women alone who have been carers.

Egalitarian: Egalitarian views are ones that endorse the equality of all humankind, and/or the principle that people should be valued equally regardless of characteristics such as ethnicity or wealth.

Egalitarianism, general: A governing principle relating to the underlying equality of humankind, and for the desirability of outcomes that approach socio-economic equality.

Egalitarianism, specific: A policy approach that seeks equality only in those areas deemed to be particularly important.

Equilibrium price: The price at which supply and demand are balanced. It represents the ideal price for goods and services in neoclassical economic theory.

Equivalisation: A process in which households' real incomes are artificially adjusted to reflect their size and make-up. This enables data to be more accurately compared across households.

Estate duty: A tax payable on the death of a person, calculated on the monetary value of their estate. It was abolished in New Zealand in 1993.

Ethnographic: Relating to the branch of anthropology that deals with the scientific description of specific human cultures.

Eurozone: The subset of the European Union which uses the Euro currency.

Eurozone crisis: An ongoing financial crisis of unbalanced trade that has left some, mainly southern European countries with unservicable private and public sector debts that cannot be addressed, as such problems can be in most other countries, through currency depreciation.

Externalities: Costs or benefits that result from activities or transactions which affect otherwise uninvolved parties who did not choose to incur that cost or benefit. For instance, any environmental damage done by greenhouse gas pollution is borne by all of society.

Factor of production: Resources used to produce goods or services. These are normally identified as labour (human resources), land (natural resources), and capital (constructed resources).

Financial sector: The institutions, instruments and markets – notably banks and other lenders – engaged in exchanging goods and services for financial assets, and exchanging certain types of assets for other types of assets. It includes the legal and regulatory framework that permits transactions to be made through the extension of credit.

Formal equality: The technical equality created by everyone being equal before the law – regardless of whether other circumstances (such as an inability to afford legal fees) prevent them from exercising their equal right to fair legal treatment. Contrast 'Substantive equality'.

Gross domestic product (GDP): The value of all the final goods and services produced for sale within an economy; in other words, the income that a country generates.

Gift duty: A tax payable on transfers of assets or money, commonly intended to prevent people avoiding estate taxes by giving away their wealth. The tax was abolished in New Zealand in 2011.

Global financial crisis (GFC): The global financial crisis of 2008 which precipitated global recession in 2009.

Great Depression: The deep and prolonged economic recession, centred on the years 1931-34, that affected all developed capitalist economies.

Goods and services tax (GST): A flat rate value-added tax levied on items of consumption in New Zealand.

High net worth individuals (HNWI): People with more than US$1 million in readily investable assets (not including the family home) and cash.

Human capital: People's skills, attributes and abilities (notably those gained through education) that augment their capacity to produce goods and services.

International Monetary Fund (IMF): An international organisation, founded as a result of the 1944 Bretton Woods conference on post-war reconstruction, tasked with maintaining world financial stability, in particular through conditional loans to countries on the verge of insolvency.

Industrial policy: A country's plan to encourage the development and growth of specific sectors of the economy.

Industry subsidies: Incentives in the form of tax discounts or the injection of financial capital to encourage industrial development.

Inequality: The extent of divergence of income and/or wealth within a society. Typically the term refers to disparities among individuals and groups, but can refer to income differences between countries.

Inequality, horizontal: Inequality between groups; also, an inequality that an individual suffers as a result of their membership of a group (for example an ethnic minority).

Inequality, vertical: Inequality between individuals, some of whom will be higher on the income 'ladder' than others.

Instrumental: Practical or evidence-based; often used to distinguish certain arguments from others that are moral or theoretical.

Kaitiakitanga: A way of managing resources, based on a Māori worldview and drawing on ideas of guardianship and protection.

KiwiSaver: A government-initiated retirement savings scheme in New Zealand in which individual contributions are augmented by contributions from the government and employers.

Liberty, negative: The idea that people have liberty as long as they are simply free *from* constraints on action, such as censorship or discrimination on the basis of ethnicity.

Liberty, positive: The idea that people have liberty only if they are helped to be free *to* carry out certain action and take advantage of theoretically available opportunities, for example through positive discrimination policies.

Long boom: Term used mainly to refer to the period of strong economic growth from the Second World War up to the 'oil crisis' of the early 1970s.

Long Depression: Worldwide economic deflation of the late nineteenth century. Many countries including New Zealand experienced minimal rates of per capita growth, with many inequalities emerging.

Longitudinal: A term that describes any study that follows its participants over a long period of time.

Macroeconomic: Relating to the aggregation of national economies – and the global economy – as a whole, rather than the behaviour of individual markets or sectors; the branch of economics that covers topics such as unemployment, inflation, balance of payments and economic growth. See also 'Microeconomic'.

Managed exchange rates: The floating exchange rates that result in part from governments 'managing' them by selling and buying financial assets denominated in various currencies, including their own.

Manaakitanga: The act of hospitality and generosity extended to guests and relations, as part of a set of reciprocal obligations, in Māori society.

Mansion tax: Any proposal to levy an annual tax on properties above a certain size – 'mansions' – so as to tax wealth more progressively.

Marginal productivity: The extra amount of goods or services produced by employing a small amount of an additional resource (typically labour), such as another worker or an existing employee working for an extra period of time.

Marginal tax rate: The amount of tax paid on extra dollars earned.

Market economies: Economies in which the major dynamic is the market, the exchange of goods and services for money; as opposed to economies based on shared production of goods and/or non-financial exchanges.

Market failure: Any situation in which the market fails to provide the ideal result that neoclassical economic theory would predict; any situation of economic inefficiency in which market processes produce too much or too little of a given good or service.

Market income: The amount of goods and services that people's market activities entitle them to – for example as wages, interest, profits and royalties – before taxes are paid and benefits received. See also 'Disposable income'.

Mass imprisonment: The situation where imprisonment rates for certain communities are significantly higher than they are for others, or were in the past, with severe consequences for the affected communities.

Mathematically tractable models: Economic models that are attractive to certain (often neoclassical) economists because they can be explained and examined using mathematical equations. See also 'Neoclassical economics'.

Mean: The arithmetic average. The number obtained by adding up a set of numbers and dividing by the number of items in that set; for instance, the mean of 3, 4 and 8 is 5, that is, (3+4+8) ÷ 3. Contrast 'Median'.

Means testing: The practice of restricting people's access to support in money or in kind – such as benefits – based on how much income and assets they have.

Median: The number that is in the mid-point of a string of numbers; for instance, the median of 3, 4 and 8 is 4, the middle number. The median is often used as a better guide to typical incomes than is the average, as it is not pulled upwards by high salaries or royalties. Contrast 'Mean'.

Microeconomic: The branch of economics dealing with individual consumers and producers and their interactions in particular markets. See also 'Macroeconomic'.

NCEA: National Certificate of Educational Achievement, New Zealand's standard system of educational assessment in secondary schools.

NEETs: Young people not in education, employment or training.

Neoclassical economics: The paradigm of economics based in large part on the assumption that individuals generally act in a calculated and self-interested way so as to maximise their well-being or 'utility'. See also 'Mathematically tractable models'.

Neoliberal: A philosophical offshoot of classical liberalism that emphasises capitalistic freedom, private property rights and limited government. It can be understood as the normative component of neoclassical economics.

New Zealand Superannuation: An indexed universal pension payable to New Zealanders over the age of 65.

Occupy movement: An international protest movement against social and economic inequality, which began in 2011.

OECD: The Organisation for Economic Co-operation and Development, a group of thirty-four developed countries, of which New Zealand is a member.

Oil shocks (1970s): The sudden and rapid increase in the cost of oil on at least two occasions in the 1970s, leading to a period of low growth and high inflation.

Otahuhu portage: Portage Road in Otahuhu, Auckland, runs across a narrow strip of land, surrounded by water on two sides. It is said to divide the greater Auckland community along socio-economic lines.

Pākehā: A Māori term for someone who is not of Māori descent.

Palagi: A Samoan term for someone of European ethnicity.

Patterned relative outcomes: Inequalities in incomes or other outcomes that are fixed or set in some way; the actual 'pattern' of incomes in a society, as opposed to the movement of people up and down through different incomes.

Penalisation: The act of imposing a penalty on a person for breaking a rule or regulation; in particular, the shift in welfare systems away from focusing on supporting people, to punishing them for not doing certain things.

PISA tests: The Programme for International Student Assessment (PISA), an OECD co-ordinated comparison of the educational abilities of students in 65 different countries, focusing on maths, science and reading skills among secondary students.

Poverty, material: Lacking the resources to acquire certain basic necessities, such as home heating and nutritious food; a synonym for material deprivation.

Poverty, relative: Lacking the resources to acquire goods and services that most others have and which, by virtue of others having them, enable full participation in society.

Price system: The market system which uses relative prices to allocate resources.

Procedural securing of opportunities: A focus on ensuring that the processes theoretically guaranteeing equal opportunities are in place, as opposed to a focus on ensuring actually equal opportunities or outcomes are achieved. See also 'Formal equality'.

Productive sector: The part of the economy that produces goods and non-financial services. See also 'Financial sector'.

Productivity: A measure of how much output (of goods and services) is produced with a given set of workers, equipment, and so on. Continued productivity growth – generating more income for each hour that people work – is generally seen as vital to improving a country's average standard of living.

Psychosocial stress: Stress generated by our sense of our social position with regards to others; in other words, the effect on our mental – and thus physical – state of comparing ourselves with others.

Quintile: A statistical value, which divides a data set into five equal proportions. See also 'decile'.

Rational maximisation: In neoclassical economics the way that people are assumed to behave – acting calculatedly to maximise their own or their household's well-being. See also 'Neoclassical economics'.

Realisation-focused comparisons: A process of choosing between options that are or might realistically be available, as opposed to seeking a perfect solution.

Regressive taxes: Taxes that extract a higher percentage of lower incomes than higher ones, for example, GST.

Second great crash: Another term for the global financial crisis (GFC) of 2008.

Socio-economic status: An economic and sociological measure that combines factors such as a person's income, education and occupation.

SROI: Social return on investment, a method that measures the broader social, environmental and economic value of an investment, rather than purely its financial return.

Substantive equality: The kind of equality people have if they are given assistance (where needed) to actually enjoy their theoretical equality with other people (for example through legal aid, or positive discrimination programmes for disadvantaged groups). See also 'Formal equality' and 'Vertical equality'.

Tangata whenua: Literally 'people of the land'. A phrase denoting the status of Māori as Aotearoa/New Zealand's indigenous people.

Tariffs: Customs duties or taxes that may be imposed on a particular imports or exports.

Tauiwi: A Māori term denoting non-indigenous New Zealanders.

Tax avoidance: Structuring one's finances, legally, to minimise the amount of tax paid.

Tax credits: Monetary payments made through Inland Revenue (or other taxation authorities); negative taxes. In New Zealand, top-up payments made to low- and middle-income households under the Working for Families scheme are called 'tax credits'.

Tax evasion: The criminal act of not paying or underpaying taxes for which a person or company is liable.

Tea Party: A US political movement that opposes 'big government' and promotes financially conservative policies. The Tea Party is often characterised as a grassroots movement, bringing together a disparate group of people, many of whom are libertarian, neo-conservative, or from the religious right.

Terms of trade: The ratio between the average prices of exports and the average prices of imports; commonly thought of as the quantity of imports that a given quantity of exports can purchase.

Thermo-regulatory: The ability of a body to keep its core temperature within a certain range, for humans typically around 37°C.

Unflued gas heaters: A heater that burns gas to produce heat but does not have a chimney to extract the combustion products away.

Working for Families: A system of government payments that top up the earnings of many people with low and middle incomes and dependent children under 19. Some components of this scheme discriminate against households whose main source of income is a benefit or is part-time employment. See also 'Tax credits'.

Endnotes

Chapter 1: Why Inequality Matters

1. Personal communications with Paul Adams, Carrus Corporation, and Phil Rhodes, Porirua City Council, May 2013.
2. Personal communication with Sharon Girvan, Housing New Zealand, 4 June 2013.
3. The number of people living on less than 60 per cent of equivalised median household income (contemporary median), after housing costs, rose from nine per cent in 1984 to 19 per cent in 2011. Bryan Perry, *Household Incomes in New Zealand: Trends in Indicators of Inequality and Hardship 1982 to 2011*, Ministry of Social Development, Wellington, August 2012, p.105. When it comes to hardship, around one-fifth of families in the lowest income groups report being unable to afford numerous basic items. Ibid., p.165.
4. Ibid., p.87; Jit Cheung, *Wealth Disparities in New Zealand*, Statistics New Zealand, Wellington, 2007, p.8. See Chapter 2 for more details.
5. On the Gini coefficient measure, though not on the 80:20 ratio. Ibid, p.10.
6. Most of that rise had taken place by the mid-1990s. Since the mid-2000s, Sweden, the Czech Republic and Finland have displaced New Zealand in the 'most increasingly unequal' stakes. OECD, *Society at a Glance 2011 – OECD Social Indicators*, 2011, http://www.oecd.org/social/soc/societyataglance2011-oecdsocialindicators.htm (accessed 26 May 2013).
7. Calculated using the average equivalised disposable income for a household in the lowest tenth ($11,000) and top tenth ($100,200). Perry, *Household Incomes in New Zealand*, p.218. In general, Perry cautions against using the above figure as a guide to the incomes of the lowest 10 per cent. However, this comparison uses it for three reasons. First, Perry's adjusted dataset is not available for 2011 to give a current comparison figure. Second, the above figure is used to ensure consistency with Chapter 2. Third, the key point across this book is the trend of a widening gap between top and lower end, which is the same regardless of which dataset is used. Figures for 2011 have been added in the Appendices to the main report, available from the MSD website at: http://www.msd.govt.nz/about-msd-and-our-work/publications-resources/monitoring/household-incomes/index.html (accessed 4 June 2013).
8. Cheung, *Wealth Disparities*, p.8.
9. For more details on these different inequalities, see Chapter 5, 'What Kind of Equality Matters?'.
10. Notable work in this field includes the Child Poverty Action Group's campaigns and supporting research, such as *Left Further Behind* (2011); the Every Child Counts campaign; and the Children's Commissioner's Expert Advisory Group on Solutions to Child Poverty in 2012.
11. The number of children deemed to be living in poverty depends on whether 'poverty' is defined as having less than 50 per cent or 60 per cent of the typical household's income, adjusted for size, and whether housing costs are deducted. See Perry, *Household Incomes in New Zealand*, p.107, or the discussion later in this chapter.
12. See Chapter 7 for further details of New Zealand's infectious disease record.
13. David Grimmond, *1000 Days to Get it Right for Every Child: The Effectiveness of Public Investment in New Zealand Children*, Infometrics Ltd for Every Child Counts, July 2011.
14. Ibid.
15. Hayley Hannan, 'Disease figures a national "embarrassment"', *New Zealand Herald*, 20 February 2012, http://www.nzherald.co.nz/nz/news/article.cfm?c_id=1&objectid=10786823 (accessed 26 April 2013).
16. Christi Parsons, 'Obama takes populist economic message to the heartland', *Los Angeles Times*, 6 December 2011, http://articles.latimes.com/2011/dec/06/nation/la-na-obama-kansas-20111207 (accessed 26 May 2013); Christine Lagarde, 'Stability and Growth for Poverty Reduction', speech to Bretton Woods Committee Annual Meeting, 15 May 2013, http://www.imf.org/external/np/speeches/2013/051513.htm (accessed 26 May 2013); The *Economist*, 'For richer, for poorer', Special Report: World Economy, 13 October 2012.

17. There are several forms of income that can be measured, including pre-tax income and 'final' income, which accounts for the value of the free public services that households consume. But the vast majority of New Zealand data is given in the form of household disposable income. Adjusting for household size is done through a process known as equivalisation, explained in Perry, *Household Incomes in New Zealand*, pp.26–29. Although this is not always the case, the equivalisation process assumes that income is shared 'reasonably equally' among household members, as a useful approximation.
18. Conversely, larger households also get economies of scale, although this only slightly offsets their extra costs.
19. For a perspective on why Māori in particular value other kinds of non-material wealth, see Poverty Action Waikato, *Talk About Poverty: Reporting Back and Moving Forward*, Hamilton, 2011, pp.6–7.
20. New Economics Foundation, *A Bit Rich: Calculating the Real Value to Society of Different Professions*, London, 2009, p.2.
21. Perry, *Household Incomes in New Zealand*, p.26. Along similar lines, the OECD has recently argued that, 'Money, while it cannot buy happiness, is an important means to achieving higher living standards.' OECD, 'Better Life Index', http://www.oecdbetterlifeindex.org/countries/new-zealand/ (accessed 29 May 2013).
22. Using the 60 per cent of after housing costs (constant value) figure. Perry, *Household Incomes in New Zealand*, p.118.
23. *Ka Tika ā Muri, Ka Tika ā Mua: Healing the Past, Building a Future: A Guide to Treaty of Waitangi Claims and Negotiations with the Crown*, Office of Treaty Settlements, Wellington, undated, p.16.
24. Ibid., pp.12–18.
25. Since 1994–95, a total of $1,484,608,102 has been provided as financial and commercial redress in historical Treaty settlements. This total includes Waikato-Tainui Raupatu ($170,000,000), Ngāi Tahu ($170,000,000), Ngāti Porou ($90,000,000) and Ngāti Toa ($70,610,000). The figures are for financial and commercial redress at the time of the settlement. These figures, covering all settlements to March 2013, were provided to the author by the Office of Treaty Settlements (personal communication, 10 April 2013). See also the settlement progress information on the Office of Treaty Settlements website: www.ots.govt.nz.
26. Human Rights Commission, *A Fair Go for All? Rite Tahi Tātou Katoa?: Addressing Structural Discrimination in Public Services*, Wellington, 2012, pp.18–19. These findings were confirmed by the United Nations Committee on the Elimination of Racial Discrimination, 'Concluding observations on New Zealand', 22 February 2013, CERD/C/NZL/CO/18-20.
27. John Gould, 'The Distribution of Personal Incomes, 1951–2006: Māori and non-Māori Compared', *New Zealand Population Review*, 33 & 34 (2007/08) pp.249–60; 2006 remains the last year for which we have data until the 2013 Census results are known.
28. Women do twice as much domestic work as men – 294 minutes a day, compared to 158 – according to the OECD's Better Life Index, http://www.oecdbetterlifeindex.org/countries/new-zealand/. The best-known account of the economic consequences of not valuing all kinds of work is in Marilyn Waring, *Counting for Nothing: What Men Value and What Women are Worth*, Allen and Unwin/Port Nicholson Press, Wellington, 1988.
29. Frank Castles, 'The Wage earners welfare state revisited', *Australian Journal of Social Issues*, 29, 2 (1994) pp.120–45; Melanie Nolan, *Breadwinning: New Zealand Women and the State*, Canterbury University Press, Christchurch, 2000.
30. Based on figures for women's average hourly earnings ($25.37) and men's ($29.28) in the quarter to March 2013, from Statistics New Zealand, 'Quarterly Employment Survey: March 2013 Quarter', 7 May 2013.
31. Women make up less than one-third of MPs, as is outlined by the Parliamentary Library, 'The 2011 General Election', Parliamentary Library Research Paper, Wellington, 2011. They also make up less than 15% of directors at our 100 largest companies, as is set out in the Human Rights Commission, *New Zealand Women's Census Participation 2012*, Wellington, 2012.
32. Damian Grimshaw and Jill Rubery, *Undervaluing Women's Work*, Equal Opportunities Commission, Manchester, 2007, v; Prue Hyman, *Women and Economics: A New Zealand Feminist Perspective*, Bridget Williams Books, Wellington, 1994, Part Two.
33. Grimshaw and Rubery, *Undervaluing Women's Work*, ix; Hyman, *Women and Economics*, p.79.
34. Sylvia Dixon, 'Pay Inequality between Men and Women in New Zealand', Department of

Labour, 2000, p.10.
35 Grimshaw and Rubery, *Undervaluing Women's Work*, viii.
36 Ronji Tanielu and Alan Johnson, *More Than Churches, Rugby & Festivals: A Report on the State of Pasifika People in New Zealand*, Salvation Army Social Policy and Parliamentary Unit, May 2013, p.42.
37 Human Rights Commission, *A Fair Go for All?*.
38 David Pearson, 'Ethnic inequalities – Ethnicity and income', Te Ara – the Encyclopedia of New Zealand, 13 July 2012, http://www.teara.govt.nz/en/ethnic-inequalities/page-5 (accessed 29 May 2013).
39 Perry, *Household Incomes in New Zealand*, pp.105–18.
40 See Chapter 2 for more details.
41 Assuming two children (one adolescent male, one ten-year-old), entitled to tax credit payments of $228, and accommodation supplement of $101. Calculations based partly on Vicki Robinson, *2011 Food Costs for Families*, Regional Public Health, 2012, p.15.
42 Department of Building and Housing, 'Market rent, 01 June 2012 – 30 Nov 2012, Porirua – Porirua East/Waitangirua', two-bedroom house, median rent, http://www.dbh.govt.nz/Utilities/marketrent/market-rent.aspx?CategoryId=258&SubCatId=6&SubCat1Id=63&SubCat2Id=71&SubCat3Id=72&ArticleId=53&Version=1.2&TLA=Porirua&RegionId=9 (accessed 11 December 2012).
43 *Information Package for Users of the Estimated Food Costs*, Department of Human Nutrition, University of Otago, 2011. Given that this study optimistically assumes that all parents have the time, skills and energy to prepare meals from scratch, and have access to low-cost supermarket food (which is not universally available), true food costs for a normal household are likely to be, in fact, substantially higher. Of course, some people can lower food costs by growing their own food. But this is not an option for the vast majority of low-income families living in inner cities, nor for anyone else who lacks the time, energy and skills for intensive gardening.
44 Calculated from *Petrol Car Operating Costs*, Automobile Association, 2012, using the 'Compact' category, and excluding interest and depreciation.
45 The Living Wage campaign calculates that a household with two wage-earners (one part-time) and two children, even if they get all their tax credits, would need $18.40 as a 'living wage', rather than the 2012 minimum wage of $13.50. For more information, see www.livingwage.org.nz.
46 More details on 'Mike' (his name has been changed) are available from the website of the Wellington soup kitchen, where he has been a regular guest: http://www.soupkitchen.org.nz/resources/living-on-a-benefit/ (accessed 26 February 2013).
47 Perry, *Household Incomes in New Zealand*, p.165.
48 Claire Smith, Winsome Parnell and Rachel Brown, *Family Food Environment: Barriers to Acquiring Affordable and Nutritious Food in New Zealand Households*, Families Commission, 2010, p.5.
49 Kristin Macfarlane, 'No food, no shoes and kids kept home', *Rotorua Daily Post*, 23 May 2012, http://www.rotoruadailypost.co.nz/news/no-food-no-shoes-and-kids-kept-home/1390496/ (accessed 8 May 2013).
50 Mark Tomlinson and Robert Walker, *Coping with Complexity: Child and Adult Poverty*, Child Poverty Action Group, London, 2009, p.16.
51 Children's Commissioner's Expert Advisory Group on Solutions to Child Poverty, *Solutions to Child Poverty in New Zealand: Evidence for Action*, December 2012, p.18.
52 Smith et al., *Family Food Environment*, p.25.
53 The figure is from Statistics New Zealand's Household Economic Survey, quoted in Child Poverty Action Group, *Hunger for Learning*, Auckland, 2011, p.16. It implies, of course, that for every stereotypical beneficiary who is spending $100 a week on alcohol, there must be at least another four spending nothing at all.
54 Ilan Katz, Judy Corlyon, Vincent La Placa and Sarah Hunter, *The Relationship Between Parenting and Poverty*, Joseph Rowntree Foundation, York, 2007, p.1.
55 Perry, *Household Incomes in New Zealand*, p.220. This figure is an average over the last three household economic surveys (2009, 2010 and 2011) and uses the 60 per cent of median after housing costs (constant value) figure.
56 Ruth Lister, *Poverty*, Polity Press, Cambridge, 2004, p.7.
57 Adam Smith, *The Wealth of Nations*, Glasgow Edition, 1976, WN V.ii.k.5, pp.869–70.
58 The 'typical' household in this case is the median one. As outlined earlier in this chapter, this measure is based on equivalised disposable income. It is calculated as a percentage of the 2011 median (the most recent available), since this, rather than the

fixed-line measures, best suits the book's focus on relative issues. In general, the after housing costs (AHC) measure is used, as it allows comparisons between groups with very different housing costs; but sometimes the before housing costs (BHC) figure is used because it is more readily understood by the general reader, who might struggle to calculate their AHC income. For a detailed discussion of how poverty lines are calculated, see Perry, *Household Incomes in New Zealand*, pp.201–6, and Robert Stephens, 'Dimensions of Poverty Measurement', *Policy Quarterly*, 9, 2 (May 2013), pp.18–23.

59 Robert Stephens, Charles Waldegrave and Paul Frater, 'Measuring Poverty in New Zealand', *Social Policy Journal of New Zealand*, 5 (December 1995), pp.88–112. Perry notes that 'more recent focus group work' confirms the importance of the 60 per cent figure. Perry, *Household Incomes in New Zealand*, p.201.

60 These figures, which are before housing costs for easier comprehension (see endnote 58), are from Perry, *Household Incomes in New Zealand*, p.96.

61 Kristie Carter and Fiona Imlach Gunasekara, 'Dynamics of Income and Deprivation in New Zealand, 2002–2009', Department of Public Health, University of Otago, Wellington, 2012.

62 David Clark, 'The PM's cleaner deserves more pay', *New Zealand Herald*, 4 September 2012, http://www.nzherald.co.nz/nz/news/article.cfm?c_id=1&objectid=10831428 (accessed 28 February 2013).

63 R.H. Tawney, quoted in Jane Franklin (ed.), *Equality*, Institute for Public Policy Research, London, 1997, p.16. Tawney was writing in 1931.

64 See, for instance, Alan B. Krueger, 'The Rise and Consequences of Inequality in the United States', speech to the Center for American Progress, 12 January 2012. Krueger draws on the 'Great Gatsby curve' created by Miles Corak, available in updated form from: http://milescorak.com/2012/01/12/here-is-the-source-for-the-great-gatsby-curve-in-the-alan-krueger-speech-at-the-center-for-american-progress/ (accessed 26 May 2013).

65 Markus Jantti et al., 'American Exceptionalism in a New Light: A Comparison of Intergenerational Earnings Mobility in the Nordic Countries, the United Kingdom and the United States', IZA DP No. 1938, Bonn, 2006.

66 Figures for investment in children's early years are in Grimmond, *1000 Days to Get it Right for Every Child*; figures for the social services spending of more egalitarian countries can be found on the OECD website, at http://stats.oecd.org/Index.aspx?DataSetCode=SOCX_AGG; and the inequality-reducing effects of egalitarian countries' welfare states are set out in Perry, *Household Incomes in New Zealand*, p.11.

67 The egalitarian Nordic societies, for instance, do as much to enable 'individual self-realization and personal autonomy' as any other country, by liberating people from dependence on employers or family members; see World Values Survey data in 'Shared Norms for the New Reality: The Nordic Way', World Economic Forum 2011, pp.15–16. Meanwhile, on Richard Florida's Global Creativity Index, three highly egalitarian countries – Sweden, Finland and Denmark – take three of the top four spots; see Richard Florida, 'The Global Creativity Index', *The Atlantic Cities*, 5 October 2011, http://www.theatlanticcities.com/jobs-and-economy/2011/10/global-creativity-index/229/ (accessed 8 May 2013). Finally, the Equality Trust notes that people in equal societies are just as likely to file high numbers of patents as those in unequal societies; see the trust's FAQs page at http://www.equalitytrust.org.uk/research/faqs (accessed 8 May 2013).

68 Deborah Coddington, 'Let's help everyone to top – not drag down wealthy', *New Zealand Herald*, 13 February 2011, http://www.nzherald.co.nz/business/news/article.cfm?c_id=3&objectid=10705861 (accessed 17 February 2013).

69 New Economics Foundation, *A Bit Rich* p.3. In this framework, 'value' is calculated by taking a broad perspective on the costs and benefits of any given activity; in particular, a range of 'externalities' are taken into account. So, for instance, bankers destroy economic value through the cost of the financial crisis on GDP and productive economic capacity, while childcare workers create value by allowing parents to keep working, promoting gender equity and enabling parents to be more focused at work.

70 'No reputable study has shown that executive pay has been successfully linked to company performance. Indeed the body of evidence challenging the link between pay and performance has become increasingly compelling.' High Pay Commission, *Cheques With Balances: Why Tackling High Pay is in the National Interest*, London, November 2011, p.43. The best New Zealand evidence is

in Helen Roberts, 'Executive Compensation in New Zealand: 1997–2002', PhD thesis, Otago University, 2007. In Chapter 3, Robert Wade also makes the point that high salaries in particular fields – notably finance – divert bright graduates from other, potentially more worthwhile professions.

71 Steven Stillman, Trinh Le, John Gibson, Dean Hyslop and David C. Maré, *The Relationship between Individual Labour Market Outcomes, Household Income and Expenditure, and Inequality and Poverty in New Zealand from 1983 to 2003*, Motu, Wellington, 2012, p.16.

72 Zaid Jilani, 'Average Japanese CEO Earns One-Sixth As Much As American CEOs', *Think Progress*, 8 July 2010, http://thinkprogress.org/politics/2010/07/08/106536/japanese-ceo-american-sixth/?mobile=nc (accessed 31 March 2013).

73 Roberts, 'Executive Compensation in New Zealand', p.4.

74 Joseph Stiglitz, 'Of the 1%, by the 1%, for the 1%', *Vanity Fair*, May 2011, http://www.vanityfair.com/society/features/2011/05/top-one-percent-201105 (accessed 25 April 2013).

75 Andrew G. Berg and Jonathan D. Ostry, 'Inequality and Unsustainable Growth: Two Sides of the Same Coin?', IMF staff discussion note, 8 April 2011, pp.9–10.

76 Raghuram G. Rajan, *Fault Lines: How Hidden Fractures Still Threaten the World Economy*, Princeton University Press, New Jersey, 2010.

77 Richard Wilkinson and Kate Pickett, *The Spirit Level: Why Equality is Better for Everyone*, Penguin, London, 2010.

78 See, for instance, Christopher Snowdon, *The Spirit Level Delusion: Fact-Checking the Left's New Theory of Everything*, Democracy Institute, 2010; and Peter Saunders, *Beware False Prophets: Equality, the Good Society and the Spirit Level*, Policy Exchange, 2010. The latter is written by the Austro-British sociologist Professor Peter Saunders, not the Australian social researcher Professor Peter Saunders. For a peer-reviewed line of argument that, in contrast to *The Spirit Level*, emphasises material poverty rather than inequality per se, see J. Lynch, G. Davey Smith, G. Kaplan et al., 'Income inequality and mortality: Importance to health of individual income, psychosocial environment or material conditions', *British Medical Journal*, 320(7243), 2000, pp.1200–1204; and J. Lynch, G. Davey Smith, S. Harper et al., 'Is Income Inequality a Determinant of Population Health? Part 1: A Systematic Review', *The Milbank Quarterly*, 82(1), 2004, pp.5–99.

79 The following discussion draws heavily on Wilkinson and Pickett, *The Spirit Level*, pp.31–45.

80 Richie Poulton, 'Expert Advisory Group on Child Poverty', presentation to Workshop on Solutions to Child Poverty in New Zealand, organised by the Institute for Governance and Policy Studies, Wellington, 19 September 2012. The Dunedin research does not identify causality, but suggests three possibilities: class-biased access to health services, class differentiated parenting practices, and stress.

81 Michael Marmot, Geoffrey Rose, Martin Shipley, and P. J. S. Hamilton, 'Employment grade and coronary heart disease in British civil servants', *Journal of Epidemiology and Community Health*, 32, 4 (December 1978), pp.244–49.

82 Paul Barber, 'How to Get Closer Together: Impacts of Income Inequality and Policy Responses', *Policy Quarterly*, 7, 4 (November 2011), p.63.

83 Wilkinson and Pickett, *The Spirit Level*, p.176.

84 Ibid., pp.49–62.

85 Ibid., p.230.

86 Levels of trust have traditionally been high: New Zealand Treasury, 'Living Standards Background Note: "Increasing Equity"', January 2013, p.22. However, in the most recent New Zealand Quality of Life survey, the percentage who say other people can be trusted fell from 77% in 2008 to 62% in 2012. Since this may be connected to, among other things, the recent finance company collapses, and since the 2004 figure was 69%, the link with inequality is not proven. But it is a worrying fall nonetheless. The Quality of Life surveys are available at: http://www.qualityoflifeproject.govt.nz/survey.htm (accessed 29 May 2013).

87 Wilkinson and Pickett, *The Spirit Level*, pp.52–53.

88 Deb Schwarz and Charles Crothers, *Macro Auckland: Informing and Inspiring Generosity – summary report*, Auckland Communities Foundation, 2011, p.33.

89 Paul White, Jinny Gunston, Clare Salmond, June Atkinson and Peter Crampton, *Atlas of Socioeconomic Deprivation in New Zealand NZDep2006*, Ministry of Health, Wellington, 2008, p.136.

90 Ibid., pp.51–54.

91 Jonathan Boston, 'The Challenge of Securing Durable Reductions in Child Poverty in New Zealand', *Policy Quarterly*, 9, 2 (May 2013), p.9.

92 The best-known exploration of this phenomenon is in Robert Putnam, *Bowling Alone: The Collapse and Revival of American community*, Simon & Schuster, New York, 2000.
93 Brett Parker, 'Very long-term jobseekers' barriers to employment: a nationwide survey', *Labour Market Bulletin*, 1997/1, pp.63–79.
94 Strategic Review of Health Inequalities in England post 2010, *Fair Society, Healthy Lives: The Marmot Review – Executive Summary*, London, 11 February 2010.
95 Vicki Robinson, 'Factors influencing (barriers and promoters) the stocking, promotion and pricing of "healthy" foods by small store owners in Eastern Porirua, Wellington', research project for a Masters of Health Sciences at the University of Otago, Dunedin, November 2011.
96 Patrick Wintour, 'A cerebral address on moral limits of markets', *Guardian*, 30 September 2012, http://www.guardian.co.uk/politics/2012/sep/30/labour-conference-2012-markets?INTCMP=ILCNETTXT3487 (accessed 28 February 2013).
97 One recent example is Michael Kumhof and Romain Ranciére, 'Inequality, Leverage and Crises', IMF Working Paper, November 2010. A slightly older review of the evidence finds significant support for claims that inequality limits growth, though also counter-arguments; see Cesar Gallo, 'Economic growth and income inequality: theoretical background and empirical evidence', Development Planning Unit, University College London, Working Paper No. 119. See also the IMF research by Berg and Ostry, and Joseph Stiglitz's *The Price of Inequality*, both referenced below.
98 Andrew G. Berg and Jonathan D. Ostry, 'Inequality and Unsustainable Growth: Two Sides of the Same Coin?', IMF staff discussion note, 8 April 2011.
99 OECD, 'Income inequality and poverty rising in most OECD countries', press release, 21 October 2008, http://www.oecd.org/els/soc/incomeinequalityandpovertyrisingin mostoecdcountries.htm (accessed 8 May 2013).
100 David MacLeod and Nita Clarke, *Engaging for Success: Enhancing Performance Through Employee Engagement*, Department for Business, Innovation and Skills, London, 2009.
101 Joseph E. Stiglitz, *The Price of Inequality*, Allen Lane, London, 2012, pp.94–95 in particular but also throughout.
102 Kumhof and Ranciere, 'Inequality, Leverage and Crises'.
103 See, for instance, Stephen Knowles, 'Inequality and Economic Growth: The Empirical Relationship Reconsidered in the Light of Comparable Data', Centre for Research in Economic Development and International Trade, University of Nottingham, CREDIT Research Paper No. 01/03, March 2001, p.3. See also Viewpoint 11.
104 Tim Hazledine, *Taking New Zealand Seriously: The Economics of Decency*, HarperCollins, Auckland, 1998.
105 ECE Taskforce, *An Agenda for Amazing Children: Final Report of the ECE Taskforce*, June 2011, p.63.

Chapter 2: Inequality and New Zealand

1 The figures here and in the following paragraphs are based on the 3.4 million tax returns filed with the Inland Revenue for the year to March 2011, and therefore do not cover all income. However, they are used here in preference to the other figures because they give vastly more detail on top incomes. See Inland Revenue data, http://www.ird.govt.nz/aboutir/external-stats/revenue-refunds/inc-dist-of-ind/ (accessed 23 May 2013).
2 Ministry of Social Development, 'Benefit rates at 1 April 2012', http://www.msd.govt.nz/documents/about-msd-and-our-work/newsroom/media-releases/2012/benefit-rates-table-april-2012.pdf (accessed 15 May 2013).
3 Kate Shuttleworth, 'Battle for a living wage: Ghosts in corridors of power highlight disparities in pay', *New Zealand Herald*, 13 February 2013, http://www.nzherald.co.nz/nz/news/article.cfm?c_id=1&objectid=10865001 (accessed 29 May 2013).
4 A senior firefighter gets a maximum of $1,086 a week, or $56,472 annually. Personal communication with New Zealand Professional Firefighters Union, 4 June 2013.
5 Teachers' salary figure from Post Primary Teachers' Association (PPTA) collective contract, http://ppta.org.nz/index.php/collective-agreements/stca/90-part-four?start=1 (accessed 21 May 2013).
6 Solicitors with at least five years' experience typically earn $90,000–175,000, according to the Careers NZ website, http://www.careers.govt.nz/jobs/law/solicitor/about-the-job (accessed 21 May 2013).
7 From the Parliamentary Salaries and Determinations Allowances 2011, http://www.legislation.govt.nz/regulation/

public/2011/0410/latest/DLM4148103.html (accessed 21 May 2013).
8. Finance managers with more than six years' experience typically earn over $150,000, according to the Careers NZ website, http://www.careers.govt.nz/jobs/finance/chief-financial-officer/ (accessed 29 May 2013).
9. Principal accountants earn $130,000–200,000, according to the Careers NZ website, http://www.careers.govt.nz/jobs/finance/accountant/ (accessed 21 May 2013).
10. These figures cover only the public service and state sector, and therefore do not include salaries at, for example, state-owned enterprises. State Services Commission, 'Remuneration of Public Service and State sector senior staff as at 30 June 2012', September 2012.
11. Christopher Adams, 'CEO Pay Survey: Salaries stall for NZ's top bosses', *New Zealand Herald*, 8 June 2012, http://www.nzherald.co.nz/business/news/article.cfm?c_id=3&objectid=10811482 (accessed 15 May 2013).
12. These figures are derived from Bryan Perry, *Household Incomes in New Zealand: Trends and Indicators of Inequality and Hardship 1982 to 2011*, Ministry of Social Development, Wellington, 2012, p.45. The weekly figures are derived by dividing Perry's figures by 52.
13. Jit Cheung, *Wealth Disparities in New Zealand*, Statistics New Zealand, Wellington, 2007, p.8. These figures are based on the 2003–4 Survey of Family, Income and Employment, and cover the 2.9 million people aged 15 and over normally resident in New Zealand at the time of the survey.
14. The 'typical' household here is the median. Ibid., p.5.
15. Like all measures, the Gini coefficient has particular features; notably, it is more sensitive to changes in the middle of the income distribution than at the ends. But while other measures have been developed, such as the Theil and Atkinson indexes, the Gini remains the most commonly used.
16. Pareto-Lorenz coefficients tabled in the World Top Incomes Database (http://topincomes.g-mond.parisschoolofeconomics.eu) show New Zealand did have one of the lowest, or indeed *the* lowest, concentrations of income in the 1950s and 1960s (among developed, non-Soviet countries), but was slipping down the rankings even by the 1970s. This is backed by Gini coefficient data from the OECD (http://stats.oecd.org/Index.aspx?QueryId=26068), which shows that New Zealand was, by the mid-1980s, still one of the most equal countries, but well behind the Scandinavian nations.
17. The graph is derived from the figures and data in OECD, *Crisis Squeezes Income and Puts Pressure on Inequality and Poverty*, May 2013, Figure 4, 'Gini Coefficient of Household Disposable Income and Gap Between Richest and Poorest 10%, 2010', http://www.oecd.org/els/soc/OECD2013-Inequality-and-Poverty-8p.pdf (accessed 28 May 2013).
18. New Zealand's Gini coefficient, as recorded in Perry, *Household Incomes in New Zealand*, p.83, was 30.9 in 2010 and 33.3 in 2011. But because the OECD uses a different equivalence scale, as Perry notes, around 0.8 must be added to his figure for New Zealand's Gini coefficient to get the equivalent OECD figure; hence, the stated figures of 31.7 in 2010 and around 34 in 2011.
19. Both the *Dominion Post* and the *New Zealand Herald* now publish annual stories on chief executive pay; 2012's versions at http://www.stuff.co.nz/business/money/7366296/Growing-pay-gap-between-CEOs-staff and http://www.nzherald.co.nz/business/news/article.cfm?c_id=3&objectid=10811482 (accessed 28 May 2013). Significant research into social mobility has recently been carried out by Kristie Carter at the University of Otago and Matthew Gibbons at the Treasury. Others at the Treasury, including Omar Aziz, Emma Ball, Gerald Minnee, Chris Ball and Emma Gorman, have researched the inequality-reducing effect of government action. The pioneering poverty research of Bob Stephens, Charles Waldegrave and Paul Frater must also be acknowledged. Statistics New Zealand's *Wealth Disparities in New Zealand*, compiled by Jit Cheung, remains the best work on wealth inequality. Peter Skilling at AUT is embarking on a three-year project to improve our understanding of New Zealanders' attitudes towards inequality. And the most comprehensive work for income inequality is the Ministry of Social Development's *Household Incomes in New Zealand*, prepared annually by Bryan Perry.
20. Grahame Armstrong, 'Spotlight to fall on tax dodgers', *Sunday Star-Times*, www.stuff.co.nz/national/2998145/Spotlight-to-fall-on-tax-dodgers (accessed 11 December 2012)
21. Helen Roberts, 'Executive Compensation in New Zealand: 1997–2002', PhD thesis, Otago University, 2007.
22. Cheung, *Wealth Disparities in New Zealand*

23. Unicef, 'Child well-being in rich countries', April 2013, http://www.unicef-irc.org/ReportCard-11/ (accessed 29 May 2013).
24. Pareto-Lorenz coefficients in the World Top Incomes Database (http://topincomes.g-mond.parisschoolofeconomics.eu) show New Zealand had one of the lowest, or indeed *the* lowest, concentrations of income in the 1950s and 1960s (among developed, non-Soviet countries), but was slipping down the rankings by the 1970s. Gini coefficient data from the OECD (http://stats.oecd.org/Index.aspx?QueryId=26068) show that New Zealand was, by the mid-1980s, still one of the most equal countries, but well behind the Scandinavian nations.
25. Bronwyn Labrum, 'The Changing Meanings and Practices of Welfare', p.400, in Giselle Byrnes (ed.), *The New Oxford History of New Zealand*, Oxford University Press, Melbourne, 2009.
26. Ibid., p.118.
27. Steven Eldred-Grigg, *The Rich: A New Zealand History*, Penguin, Auckland, 1996.
28. Carpenter Samuel Parnell established the eight-hour working day by refusing to work longer while building a store for the merchant George Hunter. The trade union movement then extended the right to other workers. See 'Fighting for the Eight-hour Working Day', New Zealand History Online, http://www.nzhistory.net.nz/politics/labour-day (accessed 14 March 2013).
29. Melanie Nolan, 'The Reality and Myth of New Zealand Egalitarianism: Explaining the Pattern of a Labour Historiography at the Edge of Empires', *Labour History Review*, 72, 2 (August 2007), p.114.
30. Leslie Lipson, *The Politics of Equality: New Zealand's Adventures in Democracy*, Victoria University Press, Wellington, 2011, p7.
31. Nolan, 'The Reality and Myth of New Zealand Egalitarianism', p.127.
32. Tom Brooking, '"Bursting-Up" the Greatest Estate of All', pp.166–83, in Judith Binney (ed.), *The Shaping of History: Essays from the New Zealand Journal of History*, Bridget Williams Books, Wellington, 2001.
33. Nolan, 'The Reality and Myth of New Zealand Egalitarianism', p.124.
34. Graph compiled from figures in the World Top Incomes Database, for New Zealand, 1921–2009, top 1 per cent income share, http://topincomes.g-mond.parisschoolofeconomics.eu/ (accessed 14 March 2013). The spike near the end was caused by the wealthy declaring income before it could be hit by the incoming Labour Government's 39 per cent tax rate.
35. Paul Krugman, *The Conscience of a Liberal*, W.W. Norton & Company, New York, 2007.
36. Stewart Lansley, *The Cost of Inequality: Why Economic Equality Is Essential for Recovery*, Gibson Square, London, 2012, p.126.
37. As is explained below, before the changes of the 1980s and 1990s, 60 per cent of national income went to labour as opposed to capital.
38. John Gould, 'The Distribution of Personal Incomes, 1951 – 2006: Māori and non-Māori Compared', *New Zealand Population Review*, 33 & 34, 2007/08, pp.252–54.
39. See, for instance, Alan S. Blinder and Jeremy B. Rudd, 'The Supply-Shock Explanation of the Great Stagflation Revisited', Center for Economic Policy Studies, CEPS Working Paper No. 176, November 2008.
40. Colin James, *The Quiet Revolution: Turbulence and Transition in Contemporary New Zealand*, Allen & Unwin/Port Nicholson Press, 1986, pp.57–66.
41. Paul Dalziel and Ralph Lattimore, *The New Zealand Macroeconomy: A Briefing on the Reforms*, Oxford University Press, Auckland, 1999, pp.16–19.
42. National income is a shorthand for GDP. From the Treasury's historical fiscal data, www.treasury.govt.nz/government/data/fiscaltimeseries1972-2012-yearend12.xls (accessed 3 May 2013).
43. David Lange, *My Life*, Penguin, Auckland, 2005, pp.174–76.
44. Dalziel and Lattimore, *The New Zealand Macroeconomy*, ix.
45. An extensive literature on these structural changes includes Dalziel and Lattimore, *The New Zealand Macroeconomy;* Jane Kelsey, *The New Zealand Experiment: A World Model for Structural Adjustment?*, Bridget Williams Books, Wellington, 1995; Chris Rudd and Brian Roper (eds), *The Political Economy of New Zealand*, Oxford University Press, Auckland, 1997; Brian Easton, *In Stormy Seas: The Post-War New Zealand Economy*, Otago University Press, Dunedin, 1997; OECD, *OECD Economic Surveys: New Zealand 1993*, Paris, 1993; and The Treasury, *Government Management: Brief to the Incoming Government 1987*, The Treasury, Wellington, 1987.
46. The Treasury, *Working Towards Higher Living Standards for New Zealanders*, New Zealand Treasury Working Paper 11/02, Wellington, 2011, p.33.
47. What is represented is equivalised median

household income, which is not in fact quite the same as the average income of single-person households. But it is the closest approximation in everyday language.

48 Figures for the real equivalised household disposable incomes of the lowest 10 per cent (decile 1), middle (the average of deciles 5 and 6) and top (decile 10) are taken from the 'Decile means' table in Perry, *Household Incomes in New Zealand*, p.218. Decile means, rather than decile boundaries, are used because they show the income of the typical person within that decile, rather than the person at the edge of that decile. For a range of reasons, incomes in decile 1 are not always a reliable guide to the resources available to these households (ibid., pp.208–13). To help address this issue, Perry uses a modified dataset with information about household expenditure to better estimate resources available to these households. While this changes the year-on-year picture and smooths the trend line, the long-run change is very similar whichever approach is used (a 13–14 per cent rise in real terms from 1984 to 2010). Meanwhile, the figures for the top 1 per cent come from the World Top Incomes database (http://topincomes.g-mond. parisschoolofeconomics.eu/), and measure *pre-tax* income as opposed to disposable, or *post-tax*, income. Post-tax incomes for the top 1 per cent are not available; but this is not critical, for two reasons. First, the graph aims above all to show trends, and since the top 1 per cent probably now pay less tax (proportionately) than they did in 1984, the trend of their incomes more than doubling, pre-tax, would undoubtedly be equally (or even more) true for post-tax income. Second, while taxation would reduce the declared average incomes of the top 1 per cent below $300,000, these figures cover only declared income, and thus exclude capital gains, which have presumably increased significantly. These figures may therefore significantly *understate* the top 1 per cent's income gains. Figures for 2011 have been added in the Appendices to the main report, available from the MSD website at: http://www.msd.govt.nz/about-msd-and-our-work/publications-resources/monitoring/household-incomes/index.html (accessed 4 June 2013).

49 Gould, 'The Distribution of Personal Incomes, 1951–2006', pp.252 and 254.

50 Paul Dalziel argues that there is a clear case for linking the two. Paul Dalziel, 'New Zealand's Economic Reforms: an assessment', *Review of Political Economy*, 14, 1, 2002. A 2003 Motu analysis, in contrast, finds that 'changes in household structure and in the socio-demographic characteristics of households' are the main factors behind widening inequality. Dean R. Hyslop and David C. Maré, 'Understanding New Zealand's Changing Income Distribution 1983–98: A Semiparametric Analysis', Motu Working Paper 2003-16, October 2003. However, a later Motu paper from 2012 finds that 'controlling for changes in household composition, demographics, education, and employment rates does not explain the increase in poverty that occurred in the 1980s', and that 'the structural reforms undertaken in the 1980s led to permanent changes in the distribution of resources across households in New Zealand, in particular a reduction in resources for the poorest households'. Steven Stillman, Trinh Le, John Gibson, Dean Hyslop, and David C. Maré, 'The Relationship between Individual Labour Market Outcomes, Household Income and Expenditure, and Inequality and Poverty in New Zealand from 1983 to 2003', Motu Working Paper 12-02, February 2012.

51 Perry, *Household Incomes in New Zealand*, p.155.

52 Based on GDP per capita growth rates, 1960–2011, using figures from both the United States Bureau of Labor (http://www.bls.gov/ilc/intl_gdp_capita_gdp_hour.htm#table01) and the OECD (figures for GDP per capita, US dollars, current prices and PPPs, at http://www.oecd.org/statistics/). Robert Wade makes a similar point in Chapter Three.

53 Perry, *Household Incomes in New Zealand*, p.72.

54 Jonathan Boston, 'The Challenge of Securing Durable Reductions in Child Poverty in New Zealand', *Policy Quarterly*, 9, 2, May 2013, p.8.

55 For Māori unemployment figures, see Te Ara, 'Economic restructuring: Māori and total unemployment, 1986–2007 (2nd of 2)', http://www.teara.govt.nz/en/graph/30741/economic-restructuring-maori-and-total-unemployment-1986–2007 (accessed 29 May 2013); for Pacific peoples' unemployment figures, see Chapter 6.

56 Figure derived from 251,400 jobless and 83,300 underemployed. Statistics New Zealand, 'Quarterly Household Labour Force Survey', March 2013 Quarter, 9 May 2013, tables 8 and 11.

57 However, the numbers on some benefits, particularly the DPB, had already been rising

during the 1970s. Welfare Working Group, *Long-Term Benefit Dependency: The Issues – Summary Paper*, August 2010, p.9.
58 Kelsey, *The New Zealand Experiment*, p.276. The cuts were even more severe – around 25 per cent – for unemployment beneficiaries aged 20–24.
59 An Inland Revenue report notes that the value of housing-related payments under Working for Families was eroded by increased housing costs. *Inland Revenue, Changing Families' Financial Support and Incentives for Working: The Summary Report of the Evaluation of the Working for Families Package*, Wellington, July 2010, viii. For further evidence of costs increases hitting people on low incomes, see Amelia Wade, 'Price rises bite middle- and low-income earners', *New Zealand Herald*, 23 March 2013, http://www.nzherald.co.nz/nz/news/article.cfm?c_id=1&objectid=10873038 (accessed 4 June 2013); and Rob Stock, 'NZ families feel the income squeeze', *Dominion Post*, 4 December 2011, http://www.stuff.co.nz/business/money/6081835/NZ-families-feel-the-income-squeeze (accessed 4 June 2013).
60 Rob Salmond, *The New New Zealand Tax System: New Zealand Taxes in Comparative Perspective*, Institute of Policy Studies, Wellington, 2011, p.34.
61 Stillman et al., 'The Relationship between Individual Labour Market Outcomes', p.22.
62 Omar A. Aziz, Matthew Gibbons, Chris Ball and Emma Gorman, 'Fiscal Incidence in New Zealand: The Distributional Effect of Government Expenditure and Taxation on Household Income, 1988 to 2010', paper presented at the 53rd New Zealand Association of Economists Annual Conference, Palmerston North, 27–29 June 2012, p.7.
63 The OECD's analysis is that evidence on the causes of growing inequality is 'inconclusive', but suggests a role for a combination of globalisation and skills-based changes. OECD, *Divided We Stand: Why Inequality Keeps Rising*, OECD Publishing, 2011, pp.24–26.
64 David Grusky, 'Taxing Away Inequality: A Conversation with Emmanuel Saez', *Boston Review*, 28 February 2013, http://www.bostonreview.net/BR38.1/emmanuel_saez_david_grusky_income_inequality_taxes_rent_seeking.php (accessed 31 March 2013).
65 Jacob S. Hacker and Paul Pierson, *Winner-Take-All Politics: How Washington Made the Rich Richer – And Turned Its Back on the Middle Class*, Simon & Schuster, New York, 2010, pp.34–40.
66 New Zealand has the lowest 'earnings premium' in the OECD for people with tertiary education, according to figures published in September 2012, http://www.oecd.org/education/educationataglanceindicatorsrawdata.htm (accessed 26 May 2013).
67 Lawrence Mishel, John Schmitt, and Heidi Shierholz, 'Assessing the job polarization explanation of growing wage inequality', Economic Policy Institute Working Paper #295, 11 January 2013.
68 New Zealand Council of Trade Unions, *Submission to the Children's Commissioner's Experts Advisory Group on Solutions to Child Poverty*, Wellington, 2012, p.13. These figures have been adjusted to March 2011 dollars.
69 Historical average wage data from Ralph Lattimore and Shamubeel Eaqub, *The New Zealand Economy: An Introduction*, Auckland University Press, 2011. Data available at https://sites.google.com/site/eaqubs/.
70 Some research attributes up to one-third of the fall in inequality to weakened unions. Bruce Western and Jake Rosenfeld, 'Unions, Norms, and the Rise in U.S. Wage Inequality', *American Sociological Review*, 76, 4 (2011), pp.513–37. Other research indicates that declining union membership accounts for a 'substantial' part of the growth in market income inequality, among men at least. David Card, Thomas Lemieux and W. Craig Riddell, 'Unionization and Wage Inequality: A Comparative Study of the U.S, the U.K., and Canada', NBER Working Paper No. 9473, February 2003.
71 According to OECD data on trade union density, http://stats.oecd.org/Index.aspx?QueryId=20167# (accessed 31 March 2013).
72 Based on OECD figures, 'Unit Labour Costs – Annual Indicators: Labour Income Share Ratios', 1980–2012, http://stats.oecd.org/Index.aspx?queryname=345&querytype=view# (accessed 21 May 2013).
73 OECD, 'Labour Losing to Capital: What Explains the Declining Labour Share?', in *OECD Employment Outlook*, 2012, p.113.
74 Boston, 'The Challenge of Securing Durable Reductions', pp.5–8.
75 The median house price, for instance, has risen from twice the median income in 1980 to 5.3 times the median income today. See Chapter 7 for more details.
76 Reserve Bank of New Zealand, 'Key graphs –

77 Perry, *Household Incomes in New Zealand*, p.70.
78 Ben Heather and Rob Stock, 'Cash flow stress hits one in two Kiwis', *Dominion Post*, 26 April 2013, http://www.stuff.co.nz/dominion-post/news/8598046/Cash-flow-stress-hits-one-in-two-Kiwis (accessed 2 May 2013).
79 James, *The Quiet Revolution*, back cover text.
80 Bruce Jesson, *Behind the Mirror Glass: The Growth of Wealth and Power in New Zealand in the Eighties*, Penguin, Auckland, 1987, p.129.
81 Adams, 'CEO Pay Survey'.
82 Roberts, 'Executive Compensation in New Zealand'.
83 Vaimoana Tapaleao and Christopher Adams, 'Rise of the $1m salaries: top boss says enough', *New Zealand Herald*, 5 November 2012, http://www.nzherald.co.nz/business/news/article.cfm?c_id=3&objectid=10845155 (accessed 15 May 2013).
84 Fiona McAlister, Debasis Bandyopadhyay, Robert Barro, Jeremy Couchman, Norman Gemmell and Gordon Liao, 'Average Marginal Income Tax Rates for New Zealand, 1907–2009', New Zealand Treasury Working Paper 12/04, September 2012, p.9. The top tax rate was in fact 66 per cent at that stage, but only as a result of a temporary surcharge imposed in 1982.
85 Salmond, *The New New Zealand Tax System*, pp.116–17.
86 International evidence shows that capital gains are disproportionate to those higher up the income scale, and make up several percentage points of their income. It seems plausible that, if measured here, capital gains could reduce top earners' effective tax rate from 34 per cent to below 30 per cent. In the absence of actual figures, however, this remains speculative.
87 Based on figures from the OECD Tax Database, New Zealand has one of the developed world's lowest 'all-in' (combined) top rate of tax for personal income. See the section entitled, 'Top marginal combined personal incomes tax rates on gross wage for a single individual' at http://www.oecd.org/tax/tax-policy/oecdtaxdatabase.htm (accessed 27 May 2013).
88 Bryan Perry, *Household Incomes in New Zealand*, p.81.
89 Analysis of the New Zealand results of the International Social Survey Programme, 1992, 1999 and 2009, provided by Philip Gendall of Otago University, personal correspondence with the author.
90 Jon Johanssen, Introduction to Lipson, *The Politics of Equality*, xix.
91 Deborah Coddington, 'Let's help everyone to top – not drag down wealthy', *New Zealand Herald*, 13 February 2011, see http://www.nzherald.co.nz/business/news/article.cfm?c_id=3&objectid=10705861 (accessed 17 February 2013).
92 R.H. Tawney, *Equality*, quoted in John Hills et al., *An Anatomy of Economic Inequality in the UK: Report of the National Equality Panel*, Government Equalities Office, London, 2010, p.1.
93 Perry, *Household Incomes in New Zealand*, p.70. The recent Quality of Life Survey showed that, in 2012, some 22 per cent of people felt they did not have enough money 'to cover everyday needs', up from 13 per cent in 2010. See http://www.qualityoflifeproject.govt.nz/media.htm (accessed 31 March 2013).
94 Christopher Adams, 'Pay rises for bosses surge ahead of ordinary Kiwis', *New Zealand Herald*, 30 April 2011, http://www.nzherald.co.nz/business/news/article.cfm?c_id=3&objectid=10722406 (accessed 29 May 2013).
95 On another key measure, the 80:20 ratio, inequality has risen in the last year of data available, but is not at record levels. Perry, *Household Incomes in New Zealand*, pp.80–83.
96 The top 10 per cent received 40 per cent of the value of the tax cuts; indeed the top 1 per cent got one dollar of every eight – more than the lower half of the country. New Zealand Council of Trade Unions, 'The Growing Gap Between Rich and Poor', 2010, http://union.org.nz/vote-fairness/growing-gap-between-rich-and-poor, (accessed 31 March 2013).
97 Ibid.
98 The Treasury, 'Living Standards Background Note: "Increasing Equity"', Treasury, Wellington, 2013, p.3. Some limitations of this argument are addressed in Chapter One.
99 Ruth Laugesen, 'More Unequal than Others', *Listener*, 18 February 2012, p.26.

Chapter 3: Inequality and the West
This chapter draws on some of the author's earlier essays, including R.H. Wade, 'On the Causes of Increasing Poverty and Inequality, or Why the Matthew Effect Prevails', *New Political Economy*, 9, 2 (June 2004), pp.163–88; 'Should We Worry about Income Inequality?', in David Held and Ayse Kaya (eds), *Global Inequality: Patterns and Explanations*, Polity Press, Cambridge, 2006, pp.104–31; 'From

Global Imbalances to Global Reorganizations', *Cambridge Journal of Economics,* 33, 4 (July 2009), pp.539–62; 'Global Trends in Income Inequality: What is Happening and Should We Worry?', *Challenge*, 54, 5 (September–October 2011), pp.54–75; 'Globalization, Growth, Poverty, Inequality, Resentment and Imperialism', in J. Ravenhill (ed.), *Global Political Economy*, 3rd edition, Oxford University Press, Oxford, pp.372–415.

1. J. Roemer, 'Ideological and Political Roots of American Inequality', *Challenge*, 54, 5 (September–October 2011), pp.76–98.
2. J. Treanor, 'World's wealthiest people now richer than before the credit crunch: World Wealth Report reveals soaring numbers of rich individuals in Asia Pacific region – But slower growth in Britain', *Guardian*, 22 June 2011.
3. J. Goldfarb, 'The Sweet Life of the 0.001%', *International Herald Tribune*, 15 November 2011.
4. This chapter concentrates on inequality within developed countries and says little about inequality within countries of the rest of the world or inequality between countries.
5. A. Coghlan and D. MacKenzie, 'Revealed – the capitalist network that runs the world', *New Scientist*, 19 October 2011.
6. P. Krugman, 'Superlow taxes at the top', *International Herald Tribune*, 21–22 January 2012.
7. J. Kampfner, 'The wealthy should pay more tax. Why has it taken so long?', *Independent*, 26 August 2011.
8. G. Lakoff, *Moral Politics: How Liberals and Conservatives Think*, 2nd edn, University of Chicago Press, Chicago, 2002.
9. Ibid.
10. So called after John Maynard Keynes, whose work provided intellectual justification for the 'mixed economy' and social democratic policies from the late 1930s to the 1970s.
11. D. Kahneman, *Thinking, Fast and Slow*, Allen Lane, London, 2011.
12. See K. Phillips-Fein, *Invisible Hands: The Making of the Conservative Movement from the New Deal to Reagan*, Norton, New York, 2009; and Roemer, 'Ideological and Political Roots of American Inequality'.
13. Roemer, 'Ideological and Political Roots of American Inequality'.
14. Asked what attainments contribute to success in the profession, only 3 per cent of 212 graduate students in American economics departments said that 'having a thorough knowledge of the economy' was 'very important', and 68 per cent said it was 'unimportant': D. Colander and A. Klamer, 'The Making of an Economist', *Journal of Economic Perspectives*, 1 (Fall 1987), p.100. The economics department of Cambridge University (Keynes's base) teaches no Keynesian economics at graduate or undergraduate level, despite student demand for it.
15. R. Liddle, *Creating a Culture of Fairness. A Progressive Response to Income Inequality in Britain*, Policy Network, London, December 2007, p.2.
16. S. Buckler and D. Dolowitz, 'Theorizing the Third Way', *Journal of Political Ideologies*, 5, 3 (2000), p.309.
17. F. Alvaredo et al., *The World Top Incomes Database*, 2012, http://g-mond.parisschoolofeconomics.eu/topincomes/ (accessed 25 April 2013).
18. Roemer, 'Ideological and Political Roots of American Inequality'.
19. C. Goldin and L. Katz, 'Transitions: Career and Family Life Cycles of the Educated Elite', *American Economic Review*, 98, 2 (May 2008), pp.263–69.
20. N. Kristof, 'Banking is No Evil', *International Herald Tribune*, 20 January 2012.
21. Cited in G. Monbiot, 'The 1% are the very best destroyers of wealth the world has ever seen', *Guardian*, 8 November 2011.
22. S. Lansley, 'Tinkering on the brink', *Guardian*, 5 October 2011.

Chapter 4: The Cost of Inequality

1. J.M. Keynes, *The General Theory of Employment, Interest and Money*, Chapter 24, Part V, MacMillan, London, 1936, p.383.
2. Admittedly, the textbook purist will point out that the 'winners' are supposed to compensate the 'losers', so that no one is left worse off as a result of the policy. However, the level and distribution of compensation (to displaced firms and workers) remain a secondary consideration (if they appear at all) in the economic advisor's policy decisions.
3. *Improving the Living Standards of New Zealanders: Moving from a Framework to Implementation*, conference paper, The Treasury, Wellington, June 2012. This, and related papers, http://www.treasury.govt.nz/abouttreasury/higherlivingstandards (accessed 24 April 2013).
4. With minimal government interventions.
5. Any standard microeconomic textbook will provide the details. I was schooled

in Nicholson, a recent edition of which is W. Nicholson and C. Snyder, *Intermediate Microeconomics and its Application*, 11th edition, South-Western College Publishing, Boston, 2009.

6 For economists, I am referring to the *micro*economic analysis of choices of points on the production possibility frontier; while points inside the frontier are assumed away as somebody else's (the *macro*economist's) problem.

7 Just as the pure perfect market does not exist in the real world either.

8 Adam Smith, *An Inquiry into the Nature and Causes of the Wealth of Nations*, Book I, Chapter X, Modern Library Edition, New York, 2000, p.148.

9 Or, more correctly, a firm that is operating in a sector that exhibits some monopoly characteristics.

10 Calculated using Statistics New Zealand GDP and Household Labour Force Survey data.

11 Or, in the economist's jargon, 'crowd out'.

12 Laura Vartia, *How Do Taxes Affect Investment and Productivity? An Industry-Level Analysis of OECD Countries*, OECD Economics Department Working Papers, No. 656, OECD Publishing, Paris, 2008, http://dx.doi.org/10.1787/230022721067 (accessed 24 April 2013).

13 Institute of Taxation and Economic Policy, *States with 'High Rate' Income Taxes are Still Outperforming No-Tax States*, http://www.itep.org/pdf/lafferhighrate.pdf (accessed 24 April 2013).

Chapter 5: What Kind of Equality Matters?

1 I would like to thank Andrew Bradstock, David Bromell, Max Rashbrooke, Tom Rennie and Ben Stephenson for their constructive and helpful comments on earlier versions of this chapter. Parts of this chapter are based on Jonathan Boston, 'Comment: Reflections on Equality and Citizenship', in Claire Charters and Dean Knight (eds), *We, The People(s): Participation in Governance*, Victoria University Press, Wellington, 2011, pp.208–21.

2 See, for instance, Brian Barry, *Why Social Justice Matters*, Polity Press, Cambridge, 2005; Jane Franklin (ed.), *Equality*, Institute for Public Policy Research, London, 1997; David Miller, *Principles of Social Justice*, Harvard University Press, Cambridge, Mass., 1999; Robert Nozick, *Anarchy, State, and Utopia*, Basil Blackwell, Oxford, 1974; John Rawls, *A Theory of Justice*, Harvard University Press, Cambridge, Mass., 1972; Michael Sandel, *Justice: What's the Right Thing to Do?*, Penguin, London, 2009; Amartya Sen, *The Idea of Justice*, Allen Lane, London, 2009; Michael Walzer, *Spheres of Justice: A Defense of Pluralism and Equality*, Basic Books, New York, 1983.

3 Sen, *The Idea of Justice*, esp. pp.1–27.

4 Ibid., p.291.

5 John Rawls, *Political Liberalism*, Columbia University Press, New York, 1993, p.291.

6 See J. Cohen, 'Money, Politics, Political Equality', in A. Byrne, R. Stalnaker and R. Wedgwood (eds), *Fact and Value: Essays on Ethics and Metaphysics for Judith Jarvis Thomson*, The MIT Press, London, 2001; and Jonathan Boston and Alec Mladenovic, 'Political Equality and the Regulation of Election Spending by Parallel Campaigners', *Australian Journal of Political Science*, 45, 4 (2010), pp.623–42.

7 Rawls, *A Theory of Justice*, p.225.

8 Joseph Stiglitz, *The Price of Inequality*, Allen Lane, London, 2012.

9 Sen, *The Idea of Justice*, esp. pp.225–68.

10 For a brief analysis of the relationship between child poverty and educational opportunities and outcomes, see Helen Ladd, 'Education and Poverty: Confronting the Evidence', *Journal of Policy Analysis and Management*, 31, 2 (2012), pp.203–27.

11 Rawls, *A Theory of Justice*, p.73.

12 Royal Commission on Social Policy, *Summary Report*, Government Printer, Wellington, 1988, pp.31–32.

13 James Tobin, 'On Limiting the Domain of Inequality', *Journal of Law and Economics*, 13 (1970), p.363.

14 The Treasury, 'Living Standards Background Note: "Increasing Equity"', January 2013, http://www.treasury.govt.nz/abouttreasury/higherlivingstandards/hls-bg-equity-jan13.pdf (accessed May 2013).

15 Royal Commission on Social Security, *Report on Social Security in New Zealand*, Government Printer, Wellington, 1972, p.65.

16 Ibid.

17 See especially Stiglitz, *The Price of Inequality*; and Richard Wilkinson and Kate Pickett, *The Spirit Level: Why Equality is Better for Everyone*, Penguin, London, 2010.

18 Miller, 'What Kind of Equality Should the Left Pursue?', in Franklin (ed.), *Equality*, p.83.

19 Michael Walzer, *Spheres of Justice*.

20 David Miller, 'What Kind of Equality Should the Left Pursue?', p.95.

21 Walzer, *Spheres of Justice*, p.19.

22. Joseph Raz, *The Morality of Freedom*, Clarendon Press, Oxford, 1986, p.235.
23. See Expert Advisory Group on Solutions to Child Poverty, *Solutions to Child Poverty in New Zealand: Evidence for Action*, Office of the Children's Commissioner, Wellington, 2012.

Chapter 6: Only One Deck

1. Words and music by Alan Jansson / Paul Fuemana. © Universal Music Publishing Pty Ltd. All rights reserved. International copyright secured. Reprinted with permission.
2. Comprising 7 per cent of the total New Zealand population, Pacific peoples are Oceanic migrants from New Zealand's neighbouring regional islands, atolls, archipelagoes and territories in the Pacific Ocean, more than half of whom are Samoan: Statistics New Zealand, *QuickStats about Pacific Peoples*, Statistics New Zealand, Wellington, 2008.
3. Ministry of Social Development, *Non-income Measures of Material Wellbeing and Hardship: First Results from the 2008 New Zealand Living Standards Survey, with International Comparisons*, Ministry of Social Development, Wellington, 2009.
4. Statistics New Zealand, *Demographic Trends: 2012*, http://www.stats.govt.nz (accessed 26 April 2013).
5. The term 'Pacific peoples' is pluralised to emphasise the cultural and linguistic diversity under the 'pan-Pacific' umbrella. Unlike Māori, they are not indigenous to New Zealand, but are considered indigenous to the Pacific region. In New Zealand, they constitute a visible ethnic minority that has experienced significant and enduring socio-economic, health and educational disadvantage.
6. Risk ratio calculated by the Ministry of Social Development using standardised criteria for hardship: Ministry of Social Development, *Non-income Measures of Material Wellbeing and Hardship*.
7. For example, a study of health inequalities for young people, based on hospital admission, census and educational data, showed a recurring pattern of either Pacific or Māori having the poorest health outcomes of all ethnic groups. A frequent pattern was that Pacific young people had an 'intermediary' profile; Māori experienced, fairly consistently, the poorest health profile; and European young people, for the most part, enjoyed the best health profile. See E. Craig, S. Taufa, C. Jackson and D. Yeo-Han, *The Health of Pacific Children and Young People in New Zealand*, Department of Paediatrics, School of Population Health, Auckland, 2008.
8. Karlo Mila, 'For Sia Figiel', *Dream Fish Floating*, Huia, Wellington, 2005, p.13. Povi masima is a cheap and very fatty form of salted beef, sold in clear plastic buckets in some supermarkets.
9. See B. Swinburn, I. Caterson et al., 'Diet, Nutrition and the Prevention of Excess Weight Gain and Obesity', *Public Health Nutrition*, 7, 1 (2003), pp.123–46. They write that the idea of people with limited resources being forced to take 'default choices' on offer in an obesogenic environment may be more useful in understanding the situation of Pacific peoples, than notions of 'lifestyle' that imply unrestrained freedom and power to make choices that affect life, health and well-being.
10. J. Connell, 'Migration, Dependency and Inequality in the Pacific: Old Wine in Bigger Bottles? (Part 1)', in Stewart Firth (ed.), *Globalisation and Governance in the Pacific Islands*, ANU E-Press, Canberra, 2006, p.60.
11. P. Ongley, 'Immigration, Employment and Ethnic Relations', in P. Spoonley, C. Macpherson and D. Pearson (eds), *Nga Patai: Racism and Ethnic Relations in Aotearoa/New Zealand*, Dunmore Press, Palmerston North, 1996, pp.17–36.
12. C. Macpherson, 'Pacific Islands Identity and Community', in Spoonley et al., *Nga Patai*, pp.124–43.
13. G. Lay, *Pacific New Zealand*, David Ling, Auckland, 1996, p.13.
14. See C. Small, *Voyages from Tongan Villages to American Suburbs*, Cornell University Press, Ithaca, New York, 1997.
15. Ongley, 'Immigration, Employment and Ethnic Relations'.
16. A.D. Trlin, 'New Zealand's Admission of Asians and Pacific Islanders', in J.T. Fawcett and B.V. Carino (eds), *Pacific Bridges: The New Migration from Asia and the Pacific Islands*, Center for Migration Studies, New York, 1987, pp.199–227.
17. Ongley, 'Immigration, Employment and Ethnic Relations', p.20.
18. P. Spoonley, 'Racism and Ethnicity', in P. Spoonley, D. Pearson and I. Shirley (eds), *New Zealand Society*, Dunmore Press, Palmerston North, 1994, pp.81–97.
19. Ibid.
20. A. Ballara, *Proud to be White? A Survey of Pakeha Prejudice in New Zealand*, Heinemann, Auckland, 1986, p.160.

21 Lay, *Pacific New Zealand*, p.13.
22 P. Ongley, 'Ethnicity, Migration and the Labour Market', in P. Spoonley, C. Macpherson and D. Pearson (eds), *Tangata Tangata: The Changing Ethnic Contours of New Zealand*, Thomson/Dunmore Press, Melbourne/Palmerston North, 2004, pp.199–220.
23 R.D. Bedford, 'Pacific Islanders in New Zealand', *Espaces Populations Societes*, 2 (1994), pp.187–200.
24 Ongley, 'Ethnicity, Migration and the Labour Market'.
25 J. de Raad and M. Walton, *Pacific People in the New Zealand Economy: Understanding Trends and Linkages*, paper presented at Thought Leaders Dialogue, NZIER, Wellington, 30–31 August 2007.
26 Ongley, 'Ethnicity, Migration and the Labour Market'.
27 Spoonley, 'Racism and Ethnicity'.
28 P. Callister and R. Didham, 'Emerging Demographics and Socioeconomic Features of the Pacific Population in New Zealand', in A. Bisley (ed.), *Pacific Interactions: Pacific in New Zealand: New Zealand in Pacific*, Institute of Policy Studies, Wellington, 2008, pp.13–40.
29 The most recent census showed that Pacific men were most likely to be labourers (23 per cent), machinery operators and drivers (21 per cent), and technicians and trade workers (20 per cent); Pacific women showed greater diversity: labourers (19 per cent), clerical or administrative workers (19 per cent), professionals (15 per cent), and community and personal service workers (15 per cent): Statistics New Zealand, *QuickStats about Pacific Peoples*.
30 Words and music by Alan Jansson / Paul Fuemana. © Universal Music Publishing Pty Ltd. All rights reserved. International copyright secured. Reprinted with permission.
31 Callister and Didham, 'Emerging Demographics'.
32 de Raad and Walton, *Pacific People in the New Zealand Economy*.
33 Statistics New Zealand, *QuickStats about Pacific Peoples*.
34 This figure is for children living in households with less than 60 per cent of equivalised median income *before* housing costs. The figure of 270,000 used elsewhere is *after* housing costs.
35 M. Henare, A. Puckey, A. Nicholson, C. Dale and R. Vaithianathan, *He Ara Hou: The Pathway Forward. Getting it Right for Aotearoa New Zealand's Māori and Pasifika Children*, Every Child Counts, Auckland, 2011.
36 P. White, J. Guston, C. Salmond et al., *Atlas of Socioeconomic Deprivation in New Zealand NZDep2006*, Ministry of Health, Wellington, 2008.
37 Henare et al., *He Ara Hou*.
38 Statistics New Zealand, *QuickStats about Pacific Peoples*.
39 M. Baker, L. Barnard, A. Kvalsvig, A. Verrall, J. Zhang, M. Keall, N. Wilson, T. Wall and P. Howden-Chapman, 'Increasing Incidence of Serious Infectious Diseases and Inequalities in New Zealand: A National Epidemiological Study', *The Lancet*, 379, 9,821 (24 March 2012), pp.1112–19.
40 R. Wilkinson and K. Pickett, *The Spirit Level: Why Equality is Better for Everyone*, Penguin, London, 2010.
41 M. Zhou, 'Segmented Assimilation: Issues, Controversies, and Recent Research on the New Second Generation', *International Migration Review*, 3, 4 (1997), p.986.
42 Statistics New Zealand, *QuickStats about Pacific Peoples*. Tongans, Samoans, Niueans and Cook Islands people are more likely to live in Manukau than any other city (p.3).
43 Consistent scores of 9 on a community resiliency index scale: Rodney City Council, North Shore City Council, Waitakere City Council, Auckland City Council, Manukau City Council, Hamilton City Council, Tauranga City Council, Hutt City Council, Wellington City Council, Christchurch City Council, Dunedin City Council: Quality of Life Project, *Quality of Life '07 in Twelve of New Zealand's Cities*, Ministry of Health, Wellington, 2007, p.135.
44 A consistent score of 39 per cent: Rodney City Council, North Shore City Council, Waitakere City Council, Auckland City Council, Manukau City Council, Hamilton City Council, Tauranga City Council, Hutt City Council, Wellington City Council, Christchurch City Council, Dunedin City Council: Quality of Life Project, *Quality of Life '07*, p.217.
45 K. Mila-Schaaf, E. Robinson, D. Schaaf, S. Denny and P. Watson, *A Health Profile of Pacific Youth: Findings of Youth2000. A National Secondary School Youth Health Survey*, University of Auckland, Auckland, 2008, p.40.
46 Rodney City Council, North Shore City Council, Waitakere City Council, Auckland City Council, Manukau City Council, Hamilton City Council, Tauranga City Council, Hutt City Council, Wellington City Council, Christchurch City Council, Dunedin City

Council: Quality of Life Project, *Quality of Life '07*, p.19.

47 A total of 85 per cent of Pacific children compared to 95 per cent for total population: Ministry of Education, ECE Participation Fact Sheet, Ministry of Education, Wellington, 2010.

48 Ministry of Education, *Pasifika Education Plan Monitoring Report 2010*, Ministry of Education, Wellington, 2012.

49 See Department of Labour, Pacific Peoples Labour Market Factsheet, Department of Labour, Wellington, March 2012. Among 15–24-year-olds, in the year to March 2012, 21.1 per cent of Pacific females and 15.2 per cent of Pacific males were NEET, compared with 14.6 per cent of all females and 11.5 per cent of males in this age group.

50 W. Darity and J. Nembhard, 'Racial and Ethnic Economic Inequality: The International Record', *American Economic Review*, 90, 2 (2000), p.310.

51 Ministry of Education, *Pasifika Education Plan Monitoring Report 2010*.

52 Darity and Nembhard, 'Racial and Ethnic Economic Inequality', p.310.

53 Lyrics by Tyree Tautogia of Smashproof. With permission of Woodcut Productions, Auckland.

54 Ministry of Education, *Pasifika Education Plan Monitoring Report 2010*.

55 See Greg Clydesdale, 'New Zealand Immigration Policy', Discussion Paper, Department of Management and International Business, Massey University, Palmerston North, 2008.

Viewpoint 6: Chris Harris

1 'Developer left holding unwanted properties', *New Zealand Herald*, 5 November 2009, http://www.nzherald.co.nz/property/news/article.cfm?c_id=8&objectid=10608592 (accessed 16 May 2013).

2 Sixteen out of the 26 had never previously been to downtown Wellington. 'Poverty and Education', *Insight*, Radio New Zealand, 8 October 2012.

Chapter 7: Building Inequality

We would like to acknowledge the insightful comments on our chapter by Ben Schrader, Ralph Chapman, Keri Lawson-Te Aho and Geoff Fougere.

1 Waitangi Tribunal, *Te Whanganui a Tara Me Ona Takiwa: Report on the Wellington District* (WAI 145), Legislation Direct, Wellington, 2003.

2 Pierre Bourdieu, *Social Structure of the Economy*, Polity Press, Cambridge, 2005, p.16.

3 Ben Schrader, *We Call it Home: A History of State Housing in New Zealand*, Reed Books, Wellington, 2005.

4 Robert Chapman, 'New Zealand Since the War', *Landfall*, 63 (1962), pp.252–77.

5 Gael Ferguson, *Building the New Zealand Dream*, Dunmore Press, Palmerston North, 1994, p.29.

6 Department of Health, Maori Hygiene – Maori Welfare – Housing, H1 194/18, Archives New Zealand, Wellington (ANZ).

7 Ibid.

8 S. Bierre, P. Howden-Chapman, L. Signal and C. Cunningham, 'Institutional Challenges in Addressing Healthy Low-cost Housing For All – Learning from Past Policy', *Social Policy Journal of New Zealand*, 30 (2007), pp.42–64.

9 Bierre et al., 'Institutional Challenges in Addressing Healthy Low-cost Housing For All', p.56. The explanations in parentheses are gathered from a file from the Department of Māori Affairs that also holds the referenced letter, SAC 1 32/1/5, ANZ.

10 H. Chappell, 'Notes on the Hokianga Maori Housing and Housing Problems Generally', in G.M. Smith, W.W. Grant and H. Chappell (eds), *Plans, Plots and Appraisals from the Backblocks*, Caxton Press, Christchurch, 1945, p.25.

11 Joan Metge, 'The Maori Population of Northern New Zealand', *New Zealand Geographer*, 8, 2 (1952), p.124.

12 W.H Pearson, *Review of The Fern and the Tiki. An American View of New Zealand: National Character, Social Attitudes and Race Relations*, by David Ausubel. *Journal of the Polynesian Society*, 69, 4 (1960), p.425.

13 Apirana Ngata, *The Price of Citizenship*, Whitcombe & Tombs, Wellington, 1943.

14 G.V. Butterworth and H.R. Young, *Maori Affairs: A Department and the People Who Made It*, GP Books for Iwi Transition Agency, Wellington, 1990.

15 Ibid.

16 Jane Kelsey, *Rolling Back the State*, Bridget Williams Books, Wellington, 1993.

17 Campbell Roberts, 'Housing', in Royal Commission on Social Policy, *The April Report: Report of the Royal Commission on Social Policy*, Government Printer, Wellington, 1988, p.184.

18 Ibid.

19 Kelsey, *Rolling Back the State*, p.88.

20 A. Davidson, *A Home of One's Own: Housing*

Policy in Sweden and New Zealand from the 1840s to the 1990s, Almqvist & Wiksell International, Stockholm, 1994; M. Reddell and C. Sleeman, 'Some Perspectives on Past Recessions', *Reserve Bank of New Zealand Bulletin*, 71, 2 (2008), pp.5–21.
21 Davidson, *A Home of One's Own*.
22 New Zealand Productivity Commission, *Housing Affordability*, New Zealand Productivity Commission, Wellington, 2012.
23 Ferguson, *Building the New Zealand Dream*.
24 Schrader, *We Call it Home*.
25 Sarah Widmer, *Household Crowding in New Zealand in the 1990s: Was it Driven by Housing Policy?*, Department of Public Health, Wellington School of Medicine and Health Sciences, University of Otago, 2006; M. Baker, R. Goodyear, L. Telfar Barnard and P. Howden-Chapman, *The Distribution of Household Crowding in New Zealand: An Analysis Based on 1991 to 2006 Census Data*, He Kainga Oranga/Housing and Health Research Programme, Wellington, 2012.
26 New Zealand Productivity Commission, *Housing Affordability*.
27 Demographia, 9th Annual Demographia International Housing Affordability Survey, 2013, http://www.demographia.com/dhi.pdf (accessed 26 April 2013).
28 David C. Thorns, 'Housing Booms and Changes to New Zealand Housing Affordability: The Policy Challenge', *Journal of Asian Public Policy*, 2, 2 (2009), pp.171–89; Davidson, *A Home of One's Own*.
29 Schrader, *We Call it Home*.
30 C.W. Cunningham and S. Triggs, *Best Outcomes for Māori: Te Hoe Nuku Roa. Summary of the Regional Results for Wave 4*, Research Centre for Māori Health and Development, Wellington, 2011.
31 Ministry of Social Development, *The Social Report 2005*, Ministry of Social Development, Wellington, 2005.
32 David Law and Lisa Meehan, 'Housing Affordability in New Zealand: Evidence from Household Surveys', in *New Zealand Association of Economists Conference*, New Zealand Productivity Commission/The Treasury, Wellington, 2012.
33 Judith MacDonald, *Racism and Rental Accommodation*, Social Development and Research Trust, Auckland, 1986.
34 R. Harris, M. Tobias, M. Jeffreys, K. Waldegrave, S. Karlsen and J. Nazroo, 'Effects of Self-reported Racial Discrimination and Deprivation on Maori Health and Inequalities in New Zealand: Cross-sectional Study', *The Lancet*, 367, 9,527 (2006), pp.2005–2009; R.Harris, D. Cormack, M. Tobias, Li-Chia Yeh, N. Talamaivao, J. Minster and R. Timutimu, 'The Pervasive Effects of Racism: Experiences of Racial Discrimination in New Zealand Over Time and Associations with Multiple Health Domains', *Social Science & Medicine*, 74 (2012), pp.408–15.
35 K. Amore, M. Baker, P. Howden-Chapman and H. Viggers, 'Severe Housing Deprivation: The Problem and its Measurement', in *Official Statistics Research Series*, 6, forthcoming, from Statistics New Zealand's website, http://www.statisphere.govt.nz (accessed 26 April 2013).
36 Statistics New Zealand, *New Zealand Definition of Homelessness*, Statistics New Zealand, Wellington, 2009.
37 K. Amore, *Everybody Counts: Defining and Measuring Severe Housing Deprivation*, PhD Thesis, Department of Public Health, University of Otago, Wellington, 2013.
38 N.R. Buckett, M.S. Jones and N.J. Marston, *BRANZ 2010 House Condition Survey – Condition Comparison by Tenure*, Wellington Building Research Association of New Zealand, Wellington, 2012.
39 Bierre et al., 'Institutional Challenges in Addressing Healthy Low-cost Housing For All'.
40 Philippa Howden-Chapman and Penelope Carroll, *Housing and Health: Research, Policy and Innovation*, Steele Roberts, Wellington, 2004.
41 P. Howden-Chapman, C. Ruthe and S. Crichton, 'Habitable Houses: Lessons Learned?', in *The Leaky Building Crisis: Understanding the Issues*, Thomson Reuters, Wellington, 2011, pp.303–15.
42 Buckett et al., *BRANZ 2010 House Condition Survey*.
43 Statistics New Zealand, *New Zealand General Social Survey: 2010*, Statistics New Zealand, Wellington, 2011, http://www.stats.govt.nz/browse_for_stats/people_and_communities/Households/nzgss_HOTP2010.aspx (accessed 26 April 2013).
44 Bryan Perry, *Household Incomes in New Zealand: Trends in Indicators of Inequality and Hardship 1982 to 2011*, Ministry of Social Development, Wellington, 2012.
45 T. Jelleyman and N. Spencer, 'Residential Mobility in Childhood and Health Outcomes: A Systematic Review', *Journal of Epidemiology and Community Health*, 62 (2008), pp.584–92.
46 Kay Saville-Smith and Bev James, *Building*

Attachment in Communities Affected by Residential Movement: An Introduction to the Final Papers, 2011, http://www.cresa.co.nz/projects-and-publications/ (accessed 26 April 2013); Helen Viggers and Philippa Howden-Chapman, 'Home-sick: Residential Movement and Health Status', in Kay Saville-Smith (ed.), FRST Building Attachment in Families and Communities Affected by Transience and Residential Movement, He Kainga Oranga/Housing and Health Research Programme, Wellington, 2007.

47 M. Baker, L. Telfar Barnard, A. Kvalsvig, A. Verrall, J. Zhang, M. Keall, N. Wilson, T. Wall, and P. Howden-Chapman. 'Increasing incidence of serious infectious diseases and inequalities in New Zealand: a national epidemiological study', *The Lancet*, 379 (2012), pp.1112–19.

48 Michael Baker, Michael Keall, Ee Lyn Au and Philippa Howden-Chapman, 'Home is where the heart is – Most of the time', *New Zealand Medical Journal*, 120 (2007), p.1264.

49 A. Marsh, D. Gordon, C. Pantazis and P. Heslop, *Home Sweet Home? The Impact of Housing on Health*, Policy Press, Bristol, 2000; Children's Commissioner's Expert Advisory Group on Solutions to Child Poverty, *Solutions to Child Poverty in New Zealand: Evidence for Action*, Office of the Children's Commission, Wellington, 2012.

50 World Health Organization Regional Office for Europe, *WHO Guidelines for Indoor Air Quality: Dampness and Mould*, WHO Europe, Copenhagen, 2009; Matthias Braubach, David E. Jacobs and David Ormandy, *Environmental Burden of Disease Associated with Inadequate Housing: A Method Guide to the Quantification of Health Effects of Selected Housing Risks in the WHO European Region*, World Health Organization Regional Office for Europe, Geneva, 2011.

51 Statistics New Zealand, *New Zealand General Social Survey: 2010*.

52 Gina Pene, Marisa Peita and Philippa Howden-Chapman, 'Living the Tokelauan Way in New Zealand', *Social Policy Journal of New Zealand*, 35 (2009), pp.79–92.

53 Baker et al., *The Distribution of Household Crowding in New Zealand*.

54 M. Baker, D. Das, K. Venugopal and P. Howden-Chapman, 'Tuberculosis Associated with Household Crowding in a Developed Country', *Journal of Epidemiology and Community Health*, 62 (2008), pp.715–21; M. Baker, A. McNicholas, M.H. Garrett, N. Jones, J. Stewart, V. Koberstein and Diana Lennon, 'Household Crowding a Major Risk Factor for Epidemic Meningococcal Disease in Auckland Children', *Pediatric Infectious Disease Journal*, 19, 10 (2000), pp.983–90; Baker et al., *The Distribution of Household Crowding in New Zealand*.

55 Baker et al., 'Increasing incidence of serious infectious diseases and inequalities in New Zealand: a national epidemiological study'.

56 Lawrence Murphy and Dorothy Cloher, 'Economic Restructuring, Housing Policy and Maori Housing Policy in Northland', *New Zealand Geoforum*, 26, 4 (1995), pp.325–36.

57 M. Keall, M.G. Baker, P. Howden-Chapman, M. Cunningham and D. Ormandy, 'Assessing Housing Quality and its Impact on Health, Safety and Sustainability', *Journal of Epidemiology and Community Health*, 64, 9 (2010), pp.765–71.

58 P. Howden-Chapman, A. Matheson, H. Viggers, J. Crane, M. Cunningham, T. Blakely, D. O'Dea, C. Cunningham, A. Woodward, K. Saville-Smith, M. Baker and N. Waipara, 'Retrofitting Houses With Insulation to Reduce Health Inequalities: Results of a Clustered, Randomised Trial in a Community Setting', *British Medical Journal*, 334 (2007), pp.460–64; Philippa Howden-Chapman, Nevil Pierse, Sarah Nicholls et al., 'Effects of Improved Home Heating on Asthma in Community Dwelling Children: Randomised Community Study', *British Medical Journal*, 337 (2008), pp.852–55; R. Chapman, P. Howden-Chapman, H. Viggers, D. O'Dea and M. Kennedy, 'Retrofitting Housing With Insulation: A Cost-Benefit Analysis of a Randomised Community Trial', *Journal of Epidemiology and Community Health*, 63 (2009), pp.271–77.

59 A. Grimes, T. Denne, P. Howden-Chapman, R. Arnold, L. Telfar-Barnard, N. Nicholas Preval and C. Young, *Cost Benefit Analysis of the Warm Up New Zealand: Heat Smart Programme*, Report for Ministry of Economic Development, Motu Economic and Public Policy Research, Wellington, 2011.

60 Michael Baker, Jane Zhang and Philippa Howden-Chapman, *Health Impacts of the Healthy Housing Programme on Housing New Zealand Tenants: 2004–2007*, He Kainga Oranga/Housing and Health Research Programme, Wellington, 2010.

Viewpoint 7: Mary Richardson

1 S. Bidwell, *Long Term Planning for Recovery after Disasters: Ensuring Health in All*

Policies, Canterbury District Health Board, Christchurch, 2011; A. Richardson, *Review of Community Recovery Initiatives*, Canterbury District Health Board, Christchurch, 2010; D. Hutton, *Psychosocial Aspects of Disaster Recovery: Integrating Communities into Disaster Planning and Policy Making*, Institute for Catastrophic Loss Reduction, Montreal, 2001; K. F. Gotham and M. Greenberg, 'From 9/11 to 8/29: Post-Disaster Recovery and Rebuilding in New York and New Orleans', *Social Forces*, 87, 2 (2008), pp.1039–1062; J. F. Pais and J. R. Elliott, 'Places as Recovery Machines: Vulnerability and Neighborhood Change after Major Hurricanes', *Social Forces*, 86, 4 (2008), pp.1415–1453.

Chapter 8: Crime, Imprisonment and Poverty

1. See http://www.police.govt.nz/sites/default/files/resources/crime-statistics/00-national-2011-12-crime-stats.pdf, p.16 (accessed 26 April 2013).
2. Kim Workman, 'The Future of Restorative Justice', paper presented to the Annual Conference of Restorative Justice Aotearoa, Hamilton, September 2008.
3. 'Prisons: 'moral and fiscal failure'?', *Otago Daily Times*, 24 May 2011, http://www.odt.co.nz/opinion/editorial/161773/prisons-moral-and-fiscal-failure (accessed 10 February 2013).
4. P. Mayhew and J. Reilly, *The New Zealand Crime and Safety Survey 2006*, Ministry of Justice, Wellington, 2007, p.46.
5. Tony Paine, 'Victim Support, Victims Rights: An Agenda for Prevention', paper presented to Addressing the Underlying Causes of Offending: What is the Evidence?, Institute of Policy Studies, Victoria University of Wellington, 26 and 27 February 2009.
6. The authors recognise that there are many forms of sanctioned punishment in New Zealand. The focus on imprisonment recognises the place it plays in the collective imagination on discussions of punitive responses to crime.
7. Department of Corrections, *Prison Facts and Statistics – March 2012*, http://www.corrections.govt.nz/about-us/facts_and_statistics/prisons/ps-march-2012.html (accessed 29 April 2013).
8. National Health Committee, *Review of Research on the Effects of Imprisonment on the Health of Inmates and Their Families*, Ministry of Health, Wellington, 2008, p.6.
9. Department of Corrections, *Growth of Women in Prison Nearly Double that of Men*, http://www.corrections.govt.nz/news-and-publications/media-releases/2010-media-releases/growth-of-women-in-prison-nearly-double-that-of-men.html (accessed 26 April 2013).
10. OECD imprisonment rates as of May 2011, http://www.teara.govt.nz/en/graph/36752/imprisonment-rates-for-oecd-countries-may-2011 (accessed 26 April 2013).
11. 'NZ Crime Rate at All Time Low – Police', *New Zealand Herald*, 1 October 2012, http://www.nzherald.co.nz/nz/news/article.cfm?c_id=1&objectid=10837671 (accessed 26 April 2013) and see http://www.police.govt.nz/sites/default/files/resources/crime-statistics/00-national-2011-12-crime-stats.pdf, p.16 (accessed 26 April 2013).
12. See http://www.police.govt.nz/sites/default/files/resources/crime-statistics/00-national-2011-12-crime-stats.pdf (accessed 26 April 2013).
13. David Brown, 'The Limited Benefit of Prison in Controlling Crime', in Gabrielle Maxwell (ed.), *The Costs of Crime: Towards Fiscal Responsibility*, Institute of Policy Studies, Wellington, 2011, pp.49–68.
14. M. Levy, 'Children of Prisoners: An Issue for Courts to Consider in Sentencing', paper presented to Federal Criminal Justice Forum, Canberra, 29 September 2008.
15. H. Blagg, 'Colonial Critique and Critical Criminology: Issues in Aboriginal Law and Aboriginal Violence', in T. Anthony and C. Cunneen (eds), *The Critical Criminology Companion*, Hawkins Press, Sydney, 2008, p.131.
16. Expert Advisory Group on Solutions to Child Poverty, *Solutions to Poverty: Evidence for Action*, Office of the Children's Commissioner, Wellington, 2012.
17. R. Berk, K. Lenihan and P. Rossi, 'Crime and Poverty', *American Sociological Review*, 45, 5 (1980), pp.766–86.
18. Gabrielle Maxwell, 'Inequality and Criminal Justice', paper presented at the forum 'Does Inequality Matter?', Institute for Policy Studies, Wellington, 16 November 2010.
19. Department of Corrections, 'About Time – Turning People Away from a Life of Crime and Reducing Re-offending: A Report to the Minister of Corrections', Department of Corrections, Wellington, May 2001, pp.27–28.
20. Ibid.
21. See, for example, John Pratt et al. (eds), *The New Punitiveness: Trends, Theories, Perspectives*, Willan, London, 2005; John Pratt, *Penal Populism*, Routledge, London, 2007; J.

Pratt, 'The Power and Limits of Populism: An Illustration from Recent Penal Developments in New Zealand', in S. Karstedt, I. Loader and H. Strang (eds), *Emotions, Crime and Justice*, Hart, Oxford, 2011, pp.331–46.

22 R.D. Putnam, *Bowling Alone: The Collapse and Revival of American Community*, Simon and Schuster, New York, 2000.

23 David Garland, *Punishment and Modern Society*, Clarendon Press, Oxford, 1990, p.252; Michael Ignatieff, *A Just Measure of Pain: The Penitentiary in the Industrial Revolution 1750–1850*, Macmillan, London, 1978.

24 Kim Workman, 'Politics and Punitiveness – Limiting the Rush to Punish', paper presented at the Australian and New Zealand Association of Psychiatry, Psychology and Law (ANZAPPL New Zealand) and the Royal Australian and New Zealand College of Psychiatrists (Faculty of Forensic Psychiatry) Conference, 'The Rising Punitiveness', Wellington, 17–19 November 2011 and 'Politicians feel heat over housing project', *New Zealand Herald*, 10 November 2011, http://www.nzherald.co.nz/nz/news/article.cfm?c_id=1&objectid=10764993 (accessed 26 April 2013).

25 'Labour hammers govt over unemployment rate', New Zealand Press Association, 5 February 2010, http://www.guide2.co.nz/politics/news/labour-hammers-govt-over-shocking039-unemployment-rate/11/13981 (accessed 26 April 2013).

26 Welfare Working Group Executive Summary, http://img.scoop.co.nz/media/pdfs/1102/WWGFinalRecommendations22February2011.pdf (accessed 26 April 2013).

27 'Drive to stem generations of welfare dependency', *New Zealand Herald*, 10 August 2011, http://www.nzherald.co.nz/nz/news/article.cfm?c_id=1&objectid=10664895 (accessed 26 April 2013).

28 'Housing NZ drops mob eviction bid', *New Zealand Herald*, 1 September 2011, http://www.nzherald.co.nz/nz/news/article.cfm?c_id=1&objectid=10748731 (accessed 26 April 2013); 'State housing ban for bad tenants', *New Zealand Herald*, 6 November 2011, http://www.stuff.co.nz/sunday-news/news/5916012/State-house-ban-for-bad-tenants (accessed 26 April 2013).

29 The Green Paper on Vulnerable Children, http://www.childrensactionplan.govt.nz/ (accessed 26 April 2013).

30 Richard Wilkinson and Kate Pickett, *The Spirit Level: Why Equality is Better for Everyone*, Penguin, London, 2010, p.148.

31 Workman, 'Politics and Punitiveness – Limiting the Rush to Punish'.

32 Wilkinson and Pickett, *The Spirit Level*, p.151.

33 B. Morrison, *Identifying and Responding to Bias in the Criminal Justice System: A Review of International and New Zealand Research*, Ministry of Justice, Wellington, 2009.

34 Ministry of Justice, personal communication, 5 May 2011.

35 Pita Sharples, 'Tackle prejudice in justice system', *New Zealand Herald*, 10 October 2011, http://www.nzherald.co.nz/nz/news/article.cfm?c_id=1&objectid=10757807 (accessed 26 April, 2013).

36 L. Gordon and L. MacGibbon, *A Study of the Children of Prisoners*, Te Puni Kōkiri, Wellington, 2009.

37 D. Garland (ed.), *Mass Imprisonment: Social Causes and Consequences*, Sage, London, 2001.

38 T. McIntosh, 'Marginalisation: A Case Study: Confinement', in T. McIntosh and M. Mulholland (eds), *Māori and Social Issues*, Huia, Wellington, 2011, p.273.

39 National Health Committee, *Health in Justice: Kia Piki te Ora, Kia Tika!: Improving the Health of Prisoners and Their Families and Whānau: He Whakapiki i t e Ora o Ngā Mauhere Me ō Rātou Whānau*, Ministry of Health, Wellington, 2010, p.112.

40 D.R. Rose and T.R. Clear, 'Incarceration, Social Capital, and Crime: Implications for Social Disorganization Theory', *Criminology*, 36, 3 (1998), p.457.

41 D. Stemen, *Reconsidering Incarceration: New Directions for Reducing Crime*, Vera Institute of Justice, New York, 2007.

42 Lucia Zedner, 'Dangers of Dystopia in Penal Theory', *Oxford Journal of Legal Studies*, 22, 2 (2002), p.356.

43 Ministry of Justice, *Reoffending Analysis for Restorative Justice Cases: 2008 and 2009 – A Summary*, Ministry of Justice, Wellington, June 2011.

44 B.J. Winick and D.B. Wexler, *Judging in a Therapeutic Key: Therapeutic Jurisprudence and the Courts*, Carolina Academic Press, Durham, NC, 2003.

45 See http://www.nzherald.co.nz/nz/news/article.cfm?c_id=1&objectid=10723259 (accessed 29 April 2013).

46 Ibid.

47 Rethinking and Crime and Punishment, 2012. http://www.rethinking.org.nz/Default.aspx?page=3655.

48 Andrew Coyle, 'New Approaches to Crime

and Justice', paper presented to the Prison Fellowship New Zealand 25th Anniversary Conference, 'Changing the Landscape', 17 May 2008, Upper Hutt.
49 Waitangi Tribunal, *Ko Aotearoa Tēnei: A Report into Claims Concerning New Zealand Law and Policy Affecting Māori Culture and Identity (Wai 262)*, Waitangi Tribunal, Wellington, 2011. Te Taumata Tuatahi, xviii.

Chapter 9: Schools and Inequality
1 Children and young people are defined here as being under the age of 18.
2 Bryan Perry, *Non-income Measures of Material Wellbeing and Hardship: First results from the 2008 New Zealand Living Standards Survey, with International Comparisons*, Ministry of Social Development, Wellington, 2009, see pp.54–55.
3 OECD, 'How Pronounced is Income Inequality Around the World – and How Can Education Help Reduce it?', Education Indicators in Focus, 4 (April 2012), http://www.oecd.library.org/docserver/download/5k97krntvqtf.pdf?expires=1359251969&id=id&accname=guest&checksum=6E21AA297889F555632C334A5A98334D (accessed 12 June 2012).
4 Emma Davies, Charles Crothers and Kirsten Hanna, 'Preventing Child Poverty: Barriers and Solutions', *New Zealand Journal of Psychology*, 39, 2 (2010), pp.20–31; Susan Mayer, *The Influence of Parental Income on Children's Outcomes*, Ministry of Social Development, Wellington, 2002; OECD, *Doing Better for Children*, OECD, Paris, 2009.
5 W. Steven Barnett, *Preschool Education and its Lasting Effects: Research and Policy Implications*, Education and the Public Interest Center & Education Policy Research Unit, Boulder and Tempe, 2008; Early Childhood Education Taskforce, *An Agenda for Amazing Children, Final report of the ECE taskforce*, Early Childhood Taskforce, 2011 (see particularly 'The Case for Investing in Early Childhood Education', pp. 21–28); Linda Mitchell, Cathy Wylie and Margaret Carr, *Outcomes of Early Childhood Education: Literature Review*, Ministry of Education, Wellington, 2008; Cathy Wylie and Edith Hodgen, *The Continuing Contribution of Early Childhood Education to Young People's Competency Levels*, Ministry of Education, Wellington, 2007.
6 Di Davies, *School Entry Assessment: June 1997–December 2000*, Research Division, Ministry of Education, Wellington, 2001, p.37. ('Decile' refers to the way schools are ranked into ten groups, according to their socio-economic intake, for funding allocation purposes.)
7 See, for example, Cathy Wylie, *Eight Years Old & Competent*, New Zealand Council for Educational Research, Wellington, 1999.
8 Nikki Turner and Innes Asher, 'Health Perspectives on Child Poverty', in Susan St John and Donna Wynd (eds), *Left Behind: How Social and Income Inequalities Damage New Zealand Children*, Child Poverty Action Group, Auckland, 2008, pp.73–90.
9 Jane Gilbert, *Educational Issues for Communities Affected by Transience and Residential Mobility*, New Zealand Council for Educational Research, Wellington, 2005, http://www.nzcer.org.nz/pdfs/14354.pdf, p.26 (accessed 20 November 2012).
10 Expert Advisory Group on Solutions to Child Poverty, *Lifecourse Effects on Childhood Poverty*, Working paper no. 2, and *What Causes Child Poverty? What are the Consequences? An Economic Perspective*, Working paper no. 3, Office of the Commissioner for Children, Wellington, August 2012.
11 Cathy Wylie, Hilary Ferral, Edith Hodgen and Jean Thompson, *Competencies at Age 14 and Competency Development for the Longitudinal Competent Children, Competent Learners Study Sample*, New Zealand Council for Educational Research, Wellington, 2006, p.18.
12 Martin Thrupp, 'Some Inconvenient Truths about Education in Aotearoa-New Zealand', in St John and Wynd (eds), *Left Behind*, pp.109–19; Cathy Wylie, *Vital Connections: Why We Need More than Self-managing Schools*, NZCER Press, Wellington, 2012.
13 Cathy Wylie, *Secondary Schools in 2012: Main Findings from the NZCER National Survey*, New Zealand Council for Educational Research, Wellington, 2013.
14 Ibid.
15 Simon Denny, Elizabeth Robinson, Taciano Milfont and Sue Grant, *Youth'07: The Social Climate of Secondary Schools in New Zealand*, University of Auckland, Auckland, 2009, p.34, table 14.
16 Cathy Wylie, *Secondary Schools in 2012: Main Findings from the NZCER National Survey*.
17 Jane Blaikie, 'Rich Kids Still Get More', *Education Aotearoa*, 3, 4 (2012), pp.13–15.
18 William J. Mathis, 'After five years: Revisiting the costs of the No Child Left Behind Act', in Jennifer King Rice and Christopher F. Roellke (eds), *High Stakes Accountability: Implications for Resources and Capacity*,

Information Age Publishing, Charlotte, New Carolina, 2009, pp.197–224.
19 Source: New Zealand Council for Educational Research, data from schools using its online marking service.
20 Stuart McNaughton, *Designing Better Schools for Culturally and Linguistically Diverse Children*, Routledge, New York, 2011, pp.70–71.
21 Ibid, pp.158–60.
22 Ministry of Education, *Developing Communities of Mathematical Inquiry*, Ministry of Education, Wellington, 2012, http://www.educationcounts.govt.nz/__data/assets/pdf_file/0010/88075/Case1-Developing-Mathematical-Communities.pdf (downloaded August 2012).
23 Wylie, *Vital Connections*, p.197.
24 Wylie, *Vital Connections*.
25 Source: Ministry of Education, http://www.educationcounts.govt.nz/publications/ece/2567/11780 (accessed 20 April 2013).
26 Irena Madjar, Elizabeth McKinley, Seini Jensen, Alice Van Der Merwe, *Towards University: Navigating NCEA Course Choices in Low-Mid Decile schools*. Starpath Project, University of Auckland, Auckland, 2009.
27 'Northland College Tops List of NCEA Big Movers', *Northern Advocate*, 29 April 2010.
28 New Zealand Qualifications Authority, *Annual Report on NCEA and New Zealand Scholarship Data and Statistics 2011*, Wellington, 2012, http://www.nzqa.govt.nz/assets/About-us/Publications/stats-reports/ncea-annualreport-2011.pdf (accessed November 2012).

Chapter 10: Inequality and Māori

1 See R. Miles, 'Summoned by Capital: The Political Economy of Labour Migration', in P. Spoonley, C. Macpherson, D. Pearson and C. Sedgwick (eds), *Tauiwi: Racism and Ethnicity in New Zealand*, Dunmore Press, Palmerston North, 1984, pp.223–43; R. Miles, *Racism and Migrant Labour*, Routledge & Kegan Paul, London, 1982, pp.95–150; R. Miles, *Racism after 'Race' Relations*, Routledge, London, 1993, pp.107–27; R. Miles and P. Spoonley, 'The Political Economy of Labour Migration: An Alternative to the Sociology of "Race" and "Ethnic Relations" in New Zealand', *Journal of Sociology*, 21, 1 (1985), pp.3–26; D. Pearson, 'Two Paths of Colonialism: Class, "Race", Ethnicity and Migrant Labour in New Zealand', in Spoonley et al., *Tauiwi*, pp.203–21; D. Pearson, *A Dream Deferred: The Origins of Ethnic Conflict in New Zealand*, Allen & Unwin, Wellington, 1990, Chapters 2 and 4, pp.38–72, pp.106–43; P. Spoonley, *Racism and Ethnicity*, 2nd edn, Oxford University Press, Auckland, 1993, pp.5–16; E. Poata-Smith, 'The Political Economy of Inequality Between Māori and Pākehā', in C. Rudd and B. Roper (eds), *The Political Economy of New Zealand*, Oxford University Press, Auckland, 1997, pp.160–79.
2 I.H.G. Sutherland, 'Maori and European' (A paper read before the Social Sciences Section of the N.Z. Science Congress in Christchurch, May, 1951), *The Journal of the Polynesian Society*, 61, 1 & 2, 1952, pp.136–155.
3 J.E. Ritchie (ed.), *Race Relations: Six New Zealand Studies*, Victoria University of Wellington Publications in Psychology, No. 16, Wellington, 1964 cited in E. Schwimmer, *The Maori People in the Nineteen-Sixties: A Symposium*, Longman Paul, Auckland, 1968, p.61.
4 D. Ausubel, *The Fern and the Tiki: An American View of New Zealand National Character*, Holt, Rinehart and Winston, New York, 1965, p.215.
5 J. Boston, *Incomes Policy in New Zealand: 1968-1984*, Institute of Policy Studies, Wellington, 1984, p.93. See also J. Gould, *The Rake's Progress?*, Hodder & Stoughton, Auckland, 1982, pp.32–36; and B. Easton, *Income Distribution in New Zealand*, NZIER Research Paper 28, NZIER, Wellington, 1983, p.188.
6 W.B. Sutch, *The Quest for Security in New Zealand, 1840–1966*, Oxford University Press, Wellington, 1966, p.452.
7 J.K. Hunn, *Report on Department of Maori Affairs: With Statistical Supplement*, Government Printer, Wellington, 1961.
8 It became increasingly clear, however, that the 'integration' paradigm that was being proposed as an alternative was really assimilation in disguise.
9 Hunn, *Report on Department of Maori Affairs*, p.31.
10 P. Armstrong, A. Glyn and J. Harrison, *Capitalism Since 1945*, Blackwell, Oxford, 1991, p.117.
11 B. Roper, 'The End of the Golden Weather: New Zealand's Economic Crisis', in B. Roper and C. Rudd (eds), *State and Economy in New Zealand*, Oxford University Press, Auckland, 1993, pp.1–25.
12 J.K. Hunn, *Report on Department of Maori Affairs*; Eru Pomare et al., *Hauora Māori Standards of Health III: A Study of the Years 1970–1991*, Te Rōpū Rangahau Hauora a Eru Pōmare, Wellington, 1995; Te Puni Kōkiri, *He*

Kākano: A Handbook of Māori Health Data, Government Printer, Wellington, 1993; Te Puni Kōkiri, *Progress Towards Closing the Gaps, Between Māori and Non-Māori*, Te Puni Kōkiri, Wellington, 1999; Te Puni Kōkiri and Ministry of Women's Affairs, *Māori Women in Focus: Titiro Hāngai, Ka Mārama*, Te Puni Kōkiri, Ministry of Women's Affairs, Wellington, 1999; Te Puni Kōkiri, *Māori in the New Zealand Economy*, 2nd edn, Te Puni Kōkiri, Wellington, 2000.

13 B. Roper, 'The End of the Golden Weather: New Zealand's Economic Crisis', p.2.

14 J. Boston and P. Dalziel (eds), *The Decent Society? Essays in Response to National's Economic and Social Policies*, Oxford University Press, Auckland, 1992; J. Boston, P. Dalziel and S. St John (eds), *Redesigning the Welfare State in New Zealand: Problems, Policies, Prospects*, Oxford University Press, Auckland, 1999.

15 Based on equivalised disposable income.

16 See P. Dalziel and R. Lattimore, *The New Zealand Macroeconomy: A Briefing on the Reforms and their Legacy*, 4th edn, Oxford University Press, Auckland, 2001.

17 Te Puni Kōkiri, *Progress Towards Closing Social and Economic Gaps Between Māori and Non-Māori: A Report to the Minister of Māori Affairs*, Te Puni Kōkiri, Wellington, 1998, p.1.

18 Minister of Finance, Michael Cullen, Budget 2000 Speech, The Treasury, Wellington, 2000, p.7.

19 Ibid.

20 See E. Poata-Smith, 'Ka Tika a Muri, Ka Tika a Mua? Māori Protest Politics and The Treaty of Waitangi Settlement Process', in P. Spoonley, C. Macpherson and D. Pearson (eds), *Tangata Tangata: The Changing Ethnic Contours of New Zealand*, Thomson/Dunmore Press, Melbourne/Palmerston North, 2004, pp.59–88.

21 The objectives included: better health and reduced inequalities in health; positive parenting and a reduced incidence of abuse and neglect; high levels of participation in education and improved educational achievement; improved labour market participation, greater access to 'sustainable employment' opportunities and reduced unemployment; higher overall living standards and reduced poverty across the community; affordable housing of an adequate standard; reduced criminal victimisation and violence; the valuing of cultural and ethnic identities; greater social capital and reduced social isolation.

22 B. Roper, *Prosperity for All? Economic, Political and Social Change in New Zealand Since 1935*, Thomson/Dunmore Press, Melbourne/Palmerston North, 2005, p.222.

23 B. Perry, *Household Incomes in New Zealand: Trends in Indicators of Inequality and Hardship 1982 to 2011*, Ministry of Social Development, Wellington, August 2012 (updated 3 October 2012), p.10.

24 J. Kelsey, 'The Dilemma of Social Justice in the Global Market Era: A Response to Charles Waldegrave: 'Reflections on the Implications of Indigenous Notions of Peace and Conflict Resolution for the Church and Political Society"', in Efi, Tuiatua Tupua Tamasese (ed.), *Pacific Indigenous Dialogue: on Faith, Peace, Reconciliation and Good Governance*, University of the South Pacific, Apia, Samoa, 2007, pp. 109–113.

25 D. Wynd, 'Committed to Fairness and Opportunity? A Brief Analysis of the Impact of the Work Payment on Māori and Pasifika Families', Child Poverty Action Group, Auckland, April 2006.

26 S. Collins, '"Closing the Gaps" policy fails Maori, report shows', *New Zealand Herald*, 9 August 2006.

27 Bill English, *Fiscal Strategy Report: Budget 2012*, The Treasury, Wellington, 24 May 2012, pp.3–11.

28 Bill English, *Budget Policy Statement: Budget 2013*, The Treasury, Wellington, 18 December 2012, p.5, http://www.treasury.govt.nz/budget/2013/bps/bps13.pdf (accessed 26 April 2013).

29 English, *Fiscal Strategy Report: Budget 2012*, p.11.

30 D. Harvey, *A Brief History of Neoliberalism*, Oxford University Press, Oxford, 2005; J.K. Galbraith and M. Berner (eds), *Inequality and Industrial Change: A Global View*, Cambridge University Press, Cambridge, 2001.

31 Bryan Perry, *Household Incomes in New Zealand*, p.10.

32 Department of Labour, *Māori Labour Market Fact Sheet March 2012*, Department of Labour, Wellington, May 2012, http://www.dol.govt.nz/publications/lmr/quick-facts/lmr-fs-maori-mar12.pdf (accessed 23 April 2013).

33 Ibid.

34 Statistics New Zealand, *New Zealand Now: Incomes*, Statistics New Zealand, Wellington, 1999, p.85.

35 M. Mowbray, *Distributions and Disparity: New Zealand Household Incomes*, Ministry of Social Policy, Wellington, 2001.

36 Ibid.
37 D. O'Dea, 'The Changes in New Zealand's Income Distribution', Treasury Working Paper 00/13, The Treasury, Wellington, 2000.
38 Perry, *Household Incomes in New Zealand*, p.11.
39 The Gini coefficient has a theoretical range between 0 and 1: the closer the value to 1, the greater the inequalities (see Chapter 2). The Gini coefficient is calculated here at 0.693, a level comparable to the 2001 Household Savings Survey of 0.689 for all economic units (Statistics New Zealand, *The Net Worth of New Zealanders*, Statistics New Zealand, Wellington, 2002). The result confirms that inequalities of net worth have persisted between the two surveys.
40 E. Poata-Smith, 'Closing the Gaps', in N. Lunt, M. O'Brien and R. Stephens (eds), *New Zealand, New Welfare*, Cengage Learning, South Melbourne, 2008, pp.106–8. See also T. O'Reilly and D. Wood, 'Biculturalism and the Public Sector', in J. Boston, J. Martin, J. Pallott and P. Walsh (eds), *Reshaping the State: New Zealand's Bureaucratic Revolution*, Oxford University Press, Auckland, 1991, p.323; J. Martin, 'Devolution and Decentralization', in Boston et al. (eds), *Reshaping the State*, p.286; A. Fleras and P. Spoonley, *Recalling Aotearoa: Indigenous Politics and Ethnic Relations in New Zealand*, Oxford University Press, Auckland, 1999, p.128.
41 E. Poata-Smith, 'Ka Tika a Muri, Ka Tika a Mua? Māori Protest Politics and The Treaty of Waitangi Settlement Process', in P. Spoonley, C. Macpherson and D. Pearson (eds), *Tangata Tangata: The Changing Ethnic Contours of New Zealand*, Thomson/Dunmore Press, Melbourne/Palmerston North, 2004, pp.59–88. See also, Annette Sykes, Bruce Jesson Memorial Lecture 2010: 'The Politics of the Brown Table', University of Auckland, 27 October 2010, https://www.artsfaculty.auckland.ac.nz/special/lectures/?view=1 (accessed 23 May 2013).
42 D. Brash, 'Nationhood', A transcript of an address by Don Brash, Leader of the National Party, to the Orewa Rotary Club, 27 January 2004, http://www.nzherald.co.nz/storyprint.cfm?ID=3545950 (accessed 10 March 2004).
43 Te Puni Kōkiri, *Māori in the New Zealand Economy*, 2nd edn, Te Puni Kōkiri, Wellington, 2000.

Chapter 11: Reducing Inequality

1 *Vulnerability Report*, Issue 13, NZCCSS, July 2012.
2 www.closertogether.org.nz/take-action/champions-for-closer-together/ (accessed September 2012).
3 John Pearce, *An Estimate of the National Costs of Child Poverty in New Zealand*, Analytica, Auckland, 2011.
4 Paul Barber is a policy advisor at the New Zealand Council of Christian Social Services (NZCCSS) and leads the council's flagship programme, *Closer Together Whakatata Mai – reducing inequalities*.
5 The Global Ethic movement has explored this deep moral connection between the world's major faith traditions and explores how this also translates into our economic relationships: see http://www.global-ethic-now.de/index-eng.php (accessed 29 April 2013).
6 David Fischer, *Fairness and Freedom: A History of Two Open Societies, New Zealand and the United States*, Oxford University Press, New York, 2012.
7 Jonathan Boston and Alan Cameron (eds), *Voices for Justice*, Dunmore Press, Palmerston North, 1993.
8 Fischer, *Fairness and Freedom*.
9 Brian Easton, 'Fairness and Community', 2012, http://www.eastonbh.ac.nz/2012/07/fairness-and-community/ (accessed December 2012).
10 New Zealand Church Leaders' Social Justice Statement, 11 July 1993, http://www.justice.net.nz/justwiki/social-justice-statement-1993/ (accessed September 2012).
11 'Church Leaders' Visions for a Fairer Society', October 2011, www.nzccss.org.nz (accessed September 2012).
12 Richard Wilkinson and Kate Pickett, *The Spirit Level: Why Equality is Better for Everyone*, Penguin, London, 2010.
13 Paul Callaghan, 'Sustainable Economic Growth For New Zealand: An Optimistic Myth-Busting Perspective', StrategyNZ: Mapping Our Future, Contributing Paper 2011/01, McGuinness Institute, Wellington, March 2011.
14 For a discussion of this and how it relates to official income inequality data, see Chapter 2.
15 Arni Hole, speech to Countess Markievicz School, Teachers Club, Dublin, 4 June 2011, http://vimeo.com/25742261 (accessed 19 April 2013).
16 'Debt and Why the Government is Different', *Economic Bulletin*, New Zealand Council of Trade Unions, Wellington, March 2011.
17 Figures based on calculations from Inland Revenue data by Bill Rosenberg, Policy Director, New Zealand Council of Trade Unions.

18 Council of Trade Unions, 'How Many of the Rich List Pay a Fair Tax?', 27 July 2012, http://www.scoop.co.nz/stories/PO1207/S00367/how-many-of-the-rich-list-pay-a-fair-tax.htm (accessed 31 December 2012).

19 Rob Salmond, *The New New Zealand Tax System: New Zealand Taxes in Comparative Perspective*, Institute of Policy Studies, Wellington, 2011, p.54.

20 Richard Florida, 'Creativity and Prosperity: The Global Creativity Index', Martin Prosperity Institute, Toronto, January 2011.

21 Helen Roberts, 'Executive Compensation in New Zealand: 1997–2002', PhD thesis, Otago University, Dunedin, 2007.

22 David MacLeod and Nita Clarke, *Engaging for Success: Enhancing Performance Through Employee Engagement*, Department for Business, Innovation and Skills, London, 2009.

23 Philip Gendall and Nicola Murray, 'Social Inequality in New Zealand', International Social Survey Programme, Massey University, Palmerston North, March 2010.

24 Penelope Carroll, Sally Casswell, John Huakau, Philippa Howden-Chapman, and Paul Perry, 'The Widening Gap: Perceptions of Poverty and Income Inequalities and Implications for Health and Social Outcomes', *Social Policy Journal of New Zealand*, 37 (May 2011), pp.111–121.

25 Tracy Watkins, 'Key battle lines drawn in early political poll', *Dominion Post*, 30 July 2012, http://www.stuff.co.nz/national/politics/7372956/Key-battle-lines-drawn-in-early-political-poll (accessed 31 December 2012).

26 Paul Perry, personal communication. Items on poverty and income inequality from the New Zealand Study of Values survey, School of People, Environment and Planning, Massey University, Palmerston North.

27 Carroll et al., 'The Widening Gap'.

28 Joseph Stiglitz, *The Price of Inequality*, Allen Lane, London, 2012, p.288.

29 David Frumm, 'The Vanishing Republican Voter', *New York Times Magazine*, 5 September 2008, http://www.nytimes.com/2008/09/07/magazine/07Inequality-t.html?pagewanted=all&_r=0 (accessed 29 April 2013).

30 Ruth Laugesen, 'The Overpaid Executive', *New Zealand Listener*, 18 February 2011.

31 Louise Bamfield and T. Horton, *Understanding Attitudes to Tackling Economic Inequality*, Joseph Rowntree Foundation, London, June 2009.

32 Expert Advisory Group on Solutions to Child Poverty, *Solutions to Child Poverty in New Zealand: Evidence for Action*, Office of the Children's Commissioner, Wellington, 2012.

33 Girol Karacaoglu, *Financial Summit on Problem Credit: Background Paper*, November 2011, http://www.consumeraffairs.govt.nz/legislation-policy/policy-development/financial-summit (accessed 29 April 2013).

34 The effect has been demonstrated internationally; Nick Bailey, Maria Gannon, Ade Kearns, Mark Livingston and Alistair H. Leyland, 'Living apart, losing sympathy? How neighbourhood context affects attitudes to redistribution and recipients', *Environment and Planning A*, 45, 2013, pp.1–22.

35 Wilkinson and Pickett, *The Spirit Level*, Chapter 15. See also Bob Hughes, 'Inequality Costs the Earth', *New Internationalist*, 433 (June 2010).

36 See Roy Morgan poll research, July 2012, http://www.roymorgan.com/news/polls/2012/4800/ (accessed 29 April 2013).

37 Find out more at www.livingwage.org.nz (accessed 29 April 2013).

38 Peter King and Charles Waldegrave, *Report of an Investigation into Defining a Living Wage for New Zealand*, Family Centre Social Policy Research Unit, Lower Hutt, December 2012.

Viewpoint 11: Kate Frykberg

1 See http://www.ocvs.govt.nz/work-programme/building-knowledge/giving-research/qqi-march-2011.html (accessed 6 May 2013).

2 See www.giving.org.nz/thoughtfulgiving/steps-to-giving (accessed 6 May 2013).

3 Barbara Kingsolver, *High Tide In Tucson: Essays From Now or Never*, Thorndike Press, Maine, 1996.

Chapter 12: Education and Skills

The author acknowledges financial support from the New Zealand Ministry of Business, Innovation and Employment under research programme LINX0603. He is grateful to fellow objective leaders in that programme, Jane Higgins, Hazel Phillips and Karen Vaughan, for many insightful discussions on the theme of this chapter. He also thanks Peter Conway, Julie Fry, Stuart Middleton, Max Rashbrooke, Tom Rennie, Bill Rosenberg, Shaun Twaddle and anonymous peer reviewers who generously commented on earlier drafts to improve the material presented in this chapter.

1 OECD, *Better Skills, Better Jobs, Better Lives: A Strategic Approach to Skills Policies*,

OECD Publishing, Paris, 2012, http://dx.doi.org/10.1787/9789264177338-en, p.3 (accessed 23 April 2013).

2. For a summary of recent New Zealand research, see J. Whatman, H. Potter and S. Boyd, *Literacy, Language and Numeracy: Connecting Research to Practice in the Tertiary Sector*, Ako Aotearoa, Wellington, March 2011, http://akoaotearoa.ac.nz/download/ng/file/group-4/literacy-language-and-numeracy-research-summary.pdf (accessed 23 April 2013).

3. Ithaca Group, *Employability Skills Framework – Stage 1: Final Report*, Department of Education, Employment and Workplace Relations, Canberra, January 2012, http://foi.deewr.gov.au/system/files/doc/other/employability_skills_framework_stage_1_final_report.pdf (accessed 23 April 2013).

4. See http://www.immigration.govt.nz/migrant/general/generalinformation/review.htm (accessed 23 April 2013).

5. P. Dalziel and C. Saunders, 'Equity and Sustainable Development', in J. Boston, A. Bradstock and D. Eng (eds), *Ethics and Public Policy: Contemporary Issues*, Victoria University Press, Wellington, 2011, pp.297–323.

6. See http://www.eel.org.nz (accessed 23 April 2013).

7. See the following publications by the author: 'Developing the Next Generation: Employer-led Channels for Education Employment Linkages', in J. Bryson (ed.), *Beyond Skill: Institutions, Organisations and Human Capability*, Palgrave Macmillan, London, 2010, pp.154–75; *Towards a New Zealand System of Skill Ecosystems*, EEL Research Report No. 11, AERU, Lincoln University, 2012, http://www.eel.org.nz; and 'Education and Qualifications as Skills', in J. Buchanan, D. Finegold, K. Mayhew and C. Warhurst (eds), *Oxford Handbook of Skills and Training*, Oxford University Press, Oxford, forthcoming November 2013.

8. Education Review Office, *Evaluation at a Glance: Priority Learners in New Zealand Schools*, Education Review Office, Wellington, 2012, p.13.

9. An important reference for anyone concerned about improving learning outcomes for Māori students, for example, is R. Bishop and M. Berryman, *Culture Speaks: Cultural Relationships and Classroom Learning*, Huia, Wellington, 2006. A recent report priviliging the voices of Māori rangatahi and Pacific young people on this issue is H. Phillips and M. Mitchell, *Kei Hea te Tuna? Māori and Pacific Island Young People's Experiences of Education Employment Linkages: Two Case Studies*, EEL Research Report No. 10, 30 September 2012, http://www.eel.org.nz.

10. M. Oldershaw, *Changes to the School System will Support Youth Employment*, Media Statement released by the Industry Training Federation, 19 February 2012, http://www.itf.org.nz (accessed 23 April 2013). This view is supported in P. Dalziel, *Education Employment Linkages: Perspectives from Employer-Led Channels*, EEL Research Report No. 5, 1 July 2010, http://www.eel.org.nz.

11. See J. Higgins, 'Young People and Transitions Policies in New Zealand', *Social Policy Journal of New Zealand*, 18 (2002), pp.44–61. The National Administration Guidelines for schools continue to retain an echo of that period by requiring 'a particular emphasis on specific career guidance for those students who have been identified by the school as being at risk of leaving school unprepared for the transition to the workplace or further education/training'.

12. For an insightful discussion on the resulting outcomes and how to reduce youth disadvantage, see R. Boven, C. Harland and L. Grace, *More Ladders, Fewer Snakes: Two Proposals to Reduce Youth Disadvantage*, Discussion paper 2011/1, New Zealand Institute, Auckland, 2011.

13. See http://www.youthguarantee.net.nz (accessed 23 April 2013). This discussion draws on a PowerPoint presentation by the Ministry of Education to a symposium on the secondary tertiary interface on 5 April 2012, organised by the Centre for Studies in Multiple Pathways, http://csmp.manukau.ac.nz/__data/assets/pdf_file/0006/83499/MITatCPIT-April-5-2012-2.pdf (accessed 23 April 2013).

14. See, for example, Stuart Middleton's Occasional Papers, *Multiple Pathways* and *Background to the Tertiary High School at Manukau Institute of Technology*, both published in November 2010, http://csmp.manukau.ac.nz/. Middleton's personal website is at http://www.stuartmiddleton.co.nz (accessed 26 April 2013) and his blog is at http://www.EdTalkNZ.com

15. The terms of reference and other published material relevant to the review can be found at http://www.minedu.govt.nz/NZEducation/EducationPolicies/TertiaryEducation/

PolicyAndStrategy/ReviewIndustryTraining. aspx (accessed 23 April 2013).
16 This paragraph draws on P. Dalziel, *Integrating Employment, Skills and Economic Development: New Zealand*, A report prepared for the OECD Local Economic and Employment Development (LEED) Programme, Department of Labour, Wellington, 2007, http://www.dol.govt.nz/publications/general/iesed/summary.asp (accessed 23 April 2013).
17 NZCTU 'Proposal to Improve the Performance of the Government's Investment in Industry Training', Submission of the New Zealand Council of Trade Unions Te Kauae Kaimahi to the Industry Training Review, 12 September 2012, par. 5.2.
18 Green Growth Advisory Group, *Greening New Zealand's Growth*, Green Growth Advisory Group Secretariat, Wellington, December 2011, http://www.med.govt.nz/sectors-industries/environment/green-growth (accessed 23 April 2013); Pure Advantage, *New Zealand's Position in the Green Race*, Pure Advantage, Auckland, 2012; and Vivid Economics and Energy Centre, University of Auckland Business School, *Green Growth: Opportunities for New Zealand*, report prepared for the New Zealand Green Growth Research Trust, Auckland, November 2012, http://www.pureadvantage.org (accessed 23 April 2013).
19 This section is based on the author's contribution to an OECD study, G. Miranda, P. Dalziel, C. Estolano, K. Krasnowski and G. Larcombe, *Climate Change, Employment and Local Development*, Sydney, Australia, OECD Local Economic and Employment Development (LEED) Working Papers, 2011/14, OECD Publishing, Paris, 2011, http://dx.doi.org/10.1787/5kg20639kgkj-en (accessed 23 April 2013).
20 See http://www.innovation.gov.au/Skills/SkillsTrainingAndWorkforceDevelopment/ClimateChangeAnd SkillsForSustainability/Pages/GreenSkillsAgreement.aspx (accessed 23 April 2013). For an overview of how the TAFE sector responded, see G. McDonald, L. Condon and M. Riordan, *The Australian Green Skills Agreement Policy and Industry Context, Institutional Response and Green Skills Delivery*, TAFE Directors Australia, Broadway, NSW, March 2012, http://www.tda.edu.au/cb_pages/files/APEC%20Australia%20TDA%20Green%20Skills%20Agreement%202012.pdf (accessed 23 April 2013). Green skills training has also been used to target young adults from communities with high poverty levels; see, for example, the Green City Force programme in New York at www.greencityforce.org/ (accessed 23 April 2013).

Chapter 13: The Rewards of Work

1 Labour productivity is the goods and services that a person generates in each hour of work.
2 See, for example, Endnotes 3 and 10 below.
3 Engelbert Stockhammer and Ozlem Onaran, 'Wage-led Growth: Theory, Evidence, Policy', Working Paper Series Number 300, Political Economy Research Institute, University of Massachusetts, Amherst, Massachusetts, 2012, pp.15–18.
4 Goran Roos, 'Is Manufacturing in Decline?', EPMU/CTU Workshop, June 2012, Auckland.
5 Nigel Haworth. 'Economic transformation, productivity and employment relations in New Zealand 1999–2008' In E. Rasmussen (ed.) *Employment Relationships: Workers, Unions and Employers in New Zealand*, AUP, Auckland, p 149–67.
6 Eileen Appelbaum, (ed.), *Manufacturing Advantage: Why High Performance Work Systems Pay Off*. ILR Press, Ithaca, 2000.
7 David Wan and Chin Huat Ong, 'Compensation Systems in Singapore', *Compensation and Benefits Review*, 34, 4 (2002), p.25.
8 See the NZCTU 2012 Submission on the Minimum Wage (pp.54–67 especially) for an overview of the literature on the labour market impacts of the minimum wage: NZCTU, 'Submission to the Minimum Wage Review', Wellington, December 2012, http://union.org.nz/sites/union.org.nz/files/NZCTU%20Minimum%20Wage%20Review%202012%20submission.pdf (accessed 31 December 2012).
9 See, for example, Olivier Blanchard, Florence Jaumotte and Prakash Loungani, 'Labor Market Policies and IMF Advice in Advanced Economies During the Great Recession', IMF Research Department, March, 2013.
10 Marc Lavoie and Engelbert Stockhammer, 'Wage-led Growth: Concept, Theories and Policies', Conditions of Work and Employment Series No. 41, International Labour Office, Geneva, 2012, pp. 24–25.

Viewpoint 13: DSK Engineering

1 Ernst & Young, 'What Makes New Zealanders Productive?', *New Zealand Productivity Pulse*, 1, (May 2012), p.1.

Chapter 14: A Better Welfare System

1 Government actions are not necessarily benevolent or intended to create greater equality, but only government has the power

to alter market distribution. The purpose and outcome of government action is the subject of wide argument; space makes it impossible to cover those arguments here.

2. A good account of this is provided in T. Shildrick, R. MacDonald, C. Webster and K. Garthwaite, *Poverty and Insecurity: Life in Low-pay, No-pay Britain*, Policy Press, Bristol, 2012.

3. Shildrick et al., *Poverty and Insecurity*.

4. 'Social investment' in the international discussions has a much wider meaning than the narrow use of 'investment' that has been part of the current government's discussions about welfare reform.

5. Jane Lewis and Rebecca Surender, *Welfare State Change*, Oxford University Press, Oxford, 2004.

6. Susan St John, 'Working for Families', in C. Dale, M. O'Brien and S. St John (eds), *Left Further Behind: How Policies Fail the Poorest Children in New Zealand*, Child Poverty Action Group, Auckland, 2011.

7. Ministry of Social Development, 'Description of Social Assistance Benefits in New Zealand', Background Document prepared for Welfare Working Group, Ministry of Social Development, Wellington, 2010.

8. See, for example, the story under the heading, 'Living on a Benefit', http://www.soupkitchen.org.nz/resources/ (accessed 21 April 2013). The University of Otago Cost of Food Survey can be found at http://nutrition.otago.ac.nz/consultancy/foodcostsurvey (accessed 21 April 2013).

9. There are good discussions of these effects in Expert Advisory Group on Solutions to Child Poverty, *Solutions to Child Poverty in New Zealand: Evidence for Action*, Office of the Children's Commissioner, Wellington, 2012; and Dale et al. (eds), *Left Further Behind*.

10. Using the most stringent measure of child poverty, namely, children living in families with less than 60 per cent of median household income (adjusted for family size), after housing costs. For a fuller discussion of the different poverty lines, see Bryan Perry, *Household Incomes in New Zealand: Trends in Indicators of Inequality and Hardship 1982 to 2011*, Ministry of Social Development, Wellington, 2012, p.107.

11. Anne Salmond, 'To the Social Policy Research and Evaluation Conference', *Social Policy Journal of New Zealand*, 20 (June 2003), http://www.msd.govt.nz/about-msd-and-our-work/publications-resources/journals-and-magazines/social-policy-journal/spj20/to-the-social-policy-research-20-pages1-5.html (accessed 26 April 2013).

12. Expert Advisory Group on Solutions to Child Poverty, *Lifecourse Effects on Child Poverty*. Commissioner for Children, Working paper no. 2. www.occ.govt.nz (accessed 20 May 2013).

13. Superannuation rates are for those with an M tax code (with no other income), and the single adult rate is for somebody living alone; there is a lower rate for a single person sharing accommodation. Rates for both groups are net.

14. St John, 'Working for Families'.

15. Shildrick et al., *Poverty and Insecurity*.

16. Statistics New Zealand, 'The New Zealand Labour Market During Recession', http://www.stats.govt.nz/browse_for_stats/income-and-work/employment_and_unemployment/nz-labour-market-during-recession.aspx (accessed 12 February 2013).

17. A good example is Bernard Orsman, 'Thousands Queue for 150 jobs', *New Zealand Herald*, 22 January 2010, http://www.nzherald.co.nz/business/news/article.cfm?c_id=3&objectid=10621612 (accessed 27 February 2013).

18. Thomas Lorentzen, 'Income Dynamics in Norwegian Families on Social Assistance: A Panel Data Study of a Social Assistance Cohort', *European Journal of Social Security*, 8, 3 (2006), pp.279–98.

19. Ministry of Social Development, *The Statistical Report for the Year Ending June 2011*, Ministry of Social Development, Wellington, 2012.

20. The figure is from Statistics New Zealand's Household Economic Survey, quoted in Child Poverty Action Group, *Hunger for Learning*, Child Poverty Action Group, Auckland, 2011, p.16.

21. R. Salmond, *The New New Zealand Tax System: New Zealand Taxes in Comparative Perspective*, Institute of Policy Studies, Wellington, 2011.

22. No Right Turn, 'Who Benefits from National's Tax Cuts?', 20 May 2010, http://norightturn.blogspot.co.nz/2010/05/who-benefits-from-nationals-tax-cuts.html (accessed 25 March 2013).

23. Salmond, *The New New Zealand Tax System*, pp.76–82.

24. Gareth Morgan and Susan Guthrie, *The Big Kahuna*, Public Interest Publishing, Wellington, 2011, pp.175–82.

25. Salmond, *The New New Zealand Tax System*, pp.105–12.

26. Whether all families would then spend that

income on their children is an important question, but one outside the scope of this chapter.

Chapter 15: The Future is Now

1. Audre Lorde 'The Master's Tools will Never Dismantle the Master's House', 1979, comments at 'The Personal and the Political' panel, Second Sex Conference, reproduced in C. Moraga and G. Anzaldua (eds), *This Bridge Called My Back: Writings by Radical Women of Color*, Kitchen Table/Women of Color Press, New York, 1981, pp.98–101.
2. Natalie Jackson, 'Māori and the Potential Demographic Dividend', session address to PANZ Conference, Auckland, 2011, National Institute of Demographic and Economic Analysis, University of Waikato, www.population.org.nz (accessed 7 May 2013).
3. L.T. Smith, M. Boler, G.H. Smith, M. Kempton, A. Ormond, H. Chueh and R. Waetford, "Do you guys hate Aucklanders too?" Youth: Voicing Difference from the Rural Heartland', *Journal for Rural Studies*, 18 (2002), pp.169–78; L.T. Smith, 'Troubling Spaces', *Journal of Critical Psychology, IV: Under the Covers* (October 2002), pp.176–82.
4. G.H. Smith, 'Manu Ao Presentation – Inclusive 360 intervention', 2011, http://www.manu-ao.ac.nz/massey/fms/manu-ao/documents/Graham%20Smith%20Powerpoint.pdf (accessed 7 May 2013).
5. Jonathan Lear, *Radical Hope: Ethics in the Face of Cultural Devastation*, Harvard University Press, Cambridge, Mass., 2006.

Index

Accident Compensation Corporation (ACC), 129
Adelaide, 102
Adenauer, Chancellor, 209
Adichie, Chimamanda, 100
alcohol: abuse, 13, 68; and crime, 129; spending on, 7, 221
apprenticeship programmes, 59, 63, 185, 190, 202
Asian people, 155, 186
Auckland, 102–3, 148; housing in, 14, 35, 54, 102–3, 149; see also Manukau City; South Auckland
Auckland Communities Foundation, 14
Auckland University of Technology, 196, 197
Australia: crime rates in, 129; equality and income levels in, 13, 23–24, 28; tax rates in, 173, 222; vocational education and training in, 184–5, 189, 193–4; see also Adelaide; Brisbane; Green Skills Agreement (Australia); Perth
Australian Chamber of Commerce, 194
Australian Council of Trade Unions, 194
Austria, 13, 24, 172
Ausubel, David, 149

Baker, Michael, 98
Beirut, 119
Belgium, 13
benefit fraud, 230
benefits, see income support
Bennett, Paula, 54
Blair, Tony, 48
borrowing: government, 27, 172; household and private, 16, 31, 44, 59, 94; see also debt
Brazil, 202
breakfast in schools scheme, see 'food in schools' strategy
Brisbane, 102
Britain; see United Kingdom
budgeting, 6–7, 35–36, 87–88, 135, 167, 221
Buiter, Willem, 39
Bush, George W., 43
Business New Zealand, 207

Callaghan, Sir Paul, 171, 173
Canada: crime rates in, 129; educational success in, 136; equality and income levels in, 13, 24, 28; tax rates in, 173
capacity-building, 194, 234
capital, cultural, human and social, 49, 101, 123, 125, 160, 231, 234
capital flight, 66, 174–5
capital gains, 40, 42–43, 54, 110; see also tax types, capital gains

capitalism, 50–53, 148–50, 156–8, 159, 176
Centre for Studies in Multiple Pathways, 191
charity and charitable trusts, 70, 175, 182, 218, 229, 230; see also KidsCan charitable organisation; philanthropy; voluntary sector
chief executives, salaries of, 10, 11, 18–19, 20, 32, 33, 39, 49, 168, 173, 175–6, 201
Child Poverty Action Group, 216
Child Welfare, 132
childcare, 5, 10, 152, 197, 214–16
children: and health, 2, 12, 24, 92, 114–15, 134–6, 167; and inequality, 2, 6–10, 14–16, 76, 85, 92–98, 112–13, 117, 134–44, 152–3, 167, 170–1, 218–20, 224; see also Child Poverty Action Group; Expert Advisory Group on Solutions to Child Poverty; mortality, infant
Children's Commissioner, 117; see also Expert Advisory Group on Solutions to Child Poverty
Chin Huat Ong, 205–6
Christchurch, 118–19
Christchurch Central Development Unit, 119
Christchurch Methodist Mission, 118–19
cigarettes, spending on, 7, 221
citizenship, rights of, 8, 75, 79, 82, 92, 109
civil society, notion of, xi, 47, 129, 130, 162, 179
Clark, Helen, 33, 110
Clear, Todd, 128
climate change, 159, 161, 162
Clinton, Bill, 43
Closer Together Whakatata Mai campaign, 179
'closing the gaps' policies, 144, 151–4
clothing costs and availability, 6–7, 29, 54, 68, 78, 88, 91, 135, 198, 217
Coddington, Deborah, 10
collective bargaining, 78, 200, 201
colonisation, 92, 105–6, 148, 157, 162, 163–4
Commerce Commission, 62
competitiveness, 46, 65, 201, 204
Connell, John, 95
Cook, Duncan, 107
corporates and multinationals, 15, 41–42, 74, 93
Coyle, Andrew, 129–30
Craig, David, 102, 103
credit downgrades and ratings, 174–5
credit subsidies, 46
crime, 16, 66, 68, 103, 120–31, 230; see also alcohol, and crime; drugs, and crime; imprisonment; justice system; violence
Cullen, Michael, 152
currency stabilisation, 202
Czech Republic, 24, 172

Dairy Workers Union, 207–8
Darling, Alistair, 43
debt: government, 27, 153, 172; private, 22, 44, 50, 94, 110, 150, 172, 208; *see also* borrowing
democracy, 14, 25, 45, 49, 51, 70, 74–75, 78, 85, 176, 206, 209
Denmark, 9–10, 13, 24, 28, 30; *see also* Scandinavia
Department of Corrections, 122–3, 127, 129
Department of Labour, 193
Department of Māori Affairs, 109, 110, 116, 149
Department of Social Welfare, 133
deregulation, 27, 42, 110, 199
disabilities, 77, 80, 81, 152, 169; *see also* income support types, disability allowance
discrimination, 4, 6, 99, 115, 168, 169, 216, 224, 230; gender, 5, 73, 76, 168; racial, 5, 25, 73, 76, 99, 108–9, 112, 115, 116, 121, 127, 149, 157, 168, 230; *see also* marginalisation, cultural; racism, general
Dobbs-Frank Act (USA), 51
domestic purposes benefit, *see* income support types, DPB
Downtown Community Ministry (DCM) (Wellington), 68–69
drugs: and crime, 68, 129; spending on, 221
DSK Engineering, 210–12
Dunedin, 185
Dunedin survey, 12, 124

Earthquake Commission (EQC), 118
East Asian financial crisis, 41
economic growth and inequality, 11, 15, 46–47, 55–67, 80, 150, 172, 174, 187–8, 201
economy, New Zealand, 11, 26–27, 150–5, 199–200
education: access to, 4, 16, 64, 144; and inequality, 83, 99, 134–44, 177, 184, 213, 224, 232–4; government funding and policy, 137–44, 153, 157, 178, 188
education types: early childhood, 16, 17, 99, 135; primary, 136, 139–41, 184; private, 146; public, 146; remedial, 61, 114; secondary, 136–43, 184, 188–92, 194; tertiary, 29, 35–36, 54, 93, 142, 184, 188–9, 191–4; vocational, 184, 189, 191–3; *see also* schools; trades skills and training
Education Review Office, 189
educational achievement and performance, 81, 134–43, 168, 192, 224, 230
educational testing, 136–9
egalitarianism, 19, 25, 28, 33, 71, 73, 79, 81, 85–86, 128, 173, 178
elderly people: and health, 2, 114, 152; and income support, 218–20; *see also* superannuation
electricity generation industry, 62; *see also* power, access and prices
employment and inequality, 125, 187–8, 199, 201–2; *see also* labour markets; unemployment; work types
employment relations systems, *see* trade unions; workplace structure and organisation
Engineering, Printing and Manufacturing Union, 207–8
English, Bill, 34, 120, 153
entrepreneurship, 65, 80, 83, 182; Māori, 158, 182
environmental issues, 160, 163, 170, 171, 172, 174, 178; *see also* climate change
Epuni Boys' Home, 133
equality, 25–26, 33, 47, 70–86, 116, 128, 170–6, 209; before the law, 72; liberties, 73–75; of opportunity, 9, 75–79, 182, 194, 224
Ernst & Young, 212
estate and gift duty, *see* tax types, estate and gift duty
Europe, 40, 48
European Union, 204, 206
Eurozone crisis, 48
exchange rates, 46, 202
Expert Advisory Group on Solutions to Child Poverty, 117, 176, 224

fairness, notions of, 33, 47, 76–78, 128, 168–71, 175–6, 223
financial crises, 12, 16, 26, 31, 39, 41, 49, 50, 51, 97, 150, 153, 162; *see also* East Asian financial crisis; Eurozone crisis; global financial crisis; Great Depression; Latin American financial crisis; Long-Term Capital Management crisis; Russian financial crisis; Wall Street crash
financial markets, 41–42, 50–51, 159–60, 162, 174, 201
Financial Times, 46
Finland, 13, 24, 136, 200
Fisher & Paykel, 204
Fletcher Building (and Construction), 32, 106
Fonterra, 32, 137, 204
food costs and availability, 7, 9, 14, 36, 68, 69, 78, 94, 134, 137, 167, 174, 217
'food in schools' strategy, 137, 167–8, 224
France, 13, 24, 30, 41
free market, 45, 51–52, 156, 206; *see also* neoliberalism
freedom of speech, 51, 73
Frumm, David, 175–6
Fuemana, Pauly, 91, 97

Galbraith, J.K., 11
gangs, 94, 124; *see also* Mongrel Mob
Garland, David, 125
General Social Survey 2008, 115
Germany, 13, 24, 40, 209; manufacturing industry in, 202; workplace structure and organisation in, 203–4
Global Creativity Index, 173

global financial crisis, 5, 12, 16, 33, 35, 41, 97, 153, 172, 175, 200
globalisation, 30–31, 34, 153, 185, 201
Goldin, Claudia, 49
goods and services tax (GST), 29, 32, 222
government intervention, 45, 50–51, 61, 62–66, 76, 83, 105, 106, 152, 155, 160, 199, 200, 208
Great Depression, 153, 225
Greece, 13, 24
Green Skills Agreement (Australia), 189, 193–4
GST, *see* goods and services tax
Gurría, Angel, 15

happiness, 71, 79–80, 83, 182, 198
Harvard study, 49–50
Hastings, 132, 210
Hawkesworth, Vince, 18
health and healthcare: and heart disease, 12; and inequality, 82, 83, 98, 125, 134–5, 167, 187–8, 195–6, 213; and infectious disease, 98, 111, 114–15, 117; and preventable disease, 2, 81, 146; availability of, 9, 25, 114; costs of, 36; government funding of, 87, 153, 157, 178; *see also* children, and health; elderly people, and health; hospital admission rates; housing, and health; life expectancy; Māori, and health; mental health issues; mortality, infant; obesity; Pacific peoples, and health
Healthy Housing Programme, 117
High Net Worth Individuals (HNWIs), 39–40
High Performance Working Initiative, 205, 210
Hole, Arni, 172
'hollowing out' of labour market, 30, 174
Holm, Nettie, 167
Holyoake, Keith, 26
home ownership, 105–17, 150, 161
homelessness, 112
homicide rates, 81
Hong Kong, 202
Hood, John, 234
hospital admission rates, 98, 114–15, 117
Household Economic Survey, 154, 221
Household Labour Force Survey, 97
Housing Corporation, 110
Housing New Zealand, 117, 197
housing: and health, 111–17, 136, 146, 195; and inequality, 64–65, 83, 105–17, 125, 146–7, 187–8; government investment in, 178; prices and costs, 29, 31, 50, 116, 146; programmes, 14, 105–6, 108–9; *see also* insulation, home; Māori, and housing; Pacific peoples, and housing; Porirua, housing in
housing types: first-home, 65, 110, 116; low-cost, 65, 116; mixed, 1, 14, 116; rental, 6, 59, 69, 88, 105, 110–17, 167, 195, 196, 217; social, 1, 116–17, 119, 125, 144, 178; state, 14, 25, 54, 106, 110, 116–17, 132
Housing Improvement Regulations 1947, 113
human rights, 168–9; *see also* rights, civil and political; Universal Declaration of Human Rights 1948
Human Rights Commission, 127
Hunn, J.K., 149
Hunt, Des, 175–6

Iceland, 24, 50
Idle No More protests, 162
Ikurere, Jaine, 9
imprisonment, 60, 68, 121–31, 133, 167, 232; *see also* crime; justice system
imprisonment rates, 13, 17, 81, 120–5; *see also* crime; justice system
incentives, role of, 46, 49–50, 53, 54, 65, 80, 85, 213, 216, 220, 226
income redistribution, 11, 42–43, 50–51, 75, 79–81, 85–86, 157, 175, 177, 222, 226; income support, 3, 4–5, 7, 16, 22, 28, 30, 55, 56, 58, 64, 65, 69, 107, 153, 174, 177, 196, 213–24, 225–7; numbers on, 10, 28–29, 216, 220–1; reductions in, 27, 29, 151–3, 157, 201, 215–17, 219, 222, 224; *see also* benefit fraud
income support types: accommodation supplement, 6, 110, 215, 217; disability allowance, 35; DPB, 20, 29, 69, 196, 197, 216, 217, 219, 221; family benefit, 25, 29, 107; invalid's benefit, 29, 217, 219; sickness benefit, 69; unemployment benefit, 6, 20, 29, 69, 215–17, 219, 221, 227; *see also* childcare, assistance with; superannuation; Working for Families
income types: household disposable, 3, 8, 21, 22, 24, 27–31, 112; individual pre-tax, 20–21, 26–28, 31–32; low, xi, 6–8, 20–22, 27–29, 32, 87–88; middle, 21–22, 27–28, 29–31, 32, 35–36, 43–44; top, 20–22, 23–24, 25–26, 27–28, 30, 31–32, 43–44
individualism; *see* self-interest and individualism
Industrial Conciliation and Arbitration Act 1894, 25
Industry Training Act 2001, 193
Industry Training Federation, 189, 190
industry training organisations (ITOs), 190–3; *see also* skills and skills training
inequality: attitudes towards, 19, 24, 33, 43–45, 48–52, 171, 175–6, 179, 229–30; definitions and understandings of, 3, 235; *see also* United States, attitudes to inequality in
inflation, 11, 26, 27, 29, 110, 153, 200, 216
inheritance, 10, 58, 59, 63, 65, 76, 77, 80, 223; *see also* tax types, estate and gift duty
Inland Revenue, 173, 196, 222
innovation and technology, 200; *see also* R&D

Institute of Taxation and Economic Policy (US), 66
insulation, home, 35, 113, 117, 223
insurance, 35, 60, 67, 88, 118
International Herald Tribune, 40
International Monetary Fund (IMF), 2, 11, 15, 16
invalid's benefit, *see* income support types, invalid's benefit
investors and investment, 11, 16, 17, 26, 50, 66, 80, 102–4, 118–19, 150, 159, 162–3, 172–5, 181–2, 198–9, 202, 206
Iraq, 43
Ireland, 13, 24, 106, 173
Italy, 13

Japan, 11, 13, 24, 30, 40, 48
Job Vacancy Monitoring Programme, 193
John Lewis Partnership (UK), 204
Johnson, Boris, 179
justice system, 4, 60, 80, 120–31; *see also* crime; imprisonment; imprisonment rates; law-and-order

Kahneman, Daniel, 45, 49
Katz, Lawrence, 49
Kerrisk, Shane, 211
Key, John, 54
Keynes, John Maynard, 45, 55–56
Keynesian ideologies, 51
KidsCan charitable organisation, 137
Kingsolver, Barbara, 182
KiwiSaver, 5, 153
KPMG Consulting, 181
Krugman, Paul, 26

Labour–Alliance coalition, 152
Labour governments, 25–27, 33, 106, 110, 148, 151–3, 157, 193
labour market, 46, 78, 96–97, 99, 149, 152, 174, 188, 199, 200, 207–9, 234; *see also* migration, of labour
Labour Party (British), 43
Lagarde, Christine, 2
Latin American financial crisis, 41
Lavoie, Marc, 208
law-and-order, costs of, 66–67, 153; *see also* police
Lay, Graeme, 96
Lear, Jonathan, 235
Lee Kuan Yew, 206
Liberal Government, 25, 106
libertarianism, 53
Liddle, Roger, 47
life expectancy, 13, 73, 81, 92, 150
Lipson, Leslie, 25
literacy, 94, 99, 143, 184, 191, 230, 234; *see also* reading recovery

Living Standards Framework, 58
Living Wage campaign, 20, 87–88, 119, 179, 207, 209
loan sharks, *see* borrowing, household and private
Long-Term Capital Management crisis, 41
Longstone, Lesley, 188–9
Lorde, Audre, 231
Lorentzen, Thomas, 220–1
Lower Manhattan Development Corporation, 119
Luxembourg Income Study, 24

management strategies, 19, 159, 163, 200, 202–5
Manahi, Glenn, 210–12
manufacturing industry, 5, 30, 95–96, 174–5, 190, 199, 202, 204, 205
Manukau City, 98–99
Manukau Institute of Technology, 191–2, 196
Māori: and education, 4, 34, 140, 150, 177, 188; and employment, 29, 96, 148–51, 153–4, 177, 186; and health, 4, 25, 34, 108, 114–15, 150, 161; and housing, 4, 25, 105, 107–9, 112–16, 148–50; and imprisonment, 4, 34, 122, 126–8, 130–1, 150, 161; and inequality, 3, 4, 25, 75, 91, 99, 105–8, 114, 123, 134, 148–58, 161–4, 171, 177, 186, 230; and land loss, 4, 25, 91, 105–6, 157; culture of, 4, 168, 171, 177; demography of, 148, 177, 232–3; economic development of, 4, 155–6, 159–63; exclusion of, 4, 6, 25, 26, 27, 102, 105, 107–8, 152–3; incomes of, 4, 5, 26, 27; urbanisation of, 25, 148–9; *see also* discrimination types, racial; entrepreneurship, Māori; protests, Māori
Māori Party, 127
Māori War Effort Organisation, 109
marginalisation, 121, 124–5, 127, 148, 157, 230
market failure, 53, 62–63, 64, 178, 209
Marmot, Michael, 12–13
Masterton, Wayne, 210–11
McIntyre, Stephanie, 68–69
McNaughton, Stuart, 139–40
means-testing, 79, 225
mental health issues, 12, 81, 167, 214, 221
mergers and acquisitions, 50, 181
meritocracy, 145, 147
Metge, Joan, 108
Mexico, 2, 24
Middleton, Stuart, 191–2
migration, 5, 6, 91, 95, 97–98, 173, 181–2, 185; and crime, 124; of labour, 66, 95–96, 97, 148–9, 185
Miller, David, 82
Ministry of Business, Innovation and Employment, 185, 192–3
Ministry of Education, 137–8, 140, 141, 142, 143, 188, 190
Ministry of Justice, 129
Ministry of Social Development, 3, 22, 23, 24, 68, 152–3, 217, 219

MMP (mixed-member proportional representation), 209
Mondragon Cooperative system (Spain), 204
Mongrel Mob, 133
monopolies, 15, 62–63
moral society, *see* civil society, notion of
Morgan, Gareth, 223
mortality, infant, 81, 92
Moskovitz, Dave, 181
Muldoon, Robert, 209
multinationals, *see* corporates and multinationals

National governments, 26, 27, 34, 96, 106, 110, 148, 151, 153, 157, 193
National Health Committee, 121, 128
Native Department, 107–8, 109
NCEA (National Certificate of Educational Achievement), 64, 142–3, 190–1, 192
neighbourhoods: low-income, 98–99, 127, 130, 134, 149; mixed, 1, 14, 116, 178; *see also* housing types, mixed
neoliberalism, 44–45, 47, 151–4, 156, 208, 229, 232
New Deal (USA), 209
New Economics Foundation, 3
New Labour Party (British), 47
Netherlands, 13, 24, 28
New York City, 163
New Zealand Company, 105–6
New Zealand Council for Educational Research, 136
New Zealand Council of Christian Social Services (NZCCSS), 167–8, 179
New Zealand Council of Trade Unions, 193, 198, 199, 222
New Zealand Crime and Safety Survey, 121
New Zealand Health Surveys, 112
New Zealand Herald, 18
New Zealand Qualifications Framework, 186–7
New Zealand Shareholders' Association, 175
Ngāi Tahu, 160–1, 164
Ngata, Sir Apirana, 109
Nolan, Melanie, 25
non-discrimination principle, 76
Northern Sydney Institute, 194
Northland, 14
Northland College, 142–3
Norway, 13, 24, 28, 172; *see also* Scandinavia
numeracy, 61, 94, 99, 141, 143, 184, 191, 234
Numeracy Development Programme, 141
nursing and nurses, 5, 87, 106, 117, 137, 190
nutrition, 6, 73, 91, 135, 224; *see also* food costs and availability; 'food in schools' strategy

Obama, Barack, 2, 40
obesity, 11, 12, 93, 161
Occupy movement, 40, 162
OECD, 16, 23, 24, 66, 110, 184, 185, 190, 194, 199
oil crises, 26–27, 96, 113, 162
Oldershaw, Mark, 189
Once Were Warriors, 94
opportunities, 2– 9, 16, 33–34, 47, 54, 55–67, 70–86, 91–101, 103, 133, 174–77, 218–19; educational, 54, 60, 65, 108, 134–44, 145–46; of employment, 66, 76–77, 103, 148, 191–92, 204, 207; *see also* equality, of opportunity
Organisation for Economic Co-operation and Development, *see* OECD
Otara Millionaires Club (OMC), 91, 97

Pacific peoples, 91–101, 102, 152–3; and education, 92–101, 140, 177, 189; and employment, 29, 34, 95–97, 151, 177, 186; and health, 98, 114–15; and housing, 98, 112–16; and inequality, 3, 5–6, 34, 75, 92–101, 114, 123, 134, 155, 171, 177, 186, 230; culture of, 168, 177; demography of, 97–99, 177, 232–3; *see also* discrimination types, racial
Paine, Tony, 121
Pakistan, 163
participation, 8, 12, 58, 64, 65, 71, 74–75, 78, 81, 100, 101, 119, 168–9, 174, 176, 179, 203–4, 214–18, 233–4
Pearson, Bill, 108–9
Perón, Eva, 100–1
Perth, 102
philanthropy, 54, 181–2
Philanthropy New Zealand, 181–2
Pickett, Kate, xi, 12–14
PISA (Programme for International Student Assessment) tests, 136–7
police, 60, 66, 122, 127, 129; *see also* law-and-order
Porirua, housing in, 1, 6, 14
Portugal, 13, 24
Positive Behaviour for Learning, 138
poverty, 1–17, 24–25, 39, 51–52, 54, 75–76, 81–82, 95, 98, 118–19, 134, 136, 145, 151, 152–3, 167–8, 181, 208, 214, 218–20, 225, 228–35; and crime, 120–5; inter-generational, 160, 228; reduction and alleviation, 48, 73, 85–86, 172–4, 220, 232, 233–4; traps, 15, 221, 225; *see also* Child Poverty Action Group; children, and inequality; Children's Commissioner; Expert Advisory Group on Solutions to Child Poverty; Māori, and inequality; Pacific peoples, and inequality
poverty statistics, 1–2, 6, 7, 8–9, 157
power, access and prices, 6, 29, 35, 88, 94, 108, 163, 167, 217
Pratt, John, 124–5
pregnancies, teenage, 81, 161
private equity funds, 50
privatisation, 27, 116
productivity, 17, 31, 46, 48–49, 50, 65, 66, 150, 172, 174, 187, 199, 201–2, 203–7, 210–11, 226

protectionism, 175
protests: global, 159, 162; Māori, 150; *see also* Idle No More protests; Occupy movement
psychosocial stress, 12; *see also* stress
Public Service Association, 207
Putnam, Robert, 15
qualifications, 76, 95–99, 142–3, 186–8, 190–2; *see also* NCEA; School Certificate examination; university entrance and University Entrance examination

race relations, 149–50, 156; *see also* discrimination types, racial
racism, 99, 157, 158, 230; *see also* discrimination types, racial
railways workshops, employment in, 190
Rajan, Raghuram, 11
Rawls, John, 73, 74, 76–77
Raz, Joseph, 83
R&D, 202, 203, 206
reading recovery, 61; *see also* literacy
Reagan, Ronald, and policies of, 44
recidivism, 122–3
reciprocity, 15, 19, 159, 162, 163, 168
Reducing Crime and Reoffending Result Action Plan, 126, 130
Regional Facilitation Programme, 193
Regional Partnerships Programme, 193
regulation, financial and government, 43, 45, 50, 51, 62–63, 66, 106, 175, 178, 179, 199, 208; *see also* deregulation
Rehabilitation Department, 109
rental accommodation, *see* housing types, rental
Report of the Royal Commission on Social Security in New Zealand 1972, 81
research and development, *see* R&D
Reserve Bank, 200
restorative justice, 128–9
rights, civil and political, 2, 5, 8, 70–75, 82, 84, 85, 92, 127, 152, 162, 168, 169, 209, 217; *see also* human rights
Ritchie, James, 149
Robinson, Dove-Myer, 102
Rose, Dina, 128
Rosenberg, Bill, 198
Royal Commission on Social Policy 1988, 78, 209
Russian financial crisis, 41

Salmond, Dame Anne, 218
Salmond, Rob, 222
Salvation Army, 5, 167
Samoa, 101
Sandel, Michael, 15
Sanitarium, 137
Scandinavia: employment relations in, 206; equality and income levels in, 13, 48–49, 172–3, 209; tax rates in, 173; *see also* Denmark; Norway; Sweden
scholarship programmes, 54, 59, 63, 93, 146
School Certificate examination, 189–90
schools: high-decile, 135–9, 143; low-decile, 7, 93, 135–44; *see also* zoning, school
self-interest and individualism, 17, 44–47, 51, 56, 61, 65–66, 68, 76, 80–86, 145–46, 168, 175
self-regulating systems, 65
Sen, Amartya, 71, 75, 86
Service and Food Workers Union, 87, 93
Sharples, Pita, 127
Singapore: currency stabilisation in, 202; employment relations system in, 205–6; equality and income levels in, 200
Skills Action Plan, 193
skills and skills training, 30, 59–60, 62–64, 66–67, 184–7, 191–4, 198, 202, 207, 214, 230; *see also* Green Skills Agreement; industry training organisations; trades skills and training
Smashproof, 99
Smith, Adam, 8, 62
Smith, Graham, 234
social cohesion, xi, 14, 82, 104, 149, 152, 170, 176, 220
social democratic policies, 45, 176, 209
social equality, *see* equality
social justice, 71, 75, 76, 78, 83, 84–85, 131
social mobility, 8–9, 16, 24, 33, 34, 54, 81–82, 85, 95, 113–14, 136, 177–8
social return on investment (SROI) model, 10, 178
Social Security Act 1938, 25
Solidere redevelopment, Beirut, 119
South Auckland, 93, 100, 102–3, 195; schools in, 139
South Korea, 13, 136
South Western Sydney Institute, 194
Spain, 13, 24, 204
St John, Susan, 215, 220
standard of living, 3, 6, 81, 157, 182, 198, 204, 213, 217, 218
State Advances Corporation, 108, 109, 116
Statistics New Zealand, 63–64
Stiglitz, Joseph, xi, 16, 74, 175
Stockhammer, Engelbert, 208
stress, 1, 12–13, 124, 134, 135, 167, 170, 196
student loans, 153
suicide, 161
superannuation, 216, 219–20, 225–6
Survey of Family, Income and Employment 2003–4, 154–5
Sutch, Dr William, 149
Suzanne Aubert Compassion Centre, 217
Sweden, 13, 24, 28; *see also* Scandinavia
Switzerland, 13, 24, 202
Sydney Institute, 194

tariffs, 26, 27, 46, 96, 151, 184
Tauranga hospital, 204
Tawney, R.H., 9
tax: avoidance and loopholes, 24, 32, 173, 214, 222–3; changes to, 34, 155, 225–7; credits, 3, 21, 29, 30, 106, 215–16, 220, 224; rates, 25, 27, 32, 33, 40–44, 50–51, 54, 63, 65–66, 69, 82, 172–8, 181, 213, 215, 220, 222–3, 225–7; *see also* Working for Families
tax types: capital gains, 24, 32, 40, 42, 65, 110, 173, 202, 223, 226; corporate, 155; estate and gift duty, 65, 173, 223; fringe benefit, 32; *see also* GST
Te Puni Kōkiri, 151
Te Whanau Putahi, 167
Te Whare Wānanga o Awanuiārangi, 234
Tea Party movement, 45
teachers, 20, 61, 93, 137–41, 168
Telecom, 32, 195
Tertiary Education Commission, 192
Thatcher, Margaret, 39, 44, 47, 48
therapeutic jurisprudence, 129
thinktanks, 3, 45
Tobin, James, 78–79
Tomorrow's Schools, 138
Tonga, 93
trade unions, 11, 25, 27, 31, 74, 87–88, 93, 179, 193–4, 198, 200, 201, 203, 205–8; *see also* Australian Council of Trade Unions; Dairy Workers Union; Engineering, Printing and Manufacturing Union; New Zealand Council of Trade Unions; Service and Food Workers Union
trade, New Zealand, 27, 28–29, 30, 57, 150, 174, 184
trades skills and training, 60, 143, 186, 187, 189, 191–2, 193–4; *see also* Green Skills Agreement; industry training organisations; skills and skills training
Treasury, 34, 58, 81, 179; *see also* Living Standards Framework
Treaty of Waitangi and settlement process, 4, 92, 148, 155–60, 169
'trickle-down' effect, 46, 150, 158
Truman, President Harry, 100
TrustPower, 18
Turkey, 2, 24

unemployment, 5–6, 28–29, 44, 80, 121, 125, 149–51; *see also* Māori, and employment; Pacific peoples, and employment
unemployment benefit, *see* income support types, unemployment benefit
unemployment rates, 5–6, 63–64, 96–97, 111, 125, 148–54, 200, 216, 220; rural, 148; youth, 118, 190
United Kingdom, 16, 25; equality and income levels in, 13, 24, 27, 28, 39–43, 48; house prices in, 50; poverty in, 7; tax rates in, 41, 42, 173; *see also* John Lewis Partnership (UK); Vickers Commission report (UK)
United States, 2, 25; attitudes to inequality in, 44–45, 209; campaign spending in, 74; crime rates in, 129; equality and income levels in, 9, 11, 13, 16, 24, 28, 39–40, 42–43, 48; financial markets in, 41–42; house prices in, 50; imprisonment rates in, 122; tax rates in, 173; unemployment in, 200; *see also* New York City; Volcker Rule (USA); Wall Street crash
United States Supreme Court, 51, 74
Universal Declaration of Human Rights 1948, 209
university entrance and University Entrance examination, 99, 146, 190
University of Auckland, 139, 234
University of Otago Cost of Food Survey, 217
urban planning, 14, 102–4, 118–19
urbanisation, *see* Māori, urbanisation of

Vickers Commission report (UK), 51
Victim Support, 121
violence, 68, 120–31, 208
vocational education and training (VET) sector, 177, 184, 189–94
Vocational Pathways, 189–91
Volcker Rule (USA), 51
voluntary sector, 70, 177

wages, 4–5, 26, 29, 30–31, 42, 88, 184–5, 187, 199, 201–9, 216–17, 220; minimum, 6, 20, 29, 179, 186, 201, 205, 207–9; average, 31, 216–17, 219, 222; wage-led growth, 201–2; *see also* Living Wage campaign
Waikeria Borstal, 133
Waitangi Tribunal, 106, 130–1
Wall Street crash, 39
Walzer, Michael, 82–83
Wan, David, 205–6
Waugh, Pam, 167
welfare dependency, 214
welfare state, 25, 47, 106, 152, 172, 184, 187
Wellington, 68–69, 103–4, 149, 181, 217
Wellington City Council, 68–69
Wellington Town Belt, 106
Whānau Ora, 4, 234–5
Whanganui, 35–36
Wilkinson, Richard, xi, 12–14
women: economic participation of, 4–5, 6, 11, 17, 25, 26, 27, 87, 189, 214; imprisonment of, 121–2, 126
Work and Income New Zealand, 195, 196
work ethic, 10, 169, 214, 220
work types: casual, 15, 201, 205, 215; low-paid, 5, 9, 30, 54, 87–88, 103, 149, 185–6, 199, 220; part-time, 5, 214–15; skilled, 184–7; unpaid

domestic, 4–5, 177; unskilled, 30, 95, 97, 184, 187; voluntary, 177
Working for Families, 5, 6, 21, 29, 30, 33, 35, 87, 152–3, 196, 215, 216
workplace structure and organisation, 11, 173, 177, 198–212
World Bank, 51

Youth Guarantee policy, 190
youth justice system, *see* justice system'

zero tolerance' strategies, 122
zoning, school, 144, 146–7